MODERN JAPAN

MODERN JAPAN

Aspects of History, Literature and Society

EDITED BY

W. G. BEASLEY

UNIVERSITY OF CALIFORNIA PRESS

Berkeley and Los Angeles

©George Allen & Unwin Ltd. 1975

University of California Press
Berkeley and Los Angeles, California

First Paperback Edition, 1977
ISBN: 0-520-03495-3
Library of Congress Catalog Card No: 74-29802

1 2 3 4 5 6 7 8 9 0

Printed in the United States of America

PREFACE

In April 1973, as a result of initiatives taken by the Japan Library Group of the United Kingdom, representing university and national libraries with collections relating to Japan, a conference on Modern Japan was held in Oxford and London. The principal part of the conference, at which meetings were organised mainly in three sections (History; Language and Literature; Social Sciences), took place at St Antony's College, Oxford. A final session on 'Japan in the Seventies' took place at the School of Oriental and African Studies, University of London. This volume comprises a selection of the papers presented on those occasions.

The conference, during which a decision was taken to form a European Association for Japanese Studies, was attended by some sixty persons, drawn from many of the countries of Europe, plus Israel and Japan. It was financed by grants from the School of Oriental and African Studies, London; St Antony's College, Oxford; and the University of Sheffield (Centre for Japanese Studies). In addition, the School of Oriental and African Studies has sponsored the publication of this volume. It therefore seems appropriate here to express our thanks for this financial help and also to record the names of those who took part in organising the conference. They were Professor G. Bownas (Sheffield), Mr D. G. Chibbett (British Museum), Professor C. J. Dunn (London, S.O.A.S.), Mr K. B. Gardner (British Museum), Professor P. G. O'Neill (London, S.O.A.S.), Dr B. Powell (Oxford), Mr J. Sargent (London, S.O.A.S.), Dr W. E. Skillend (London, S.O.A.S.), Dr G. R. Storry (Oxford) and Mr K. Thurley (London, L.S.E.).

W. G. Beasley

London, 1974

CONTENTS

CONTRIBUTORS

PROFESSOR W. G. BEASLEY: *Professor of the History of the Far East, School of Oriental and African Studies, University of London.*

DR CHARLES D. SHELDON: *University Lecturer in Japanese History, University of Cambridge.*

DR ALBERT A. ALTMAN: *Senior Lecturer in Japanese History and Language, Hebrew University of Jerusalem.*

DR I. H. NISH: *Reader in International History, London School of Economics, University of London.*

DR BEN-AMI SHILLONY: *Senior Lecturer in Japanese History, Hebrew University of Jerusalem.*

DR R. L. SIMS: *Lecturer in the History of the Far East, School of Oriental and African Studies, University of London.*

DR GORDON DANIELS: *Senior Lecturer in Modern Far Eastern History, Centre of Japanese Studies, University of Sheffield.*

DR BRIAN POWELL: *Fellow of St Antony's College and Lecturer in Japanese, University of Oxford.*

MRS A. HORIE-WEBBER: *Doctoral candidate, Department of Dramatic Art, University of California, Berkeley; teacher of Japanese at University of Cambridge, 1971–3.*

MR HISAAKI YAMANOUCHI: *Doctoral candidate and Lector in Japanese, University of Cambridge, 1968–73.*

DR EIMI WATANABE RAJANA: *Former Part-time Lecturer in Japanese, School of Oriental and African Studies, University of London.*

DR SEPP LINHART: *Lecturer and Research Assistant, Institut für Japanologie, University of Vienna.*

DR R. C. CLARK: *Former doctoral candidate, School of Oriental and African Studies, University of London; subsequently with Jardine Fleming (Far East) Limited, Tokyo.*

MR JOHN SARGENT: *Lecturer in Geography with reference to the Far East, School of Oriental and African Studies, University of London.*

DR C. B. HOWE: *Reader in Economics with reference to Asia, School of Oriental and African Studies, University of London.*

INTRODUCTION

MODERN JAPAN:
AN HISTORIAN'S VIEW

W. G. BEASLEY

Japan, it has often been said, moved from feudalism to capitalism—to an advanced form of capitalism—in little more than a hundred years. In the process she transformed a traditional, Asian culture into a 'modern', predominantly Western one. Nevertheless, both these statements, broadly tenable though they are, prove on closer inspection to need qualification. Japanese feudalism and Japanese capitalism have had distinctive features that put in question some of the assumptions (derived from Western society) on which our labelling of institutions and processes is based. Moreover, it quickly appears that a *cultural* definition of 'modern' is as difficult to identify for Japan as it is for the West; in neither context can one disregard or readily disentangle the influence of tradition, which is both specific and indigenous. Hence the study of modernisation in Japan involves a study of concepts, as well as of Japanese society. It is perhaps for this reason that it appeals to scholars of many different kinds: students of history, of literature, of geography, of economics, of sociology have contributed to this volume, each writing from a different academic viewpoint, but each adding to the understanding of problems that all recognise and to some extent share.

As an historian, I hold it to be necessary to begin discussion of this subject with a look at the kind of society from which that of modern Japan has evolved, namely the society of the Tokugawa period (1600–1868). What do we mean when we call this 'feudal'? Firstly, I think, that political authority was in large measure decentralised in the hands of hereditary lords who were the ruler's vassals. Secondly, that the economy was agrarian, dominated by a military (samurai) class whose power rested on control of the land and its cultivators. Yet even at this level one needs to qualify. There were two rulers: a *de jure* sovereign, the Emperor; and a *de facto* monarch, the Shogun. The latter's power over the lords, and the power of the lords over their retainers, were greater than was common in medieval Europe. More fundamentally, the samurai were for the most part divorced from the land, living in castle towns, from which they exercised

13

authority over the countryside as officials, collecting dues that were more akin to tax than rent.

Several consequences followed from this. One was the gradual bureaucratisation of the samurai, in the sense that civil office became more his preoccupation than military prowess. This weakened the personal element in the feudal relationship and introduced a conflict between inherited ethos and contemporary reality, slowly undermining the cohesion and self-confidence of the ruling class. Simultaneously, the growth of commerce—a tribute to the samurai's success in maintaining order and avoiding civil war—was changing other class relationships. By the eighteenth century it had produced a sizable body of merchants whose wealth greatly exceeded their formal status. This is seemingly a classic ingredient in the destruction of a feudal state; but in Japan, unlike Europe, the result was not that merchants developed an independent power base in the towns from which to overthrow feudalism. The towns, after all, were already the centres of samurai authority. Instead, urban merchants entered into a symbiotic relationship with urban samurai, in which the wealth of the one reinforced and was reinforced by the political authority of the other. What is more, the samurai's absence from the village allowed a measure of power there to fall into the hands of a local élite, consisting originally of village headmen and the richer farmers (often of samurai descent), but supplemented as time went on by emergent landlords and rural entrepreneurs. These groups, too, recognising feudal authority as the condition for their own superiority in the countryside, accepted symbiosis with it.

Such changes inevitably produced disorder and turbulence of a kind that seemed to threaten the regime's stability: the acquisition by marriage or purchase of a degree of samurai status by the non-samurai rich; competition for office within the village and castle town; a rising level of peasant revolt, directed against both the old forms of exploitation and the new. Japanese historians have frequently seen the nineteenth century in these terms, that is, as the interaction of non-feudal challenge and feudal response, paralleling the shift that took place from 'feudal' to 'modern' (or 'capitalist') in Europe several centuries earlier.

To view it in this way, however, is not only to ignore the differences in urban and rural patterns between Europe and Japan (which might have led the latter to some kind of neo-feudalism). It is also to leave aside the impact of the West. During the 1850s Japan was brought within the scope of a system of international treaties, essentially the same as that the powers had imposed on China. Like China, she was brought to this unwillingly, as a result of gunboat diplomacy and commercial pressures. Like China, she was thereby

14

subjected to influences—political, economic and cultural—that were to shape her subsequent history.

Politically, the 'unequal treaties' of 1858 gave a sharper focus to the struggle for power which was already implicit, and had become in some respects explicit, in late Tokugawa society. They prompted heated policy debates and a realignment of forces, directed to a search for national unity and strength. It was widely recognised, especially by samurai, that only these qualities would enable Japan to resist Western encroachment and eventually meet the West on equal terms. Less widely, it was also acknowledged that neither unity nor strength could be won without institutional change, though there was bitter disagreement about the form that change should take. Vested interests and conservatism argued for a minimum. Ambition on the part of men who had a smaller stake in things as they were, or enthusiasm on the part of men for whom the study of the West was opening up new worlds, brought plans that were far more sweeping. Ambition and enthusiasm won. In a series of crises during 1867–8 the Tokugawa government was overthrown and a new regime emerged (ostensibly based on direct Imperial rule) in which the root-and-branch reformers gained an important voice. Thus Japan was set on a new course: to 'use the barbarian to control the barbarian', that is, to adopt the West's military technology, economic processes and political institutions as sources of Japanese strength.

All this was not achieved without force, as Dr Sheldon's paper shows (pp. 27–51). The civil war of 1868–9 played a part in defeating the more moderate reformers, as well as the Tokugawa, thereby initiating an era of great political change. One aspect of it was the abolition of the domains (1871), undertaken on the grounds that feudalism was an inefficient and divisive form of government. Another was the gradual recognition of the 'hidden' changes in Tokugawa society. The creation of a Western-style bureaucracy and conscript army had the effect (at various levels) of giving power openly to samurai who had already begun to wield it in the name of their lords, emphasising efficiency, rather than birth, as the criterion of appointment and promotion. Those who lacked this virtue found their privileges taken away, even to hereditary stipends. Similarly, the men who dominated the village had their economic position confirmed by a land-tax reform that could well be called a landlord's bill of rights (though it was also a secure base for government revenue). A national education system opened a way for their sons into officialdom, as it did also for sons of the well-to-do of the towns. Moreover, the government's promotion of industry and commerce gave both groups the opportunity to gain status, setting the seal on wealth.

In sum, the Meiji policies had the effect of shifting the centre of power downwards within the former ruling class; of widening recruitment to it, albeit fairly narrowly; and of putting privilege related to function in the place of an hereditary authority. These were all 'modern' characteristics, in the sense of being departures from feudal norms. They were also in large part 'Western'—and therefore anathema to many by virtue of precisely the same nationalist prejudices and emotions as prompted the reforms themselves. This posed difficult problems of public education for the Meiji leadership. One way of overcoming them was to use the schools, through which a rising generation was taught to combine a traditional ethic with patriotic open-mindedness in 'practical' learning. Another, as Dr Altman's paper shows (pp. 52–66), was the Western-style newspaper, consciously an instrument of 'enlightenment'. Yet both tools proved double-edged. In the twentieth century, the mass patriotism fostered in this way was to endanger the structure it was designed to support, while consciousness of a conflict between inherited and imported values was to bring a crisis of identity, both national and personal, to a generation or more of the country's intellectuals.

Before turning to these matters, however, let us briefly round out our survey of nineteenth-century Japanese society. The economy, like the polity, entered a new era with the coming of the West. Partly this occurred through the workings of foreign trade, notably exports of silk and imports of cotton and cotton goods, which gave a stimulus to exactly those sectors in which capitalism had already begun to emerge. The result was to create a 'leading sector', vital to economic growth, which by the 1890s had linked Western-style institutions (like banks) and machine technology to the most vigorous parts of the pre-modern economy.

Indirectly, but more pervasively, the West gave an encouragement to economic initiatives by example, that is by its overwhelming military and political power, which its own writers attributed to 'trade and industry'. Reinforcing this, it furnished models—specific economic devices by which such strength was to be won—and provided help in the form of experts and machinery. It thereby promoted new forms of economic enterprise, which were made acceptable in Japan by being associated in men's minds with the country's international aspirations; in effect, harnessing nationalism to growth. There followed an exceptionally rapid development of capitalism, starting from the foundations Tokugawa Japan had laid.[1]

It was because political and economic changes reinforced each other that Japan departed so decisively from traditional institutions and ideas in many fields. Yet the process was still at this stage incomplete. There was, for example, no effective transfer of power to a bourgeoisie. Landlords and merchants certainly exercised more influence after the Meiji Restoration than they had before it, but they did not control policy; they neither furnished nor dominated the men who made the crucial decisions. Indeed, it could be argued that they entered into very similar symbiotic relations with the new government and bureaucracy as their predecessors had enjoyed with former samurai (from whose ranks ministers and the higher bureaucracy were still substantially drawn). Down to 1900, at least, changes in the social distribution of power took the form, not of a sudden, revolutionary replacement of one class structure by another, but of the recognition and legal confirmation of patterns that had long been taking shape beneath the surface of Japan's society. The result was neither 'feudal' nor 'bourgeois', but a hybrid that Japanese Marxists now call bureaucratically 'absolutist' (*zettaishugi*) in the manner of *Eighteenth Brumaire*.

Nor was the Japanese economy at this time fully 'modern'. For a variety of reasons, which include the nature of landlordism and of the Meiji land settlement, traditional agriculture was intensified, rather than destroyed, by economic modernisation. It retained, for example, a much larger proportion of the work force than is normal in an industrial state. It might even be claimed that Japan achieved agricultural growth without agrarian revolution. Industrial organisation for its part reflected the unusual measure of state intervention that was occasioned by the influence of nationalism on economic policy. This was manifested not only in the emergence of giant, government-favoured concerns (*zaibatsu*), dominating capital-intensive industry (and much else), but also in the exceptional economic functions performed by the bureaucracy. What is more, in business, as in politics, one can detect almost everywhere the presence of pre-modern values: intense group loyalties; quasi-familial ties; the Confucian ethic.

This is to speak as if Meiji society was the end-product of modernisation, whereas in reality, of course, it was no more than an intermediate stage; the first part of the twentieth century saw the continuation and extension of many of the developments we have been discussing. In Rostow's terms, economic take-off was followed by self-sustaining growth, moving Japan into industrialisation on an ever increasing scale. Meanwhile, politically and socially what had been built by the Meiji leaders was consolidated by their heirs. Or so at first it seemed. Within a generation, however, it was becoming apparent that the very success of Meiji policies was threatening to undermine the balance of forces on which they rested. It was not only economically that growth was self-sustaining. The greater importance of trade and industry soon gave the bourgeoisie a base from which to challenge the ex-samurai élite, as was demonstrated in the composition and aims of the political parties. By the 1920s they were in a position to demand party cabinets. Simultaneously, liberalism and individualism—the ideals of bourgeois society in the West—made further inroads into the traditional ethic. And logically enough, the same economic phenomena that prompted all this produced unrest among tenant-farmers and the new urban proletariat, marching under various socialist banners.

The simple and reasonable interpretation of these developments is that capitalism, once established, had proceeded to move Japan, somewhat unevenly, along the paths that industrial countries of the West had earlier taken, steadily removing the 'anomalies' of the Meiji settlement. Clearly there is a good deal of truth in this. Moreover, the nature of twentieth-century opposition bears it out. In Japan, as in Europe, the rise of the bourgeoisie created proletarian politics, and both together provoked resistance from conservatives. Since the latter sought to defend traditional values (and the distribution of power they served), this situation set elements within the Court, the bureaucracy and the armed forces against the Diet, as much as it did liberals against socialists, old against young, 'modern' against 'old-fashioned'. It is not difficult on the face of it to find parallels in Western Europe between the wars.

Japan, however, had an ingredient Europe lacked. In Japan, the conflict between modern and traditional was also a conflict between alien and Japanese, arousing once again the emotions of the Meiji struggles. Accordingly, conservatism was argued not only in terms of political antiquarianism, but also in those of 'national essence' and cultural purity. This put the debate about the nature of Japanese society into the context of resistance to the West and an assertion of Japan's international rights, a framework within which socialists could support imperialism and army officers could demand the confiscation of excess wealth. In this sense, Japanese politics in the years before the Second World War have a flavour all their own.

Recent studies of the events leading to Japanese participation in the war have for the most part been revisionist. It is now quite generally accepted, for example, that Japanese expansion in East Asia derived, not from sheer megalomania on the part of her military leadership, but at least partly from a long series of rational—if sometimes mistaken—assessments of defence needs and resources by men acting in the 'great power' tradition. Dr Nish's paper (pp. 67–80) exemplifies an early stage of this; and professional disagreements of the kind he describes continued until the eve of Pearl Harbor.

Complicating them were the activities of the more irrational elements in Japanese public life, those associated with ultranationalism, or in Maruyama's phrase, 'fascism from below'. As Dr Shillony argues (pp. 81–8), these never really achieved a position from which they could decide the course of history, despite the myths that have grown up about them. They were neither as menacing nor as romantic as they have been made to seem. Nor did their activities, coupled with those of the army high command, have quite such a stifling effect on the parties as has commonly been said. Dr Sims's study of Akita in the 1930s (pp. 89–112) shows the Seiyūkai and Minseitō still to be the main focus of politics locally—and not differing greatly from earlier years in methods or slogans—despite the weakening of the Diet as an institution and therefore, supposedly, a decline in the influence of the party leaders in the capital.

It is probably too soon to attempt a full reassessment of Japanese history in the years between the wars, especially in its domestic aspects, but, as these papers and a number of recent monographs suggest, a pattern is beginning to emerge. As in the Meiji period, it is a pattern of incompleteness, viewed conceptually. Traditionalist reaction, manifested at times as nationalist hysteria, did not prove strong enough wholly to turn the clock back on the development of a bourgeois society, but it was able to check it in some respects, distort it in others. Thus the intervention of the army re-established something like a Meiji relationship between government, business and party politics, a relationship that in the 1920s had seemed likely to be destroyed or wither away. The business world accepted the primacy of *raison d'état* in return for retaining some of its economic freedoms; the political establishment devised a new balance between its various components and sacrificed restraint in foreign policy as the price of maintaining it; building a 'New Order' overseas and reviving tradition at home diverted the energies of the radical right; and the police suppressed the revolutionary left. In other words, one strand from the Meiji heritage, that of national strength, was emphasised at the expense of others, namely economic growth and 'enlightenment'. And it must be doubted whether this result was truly fascist, except in so far as Maruyama's other phrase, 'fascism from above', might be taken to identify something distinct from Europe's experience.

This phase of Japan's modern history ended, as it had begun, in war. There is even a case for saying, *vide* Dr Daniels's paper (pp. 113–31), that it ended in holocaust, literally and metaphorically. Indeed, at first sight the Second World War brought not only defeat, but also the destruction of everything that had been achieved since Meiji—

empire, structure of government, industry, self-confidence—leaving only the ashes on which to build anew. 1945, it seemed, was to mark as great a turning-point as 1868 had done.

Yet was it? From the perspective of the 1970s one can identify a greater continuity in Japan than ever seemed likely twenty-five years ago. American military occupation, for example, while seeking to reinforce democracy, did much to put the clock back to the 'liberal' years before the Manchurian Incident, restoring the political parties (and the bourgeois elements they largely represent) to a position of influence. This influence has been all the greater because some of the parties' rivals, notably those connected with the military and the Court, were deliberately weakened. Similarly, land reform, by reducing the power of landlords in the village, eliminated some of the tensions within Japanese capitalism on which pre-war anti-business groups had relied. Hence the obstacles to the emergence of a business-dominated society, towards which Japan had appeared to be moving after 1918, were substantially removed between 1945 and 1951.

At this point a different kind of continuity manifested itself: a resurgence of the country's industrial economy, modified by the emphasis on heavy industry given by the war and preparations for it, but dependent on inherited supplies of skilled labour and management. Luck played a part in this resurgence (the Korean War; the Suez crisis), as did American aid. However, our concern here is not with the causes of the change, but with its results. And these are evident enough. During the 1960s Japan entered a period of rapid economic growth, overtaking most of the advanced economies of Western Europe in terms of gross national product and moving almost at a leap into the world of great corporations and the mass consumer. Her overseas trade quickly adjusted to this situation, eventually causing great difficulties in international markets and the balance of payments. These are analysed in the paper by Dr Howe (pp. 244–63). Politics adjusted, too: power became unshakably vested in a conservative government and an élite bureaucracy, which both maintain close connections with the business community. In addition, Japan acquired vast environmental problems, arising, as they had after the First World War, from urbanisation, but acuter now because of greater pace and scale. As Mr Sargent shows (pp. 227–43), these have become a main preoccupation of politicians and planners.[2]

It is tempting to sum up these developments by saying that conditions since 1945 have been such as to encourage the resumption of the country's progress towards a characteristically bourgeois society, that is, the course which was set by the Meiji reforms, but diverted in the 1930s by the moves towards war. This would be to designate the period from 1930 to 1945 as a kind of blind alley, leading off at a tangent from the main path of modern Japanese history, which was subsequently resumed. However, such an argument cannot fully be sustained. Clearly, the factors making for war before 1941 were as much the product of the Meiji settlement as bourgeois society itself has been. Therefore, what we have in actuality to consider are variant paths of development from Meiji, which are not necessarily 'main' and 'subsidiary' ones. We must re-word the proposition so as to ascribe changes of direction to differences of emphasis within a complex continuity, not to intermittent acceptance or rejection of conflicting wholes.

In such a context it is possible to examine other strands of continuity, for which war and defeat have not had the same relevance as they have had for politics. One is the problem of cultural assimilation, almost as difficult for the Japanese of the 1970s as it was for those of the 1880s, when the West was first being critically appraised. Literature and the arts both exemplify it. Dr Powell's paper (pp. 135–46), discussing the actress, Matsui Sumako, shows how coming to terms with Western dramatic techniques involved Meiji Japanese not only in rethinking the bases of their own, but also in accommodating themselves to some disturbing social novelties. Nor was it a once-for-all adjustment. As Mrs Horie-Webber demonstrates (pp. 147–65), attitudes that were taken up at the end of the Meiji period were constantly subject to revision thereafter, as fresh Western models emerged; but this was not in itself a guarantee that the transition to Western practices would be smooth. The ideas built into the new drama, divorced as they were from traditional concepts (to some of which the public remained attached), were grafted on to a very Japanese form of professional organisation, so that the ideology of the plays and the social structure of the companies performing them were thoroughly at odds. In recent years this has produced a general turbulence and bitter controversy.

Disputes of this kind, in which the West's ideological quarrels are apparently made sharper by being transplanted into a Japanese *milieu*, are not confined to the theatre by any means. The student movement affords a plethora of examples. Moreover, Japanese intellectuals are also bedevilled—and have been for the past hundred years—by another product of Westernisation: the problem of knowing what it is to be 'Japanese', when Japaneseness has in every ordinary sense come to incorporate (in varying proportions for different persons at different times) a number of alien elements. It is an inescapable problem for the writer, especially the novelist, who comments on the contemporary scene. Mr Yamanouchi (pp. 166–84) examines two such men: Abe Kōzō, whose alienation from Japan-as-it-is leads him to devise an abstract, non-Japanese, non-Western world; and Ōe Kenzaburō, who seeks, more narrowly, a fresh concept of a Japanese community to which he might better feel able to belong. Both are concerned with questions of national and individual identity that have preoccupied many of their predecessors (for example, Tanizaki Junichirō, Kawabata Yasunari and Mishima Yukio, to name only three).

In discussing these aspects of the drama and the novel one tends almost inevitably to emphasise the tensions that have arisen between traditional and modern in Japan (impelled in that direction partly by the evidence of unhappiness in the personal lives of those concerned). To do so is to highlight the cultural break between Meiji and everything that went before, rather than subdivisions of the modern period; that is, to dwell upon the major discontinuities caused by the introduction of ideas and institutions from the West. Yet there is a sense in which such an emphasis can be misleading. It is not only that tradition has 'survived' in certain fields: for example, in music, in which old and new exist side by side, having remarkably little effect on each other. It is also that tradition is not invariably in conflict with what is 'modern'. In some cases it has become established *within* the new, genuinely assimilated, so that one gets the phenomenon, familiar to many visitors to Japan, of apparently Western mechanisms working in a 'Japanese' way. These forms of continuity are now being increasingly studied.

Significantly, they occur most in those social institutions that involve the functioning of the group. It has become a commonplace to say that the Japanese have not found it easy to accept the Western concept of the individual and his role in society. They give a priority to membership of the group—the ministry or department to which a man belongs, his firm or trade union, his school or school year—that parallels and derives from the loyalties which in an earlier scheme of things were due to domain and village and family. As a phenomenon of bureaucracy this is not unknown in the West. Economically and socially, however, it produces in Japan features that to a Westerner are surprising, even contradictory. One of them is the relative absence of outstanding individual entrepreneurs in what is, after all, a highly capitalist society (though Japanese-type business leadership is rapidly becoming a worldwide norm, which suggests that its coincidental relevance to the working of large concerns may be a factor in Japan's economic success). There is also the special character that a sense of 'belonging' to firm or factory gives to the relations of management and labour with each other. Dr Clark's paper (pp. 209–26) examines an example of this in considerable detail. Dr Linhart (pp. 198–208) shows that some features of the Japanese approach to

22

leisure are related to the same set of attitudes. And Mrs Rajana (pp. 187–97), discussing the new religions that have flourished in post-war Japan, notes that these, too, have their part in the pattern; in many instances they reflect a search for integration into a group, through which the alienated individual—often alienated by the consequences of modernisation—can achieve integration in society.

These studies deal with fundamental aspects of culture and society that need much fuller analysis, historically and sociologically, before we can be confident about the nature of change in modern Japan. In a different perspective, they suggest, by contradicting some Western assumptions, that the concept of modernity needs re-examining in the West as well. Indeed, the question needs to be asked of *all* the societies that have been brought into closer contact with the West and with each other by a century or more of Western influence and expansion, thereby entering upon what we call 'modernisation': do the differences between them chiefly reflect location at different stages along a single path of 'modern' development, or are they primarily to be taken as evidence that variant pre-modern traditions react differently with—and in the end contribute differently to—an entity identifiable as 'the modern'? The question was already being asked by Japanese as early as the Meiji period. It is being posed again by the character of Japanese society now.

PART I

HISTORY

1

THE POLITICS OF THE CIVIL WAR
OF 1868

CHARLES D. SHELDON

The year 1868 was a time of extreme trials for the new Meiji government. Perhaps because these trials were ultimately weathered, historians have tended to underemphasise their importance, and the importance of the civil war itself. Within the new government there were two closely balanced opposing forces: the group led by Chōshū and Satsuma leaders, chiefly Ōkubo Toshimichi, Saigō Takamori, both of Satsuma, and Kido Kōin of Chōshū, and usually associated with the crafty and influential court noble Iwakura Tomomi. This group is often called in Japanese buryoku tōbaku-ha (the faction favouring bringing down the Bakufu—the Shogunate—by military force). For convenience, as this is a bit unwieldy in English, I will refer to this faction as the Ōkubo group. It is the party associated with a policy of thorough and uncompromising centralisation of the country under the Emperor, and, increasingly, with an anti-feudal policy and modernisation on the Western model.

The other group, kōgi seitai-ha in Japanese, the faction advocating a political structure based on consultation, consisted of a loose alignment of moderate and conservative forces. It was not nearly so singleminded, but in numbers it was vastly superior to the Ōkubo group. Its numerical advantages were, however, largely outside the government. It favoured compromise, clemency to the Tokugawa, and maintenance of a modified, more centralised feudal system. I will use the term 'moderate group' to characterise this faction.

Despite strong pressure for a moderate solution, the Ōkubo group won in the end due to determination and willingness to use force, to a clearsighted policy, and also, as is often the case in human affairs, to simple good luck as well. Three events played a crucial role in this success: the victories of the Imperial forces in the battles at Toba and Fushimi (27–30 January 1868)—this, in fact, was a virtually independent action of Satsuma and Chōshū forces—in the one-day battle of Ueno in Edo (4 July), and in the taking of the castle of Wakamatsu in northern Japan (5 November) after a long and difficult campaign.*

* See Figure 1, p. 29, for domain and other geographical location.

27

Last, and most important, the challenges and opportunities offered to the government during the day-to-day hostilities created patterns which did much to determine the kind of central government which emerged, and the options open to that government.

There are two indisputable facts which no doubt have led historians to underestimate the importance of the civil war: at the very beginning, the most crucial battle, that at Toba and Fushimi, ended in a decisive victory for the new government; and the pro-Tokugawa holdouts under Admiral Enomoto, far away in Hokkaido, who were the last to surrender, were obviously no serious threat to the Meiji government. But this is to overlook the importance of the struggle that went on throughout most of 1868, which included a long and difficult campaign in the north against a large anti-government alliance. This comprised thirty-one domains, plus Aizu and Shōnai, aided by several thousand officers and men from the Bakufu, from Kuwana, Mito and other *han*, together with French 'military advisers', and by the former Bakufu fleet under Enomoto. It also misses the importance of the use of government troops to threaten or to force recalcitrant or hesitant feudal lords throughout much of the country to swear allegiance to the new government under the Emperor. Under these conditions, military considerations and military men came to the fore. Both force and the threat of force proved to be very important politically, in the effects they had on the breakdown of the feudal system and its later abolition. Ōkubo and other leaders, fully aware of the basic weakness and narrow base of the new government, took the war very seriously indeed. The nature of the war, in which both sides were striving to 'modernise', spurred on the search for new military and political methods and solutions, mostly suggested by Western experience, and the fear of foreign aid or intervention on behalf of the 'rebels', made this search all the more pressing.

The year 1868 marked the real beginning of the shift from a feudal to a modern Japan, when the political struggle which had been set off by Perry's arrival in 1853 finally broke out into an open fight. The ruling classes, the many-tiered hierarchy of warriors, were not alone involved in the fighting. Whether in the villages, towns or cities, people of all classes were involved in one way or another. The civil war served to intensify conflicts and compromises of group interests, breaking down feudal solidarity among the samurai, stimulating new ideas and innovations, and speeding the defeat of the traditional political and moral principles associated with feudalism.

However, it was not simply a struggle between progressive and unprogressive forces. The reforms of the Bakufu under the last

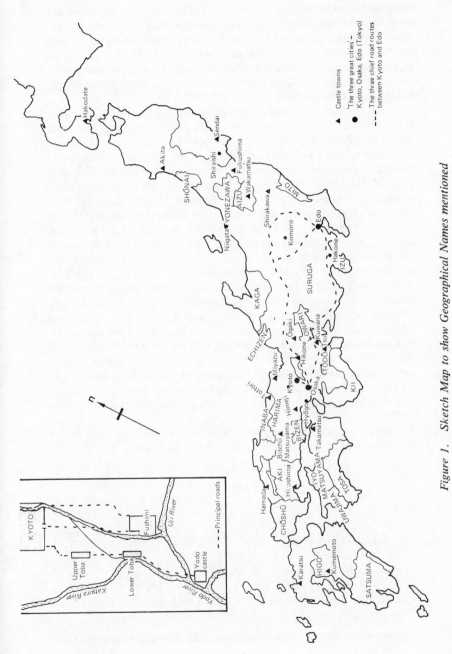

Figure 1. Sketch Map to show Geographical Names mentioned

Shogun, the vigorous and impressive Tokugawa Yoshinobu (Keiki) were in some ways surprisingly progressive. Not only were efforts made to build a modern navy (with British help) and to modernise the Bakufu army (with French aid), but Oguri Tadamasa and other Bakufu bureaucrats, under French tutelage, planned to institute a prefectural system which would have cut off the prerogatives of the feudal lords (daimyo).[1]

These reforms were making good progress until they were interrupted by the civil war. Their very successes, in the short run, and their radical nature, coupled with respect for the political abilities of Yoshinobu, provoked greater militancy on the part of the anti-Bakufu forces, and helped to bring about the Satsuma-Chōshū alliance. It is, however, problematical whether they would have been ultimately successful in reviving the Bakufu. In any case, they were interrupted by the civil war, and, aside from the basic difficulty, perhaps impossibility, for the Bakufu to dispense with the feudal system, there were many more immediate obstacles to the ultimate success of the reforms. They included the limitations of French aid, corruption in the Bakufu bureaucracy, and the fact that public opinion had already foresaken the Bakufu after the failure of the second punitive expedition against Chōshū in October 1866. Evidences of widespread disillusionment with the Bakufu include increasing disregard for Bakufu law, the lack of response by the daimyo to Bakufu requests and even orders, as well as peasant uprisings and riots which were at their worst in Bakufu territories. All this leads one to conclude that although something of the feudal system might well have been prolonged, the Tokugawa system was without doubt irretrievably lost by the time Yoshinobu became Shogun in January 1867.

Perhaps the best description of Yoshinobu comes to us from the British diplomat A. H. Mitford, later Lord Redesdale:

'[He] was a very striking personality. He was of average height, small as compared with Europeans, but the old Japanese robes made the difference less apparent. I think he was the handsomest man, according to our ideas, that I saw during all the years I was in Japan. His features were regular, his eye brilliantly lighted and keen, his complexion a clear, healthy olive colour. The mouth was very firm, but his expression when he smiled was gentle and singularly winning. His frame was well-knit and strong, the figure of a man of great activity; an indefatigable horseman, as inured to weather as an English master of hounds. . . . He was a great noble if ever there was one. The pity of it was that he was an anachronism.'[2]

The coup d'état of 3 January 1868, which secured control of the young Emperor by a small group of court nobles and representatives of the three *tozama* ('outside') *han* of Satsuma, Tosa and Aki (Hiroshima) and the Tokugawa related houses of Owari (*sanke*) and Echizen (*kamon*), proved to be the decisive date for the Restoration of the Emperor and the beginning of far-reaching changes. But, as Professor Beasley has pointed out: 'To all appearances it was no more than another palace revolution—as many of the participants must have thought it.'[3]

The decisions taken by a council, which excluded all known opponents, included stripping the former Shogun of his offices and lands. But this was understood by some to mean only part of his lands, and in any case, the decisions of the council were not made public. Chōshū, having been pardoned by the Emperor, moved troops to Kyoto, and Yoshinobu left the capital for Osaka on 7 January. Mitford, who was there, describes the scene when the former Shogun arrived at Osaka castle:

'A more extravagantly weird picture it would be difficult to imagine. There were some infantry armed with European rifles, but there were also warriors clad in the old armour of the country carrying spears, bows and arrows, curiously shaped with sword and dirk, who looked as if they had stepped out of some old pictures of the Gem-Pei wars in the Middle Ages. Their *jimbaoris* [coats worn over armour], not unlike heralds' tabards, were as many-coloured as Joseph's coat. Hideous masks of lacquer and iron, fringed with portentous whiskers and moustachios, crested helmets with wigs from which long streamers of horsehair floated to their waists, might strike terror into any enemy. They looked like the hobgoblins of a nightmare. Soon a troop of horsemen appeared. The Japanese all prostrated themselves and bent their heads in reverent awe. In the midst of the troop was the fallen Prince, accompanied by his faithful adherents, Aidzu and Kuwana. The Prince himself seemed worn and dejected . . . his head wrapped in a black cloth, taking notice of nothing. . . . At the gate all dismounted, according to custom—save only the War Lord himself; he rode in, a solitary horseman. It was the last entry of a Shogun into the grand old castle which had come into the heritage of the Tokugawa by one tragedy, and was to pass out of their possession by another.'[4]

But this was not the end of Yoshinobu as a force in Japanese politics. With less thought for himself than for the preservation of the Tokugawa clan, he turned his efforts towards a compromise settlement, with the help of Owari and Echizen, two of the *han* which had participated in the Restoration council, both related to the Tokugawa. Yoshinobu agreed to their proposal that he would give up his offices and court rank, but only enough of his domains to give the Emperor a sufficient revenue. Yoshinobu's explanation of his withdrawal to Osaka was that he wished to avoid civil war. On 14 January, he wrote a memorial to the Court interpreting the *coup d'état* as having resulted from plans, based on self-interest, of one or two *han* (a reference to Chōshū, banned from the Court, and Satsuma), brazenly making use of the boy Emperor. Yoshinobu proposed a return to the situation before the *coup*, calling a meeting of the principal lords, selecting men 'of integrity', and securing the resignation of the traitors. The memorial was received by Iwakura, who shelved it, not telling others in the government, perhaps for fear of a disturbance.[5]

In the Imperial council meeting of 18 and 19 January, the issue between the two factions on the problem of the resignation of the Shogun and the confiscation of his lands was reconsidered. Iwakura, while ostensibly carrying out the implications of the *coup d'état*, absented himself from the meeting on the pretext of illness. The meeting finally decided that, 'After an investigation into the administrative means for the distribution of lands, the matter will be decided by reference to opinion in the country', significantly omitting any reference to the return of lands to the Emperor. The efforts of the Ōkubo group and the demand for the return of lands in Iwakura's letter were swept aside by the moderate faction, now evidently in a position of predominance. Iwakura's withdrawal left a strong suspicion that the position he had taken earlier had been no more than a manoeuvre. The same day, returning to the principles of the memorial of Yamauchi Yōdō (the Tosa Memorial), on the basis of which the Shogun had resigned, the moderate faction took the lead in deciding that government expenses would be levied against the main *han*, including the Tokugawa, 'as soon as a decision in detail is taken on the problem of Yoshinobu's return of lands to the Emperor'.[6]

At this point, Yoshinobu advanced a step further. On 23 January he sent word to Tokugawa Yoshikatsu (of Owari) and Matsudaira Keiei (of Echizen), leaders of the moderate group in Kyoto, that if the expenses of the government were not met first by his order, then by the *daimyo* doing likewise, and if all did not levy an equal tax on all land in the country, it would be impossible to keep subordinates quiet. The government was apparently moving towards an acceptance of this.[7] Just before the battles of Fushimi and Toba, Iwakura agreed to a proposal that Yoshinobu be invited to come to Kyoto, and be appointed as a senior councillor (*Gijō*). He praised Yoshinobu's ability and talents, and said they would be able to do nothing without him.[8]

This shift can be seen in foreign affairs as well as in the problem of stripping the Shogun of his lands. On 11 January Yoshinobu gave an audience in Osaka to the representatives of the six powers—England, France, the U.S.A., Italy, Prussia and Holland. Giving his interpretation of the radical changes in the political structure, he voiced his dissatisfaction with the *coup d'état*, saying: 'Until, in due course, by means of the general opinion throughout the country, detailed decisions are taken about the political forms of our country, I wish to make it clear that it will be my duty to comply with the treaties, carrying out all conditions as promised, and to perfect our foreign relations.'⁹ In this he expressed his determination to remain at the centre of political power, refusing to recognise the Imperial government's authority in foreign affairs, but the government could do nothing. Further, even the proclamation to foreign countries of the restoration of Imperial rule was finally suspended due to the opposition of the moderate faction, when dissenting opinions were put forward by Matsudaira Keiei (of Echizen) and Asano Yoshiteru (of Aki), and Tokugawa Yoshikatsu and Yamauchi Yōdō joined them in refusing to sign it.¹⁰

The main point of their opposition was that it was unsuitable that such an important decision should be made by the handful of *daimyo* in Kyoto rather than by all the *daimyo*. Ōkubo, connecting this setback with Yoshinobu's announcement to the foreign representatives, remarked: 'It is certainly due to fear of the Tokugawa clan.' But it is possible that Ōkubo did not wish to make too much of an issue of this because of a letter from Terajima Munenori transmitting to him views attributed to the English, to the effect that Satow and others had told him that Yoshinobu's proclamation was sufficient, and that as the form of government had not yet been definitely decided, to proclaim this now would simply invite laughter from the foreigners.¹¹

It was clear that in the appointment of non-Satsuma-Chōshū councillors (*Gijō* and *Sanyo*), things were turning in favour of Yoshinobu and the moderate group. The attitudes of the ten *han* represented in Kyoto on 7 January changed. The military situation did not develop to the advantage of the Ōkubo group either: a number of important *daimyo*, who might have supported the new government, left the capital. Maeda of Kaga returned with a large force to his own *han*, on the excuse of not wanting to cause any incidents in Kyoto, and others such as Sakai, the lord of Himeji, and Hisamatsu of Iyo Matsuyama, joined Yoshinobu in Osaka.

The reasons for this shift towards the moderate position included the very narrow base of the new government, financial stringency leading to a need to rely on a larger base, the tendency of the majority of the *han* to be pro-Bakufu and to adopt opportunistic, 'wait-and-see' policies, and efforts to avoid a military conflict, at a time when the nation needed solidarity against the Western threat as it was seen at the time. There was a general fear both of foreign intervention and domestic disturbances.

At this point, the victory of the Ōkubo group and, *ex post facto*, of the new government in the Toba-Fushimi hostilities was decisive, bringing about a drastic loss of influence within the government by the moderate group, the grasping of control by the militant anti-Bakufu faction (the Ōkubo group), and the decision of the feudal lords of the Kinki area (around Kyoto), and to the west, to support the new government. The sudden swing back to control by the Ōkubo group resulting from this first outbreak of hostilities in the civil war is interpreted by some Japanese historians, especially Marxists like Inoue Kiyoshi, as having greatly encouraged bureaucratic absolutism and as having dealt decisive blows against the advocacy of a parliamentary political structure as a means of consulting public opinion, and against the political prerogatives of the alliance of important lords associated with this idea.[12] It is hard to avoid doubts, however, about whether one side was any more democratic than the other.

There seems to be no actual evidence that Yoshinobu approved the sudden movement of between 10,000 and 15,000 troops from Osaka towards Kyoto on 26 January. It is known that he was having trouble controlling his more zealous subordinates, especially the lords of Kuwana and Aizu, who had been the Bakufu military officers responsible for the security of Kyoto, and it is quite possible they started out without Yoshinobu's consent. On the other hand, Yoshinobu may have decided to take the initiative by permitting a demonstration of power ostensibly to strengthen further the moderate party in Kyoto,[13] but this seems somehow slightly out of character, unless it was a desperate compromise with the explosion of anger among the Tokugawa adherents over news of fighting in Edo between Satsuma and Bakufu troops who counter-attacked and burned the Satsuma residence in Edo. The latter had become the headquarters of a group of Satsuma hot-heads with a link to Saigō in Kyoto, who evidently gave the signal to begin disturbances in order to provoke the enemy into making the first move. The existence of a secret agreement between Saigō and Sagara Sōzō and others of the Sōmō Rōshitai (popular force of masterless samurai), whose activities were centred in the Satsuma residence in Edo, has been affirmed by a number of Japanese historians.[14]

Perhaps there was no time to get government approval of the dispatch of troops from Kyoto to reinforce those already guarding the southern approaches to the city. In any case, Saigō moved immediately on hearing that Aizu, Kuwana and allied troops had left Osaka. In the next few days decisive defeats were administered by the Imperial forces, mostly Satsuma units under Saigō's instructions. The two separate Bakufu columns coming from Osaka were stopped at Toba and Fushimi by the numerically inferior guard units, about 2,000 of them, who refused demands for passage through to Kyoto. In the ensuing battles, begun when Satsuma cannons were fired into the ranks of the enemy, the anti-Tokugawa forces numbering between 5,500 and 6,000 were made up of Satsuma men aided by Chōshū and Tosa troops, and, later, by smaller units from Inaba (Tottori) and Tōdō *han*, a combined force of about half the size of the pro-Tokugawa army. The defenders were in well-prepared positions, were much better equipped with rifles and cannons, and their solidarity and morale, already strong, were heightened after the first day by the bestowal of Imperial banners rushed from Kyoto. And luck was with them as well.

The historical importance of the battle at Toba and Fushimi may justify the addition of some details here. Hostilities began on 27 January at Lower Toba (see inset to map, p. 29), after long negotiations and arguments with the Satsuma guards, who resolutely refused passage. The Bakufu commanders of the Kuwana troops, former Bakufu units, Ōgaki and other *han* forces temporarily withdrew to Yodo castle. When they returned and resumed the argument, suddenly, at 5 p.m., Satsuma cannons opened fire on their ranks. An attack with spears and swords was attempted, but met rifle fire 'like rain' from the Satsuma positions, and the attackers were forced to retreat. At the entrance to Fushimi, the other column of the pro-Tokugawa forces, also under Bakufu commanders, was waiting. It was made up of the Aizu troops, Bakufu units, and troops from Hamada, Takamatsu, Toba and other *han*. The commanders were similarly demanding entrance. Shortly after the artillery fire at Toba was heard, hostilities began there as well. At Toba, there was a withdrawal by the pro-Yoshinobu troops at 10 p.m., and a short rear-guard action took place at about midnight. At Fushimi, indecisive fighting continued until about 1 a.m., followed by a withdrawal to Yodo, where Aizu, Kuwana and Bakufu commanders held a conference in Yodo castle.

The Satsuma and Chōshū forces were clearly well prepared for an attack, but Saigō planned, if things went badly, to announce an Imperial progress to Hiei, the mountain just north-east of Kyoto. Then, he planned to take the young Emperor to a strong, strategic point between Hiroshima and Okayama via the inner mountain road (the San'indō), dividing the Imperial commands into three regional ones to carry on the fight. In later years, Saigō recalled: 'I was happier at the first sound of cannon fire at Toba than I would have been if I had gained a following of a million allies.' For him, it was a sound which meant he was staking everything on victory or defeat.

The morning of the second day (28 January) began with a unit of Bakufu troops being ambushed by Satsuma and Chōshū riflemen hidden in a bamboo thicket, with disastrous effect. After a prolonged exchange of rifle fire, the Bakufu troops retreated, leaving two of the Bakufu commanders dead on the battlefield. Then, the Imperial Prince Ninnaji no Miya arrived from Kyoto and bestowed Imperial banners on the Satsuma-Chōshū command.

The Tosa commanders had no orders to participate in the battle, and knew that Yamauchi Yōdō, the active head of the *han*, preferred a peaceful settlement. The official Tosa view of the battle was that it was essentially a private one between Satsuma and Aizu, and the *han* was holding to a neutral position. But after the first day of fighting, perhaps the majority of the troops wanted to join the Satsuma and Chōshū forces. The bestowal of the Imperial banners, and persuasion from Itagaki Taisuke, who had promised Saigō his co-operation, decided two of the three commanders. Then, they were fired on by Takamatsu troops. The Tosa men repulsed them successfully, but with some loss of life. At this point the commanders decided that if the battle went badly, and their action brought trouble to Yamauchi Yōdō, they would commit suicide. But in fact they were given no further chance to play an active part in the battle.

The samurai of Kumamoto *han* (Higo) actually divided into opposing groups, one planning to attack Satsuma in Kyoto, the other intending to join Satsuma and Chōshū at Toba and Fushimi. Neither plan was actually carried out, due to prolonged arguments between the opposed groups. Among the samurai of Tōdō *han* stationed nearby at Yamazaki, across the river and just south of Yodo, some actually arranged secretly to ally with one or the other of the Kumamoto groups. The action of other domains as well was unpredictable, and depended on how the military situation developed.

On 29 January the Satsuma-Chōshū forces turned to the offensive, making good use of their superior fire power and experience with rifles. The Aizu forces under remaining Bakufu commanders were forced to retreat to Yodo castle, one of their three commanders being killed and another seriously wounded during the retreat. A fresh Satsuma unit, released from guard duty in Kyoto, arrived on the scene where about eighty Aizu spearmen were between them and the other Aizu men, some of them riflemen. The Aizu riflemen could not fire for fear of hitting their own spearmen, so Miura, the Satsuma commander, seeing his opportunity, ordered a charge. The spearmen were mostly shot down, and the other Aizu men forced to abandon their positions, including the Yodo bridge, to the Satsuma attackers.

The Bakufu, Kuwana and Aizu forces planned to make a stand in Yodo castle, and stop the attack, but this was not to be. They found the castle held by Yodo troops, their allies of yesterday, who greeted them with threats to cut them to pieces if they attempted to enter the castle. Inaba, the *daimyo* of Yodo *han*, was a Senior Councillor (*Rōjū*) in the Bakufu, but was on duty in Edo. The officers in the castle sent word that without the permission of the *daimyo*, they could not admit troops of any other *han* to the castle. In fact, they had decided not to sacrifice their *han* for an apparently doomed cause. The next day (30 January), they allied formally with Chōshū and Satsuma, the Imperial side.

Denied entrance to Yodo castle, the pro-Tokugawa troops withdrew south of the castle for the night. The following morning (30 January), from across the river, the Tōdō *han* army, having watched developments closely, opened up with cannons on the pro-Tokugawa forces. The previous day they had been visited by representatives of the old Bakufu as well as by a court noble from Kyoto. Their decision to join the fray on the Satsuma-Chōshū side proved to be the final blow. Nagai Kōshi, a Junior Councillor (*Wakadoshi-yori*) of the old Bakufu, had taken the precaution of obtaining from Yoshinobu an order to retreat. Accordingly, a retreat to Osaka was ordered on 30 January and by the morning of 31 January, all troops had returned to Osaka.

As seen from Osaka castle, defeat was certain by 30 January, and any desire to continue hostilities had been lost. Yoshinobu, suffering from a cold, listened to the battle reports with a heavy heart, not having taken a step outside the castle. Convinced by arguments that he should return to Edo, he slipped secretly out of the castle at 10 p.m. on 30 January, with a small escort. Unable to find a Bakufu ship in the dark, they spent the night on board an American warship anchored off Osaka. In the morning, joined by two *Rōjū*, Sakai and Itakura, and by the lords of Aizu and Kuwana and a few others, Yoshinobu travelled on a Bakufu ship to Edo. The wounded were taken to Edo on other Bakufu ships. The defeated troops dispersed after their return to Osaka. Chōshū units arrived late on 31 January, and when they entered the castle the following morning, they found it burned out and its famous treasures stolen. Osaka castle was formally surrendered on 5 February.[15]

During the battles of Toba and Fushimi, gale-force winds, very cold, were blowing from the north. As the Satsuma and Chōshū men advanced, they had the winds to their backs, while their enemies had to face them. The Imperial forces considered these winds providential.

Three special Bakufu units (or groups, *kumi*) fought well, especially the one which had received training from French officers, and there were many Aizu and Kuwana soldiers who fought bravely, though their morale was not nearly as high as that of the Imperial forces. In the face of withering cannon and rifle fire, they had little opportunity to show their more traditional skills. Also, other troops from various *han* who fought with them in fact contributed very little. Large numbers of spearmen tended to get in the way, and horses, frightened by the noise of cannon and rifle fire, often bolted and unseated their riders. Compared with the total of some 15,000 pro-Tokugawa troops, Satsuma apparently had only about 3,000, Chōshū about 1,500, and Tosa something over 1,000. Since Tosa was involved in only one small action, and Inaba (Tottori) and Tōdō forces were involved only after the outcome was in little doubt, the difference in totals is all the more impressive.

The advantages enjoyed by Satsuma and Chōshū included superior solidarity and spirit, better equipment and training in riflery, professional confidence in the skills of their troops, and a psychological advantage conferred by the Imperial banners proclaiming them as the Imperial army. This was an advantage both for their own morale and in persuading the undecided *han* to ally themselves with the Imperial side, or at least not to aid the side branded as 'enemies of the Court' (*chōteki*). In so designating the 'rebels', the Court held Yoshinobu responsible for the resort to arms, and ordered a punitive expedition against him and the lords of the domains who were involved, or whose men were involved on the Tokugawa side in the actual hostilities.[16]

Before the battle began, the moderate party in Kyoto, hearing of the departure of Shogunal forces from Osaka towards Kyoto, cast about for means to prevent hostilities. In a memorandum written after the event, it is recorded that Echizen proposed, in great haste, to co-operate with Owari *han* in meeting and placating the Aizu and Kuwana forces as near Osaka as possible, placing, if possible, the two armies of Owari and Echizen between the opposed forces to keep them apart. But this was seen to be impossible, due to insufficient preparation. Then, it was agreed that at Court every effort had to be made to prevent the issuance of an Imperial order for the punishment of the former Shogun. But this, too, proved impossible. The Echizen memorandum continues: 'The Tokugawa were, of course, branded as enemies of the Court. But not only that. Without asking about right or wrong, everyone who could be said to have supported the Bakufu was branded as an enemy of the Court and subjected to pressure.'[17]

After this, there was a considerable development of ideological opposition to the new government, based principally on loyalty to the Tokugawa clan, but also on feelings of resentment over the treatment of Yoshinobu. The *daimyo* of Komoro in Shinshū complains in a memorial: 'Now the lords are required to attack the Tokugawa clan. For example, Inaba and Bizen are younger brothers of the Tokugawa [i.e. of Yoshinobu]. The family of Ii [Hikone] are ministers of the Tokugawa. Others too have been followers of the Tokugawa for three hundred years. But younger brothers are caused to attack their elder brothers. Ministers are made to kill their lords. What will later generations say of this?'[18]

Back in Edo, Yoshinobu endeavoured without success to revert to the situation just before the Toba-Fushimi defeats. To strengthen his position, he took two positive steps. He asked for foreign support through the French Minister, Léon Roches, and gave orders to defend key points along the high-roads from the Kansai to Edo. Meanwhile, he sought clemency from the government through an intermediary, arranging to send as his emissary to Kyoto the Princess Kazu no Miya, younger sister of the former Emperor Kōmei who, at the age of 15, had married Iemochi, Yoshinobu's predecessor as Shogun. Then, on 5 March, he declared his absolute fidelity to the Emperor. These actions may seem contradictory, but Yoshinobu apparently wished, by resigning completely, to preserve the Tokugawa clan if at all possible. But his efforts to strengthen his position failed. No help was forthcoming from the foreign powers; the powerful lords of the central regions, including the Ii of Hikone, the largest of the *fudai daimyo*, had all pledged their allegiance to the Emperor; and he received a discouraging letter from Matsudaira Keiei telling him of the hardening attitude of the government towards him.[19] This reversal of the political situation after defeat in a battle in which both sides had some claim to be the government (and therefore, the Imperial) army, is often referred to as another example in Japanese history of the adage, *Kateba Kangun* (If you win, you are the Imperial army).

Before the Toba-Fushimi battles, the uncommitted *daimyo*, although frequently receiving orders from the Restoration government, did not necessarily follow them. After the battle, the majority of them did, and with alacrity. The powerful *han* of the Kansai and Chūbu areas (South and West Honshū and Shikoku), Aki, Bizen, Harima, Tosa, Owari and others, moved over quickly to the support of the government, and, together with Satsuma and Chōshū, played an important part in deciding the movements and actions of their neighbouring *han*, which were mostly smaller. The lords of those domains were asked point blank where they stood, and when they claimed loyalty to the Emperor, they were required to swear formal allegiance, and in some cases were given Imperial banners. In the course of organising and pushing forward the campaign against Yoshinobu, the forces moving toward Edo along the three principal road routes carried out a similar policy of assuring the absolute loyalty of ail along the way.[20]

As the Imperial armies approached, confusion in the Kantō increased. Peasant disturbances flared up in part due to change-overs in Bakufu territories which sometimes left temporary gaps in administrative control. Some *daikan* and other Bakufu officers, with their staffs, simply left their posts, mostly to collect in discontented bands in Edo. Some of the uprisings were caused by rumours that a reduction in the land taxes by half, which had been announced in some places in an irregular manner, had been retracted. Others were protests against rapidly rising prices, forced labour and special exactions required by the military, etc.; in general, conditions caused by military movements which, among other things, cut off ordinary transport and communications.[21]

Among some of the small *han* in the Kantō, confrontations between pro-Bakufu and pro-government cliques flared into open clashes,[22] and these troubles spread southward to the Izu and Hakone regions.[23] *Han* close to the Tokugawa tried to avoid being involved in anti-Tokugawa military action by asking for other duties. Some asked for, and received, orders to suppress pro-Tokugawa factions in their own domains. In the case of Owari and Mito, there was actual fighting, and a considerable loss of life. Some were permitted to make financial, rather than military, contributions to the campaign. In one case, as his son was a well-known *Rōjū* in the old Bakufu, Ogasawara Nagakuni, the lord of Karatsu *han* in Kyūshū, disowned him, and, insisting that he was not related to him, requested to be in the vanguard of the attack on the former Shogun.[24]

The government's policy was a positive one of facing directly the crisis situation, domestic and foreign. The immediate foreign crisis was caused by three incidents in the period from the end of January to April, which had an indirect relation to the civil war: in Hyōgo (Kōbe), the firing on a group of unarmed foreigners, one of whom was injured, by Bizen troops; the killing of eleven French soldiers and sailors in Sakai by Tosa troops; and the attack on the British Minister, Sir Harry Parkes, by *jōi* extremists in Kyoto. These incidents, occurring at a time when the new government, deeply involved in the civil war, lacked both solidity and recognition of legality by the foreign powers, greatly increased the fear of serious foreign intervention. To prevent this, quick action was taken. In February, the demands of the foreign representatives made after the first incident (in Hyōgo), were immediately accepted. An Imperial judgement to punish the offenders was served on Echizen, with the threat of an attack on the *han* if it was disobeyed.[25] Similarly, quick action was taken to satisfy the powers in the other incidents. After the attack on Sir Harry Parkes, notices, whose original text was submitted to and corrected by Sir Harry himself, were posted at road and street intersections throughout the country. Haraguchi Kiyoshi, describing this concession with distaste in 1963, called it 'needlessly servile'.[26]

The need for the foreigners to see the Imperial Court imposing a 'justice common to all countries' was pressed by a memorial to the government signed by five major heads of *han*, all closely associated with the government: Shimazu, Asano, Hosokawa, Matsudaira Keiei, and Yamauchi Yōdō. As we have seen, the government did not hesitate to use threats against the domains in order to placate the powers and to prevent further incidents. Soon, persuasion was added to coercion. The first formal expression by the government of ideas later seen in the Five-Article Charter Oath of 6 April 1868 was a direct result of these efforts. In the Imperial Proclamation of 11 February, an attempt was made to pacify anti-foreign elements, and a pointed suggestion was made that changes in attitudes were necessary: 'What is urgently needed now is to respond to the times with eyes open, to rid ourselves of former evil customs, and to show forth the light of virtue to all countries', ideas repeated in a public statement by the Emperor on 22 March.[27] These worries about possible foreign intervention in the civil war thus not only impelled the government to placate the powers by moving quickly against anti-foreignism, but also served to strengthen the hand of innovators in the government.

When the decision was taken, at the instigation of Iwakura, to send a large Imperial army to the Kantō, Matsudaira Keiei of Echizen wrote a dissenting memorial which was not accepted. Again, Keiei wrote a proposal on 10 March, supported by Owari and Kii, asking for the pardon of Yoshinobu, also rejected.[28] The moderate position at Court still had its spokesmen.

On 3 May, Yoshinobu, who had been working for a negotiated settlement through Katsu Awa (the naval expert and head of a 'loyalist' faction in the Bakufu which favoured a compromise settlement), surrendered Edo to the Imperial forces whose active head was Saigō Takamori. Yoshinobu's explanation of this was that it was the only way of avoiding needless bloodshed and major hostilities which could bring down upon Japan the additional calamity of foreign intervention. The agreement negotiated with the government provided for the resignation of Yoshinobu as head of the Tokugawa clan. The headship was to move to the Tayasu branch of the family, which was to hold a maximum domain of 700,000 *koku*, roughly 10 per cent of the former Shogunal holdings. This compromise settlement was not easily accepted by either side. In Kyoto, the Ōkubo group calmed the protests of unsatisfied loyalists only with difficulty. In Edo, the dissatisfaction of Tokugawa retainers led eventually to the battle of Ueno (4 July), after which Admiral Enomoto, taking part of the Bakufu fleet, fled to Ezo (Hokkaido), which he intended to preserve as a domain for Yoshinobu.[29] In the north, opposition began organising under Aizu leadership.

After the Toba-Fushimi battles, the government classified the following as enemies of the Court, in order of importance: (1) Tokugawa Yoshinobu; (2) Matsudaira Katamori (Aizu) and Matsudaira Sadaaki (Kuwana), the two former Bakufu military supervisors of Kyoto; (3) Hisamatsu Teishō (Iyo Matsuyama), Sakai Tadaatsushi (Himeji) and Itakura Katsukiyo (Bitchū Matsuyama); (4) Honjō Munetaka (Miyazu); and (5) Toda Ujitomo (Ōgaki) and Matsudaira Yoriaki (Takamatsu). Troops from all these domains had been involved against the Chōshū-Satsuma-Tosa troops at Toba-Fushimi, although some were clearly 'without instructions' from their lords.[30] It was considered that once all the *daimyo* were brought to guarantee absolute obedience to the Emperor, the government's objective in the civil war would be reached. Until a *daimyo* did this, the government was uncompromising, but once allegiance was sworn, it was prepared to be lenient.

Government army rules and regulations applying to the campaign in the north were aimed at uniting all domain units into a single command, and preventing depredations by government troops, for which severe punishments were provided. If it became necessary, the army was to suppress peasant revolts and riots. Despite regulations, however, there were cases of government troops stealing, firing on the houses of ordinary people, terrorising them, and taking part in all the other kinds of depredations that are associated with civil war (especially when one aspect of the opposition takes the form of guerrilla warfare). Although in principle, and to some extent in fact, it was a united Imperial army, its ideology and ideals did not necessarily penetrate down through the subordinate ranks. Also, there were cases of trouble between regional army commands, between Satsuma and Tosa troops, and between Satsuma and Chōshū. In the early phases of the campaign, the Imperial commands experienced many difficulties about supplies, communications and organisation.[31]

Even most Japanese writers have overlooked two important aspects of the army's role in the civil war period: propagandising the people on behalf of the new government, and transmitting orders to the *han* as well as supervising them to see that they were enforced. Towards the peasants, the ultimate weapon of propaganda was the Imperial declaration of a reduction by half in the annual taxes on crops. Such declarations were apparently reserved for particularly difficult areas, but the general effect must have been considerable, provided the peasants were disposed to believe in them. Charity for the most impoverished people was often offered, and sometimes delivered, in a conscious attempt to contrast what the government liked to call the Emperor's concern for his people with the traditional unconcern of the feudal overlords.[32]

Given the history of the success of irregular troops or auxiliary militia in Chōshū, it is not surprising that the government army included a number of such units, incorporating members of the lower classes trained mostly in the use of rifles. Some were attached as integral units of the army, others were permitted to operate independently, and it is those last which presented the greatest problems of discipline. One of these units was called the Sekibōtai, organised immediately after the Toba-Fushimi battles by Sagara Sōzō, with a nucleus of the Sōmō Rōshitai, already mentioned as the gang organised in Edo in 1867 to create disturbances on orders from Saigō Takamori. The Sekibōtai was a mixed group of about five hundred men, the majority of peasant origin. They were dedicated to fighting against supporters of the Bakufu, all those who got in their way, and those engaged in foreign trade. They collected money by force from wealthy houses, mostly of merchants, in Edo. Some were caught by Bakufu officers and executed for armed robbery.[33]

The Sekibōtai received an order from the government to be a vanguard for the Imperial army in the Kantō, and at the same time they were informed of orders to reduce by half the taxes collected from former Bakufu direct territories, and were given instructions to render material assistance to the poor. The members of the Sekibōtai were rather overzealous in spreading the word not only in former Bakufu territories, but in the *han* as well, especially in the Tōsan region. In this area, the government never acknowledged publicly that the orders were inapplicable, but it simply did not apply them, and it charged the Sekibōtai with fomenting peasant uprisings. The government's attitude towards groups like the Sekibōtai who were not exactly under military discipline changed after mid-February from making use of them to suppressing them. The domains were rapidly turning towards co-operation with the government, and there was no longer a need for these semi-independent irregulars.[34]

The problem of the final disposition of the Tokugawa clan was still open when the one-day battle took place at Ueno on 4 July. The resolute action of the government at Ueno in attacking and defeating a force of about 3,000 Tokugawa adherents opened up an escape route from its difficulties in the former Bakufu stronghold, the Kantō. First, it dealt a crushing blow to one of the largest anti-government units, which had been preparing for and carrying out attacks in the Kantō. This weakened them and restored confidence in the security of the area. There were still some small actions here and there, but nothing serious. Some groups fled from Edo to join likeminded units in the north, where they were welcomed as 'guest fighters' (*kyakuhei*). Secondly, the government army was released to apply its full power in the north. Thirdly, it had the effect of deciding the as yet uncommitted *han*, especially in the Kantō area, in favour of the government. In addition, it moved closer to possibility the plans to move Yoshinobu to a domain in Suruga and to make Edo, as Tokyo, the new capital. On 14 July, Sanjō Sanetomi was named commander-in-chief for the eight provinces of the Kantō, and the announcement was made that the Tokugawa clan had been granted a fief assessed at 700,000 *koku* in Suruga. In August, the change of capital from Edo to Tokyo was announced.[35]

On 20 September, an Imperial proclamation was issued announcing that the entire country had now been united under the Imperial government except for 'a corner of Ōu'. As this comprised most of northern Honshū, it was a rather large 'corner'! The Emperor expressed regret for this, and went on, rather pointedly, to say that the people were one family under the Emperor, that no distinction would be made among the peasants of the entire country, and that they would not be forgotten. The war was still raging in the north when the announcement was made of the change of capital, and some small operations were still continuing in the Kantō. But, although the civil war was not yet finished, the period of real danger to the new government was over.[36]

This does not mean that the outcome of the war in the north was necessarily a foregone conclusion, or that it would be easy. In fact, it proved extremely difficult. But it had the advantage for the government of being fought at a considerable distance from the strategic areas of the Kansai and the Kantō. At the same time, in military terms, the remoteness of some of the domains involved, especially Shōnai, to the north of Aizu, did pose serious problems of communications, transport and organisation, providing, incidentally, the government army and its commanders with valuable experience.

The two most aggressively anti-government domains were Aizu and Shōnai, and later, Sendai. In the early stages, Sendai and Yonezawa were only nominal supporters of the government, continually postponing action on various pretexts, the most important of which was that they did not wish to interfere with peasants during the early planting season, for fear of peasant uprisings. But basically, there was too close a balance of opinion within the samurai of these doubtful domains, between pro-government and anti-government factions, in which fear of Aizu and Shōnai, whose samurai enjoyed a high reputation for their fighting ability, played a part.[37]

In Fukushima, on the evening of 10 June, a band of samurai from Sendai assassinated Sera Shūzō, a government army staff officer. This was a move by the anti-government clique in Sendai to push Sendai *han* into the anti-government camp. Sera, in his frustration at the lack of response from Sendai to repeated calls for troops, had let slip a remark about the 'cowardice' of Sendai samurai. A Governor-General, the Court Noble Kujō, was put under house arrest in Sendai, and a staff officer, Daigo, was kidnapped with some of his men and taken to Sendai; the *han* joined the anti-government alliance. On 11 June, Aizu troops took Shirakawa castle. Communications with the large government force sent north to subdue Shōnai had been cut off, and requests for help from Akita and Hirosaki were rejected. The situation of the government army in the north in mid-June had reached its lowest point.[38]

In Aizu, solidarity and morale were high. Like Chōshū and Tosa, Aizu organised mixed militia units. These incorporated about 2,700 peasants, and a few sons of merchants and other commoners. Units of Bakufu *hatamoto*, volunteers from Kuwana (some 2,000), Mito, and many others, mostly representing defeated factions of other *han*, were organised. Special units of hunters, gamblers, wrestlers, even Buddhist and Shinto priests were used, perhaps in part for psychological effect on the enemy. The Aizu authorities bought Western rifles and ammunition from foreign merchants, mostly from a Dutch merchant in Edo named Snell. They borrowed cannons and rifles from the Bakufu pro-war faction, and continued to receive training from French military experts.[39]

The anti-government alliance was concluded on 23 June by twenty-five lords of domains in Ōu, later joined by six others. In a memorial to the Emperor, they heaped the blame on Satsuma and Chōshū, rather than on the Imperial government, for harsh terms and a dictatorial attitude towards Aizu and Shōnai, and injustice on the part of the Imperial regional commands. Citing the case of Shōnai, they charged the government with proclaiming, from a distance, the confiscation of certain lands in favour of neighbouring domains thought to be loyal, and then branding the *daimyo* as an enemy of the Court when his officials collected the annual taxes from those lands. The alliance did not include the two accused domains, Shōnai and Aizu, and was in a sense another appearance of the conservative, feudal, moderate position, pressing for the traditional methods of conciliation as a means to solve the problem. The memorial begins with a statement of basic support for the return of political power to the Emperor (ōsei fukko). It goes on with detailed complaints about obstacles to the 'great project' of building an Imperial Japan: the peremptory orders of the regional headquarters under the nominal command of Kujō, ordering various han to mount immediate attacks on recalcitrant domains; the harsh attitude of the command on the conditions for the surrender of Matsudaira Kata-mori of Aizu; the campaign against Shōnai whose guilt, chiefly of collecting their own taxes, was unclear and doubtful; and the pursuit by the regional commanders of personal enmity by means of Imperial orders. It goes on to plead for clemency towards Aizu and Shōnai, and for a just disposition granting the former Shogun Court rank and lands. It ends by pleading for the suppression of 'false Imperial soldiers' and for the establishment of a just Imperial rule in the north.[40]

As for Aizu han, the memorial states that that domain did not intend to revive the Bakufu, but merely wished to remove the charge of treachery and wrongdoing on the part of their daimyo. But it was clear that Aizu was not willing to support or participate in a government dominated by the uncompromising faction led by Satsuma and Chōshū. The headquarters of the alliance was established in Shiraishi in August, and former Bakufu Senior Councillors Itakura and Ogasawara were put in charge of the administration.[41]

To return for a moment to problems of foreign relations, the government was convinced that there was danger for Japan until all opposition to the government had been suppressed. The official neutrality of the powers, speculation about the splitting of the country, north and south, among foreigners in Japan and in the foreign press (especially newspapers published in Japan), the possibilities of Russian aid to the anti-government forces in the north, and inability to prevent the provision of arms to them by smuggling, all pointed up potential dangers in the situation.[42]

Niigata, on the Japan Sea, was scheduled to open as a treaty port for foreign trade, but its opening was postponed due to the fact that it was held by 'enemies of the Court'. This did not, however, prevent the port from being used by the northern anti-government domains for foreign trade, especially with the Dutch—the peripatetic Mr Snell again. The government informed the foreign representatives that it could not guarantee the safety of foreigners trading at Niigata, but this, again, appears not to have deterred the foreign merchants. Bakufu officials who had been negotiating the purchase from the United States of an ironclad ship, the Stonewall, declared excess after the American Civil War, continued the negotiations from Shiraishi. But the fall of Niigata to the Imperial forces on 16 September prevented completion of the purchase. Meanwhile, a joint administration of the foreign trade at Niigata was set up by the major northern anti-government domains, and trade flourished. Beginning with Snell, later traders from Prussia, America and Britain came to join in the trade, partly because of the drop in trade at the other ports due to the war.[43]

By this time, the victory in the battle of Ueno, which placed the government in a position of superiority, permitted the shifting of troops from the Kantō, and a large army was before long on its way north, later placed under the able and aggressive leadership of Saigō, sent by sea to join his forces in September for the final stages of the campaign. There was progress in foreign relations as well. In a memorial written in August, Kido Kōin emphasised the need to press the foreign governments to recognise the Imperial government as the one legal government of Japan. This would mean, he explained, that there would be no further links with the Tokugawa, and there would be no room for foreign interference and foreign aid to the enemy. Within a month, such a notification was made. In December, although the naval force under Enomoto was still holding out in Hakodate, the declaration by the foreign powers of neutrality in the civil war was cancelled.[44]

During the northern campaign, two main efforts were made to bring the common people over to the Imperial side: first, continual notices prohibiting troops from stealing and mistreating the people, plus a public demonstration of determination to punish violators; and second, proclamations of a reduction by half in the annual land taxes. In the Echigo area, permission was given to peasants to arrest any wrongdoers. In a system of joint responsibility, squad commanders were held responsible for the conduct of their men. Even these measures, however, did not prevent a large number of incidents from happening. The anti-government army had similar troubles and adopted similar policies, but with generally less success. To protect their property, women, and their own lives, some villagers organised their own defences. There were a number of peasant uprisings during the hostilities in the north, some directed against the new, some against the old, authorities and the military forces supporting them. In most places, there seemed to be more fear and resentment against the anti-government forces, which were more of a motley lot, some of them mere guerilla bands, living off the land.[45]

The small domains associated in the anti-government alliance suffered most. They had either to follow the larger *han* in the alliance, often near neighbours, or be forced by government military pressure to leave the alliance and support the government effort with man-power, supplies and money. Most domains were divided internally between pro- and anti-government factions, a confrontation which became extreme under military pressure. The *daimyo* who tried to stand between these factions would be in the most unenviable position, since compromise and neutrality proved impossible, and often disastrous. In some cases, when a domain was defeated, those pro-government groups who quickly surrendered were made into the vanguard for the next government attack. Foraging and demands for financial and material aid from defeated *han* greatly increased their difficulties.[46]

The struggle on the main islands ended completely in January 1869, after the surrender of the various northern domains by the middle of November, following the decisive victory over Aizu when the strongly defended Wakamatsu castle was taken by a large Imperial army under Saigō on 6 November. Admiral Enomoto's 'semi-feudal republic'[47] in Hakodate surrendered in July 1869.

Most histories of Japan treat the civil war as a virtually bloodless affair whose outcome from the beginning was almost a foregone conclusion. Before the Toba-Fushimi battles, it was, however, by no means a foregone conclusion. The latest study by a distinguished Japanese historian, Hirao Michio, published in 1971, refers to the risk Saigō took in pitting his forces, only about 2,000 of whom were actually available at Toba and Fushimi, against such odds. The total numbers he could rely on were about 3,000 troops from Satsuma and roughly 1,500 from Chōshū, in the Kyoto area. The position of possible allies, including Tosa, was doubtful. Hirao characterises Saigō's decision as 'staking everything on victory or defeat.'[48]

After the initial and crucial Toba-Fushimi battles, everything seemed to go well for the government. But this was really true only after a series of setbacks in the north. From Hirao's work, one can cite two evidences of the importance of the battles fought after Toba-Fushimi: the number of battles considered important enough to detail; and the numbers of killed and wounded in the civil war. As to the first, Hirao includes details of no less than twenty-four battles, two of them naval battles, and three of them involving some naval action. From incomplete statistics and estimates of casualties for 1868–9, one can reach conjectural totals of something like 10,000 dead and 12,000 wounded.[49] According to another source, during the ten years preceding 1868, more than 2,000 were killed in internal struggles in the domain of Mito alone.[50] Perhaps the civil war should no longer be characterised as 'bloodless'.

The end of the civil war meant the end of the feudal system of Bakufu and *han*. For the *han*, whether pro- or anti-government, the civil war had brought extreme impoverishment, which made the later abolition of the *han* not only easier, but in some cases even welcomed by the *daimyo*. The civil war had aroused lasting enmities among the *han*, and, more importantly, within the *han*. There was never, after the battle of Osaka in 1615, very much solidarity among the *tozama* (outer) domains, except a common hostility to the Tokugawa among a few of them. But among the Tokugawa related houses, *sanke* and *kamon*, and among the hereditary vassal *daimyo* of the Tokugawa, the *fudai*, there was a degree of solidarity which was largely destroyed during the civil war, when, under extreme stress, each *han* took a position which had much less to do with its formal classification and historical relationship to the Tokugawa clan than with immediate problems of survival. Within the domains, through the splitting into warring factions forced into the open by military pressure, the solidarity of the feudal ruling classes was even more fragmented, leaving much mutual resentment.

Even in the domains which had provided the leadership for the Restoration, Tosa, Satsuma and Chōshū, there were divisive forces at work, notably the growing gap in attitudes and ideology between those who remained in the *han* and those in the central government. Satsuma and Tosa had perhaps the greatest difficulty of all in accepting the abolition of the *han*, because pride in the part they had played in establishing the Imperial government and in winning the civil war was essentially pride in the accomplishment of their *han*. In these domains, there was actually an increase in the strength of the *han* nationalism which the government found absolutely essential to convert into an Emperor-centred nationalism in the Meiji period.

In June 1869, the government collected answers to a questionnaire asking whether the *han* should be replaced with a prefectural system. The results were as follows: Yes (102 *han*, plus the Shōheikō, the Tokugawa-founded orthodox Confucian university in Edo-Tokyo); No (113 *han*); Neither (2 *han*). Among those voting for the change, those whose finances were most adversely affected by the civil war were prominent. Among the 102 favouring the prefectural system, there were 31 *tozama*, 1 *sanke*, 11 *kamon*, and 58 *fudai*, plus Shizuoka, whose status as the Tokugawa domain was still unclear. Among the *tozama* domains, with the exception of Kaga, the largest of all, Aki, and Uwajima, both large domains, all were *han* of 50,000 *koku* and less. Conspicuously absent were Satsuma, Chōshū and Tosa. It is quite possible that some of the domains favoured the change to a prefectural system in the hope that it would end the monopoly of power by Chōshū and Satsuma leaders. This was especially true in the case of large domains such as Kii and Echizen. Those *han* who opposed the change did not want simply to preserve the feudal system as it was, but proposed major reforms to make it more logical and more effectively centralised.[51]

Obviously, the war was fought to unify the country. It began, after the outbreak of hostilities at Toba and Fushimi, as a punitive expedition against the former Shogun and other 'enemies of the Court'. But it was not aimed simply at eliminating the remaining power of the old Bakufu. It became a war against the Tokugawa as feudal lords and against the other 'enemies of the Court' as feudal lords. Until the surrender of Edo castle, the campaign went smoothly, with little opposition, and the old Bakufu system was extinguished, with few regrets. Only when it became apparent that the campaign was now aimed at depriving the Shogun of his lands did the opposition of the Tokugawa adherents begin to mount in the Kantō, and, at the same time, in the north. Their purpose was not to restore the Bakufu. On a deeper level, there was an element of self-interest in desiring to maintain the old system as much as possible, but as this was apparently not articulated, it is difficult to assess. We can say it was a desperate and emotional opposition, based on traditional feudal loyalty and prompted by fear of the extinction of the Tokugawa clan and the hope of maintaining the position of Yoshinobu (or, if necessary, another clan leader of the Tokugawa house) as a feudal lord.

Likewise, in the spring, the gathering alliance of feudal lords in the north, in an atmosphere of anger and outrage, represented a collective commitment to resort to force if necessary, to protest and, if possible, to modify the uncompromising enmity of the government, viewed as a Satsuma-Chōshū monopoly, towards the Tokugawa clan, and to expose the 'personal malice' of the regional commands toward Aizu and Shōnai. In terms of *han* interests, the lords saw in the government's disregard for the rights of the Tokugawa, inevitably, the same fate for their own domains if they did not make a stand. They felt that the moderate solution, along the lines of the Tosa Memorial, on the basis of which Yoshinobu had decided to resign as Shogun, and which had seemed certain of attainment earlier, had been overturned by what they considered the self-centred and megalomanic actions of Satsuma and Chōshū. They could see no disloyalty to the Emperor in insisting that the new dispensation be an effective, centralised alliance of domains under the Emperor. The monopoly of patriotism asserted by the Ōkubo clique raised resentments which long outlived the civil war.

The moderate party's insistence, throughout the year, on a government based on consultation, and on representative institutions suggested by European and American practice was, of course, understandable. The moderate position represented an overwhelmingly majority opinion among the ruling classes, until the civil war forced a reluctant change. The need even in present-day Japan for a consensus before important decisions are taken, and involving concessions to the weaker party, at least for the sake of face and a façade of Confucian-style harmony, is, of course, a strong and deeply traditional one, and is perhaps sufficient to explain the 'consultative' emphasis in the moderate position without requiring a thesis that they were in any way progressives committed to parliamentarism as understood in the West. It should perhaps be added that in 1868, there had not yet been time for Japanese intellectuals and officials on either side of the civil war to work out the implications of the systems of representative government which Fukuzawa Yukichi had observed and found so difficult to understand.

The struggle to reach a consensus is the key to Bakumatsu political history, and as radical change was advocated strongly by only a small, although well-organised and singleminded minority, perhaps the war was necessary. Military men like Saigō and Yamagata[52] strode to the centre of the stage during the war, and the necessary military emphasis in the first year of the new government left its stamp on modern Japan.

The resentment at being forced to change, anger and frustration at the monopoly of power by the Satsuma-Chōshū leaders, and at their non-traditional use of that power, reached its peak during the civil war. In this resentment, which long outlived the war, can be seen the beginnings of two types of often closely related anti-government movements: that of people's rights and democracy, resulting in the granting of a Constitution, and that of ultra-nationalistic opposition outside the government, whose first manifestations were Saigō's Satsuma rebellion and the other suicidal rebellions of the early Meiji period.

2

SHINBUNSHI: THE EARLY MEIJI
ADAPTATION OF THE
WESTERN-STYLE NEWSPAPER

ALBERT A. ALTMAN

In 1866, when Fukuzawa Yukichi published the first edition of his *Seiyō jijō* (*Conditions in the West*), he included a chapter on 'Newspapers'. This medium of communication had yet to take root in Japan and Fukuzawa thought it necessary to fill this gap in his readers' knowledge. A single Japanese-language newspaper, the *Kaigai shinbun*, was being published in Yokohama, but it was a strikingly unsuccessful venture in journalism since it had only two regular subscribers.[1] The English-language *Nagasaki Shipping List and Advertiser*, Japan's first newspaper in any language, first appeared on 22 June 1861.[2] When the publisher, an English commission merchant, transferred his agency from Nagasaki to Yokohama, he started producing *The Japan Herald* from 23 November 1861. By 1866, a number of English-language newspapers were being published in Yokohama, but they were intended for residents of the foreign settlement, an exotic world apart from the mainstream of Japanese life.[3] In any case, only a few Japanese could understand the language in which these newspapers were written, even if they did know about them.[4]

Fukuzawa, therefore, started from scratch, and he tried to explain what newspapers were. Apart from the great personal pleasure to be derived from reading newspapers, he wrote, they were unequalled as a tool of education and as a means of getting on in the world. The newspaper could bring the world to the reader 'though he remains indoors and does not see what goes on outside, and though he is far from home and cannot get word from there'. Reading a newspaper, he explained, tells you at a glance what is going on, since the paper 'reproduces the true state of affairs in the world' and 'it is almost as if everything were right there in front of you'. Fukuzawa also explained that Western newspapers exert great social and political influence, because they express views and opinions, 'passing judgement on the country's political affairs or on personal character'. This observation struck a true Confucian note, but when he added that 'there have been instances of newspapers influencing public sentiment and even changing government policy', he was foreshadowing the future.

Within forty years, the observation assumed an unanticipated immediacy. A Japanese press capable of stirring large numbers of people into action had come into existence. The events of the first week of September 1905 forcefully illustrate this point, and I shall recount them at some length.

In the early afternoon of 5 September 1905, a mob estimated at 30,000 pushed over a police barrier in front of the main entrance into Hibiya park in central Tokyo and held a meeting denouncing the negotiations to end the war with Russia. The mob adopted a resolution affirming its intention of destroying the 'humiliating' treaty then being considered and stated its earnest desire that the Japanese armies in Manchuria advance and utterly destroy the enemy. The press had repeated these slogans many times during the four preceding days.[5] The first definite news of the Portsmouth Treaty's contents had been disclosed to the Japanese public by the *Mainichi shinbun* in Osaka and the *Kokumin shinbun* in Tokyo. The bitter news was picked up by other papers and spread throughout Japan. On 1 September, the same day that it reported the news of the treaty contents, the *Tokyo Asahi shinbun* published a feature article, headlined 'This Humiliation', which fumed in patriotic rhetoric that '50,000,000 Japanese, without exception, deplore the ineffectiveness of the men in government . . .'. It added fuel to the fire of indignation on the same day by publishing letters from readers in many walks of life, lamenting the treaty and attacking the government for its 'stupidity'. In Osaka on the same day, the *Asahi* issued a 'Manifesto to the Entire Nation' that began by asserting, 'the Russo-Japanese War was not the fight of one or two Cabinet Ministers or the Genrō; it was the people's fight', and ended by charging the Cabinet Ministers and the Genrō with having deceived the nation. The paper also published a stirring appeal to the Emperor to denounce the humiliating treaty while it was still unsigned, and to continue the war. The press campaign against the treaty talks continued for the next three days. The tone was set by headlines such as 'The People Cannot Restrain Their Unconsolable Anger and Sorrow' and 'A Crime Neither Heaven nor Man Can Forgive'.

These sentiments were transformed into action on that afternoon of 5 September. Once the meeting was over, the mob swept out of the park into the plaza in front of the Imperial Palace, where they prostrated themselves, then rose to shout '*Banzai*' three times and moved on to a nearby Kabuki theatre for another meeting. On the way, part of the mob broke off from the main group and marched to the premises of the *Kokumin shinbun*, a newspaper which supported the government and was prepared to swallow the treaty. Stones were sent crashing through the windows, and demonstrators tried to storm the building. They forced their way in, overturned trays of type and damaged one of the presses. Police and newspaper employees prevented the mob from doing further damage. Despite the broken glass, flying stones and blocks of wood, casualties were few and only minor, and after an hour the crowd melted away when police reinforcements were summoned. At the same time, in another part of Tokyo, a mob gathered before the Minister of Home Affairs' official residence. A shower of roof tiles rained down upon the building and when mounted police surrounded the demonstrators, they, too, were attacked. The mob destroyed the windows and the iron door of the gate at the side of the residence, and tried to push its way in, but was stopped by sword-wielding police. The building was set afire but finally a detachment of the Imperial Guards arrived on the scene. At night, in different sections of Tokyo, police boxes were destroyed, police were attacked and wounded, and a mob attempted to burn down a hospital. 'The people's heart', declared the *Nihon* magazine, 'has become like a fire. Once stirred up, the tongues of flame will scorch Heaven.' On the morning of 6 September, the city of Tokyo and its environs awoke to find themselves under martial law. An Imperial Rescript forbade newspapers and magazines from printing inciting reports under penalty of suspension.

These two years, 1866 and 1905, roughly mark the time-boundaries of the generation during which the Japanese press reached maturity. It had become a force able to shape public opinion. The changes that had come over the Japanese press in that relatively short time-span occurred within the ambience of a society itself undergoing dramatic transformations. By the turn of the century, the Japanese press had already acquired in broad outline features that characterise it today. A small number of newspapers were achieving nationwide circulations. Two Osaka newspapers, the *Asahi* and the *Mainichi shinbun*, stood head and shoulders above their contemporaries, looking out over a larger number whose readers clustered in a region, or prefecture, while farther away at the periphery were papers that limited their appeal to readers in one city and its vicinity. The giants were also setting the pace in the modernity of their production methods that exploited the latest technology and in their news and sales techniques.

This chapter concentrates on the five years from 1868 to 1873 when this growth was in its early stages. During these five years there emerged news publications with the accoutrements of the Western newspaper press as these have been discriminated by students of the subject: periodical in publication, mechanical in reduplication, available to all readers willing to pay the price, miscellaneous in content, timely in material, and published by a going concern.[6] A problem of theoretical importance is thereby raised: namely the weight to be assigned to the Western model in this phenomenon. This paper attempts to make a case for the view that the Western model was of less significance than events within Japan, and that by the mid-nineteenth century, Japan had reached the communications point at which the West had arrived at the beginning of the seventeenth century.

Between the early spring and midsummer of 1868, at least seventeen *shinbunshi*, as news publications were called (the word *shinbun* meaning 'news'), were issued in Edo and two in nearby Yokohama.[7] Japan was in the grip of the civil war that flared up after the Satsuma- and Chōshū-led *coup d'état* in Kyoto in early January. Edo itself was in a state of limbo: the Tokugawa government had lost control of the city, but the armed forces of the Kyoto government had not yet gained control. In the absence of a political power able to enforce a Japanese ruler's traditional prerogative to censor the publication of information concerning affairs of state, the fledgling Edo press savoured a taste of freedom.

Outwardly, the *shinbunshi* published during this interval were hardly more than pamphlets, most of them octavo-size, bound between soft paper covers, and stitched like a usual Japanese book. They were more 'newsbooks' than 'newspapers', and were reminiscent of *zuihitsu* collections (literary miscellanies) in the variety of their contents. Like most Japanese books of the time, these *shinbunshi*, too, were printed off woodblocks, the maximum size of each issue probably being in the region of 200. Such newsbooks began appearing in Edo in mid-March 1868, about a fortnight after Keiki's decision to surrender, and as the Kyoto army's advance units entered the city's outskirts. The newsbooks are filled with reports of military engagements, Court decrees addressed to *daimyo*, calling upon them to put down 'rebellion', and the replies of *daimyo* and their retainers. These reports make dreary reading today in such large doses, but they must have been unusually interesting to those eager for any scrap of information about the course of the civil war and the latest additions to or defections from either side. Reliable news was exceedingly difficult to acquire and information of events occurring only several miles away might travel a convoluted route to reach the reader. The first issue of the *Chūgai shinbun* on 17 March, for example, reporting the arrival of the Kyoto army's advance elements at the Hakone Barrier, depended upon a letter from Kobe quoted in an English-language paper printed in Yokohama.

The Edo *shinbunshi* were short-lived. Once the Restoration forces defeated the Shōgitai, the largest of the armed bands in Edo, in the battle on Ueno Hill in midsummer, the new regime put the city under military rule. Within three weeks, on 27 July, it enforced controls on publication, and the newsbooks disappeared one by one. Despite their brief lives, however, the civil-war *shinbunshi* in Edo made at least two significant bequests to the future development of the Japanese newspaper press. The first of these was periodicity, that is, regular and continuous appearance at short intervals. Of the more substantial newsbooks, the *Naigai shinbun* came out every other day on average; the *Chūgai shinbun* and the *Kōko shinbun* every two to three days; and the *Kōshi zappō* once every three to four days.

News publications, as such, were hardly novel in Japan at that time. Broadsheets and pamphlets, some of them illustrated, which are now gathered together under the rubric of *kawaraban*, had been published intermittently during the Tokugawa period.[8] Their stock-in-trade had been what journalists now call 'human interest stories': personal tragedies, vendettas, fires, natural disasters, reports of strange omens, supernatural beasts, and morally edifying tales of filial children. Political news and comment had been taboo, as it was for all other printed matter. These broadsheets and pamphlets began moving gingerly, if not always legally, into the forbidden territory of politics towards the end of the Tokugawa period.

Although the *kawaraban* had acquired many of the characteristics of the modern newspaper press, they did not achieve periodicity. Periodicity had already characterised news publications in China and the West. By the mid-nineteenth century, time had hallowed the Ch'ing bureaucracy's practice of making available a daily budget of news of government, including copies of censors' reports, to private persons who reproduced them for sale.[9] The publicity given to the Ch'ing government's daily business stands out in sharp relief from the Bakufu practice. In Japan, the knowledge of the facts of the Bakufu's management of state affairs was considered solely the concern of officials chosen for the task. Many of the essays on problems of state and the economy that have come down to us from the Tokugawa period were written, not for publication, but for the information of the authorities. In Europe, periodicity of news publications had become common in the early seventeenth century. By the eighteenth century, the former weekly interval between consecutive issues had been narrowed down to one day.

It is intriguing to speculate why periodicity emerged when it did in China, Europe and Japan. What Eric W. Allen has said about the pioneer European press may also be applied to the Chinese and Japanese cases, namely that the insistent rush of events itself imposes a rough sort of periodicity.[10] In Europe, the trigger was a flood of war news. In China, the very volume of information about government and the government's continuous desire to make its Confucian benevolence widely known imposed periodicity. In the Japanese case, the trigger, as in Europe two and a half centuries earlier, was also war news.

Periodicity of publication, once achieved, is not an isolated, independent phenomenon. If it is to be maintained for more than a brief spurt, so must other activities that go into the making of a newspaper. Of necessity, the flow of information into the newspaper office must be regular and dependable. The preparation of this raw material for transmission to the printing shop must be kept to a deadline. The printer, in turn, must be equipped to produce the printed document in co-ordination with the paper's editorial staff and in conformity with an agreed schedule, so that the finished product may be introduced into the distribution network which, too, must be geared to getting the newspaper to its readers on time. In other words, once periodicity has been achieved, communication, which is as old as society itself and without which society cannot exist, has become in the newspaper, the object of what Benjamin Schwartz, in a discussion of the criteria of modernisation, has called 'systematic, sustained and purposeful control'.[11] Such control first became possible in Japan for more than a short interlude during the Meiji period.

The Edo newsbooks also kept alive the idea that newspapers had a social value. Ferreting out the news of events and publishing it for general consumption was not simply, or only, a private, idle curiosity, and hence potentially damnable, but rather an activity of considerable pragmatic and symbolic importance for society. A philosophy cast in Confucian terms helped absorb Western-style newspaper practice into Japan. What is perhaps the earliest attribution of social value to news was made by Ikeda Nagaaki, Chikugo no kami, upon his return from France in the summer of 1864 at the head of a Bakufu mission. Ikeda, as a *Gaikoku bugyō*, was acutely sensitive to how news and newspapers could be managed for the ends of foreign policy, and he reported to the Bakufu on the subject.[12] It is debateable whether Ikeda's proposals made any immediate impression, since he was disgraced soon after his return home. Nevertheless, they reveal a growing sophistication about Western institutions and a readiness to manipulate them for Japan's advantage.

Ikeda explained the social role of newspapers he had seen abroad in terms of a Confucian philosophy of government. Newspapers were valuable, he told his superiors, because they assisted 'those in positions of authority [to] learn of the conditions among the public'. Despite this interpretation, he did not suggest that the Bakufu sponsor newspapers in Japan. Ikeda was concerned rather with what foreign newspapers could do to further the goals of Bakufu foreign policy. He had become convinced while in Europe that the Bakufu's position on foreign problems was not getting a hearing in the countries with which Japan had treaty ties. The Bakufu had to bring its position to the foreign public's attention, he declared, and this could be done through newspapers. It was possible, Ikeda said, for a government to 'join' (*kanyū*) the newspaper enterprise upon payment of a fee and thus guarantee that its views got an airing. He proposed, therefore, that the Bakufu 'join' foreign newspaper enterprises. 'Taking up membership in such companies initially involves a trifling deposit for copying and printing . . . but in this case it is essential if Japan is to establish relations of equality with foreign countries.'

While Ikeda viewed newspapers as instruments of foreign policy, a broader outlook is discernible in Fukuzawa's *Seiyō jijō*, which has already been cited. Notions about the newspaper's social value made their way in one version or another into the civil-war newsbooks. The prospectus of the *Nichi-nichi shinbun* said that the fact that newsbooks were being published in Edo was 'truly a sign of civilisation. By bringing new information to the readers' attention and broadening their knowledge, newsbooks are naturally of great benefit to the four estates . . . in the transaction of their daily affairs. Consequently, if a great volume of news circulates among the public, the country will benefit greatly. . . .' The prospectus of the *Soyofuku kaze* echoed Fukuzawa in writing that 'there is nothing better than news to widen one's knowledge', while Fukuchi Genichirō, in his *Kōko shinbun*, said that: 'News concerns secret things, yet by writing it down for many to see, it becomes of great value.'

The link between newspapers and civilisation was soon quantified. The *Chūgai shinbun* printed a letter from a foreigner saying that 'throughout the world, wherever the government is just and the people civilised, newspapers will flourish. . . . You can judge a country's relative superiority by the number of its newspapers.'[13] This theme was repeated in another letter from a foreigner which held up Hawaii as a model. 'Forty or fifty years ago, the Hawaiians were illiterate. Today, they all eagerly buy newspapers. It is reported that copies go out to some 7,000 families. Since 7,000 families out of a total population of 80,000 take newspapers, there is hardly a family that does not buy a newspaper. You may judge from this how civilised they are.'[14] To a Japanese eager to be accounted civilised in the eyes of the Western world, here was a compelling reason to work hard at publishing newspapers.

Taking England as a model, the *Chūgai shinbun*, while also remaining within the bounds of Confucian ideology, perceived the newspaper as a potential political instrument. English newspapers, it noted, 'pass judgement on political affairs and rebuke officials without being punished in the slightest. On the contrary, what newspapers write is a guide to the government. That is why England has the most newspapers of any country in the world.'[15] Here was an authentic note heralding the not-too-distant future when the opposition would enlist the press in its struggle with the Meiji leaders. An equally authentic note was sounded by a reader of the *Chūgai shinbun* who assigned to newspapers a task in the programme of creating 'a wealthy country and strong army'. 'Newspapers', he suggested, 'should be set up in all the provinces and they should consider everything without fear of incurring the authorities' displeasure. Nothing excels a newspaper for enabling the four estates to study international conditions, and for high and low to learn about each other.'[16]

In early April 1869, the new Meiji government promulgated a set of regulations governing newsbook publication, the *Shinbunshi inkō jōrei*.[17] These regulations were the first piece of Meiji legislation concerned specifically with news publications, and they became the foundation of the legal structure within which the young Japanese press developed. The regulations were an affirmation of the government's prerogative to control the content of printed matter and, except for matters of detail, there was little in them that a publisher of the Tokugawa period would have found strange. Certain of the injunctions harked back to the decree of Kyōho VII (1722): that copies of books with certain specified subject matter had to be presented to the authorities, that all news publications indicate the true name of the author and of the woodblock owner, that slander be avoided, and that heterodox views be kept out of print.[18]

The crucial articles in the 1869 Regulations declared that 'government shall not be irresponsibly criticised' (*Seihō wa midari ni hihyō o kuwauru yurusazu*) and that 'it is strictly forbidden to make false accusations in the newspaper' (*hito no tsumi o bukoku suru koto gonkin nari*). Apart from these qualifications, and others specified in the Regulations, 'anything not socially harmful' (*koto no yo ni gainaki mono*) might be printed. Key terms like *midari ni* (irresponsibly), *hihyō* (criticism) and *gainaki* (not harmful) remained undefined. *Midari ni*, for example, which also appeared in the Kyōho decree, has a range of possible meanings: disorderly; not in accordance with law, order or custom; arbitrarily; licentiously; rudely; vainly; without permission. Such latitude left the door open to prosecutions on a number of grounds, but the general import was, nevertheless, probably clear enough to a publisher brought up in the Tokugawa tradition of government, namely print nothing likely to displease the authorities.

Nothing was to be printed in a newspaper that placed in question the government's legitimate right to rule, or the manner in which that rule was exercised, or that blemished the good name and reputation of its officials. The Regulations were later fleshed out with increasing severity, but when the 1869 Regulations were promulgated, as long as these sensitive zones were avoided, the newspaper might print almost anything and there was hardly any subject that could not be subsumed under one or another of the articles in the Regulations. It is significant that the Regulations were not promulgated in response to a demand for the right of expression in print. So weakly developed was any consciousness of such a right, that not a single editor or publisher of the civil-war newsbooks is known to have protested against the government's banning of these unlicensed publications. On the contrary, even Fukuchi Genichirō was abject in his apologies when his newsbook, the *Kōko shinbun*, was banned and he himself imprisoned for a short while, though his memoirs, written nearly half a century later, suppress any mention of such submissive behaviour.[19] None of the editors of the civil-war newsbooks, during the ten months between July 1868 and the promulgation of the Regulations, appears even to have suggested that he had the 'right' to publish his views in print. Neither has any evidence been offered that these same intellectuals were censorious of the Regulations on the ground that the government attempted to control the contents of the newspapers it was allowing to come into legal existence. These former editors were all Tokugawa intellectuals committed to the accepted ethic which emphasised responsibility and obligation rather than right. Even two years later, Mitsukuri Rinshō's neologism, *minken*, for *droit civil*, in his translation of the *Code Napoléon*, was pounced upon by those who questioned the legitimacy of the concept.[20]

It was not until August 1871, when the government abolished the feudal polity, that the idea that *shinbunshi* could be an instrument for progress fell on fertile soil. Almost immediately, an increased number of *shinbunshi* came into being. Whereas during the two previous years, some twelve had been started, the number doubled in 1871, then dipped slightly to twenty-two in 1872 and rose again to twenty-six in 1873. The increase occurred not only in Tokyo, where it was greatest, but in the newly established prefectures as well. In place of the 261 domains (*han*) a total of 302 prefectures (*ken*) and 3 cities (*fu*) had been created in August 1871, but in four months, amalgamation had reduced the unwieldy number of *ken* to 72. The publication of *shinbunshi* in the prefectures began hesitantly, with only three in 1871, all of which were published during the last two months of the year. In 1872, the movement gathered strength and within five years *shinbunshi* had been started inside the boundaries of most of the present-day prefectures.

Table 1: *Geographical Diffusion of Newspapers* (*excluding Kanagawa prefecture and Tokyo, Kyoto and Osaka*)*

YEAR OF FIRST NEWSPAPER	PREFECTURES
1868	Nagasaki
1869	—
1870	—
1871	Ishikawa, Aichi, Hiroshima
1872	Fukushima, Ibaragi, Niigata, Fukui, Yamanashi, Nagano, Mie, Hyōgo, Nara, Wakayama, Tottori, Fukuoka, Saga, Shimane
1873	Miyagi, Gumma, Saitama, Chiba, Shizuoka, Shiga, Yamaguchi, Tokushima, Kōchi, Ōita
1874	Akita, Kumamoto, Tochigi
1875	Aomori, Okayama
1876	Iwate, Ehime, Yamagata
1877	Hokkaidó
1878	—
1879	Gifu
1880	—
1881	Tōyama, Kagawa, Kagoshima
1882-7	—
1888	Miyazaki

The *shinbunshi* launched at this time were expected to furnish news, articulate ideas, and generate sentiments buttressing the modernising goals set by Japan's leaders. This expectation created a tension in official policy which was caught in the cross-current of two conflicting demands. The tradition of government to which the Meiji leaders were heirs granted them the authority to impose a blackout if they saw fit on information concerning official actions. Yet the need to encourage identification with national goals led to the wraps being removed to a degree without precedent during the Tokugawa Bakufu, and very probably in all Japanese history. Information about the new course upon which Japan was set, about the novel strands being woven into the fabric of national life, and about the international world, would have to be made available if a foundation was to be laid for new patterns of behaviour and attitude.

* Based on collection of prefectural newspaper histories in *Chihō betsu nihon shinbun shi.* It should be kept in mind that today's prefectures are the product of considerable administrative change that reduced their number from seventy-two.

The history of the stages by which these wraps were removed so that the processes of government might be more visible and the facts reported, has not yet been written.[21] No government discloses everything concerning its actions; societies differ in their definition of what government may legitimately conceal and, conversely, shall disclose. And even within a society, there are fluctuations depending upon the internal and external pressures on the making of policy and its implementation.

On 3 September 1871, five days after the new national framework had been announced in connection with the abolition of the feudal structure of domains, a Dajōkan Notice was despatched to the Kyoto authorities, enunciating the principles to guide them in their policy towards *shinbunshi*. Known as the *Shinbunshi jōrei*, these instructions reflect official thinking at the time and exceed what had been stated in the 1869 Regulations.[22] The 'object of *shinbunshi*', they affirmed, 'shall be to develop people's knowledge', and 'developing people's knowledge means destroying the spirit of bigotry and prejudice, and leading [the people] to civilisation and enlightenment'. Lest there be any misunderstanding of these high purposes, the instructions stated categorically that 'compiling a *shinbunshi* shall be considered equivalent to composing the authentic records of the times. . . . Though care must be taken not to bore readers, it is forbidden to make something out of nothing, to turn falsehood into truth, to agitate men's hearts or to deceive the public.' In other words, the *shinbunshi* were to serve state policy and not to be vehicles for the expression of discontent.

Given this definition, it comes as no surprise that the publication of many early *shinbunshi* was an act of government. In most cases, the *shinbunshi* were edited in government offices by government officials, or by persons with close ties to officialdom. The most prestigious were the metropolitan *shinbunshi* edited and published in Tokyo. The foremost example is the *Shinbun zasshi* which appeared under the patronage of Kido Kōin, who financed the publication and took great pains to fix its ideological underpinnings. Kido was acutely aware of the pressing need to stir the samurai élite into supporting the new regime. He broached the notion that a *shinbunshi* might be enlisted in this cause in January 1871 in a letter to a colleague from Chōshū, Shinagawa Yajirō, who was then on an official mission in Europe observing the progress of the Franco-Prussian War. He said he was profoundly disturbed that Japan's 'progress towards civilisation is accompanied by great difficulties. Not even 20–30 per cent of what we want to accomplish goes along as we wish. I will not speak of commoners, but even most of the officials have to be flattered. If we do not give them guidance,

affairs will not come to a satisfactory conclusion.' Kido was prepared to extend the range of subjects that might be considered in
print by having the projected *shinbunshi* 'discuss the government's
affairs to a certain degree—and even critically, if there is anything
unreasonable about them'.[23] It was Kido's intention that a *shinbunshi*
such as had in mind should educate its readers, or in his words,
should 'urge them on towards civilisation', by giving them news of
the West and of Japan.[24]

Kido himself had little to do with the day-to-day editing of the
Shinbun zasshi. He was obviously much too busy with national
affairs and, in fact, was abroad with the Iwakura Mission from late
December 1871 until his return late in July 1873. He devoted time to
recruiting foreign correspondents from among his friends in the
United States and Europe. While abroad with the Iwakura Mission,
Kido himself sent material to the *Shinbun zasshi*'s editors in Tokyo,
according to one authority.[25] Those editors about whom there is
some biographical information were bureaucrats employed in the
Ministry of Education, like Chō Sanshū who was a *Monbu shōjō*, a
fifth-grade official, Sugiyama Taketoshi and Yamagata Tokuzō. The
last two, like Kido, were both Chōshū men, no doubt of samurai
descent, while Chō, though not a Chōshū samurai by birth, had
thrown his lot in with the *han*: he had taught in the *han* school, had
taken an active part in *han* politics, and had fought in the civil war.
Later to gain fame for the beauty of his calligraphic hand, he wrote
Kido's memorials. Another Chōshū man, Shimaji Mokurai, was a
Buddhist monk of the Shinshū sect, known for his advanced views.[26]

Such men could clearly be entrusted with the responsibility of
giving the *Shinbun zasshi* the tone Kido sought for it. The newsbook
stressed the need for discarding discredited patterns from the
feudal past and for adopting the more enlightened ways of the West,
both in governmental practice and in individual behaviour. It
encouraged enthusiasm for change. The items appearing ranged
from reports and essays on the abolition of feudalism on the one
hand, to news about the homely signs of 'civilisation': watches,
haircuts, Western apparel, Western food and jinrickshas. The
Western-style leading article had not yet become part of Japanese
journalism, but in the choice of items and the manner in which they
were written, the *Shinbun zasshi* expressed its point of view and
enunciated standards as openly as do leading articles.

When the *Shinbun zasshi* first appeared in Tokyo in mid-June
1871, the only other *shinbunshi* in the city was one sponsored by the
Daigaku nankō, namely the *Kanpan Kaigai shinbun* that specialised in
news about the Franco-Prussian War. In nearby Yokohama, a
newly established type foundry was publishing the *Yokohama*

mainichi shinbun, which is reputed to be Japan's first daily.[27] The *Shinbun zasshi's* circulation soon reached some 30,000. During its first month, it came out twice, but the frequency of publication quickly increased to three or four issues monthly, rising to five, six and then seven by the autumn of 1873 and to every other day by February 1874. The greater frequency, however, was accompanied by a drastic decline in circulation, which dipped to 5,000 by 1873.

The pattern of official patronage for the *shinbunshi* was also adopted in the prefectures. As a rule, the local authorities, too, were interested in using the *shinbunshi* as a channel through which to spread information. Very often interspersed with official matter were market reports, announcements of appointments of officials, the story of the opening of a new school or hospital or the paving of a road, a few advertisements, and human interest stories that harnessed, as in the Tokyo *shinbunshi*, the ethical standards of *kanzen chōaku* (rewarding good and punishing evil) to the requirements of *bunmei kaika* (civilisation and enlightenment).

One example, the *Kyōchū shinbun* of Kōfu city, Yamanashi *ken*, will stand for many.[28] This *shinbunshi*, the venture of four men, one of them a bookdealer, first came out in August 1872. After the customary preface enlisting the newsbook in the task of enlightening its readers, the first issue carried a decree announcing the amalgamation of a number of stations on the Kōshūdō highway, a decree changing the names of *machi* in Kōfu city and an announcement of regulations governing the display of books and paintings at a monthly exhibition in a local Buddhist temple. There was also the report of two Kōfu men who had contributed 550 bales of rice to the prefectural hospital, the report ending with the comment that 'we wish others would follow their example'. Then came the story of the Kōfu man who had brought from Tokyo several dozen photographs of the Emperor. The story was used to teach a lesson in national feeling. 'Knowing that even now it is extraordinarily difficult to gaze upon the Imperial countenance in such a remote corner of the country, he ordered the photographs . . . so that he might worship the photograph and so that others who also wished to do so might be able to place one on their *kamidana*. . . . We respectfully submit', the editor added, 'that this man should be singled out and rewarded.'

The relationship of the authorities to the newspaper publishers and editors took on a number of forms depending on local conditions. But in many cases, it is difficult to disentangle the official from the private, and indeed, it may be meaningless to make this distinction, so intermeshed were official and private initiatives. In Hiroshima, the *Nichū zakki*, which was published by the prefectural *Shinbun kyoku* (News Bureau) from mid-January 1872, was distributed free of charge each month to villages (*mura*) and towns (*machi*). In Fukui, the prefectural *Shinbunsha* published the *Satsuyō shinbun* from September 1872, the editor being a school-teacher. In Niigata, the prefecture established its own printing plant in 1873 and printed the Dajōkan decrees, as well as its own decrees, notices of official appointments, and of awards and punishments, under the overall title of *Niigata kenji hōchi*.

The *Shinbun kyoku* in the Nagoya prefectural administration (the predecessor of today's Aichi *ken*) had a different purpose: the encouragement of the formation of newspaper companies and the purchase of newspapers. In December 1871–January 1872, on the occasion of the first issue of the *Nagoya shinbun*, the prefectural authorities promulgated a decree that: 'Newspapers develop wisdom and are of great benefit to human life. Each *mura* and *ku* (ward) is to purchase a copy without fail so that knowledge may be extended, the foundations of industry laid, and progress made towards civilisation. . . .' Decrees giving the prefectural stamp of approval to newspaper-reading were also issued in Ehime and Shizuoka. Occasionally, newspaper-reading was encouraged within what were known as *shinbun jūransho* or *shinbun etsuransho*, 'news-reading rooms'. Such rooms sprang into existence in 1872 and spread throughout Japan. In December 1872, the Sannuma *ken*, one of the predecessors of Fukuoka prefecture, announced that it was establishing such a *jūransho* in the prefectural office, where 'everyone, whether gentry (*shizoku*) or commoner (*heimin*), may read newspapers whenever he wishes, since newspapers develop people's knowledge and lead them on towards civilisation'. In Chikuma *ken*, now part of Nagano prefecture, the governor in 1873 ordered the establishment of *jūransho* and instructed the village headmen, teachers and prefectural employees to read newspapers.

The local authorities did not always stop at simply encouraging the establishment of such reading rooms. In some cases, they ordered that villagers were to have newspapers read to them. The role of such public newspaper readings in the maintenance of social order was dramatically displayed in Yamanashi *ken* in September–October 1872, when troops were summoned from Tokyo to quell a riot of several thousand farmers protesting against revisions in the land tax. The next month, the following instructions went out to all village headmen.

'In the present civilised times, people of the lower classes, including women and children, have absolutely no knowledge of what is going on in the world. . . . Nothing equals a newspaper for getting this knowledge. Newspapers describe in detail conditions in

Japan and abroad. They report good and evil behaviour faithfully. Good is praised and evil decried quite naturally. Newspapers are a short cut to improving manners. Furthermore, they are often useful in the family enterprise. It is regrettable, however, that there are many who are illiterate and cannot themselves read and understand. It is decreed that, henceforth, in all villages qualified persons from among the Shinto priests, Buddhist monks and farmers shall be selected to serve as reading masters to explain (at lectures held six times a month) what is printed in the newspapers.'[29]

The government split in October 1873 sounded the death knell of these officially patronised newspapers, although they continued to be published in some prefectures until well past the middle of the decade. The crisis of 1873 and the popular rights (*jiyū minken*) movement that followed helped create the climate favourable for the emergence of a different kind of newspaper, one devoted to polemic and criticism, though no less eager to give voice to an ideal. A political opposition now began to function openly and however much the government circumscribed the opposition, it had to accept them as a legitimate factor in public life, competing with the regime in its use of this new communications medium—and that with considerable success.

By 1905, the press was being used to stimulate mass reaction, not to dampen it down. But, significantly, the attainment of this power was accompanied by a profound dissatisfaction with the role of the press in society and of the journalist in the press. This dissatisfaction, which is still felt, reflected the tension between the old conception of the newspaper's function in society and the requirements of the newspaper as an enterprise. This dissatisfaction was expressed by Tokutomi Sohō in 1929 when looking back upon his long career in journalism during the Meiji period. 'Once', he wrote,

'nobody thought of journalism as *shōbai*, as business. . . . The newspaper was an instrument of polemic, "news" was less important. . . . "News" became important from the time of the Russo-Japanese War. . . . Once, the dominant figure in the world of journalism was the newspaperman who wielded the pen; today, it is the businessman who fingers the abacus. This is the great change that has overtaken newspapers and newspapermen. . . . Newspapers have changed from being organs of polemic to being purveyors of news, from instruments of the newspaperman to instruments of the businessman. . . . Newspapers once served a learned minority; today, they are for the masses. The newspaperman was once the leader of the masses; today, he provides them with one more source of amusement.'[30]

3

JAPAN AND NAVAL ASPECTS OF
THE WASHINGTON CONFERENCE

IAN NISH

The First World War and its aftermath saw a great deal of naval building activity in Japan. A leading Japanese expert differentiates between three periods: 1906–16, being a period of gradual expansion; 1917–21, a period of rapid expansion; and 1922–32, the period of adjustment to naval disarmament.[1] The programme for the building of eight battleships and eight cruisers (the so-called 'eight-eight programme') had been in the minds of naval leaders since the Russo-Japanese War and became the object of national ambitions in the Taishō period. But it was only authorised by the Diet in gradual stages. It was only in the budget for 1917 that the 'eight-four programme' was approved. It was justified to the Diet on the ground of Japan's growing wealth in the war years and the threat to Japan's security which was thought to be posed by the American naval building plans of 1916. The 'eight-six programme' quickly followed. Then the 'eight-eight programme' received Diet approval in July 1920 as a defence against the building plans announced by President Woodrow Wilson.[2]

This was an extraordinarily ambitious plan for a country which had limited resources, compared to its naval competitors. First, there were the financial problems. After her failure to obtain an indemnity from the war with Russia, Japan was in a state of indebtedness and no battleships were laid down for five years. It was only with the expansion of trading opportunities created by the First World War that her ability to finance a sustained programme of naval building improved. Secondly, there was the problem of building battleships and especially the new-style Dreadnoughts in her own dockyards. While she was able to build conventional capital ships, her naval leaders still insisted on ordering their first Dreadnought battle-cruiser, the *Kongō* (27,000 tons), in Britain in 1910. They then proceeded to build three *Kongō*-style cruisers and Dreadnought battleships in their own yards. But, even after 1919, there were question-marks against the capacity of Japanese yards which were,

67

among other things, so dependent on imports of vital raw materials. They had been the first to suffer under the American steel embargo of 1917–18. As a result of these factors, there was widespread comment on the shortfall between Japan's programmes and her accomplishments. Her shipbuilding programmes were often thought of as paper programmes, devised for political effect. In this she was by no means unique. But it lent an air of unreal debate to the controversies over naval ratios in the post-1918 period.

At the end of the war some, but not all, of these problems were solved. In November 1919 the *Nagato* was launched from the Kure yards; in 1921 the *Mutsu* was to be launched. Their tonnage of 33,800 placed them squarely in the category of post-Jutland super-Dreadnoughts, bigger than any ship other than the *Hood*. Vice-Admiral Baron Katō Tomosaburō (1861–1923), who had been the navy minister since 1914, said that Japan had taken as her ideal 'that her capital ships should equal ship for ship those of the other Powers, hence the construction of the largest type of battleships'.[3] The eight-eight plan to build sixteen of these giants by 1928 was certain to be an expensive one, which would not be easy to achieve. Thirty-two per cent of the 1922 budget was asked for naval appropriations; and these, together with the army estimates, accounted for half of the budget. Considering that there was a severe post-war depression in Japan, could she afford such a continuing investment? Were rival building programmes serious enough to warrant this?[4]

The debate within the navy and the government between limited means and international competition came to a climax in 1921 at the time of the Washington Conference, which it is the object of this paper to discuss.

Japan's anxiety was not over relations with Britain, once the strongest of the naval powers. On the one hand, her British alliance was continuing and, while it was being criticised in many quarters, there was no prospect of it being terminated or replaced until mid-summer 1921. On the other hand, it was apparent that Britain could not afford in the post-war period to be the ascendant naval power because it was impossible, in view of her indebtedness, for her to lead the world in naval building. To be sure, Britain was maintaining in Far Eastern waters a sizeable cruiser force; but this was hardly a menace to Japan. Thus, war between Britain and Japan was not regarded by Japanese strategists as a possibility for which they need prepare in the short term.

The position of the other leading naval power, the United States, was more worrying. In the view of Japan's strategists it showed up her vulnerability in the Pacific region. The theoretical problem of war with the United States was, of course, a subject of regular study at the Naval Staff College, which by 1921 had failed to reach a consensus on it. It is understood that half the officers considered that any warlike naval measures undertaken by America or Japan would end in a stalemate owing to their geographical positions, while the remainder contended that America could establish a great fleet in China, based on Hawaii and Manila, and from there fight Japan to the limit of her endurance.[5] Japan's defensive strategy —and by the Japanese the naval expansion plans were regarded as defensive—depended not only on the numerical strength of her adversary's fleet but also on the existence of bases, their effectiveness, and the range of its ships. Japan's worries on these points were used to justify the naval programmes to the Diet. In the opinion of many, however, they were exaggerated; and the expansion programmes were artificially contrived. Was the much-vaunted eight-eight plan merely a 'paper programme', passed for the purpose of propaganda?

These naval expansion programmes have to be seen in the light of Japan's deteriorating relations with the United States throughout the 1910s. In Japan's strategic thinking, the United States had been described ambiguously in 1907 as a potential naval enemy and identified in 1917 as the power most likely to be hostile to Japan, in other words the 'budgetary enemy'. There were important sections of the Japanese navy—and army, for that matter—which were disaffected to the Americans by 1920.[6] This attitude was reciprocated by the American naval attachés in Tokyo, who took a pessimistic view of Japan's long-term intentions and whose reports stand in marked contrast to those of the British attachés (who tended to give the Japanese the benefit of the doubt).[7] This is not to deny that there were others in the Japanese and American naval camps who were seeking *détente* on naval building and were playing down the heady talk of an impending naval race.

It is perhaps understandable that the proposal made on 14 December 1920 by Senator William E. Borah calling on the three great naval powers to reduce their naval building by half during the next five years should have created a wave of interest in Japan. The members of the cabinet of Hara Kei (1918–21) were immediately under pressure to state where they stood. Navy Minister Admiral Katō, who had been largely responsible for the various expansion plans, had, in speaking to the *The Times* correspondent on 8 December, admitted that 'Japan was unable, for financial and technical reasons, to equal the achievements of the leading maritime Powers' and was content with fewer vessels.[8] This interview took place a week before Borah's statement and was unspecific, but it did show that Japan was not unwilling to join the other Powers in exploring means of naval limitation.

It was in the autumn of 1920 that the first vocal opposition to naval building had developed in Japan. Strangely enough, it did not come from Hara's political rivals, the Kenseikai. In their speeches, its leaders, Viscount Katō Takaaki (12 October 1920) and Hamaguchi Yūkō (22 January 1921), while they were critical of the government and its wild expenditure, denied that they were opposed to the concept of an eight-eight squadron. Rather, opposition came from Ozaki Yukio, the maverick politician who had just been expelled from the Kenseikai and who was mobilising opinion throughout Japan by mass rallies in favour of disarmament. In a referendum taken at his meetings he had secured the support of 93 per cent of his audiences and had been emboldened to send a message to the new American President in support of Senator Borah. Early in February 1921 he introduced into the Diet a motion that the Japanese should take the initiative in proposing disarmament, but this was thrown out by a substantial majority. Despite the lack of support among politicians, he enjoyed the regular support of a large section of the press, notably *Jiji Shimpō*, *Nichi Nichi*, *Yomiuri* and *Osaka Asahi*.

Doubtless as an indirect offshoot of this, Admiral Katō himself expressed interest in disarmament. In an interview with an Associated Press correspondent on 14 March, he said:

'This is not the time for the Japanese navy which is at the moment comparatively weak, to take the lead in the restriction of armaments or in reducing plans already formulated. Should, however, the Powers reach agreement on which reliance could be placed, Japan also is prepared to limit her armaments to a proper extent. Japan would not insist on the completion of her eight-eight programme.'[9]

Earlier in January Prime Minister Hara had spoken to foreign correspondents in similar terms: 'The press message that Japan's foe is the United States is fantastic nonsense. Even when her present programme is completed, Japan's naval strength will still be far less than would be required for an attack on the United States.'[10] This accorded well with Admiral Katō's often expressed ambition 'to set to rights the many anti-Japanese opinions in America'.[11] Thus, there was within the Hara cabinet a strong desire to prevent American-Japanese hostility getting out of hand and to avoid a naval building race.

Moreover, there is some evidence that these views had filtered down within the navy itself. Thus, Captain J. P. R. Marriott, the British naval attaché in Tokyo, wrote: 'The Japanese naval staff at the moment are giving limitation of naval armaments their serious consideration and they are of opinion that such a measure brought into force would be welcomed by Japanese officers generally. Offensive militarism does not exist today in the navy. [But] Japan being the weakest of the great Naval Powers of the world will never take the initiative in asking for partial disarmament.'[12] And Captain (later Admiral) Nomura Kichisaburō, who was close to Admiral Katō, readily discussed with his British and American colleagues the form which a naval holiday might take. On the whole, the British diplomats appear to have been more ready to report these and similar feelers than their American counterparts. Doubtless there were others in Japanese naval circles who did not share these ideas and presumably did not discuss their views with the foreign attachés. But, on the whole, there was a general recognition that it was unwise to believe that Japan could compete with the Americans in naval building since they held so many of the trump cards. This had been clearly demonstrated as recently as 1917, when the United States had imposed an iron and steel embargo which had certainly affected Japan's shipbuilding output.

On 25 May 1921 the American Senate passed the Naval Estimates Bill which had been promoted by Senator Borah, and asked the President to join with Britain and Japan in arranging a conference for reducing naval armaments. Early in July President Harding sounded out opinion over a naval and Pacific conference to be held later in the year. Japan was anxious to attend a naval conference but resented very much the intrusion of irrelevant issues concerning China, the Far East and the Anglo-Japanese alliance. Nonetheless, the invitations were sent out on 13 August, and Japan accepted.

We are concerned here only with the naval aspect of the conference and initially with the mandate which was to be given to the naval delegation. On 16 August the first of a series of inter-ministry meetings was held, covering the army, navy and foreign ministries. These preliminary conferences were extremely detailed and fractious, the army and navy being especially prone to disagree. As a result, the instructions which were hammered out on the 'naval building holiday' were vague indeed: 'Although we take the eight-eight fleet as the target for naval strength, we are not bound to persist with it as originally planned. In accordance with circumstances, we will comply with any limitation treaty proposed within the context of the eight-eight fleet to the extent that it maintains a ratio of strength for us commensurate with that of Britain and America.'[13]

These instructions were adopted by the cabinet and the Gaikō Chōsakai (Advisory Council on Foreign Relations) and approved on 26 September. The navy did not surrender on the eight-eight fleet, but was prepared to suspend its plans and contemplate a ratio of naval tonnage *vis-à-vis* the other powers which was not laid down in the mandate. The formula was the result of compromise which allowed the delegates some discretion.

Turning to the question of representation, the Americans had suggested unofficially that the chief delegates should all be civilians. This posed special problems for the Japanese leaders. Considering the prerogatives of the armed services, how could the Japanese navy be represented at a naval disarmament conference by a civilian? Certainly Hara, the strong prime minister, and Uchida Yasuya, the foreign minister, declined to attend. But there was one civilian available: Baron Itō Miyoji, the best-informed member of the Gaikō Chōsakai. His candidature was backed by the Genrō, Yamagata Aritomo, by General Tanaka Giichi, and by other dissentient members of the Gaikō Chōsakai, Gotō Shimpei and Inukai Ki (Tsuyoshi). But the opinionated and 'difficult' Itō had been a thorn in the government's flesh at the time of the Paris conference; and Hara would have none of him. So on 27 September the cabinet announced Japan's delegates as the navy minister, Admiral Baron Katō Tomosaburō, Ambassador Shidehara and Prince Tokugawa.[14]

Having taken pains not to choose as plenipotentiary anyone who would rock the boat, the cabinet chose Vice-Admiral Katō Kanji (Hiroharu) to complement Baron Katō as naval adviser to the delegation. Admiral Katō was head of the Naval Staff College (1920–1). He had commanded the cruiser *Ibuki* at the battle of Cocos Islands—for which he had been awarded the K.C.M.G.—and had been in charge of the fifth squadron at Vladivostok in 1918. He had visited Europe and America in 1920; and some would date his anti-Americanism from this trip.[15] Katō was associated with Captain Suetsugu Nobumasa as the advocate of a big fleet and the opponent of naval limitation. His inclusion is therefore something of a mystery and can only be explained on the hypothesis that the Japanese in their desire for consensus wished to include representatives of discordant elements within the navy. During the absence of the navy minister overseas, Prime Minister Hara was to act as head of the ministry—a calculated infringement of the rights of the armed services, which was among the grounds on which he was attacked on Tokyo railway station on 4 November and killed. This led to confusion and weak government under Takahashi Korekiyo for the duration of the Washington Conference.

Katō Tomosaburō reached Washington on 2 November, ten days before the opening of the conference. In view of Japan's rather poor image in the United States as a whole, great importance was attached to convincing influential American opinion of her goodwill.[16] It was doubly important to impress the newspapermen who were swarming in Washington at the time. Ambassador Shidehara undertook to school Admiral Katō in the diplomatic niceties of the Wilsonian period. He urged the admiral not to wear his naval uniform—uniforms were taboo to the Americans at the conference—when receiving the greetings of officials from the State Department, but to take care to pause, smile and wave his hat to the assembled crowds. Katō followed this advice and acquired a reputation for amiability from this incident. But he later confessed to Shidehara that it went against the grain for him as a naval officer to wave his hat to crowds and he would never repeat the experience.[17]

Katō and Shidehara were able to discuss the naval position. They had been on good terms since 1918, when they had met daily while Katō was deputising for General Terauchi as prime minister and Shidehara, then foreign vice-minister, was acting for Foreign Minister Motono. Katō apparently admitted that he was doubtful whether the Japanese could attain an eight-eight fleet, and confessed that the government was thinking of giving up the programme if a suitable opportunity presented itself. This was, he said, a matter which he had discussed with Prime Minister Hara on many occasions.[18] There is no doubt that these views found favour with the ambassador. But shortly after the conference began, Shidehara became seriously ill with kidney stones and had to leave Katō to attend to naval matters on his own. It was the middle of December before he again played some part in resolving the impasse which the naval discussions had then reached.

Very soon the Japanese became suspicious of Anglo-American collaboration in the naval sphere.[19] The suspicion was that the British delegates had arrived in Washington in order to have preliminary conversations with the Americans, with whom the Japanese plenipotentiaries had been unable to have substantive conversations. Lord Beatty, the First Sea Lord, had gone to the United States a month before the conference opened at the express invitation of the American Legion. He was on good terms with many American navy men and almost inevitably discussed the naval limitation issue.[20] Lord Lee of Fareham, the First Lord of the Admiralty, Beatty's political superior, had arrived on 1 November and had spent a great deal of time with influential American friends, including Senator Henry Cabot Lodge.[21] The main delegation led by a senior member of the cabinet, Arthur James Balfour, reached Washington on 10 November, just before the Armistice Day ceremony at Arlington cemetery. But even he had an advance talk with Secretary of State Charles Evans Hughes at a dinner party on the 11th.

At the first plenary session of the conference on the following day, Hughes propounded his sensational naval scrapping formula which took most delegates by surprise. Turning to competition in naval building, Hughes proposed to 'end it now' by stopping all building of capital ships, by scrapping older vessels, and by fixing capital ship tonnage between the Powers on a proportional basis. He undertook to scrap fifteen of the older American battleships and called on Britain and Japan to make similar sacrifices. In the long run, Hughes hoped to devise a 5 : 5 : 3 (10 : 10 : 6) ratio for the United States, Britain and Japan in capital ships. In the over-heated atmosphere of the Hall of the Daughters of the American Revolution, newspapermen vied with each other to describe the facial reactions of the major delegates, especially the British and the Japanese. It was hardly worthwhile. The proposals did not commend themselves to any naval representative, being both novel and wide-ranging. But, in the mood of popular excitement, favourable appear-ances had to be preserved.

So deep had suspicion of Anglo-American collusion penetrated that the Japanese concluded that the proposals had been cleared with the British plenipotentiaries in their preliminary discussions. Embroidered in various ways, this idea came to be widely held in Japan. But Japan's suspicions seem to have been largely misplaced. It can only be said that there were informal discussions of various sorts between the British and American delegates but, so far as is known, these tended to steer clear of the naval issue on which there were thought to be inevitable disagreements. On the specific charge about the formula on scrapping and replacement, it can only be said that it came as a surprise to the British delegation.[22] Thus, Lord Lee who had an appointment to meet Theodore Roosevelt, junior, then the Assistant Secretary for the Navy, in the afternoon following Hughes's speech, cancelled the meeting in order that he could work out the implications of the American proposals—which clearly came as a surprise.[23] Japan may have been under attack at Washington, but she was not under deliberate attack by a united front of the other major naval powers.

Japan responded amicably enough. In reply to Hughes's bomb-shell speech on 12 November, Baron Katō said that, provided her security was safeguarded, Japan was prepared to agree to whatever limitations were acceptable to the other naval powers: 'her govern-ment and people had hoped that the conclusion of the Great War would bring a cessation of construction but, as the United States with her unassailable position deemed it necessary to continue her naval development, no alternative was permitted to Japan. It has never been the policy or intention of Japan to attempt to rival the two greatest navies of the world.'[24] When naval questions were referred to the technical sub-committee, on which Japan was represented by Katō Kanji, Japan's position slightly changed. Katō called for a ratio of 10 : 10 : 7 to America and Britain and would not budge. He also proposed for inclusion on the scrapping list the older *Settsu*[25] in place of the new *Mutsu*. Although the Americans argued that *Mutsu* was still 'under construction' and had not really 'joined the fleet', the Japanese claimed that she was in full commission and had cruised over 1,000 miles under her own steam. The Japanese further argued that the treatment of the *Mutsu* was a sensitive political issue, because she had been built partly from money raised by public subscription—largely by school-children—and was naturally the focus of much national pride as the world's biggest battleship. In all this, Admiral Katō was arguing his case more rigorously than his senior but, since he had been deeply involved in drawing up the mandate, he doubtless knew its loop-holes and its vagueness. Katō Kanji was only one of many hard-liners at Washington, where admirals who did not like the prospect of naval limitation were pursuing their private strategies. Pray spare a thought for this if you are tempted to consider the Japanese experience in isolation.

Deadlock having been reached in the technical committee, the problem came back to a summit conference of the leaders, Hughes, Balfour and Baron Katō. The navy minister decided to overrule Katō Kanji on grounds of principle. He was later to explain that it was his duty to interpret the national interest as distinct from the narrow sectional interest of the navy and to take account of international factors; he had to bear in mind that it was Japan's essential interest to prevent war with the United States and to avoid a naval race, in both of which Japan was bound to lose.[26] In rejecting the views of Katō Kanji, he was in effect dismissing the ideas of the *Kyōkōha* (hard-liners) within the navy. Knowing that 10 : 10 : 7 would not be accepted by Japan's naval rivals and that, if she persisted with this demand, it would only result in the conference breaking up, Baron Katō concluded that it was not in the long-term interest of Japan to allow the conference to fail in its objectives.

Moreover, there was the personal factor. Katō Kanji had graduated from the Naval Academy where he had been a student of gunnery under Baron Katō who therefore expected some respect from the younger man. Furthermore, Katō Kanji, who was a man of strong beliefs (such as his enthusiasm for Admiral Mahan's view of sea-power) and a thinker of undoubted brilliance, had just been promoted vice-admiral, equal in rank to Baron Katō. But the latter thought that Katō Kanji was being exploited by junior members of the *Kyōkōha* and is reported to have told him: 'Now that you have become vice-admiral, what about keeping those below you under control?' According to this account, he rebuked him with harsh words.[27] It was later reported that Katō Kanji had committed suicide in Washington. That was untrue, but he was unquestionably ill and was forced to leave prematurely in order to return to hospital in Japan.[28]

At the meeting of the Big Three on 2 December, Baron Katō withdrew his junior's insistence on 10 : 10 : 7. He claimed, however, that it was going to be hard to persuade his people that this was not an ignominious capitulation to pressure from America and the American press, which was carrying inspired articles that the United States should not give in over the naval ratio. With the authority of Tokyo, Baron Katō announced that Japan accepted the 10 : 10 : 6 ratio, provided that the other powers agreed to maintain the *status quo* in fortifications and bases in the Pacific and also permitted Japan to retain the *Mutsu* in place of the older *Settsu*. While the American and British delegates were with reservations ready to observe the *status quo*, it took a while for them to agree to Japan retaining the post-Jutland ships, *Nagato* and *Mutsu*. Eventually a formula was reached and the announcement on fortifications was published on 15 December. It stated: 'there shall be no increase in these fortifications and naval bases, except that this restriction shall not apply to the Hawaiian islands, Australia, New Zealand and the islands composing Japan proper.'[29]

Japan had originally urged the inclusion of Hawaii in the restricted area; but the Americans resisted this on the ground that it lay 3,374 miles from Tokyo and could not rightly be regarded as an offensive base. The Japanese did not want to concede that they could not fortify two islands which they held to be covered by the phrase 'Japan proper', Amami-Oshima and Ogasawara (Bonin islands). From discussions it was clear that the other naval powers intended to prevent Japan from fortifying them. Indeed Japan may have had no such intention; but she was offended by the others' demands for so many one-sided concessions which she regarded as discriminatory.

While the proceedings were suspended for the Christmas festivities, the chief naval delegate wrote a detailed personal memorandum from the Shoreham Hotel on 27 December. Baron Katō, feeling that the acceptance of 10 : 10 : 6 would be blamed on him in any later recriminations, decided to inform his deputy in Tokyo, Vice-Minister Ide Kenji, of his way of thinking. Choosing Captain Hōri Teikichi from his staff, he asked him to return home right away with his views, which were dictated in philosophical style and unusually non-technical language.[30] With a frankness which was rare among Japanese service ministers, Katō reviewed some of his country's weaknesses:

'One has to admit that, if one has no money, one cannot make war. Russia and Germany have lost their importance since the war and the only country with which there is now a "probability"[31] of our getting involved in war is the United States. Even if we assume that our "arms" are equal to those of the Americans, we can no longer make war on the small amount of money that we had at the time of the Russo-Japanese War. If we examine where funds can now be obtained, we cannot discover any country apart from the United States which can give us a loan. If America is to be the enemy, such funds would be frozen and Japan would have to build up her military finance from her own sources. So long as we cannot do this, we cannot make war. Britain and France cannot serve our purpose. If we argue in this way, we can only conclude that a war between Japan and the United States is something which must be avoided.'

Turning to the Washington Conference stalemate, Katō argued that there was no alternative open to Japan but to agree in principle with the American proposals; it would be disastrous for Japan if there were no understanding reached on naval limitation, and competition in naval shipbuilding continued on the lines laid down in the building programmes; she could not match the building capacity of the United States. His view was:

'One cannot do much about military preparedness if one does not have enough funds. There is no other course open to us but to avoid war with the United States and wait a considerable time. . . . It is a basic security principle nowadays that we keep our national defence in line with our national strength and try to increase our strength while avoiding war by diplomatic means. I come, therefore, to the conclusion that national defence is not a matter exclusively for soldiers.'

Evidently the purpose of this memorandum was two-fold. On the one hand, Baron Katō was aware that his delegation was divided. It cannot have been pleasant for Katō Kanji in his technical committee to be overruled by Baron Katō at the summit meetings with Hughes and Balfour. Katō Kanji—'Katō minor' as the British delegation jocularly referred to him—was creating a great deal of trouble in Washington and had succeeded in causing delays. He was also a man of power within the navy and might try to influence events in Tokyo. It was, therefore, desirable to explain at length why the more conciliatory policy had been followed. The second factor may have been that Baron Katō expected that awkward questions might be asked in the 45th Diet which had just been convened on 24 December.

Certainly reports that he was prepared to accept a 'sell-out' to America were appearing in the Japanese press from correspondents at the conference and were most damaging to the weak ministry of Takahashi. The ministry's policy was also being eroded from within. The Advisory Council on Foreign Relations whose advice it was bound to seek was ill-disposed to the settlement so far and was to hold many critical meetings in January 1922. Remember that Itō Miyoji, the candidate sponsored by Gotō Shimpei and Inukai Ki, had been passed over by Prime Minister Hara for the post of plenipotentiary to the Washington conference. He and his sponsors formed the core of the Advisory Council; and they bore a grudge. Baron Katō may have had it in mind to keep his supporters posted in order to cope with opposition within the navy ministry and the government.

It is doubtful how far Katō succeeded in these two directions. His message certainly overcame some of the problems of cable communication between Washington and Tokyo, which were chronically bad during the conference, but there is no evidence that it arrived in time to influence the Japanese government's decision on the naval treaty. Its prime interest lies in the impression which it conveys of the author.

There was a basic divergence between the approach of Katō and his home authorities. He advocated that Tokyo should not miss the wood for the trees and wreck the conference because of pettifogging detail. Tokyo and the Advisory Council wanted to be certain that Oshima and the Bonin islands were regarded as part of Japan proper, though they did not want this to be spelt out in any treaty. After abortive meetings in the specialist committee, Katō met Balfour and Hughes on 10 January 1922 and asked for a separate private document to cover Oshima and the Bonins. When the other leaders refused, Katō recommended to Prime Minister Takahashi that Japan should swallow her pride, since she had gained an American non-fortification undertaking over Guam and the Philippines. But the government could not follow why Hawaii, 2,100 miles from California, was excluded, while islands close to her main islands were to be included. At the same time it was ready to agree not to fortify Amami-Oshima and the Bonins. It seems, therefore, to have been more a matter of *amour propre*, arising from the fear of discrimination against Japan, than a genuine matter of substance.

The leaders of the government, Takahashi and Uchida, were in a quandary between the delegates and their Tokyo advisers. On the one hand, Baron Katō, joined by Shidehara who had now recovered, felt that Tokyo was ready to wreck the conference and thus sacrifice some of the real advantages which Japan had won. On 18 January he proposed to resign rather than comply with Tokyo's orders. As for Shidehara, *i-ku dō-on*: he had a different voice but made the same sound.[32] The chief delegates at Washington were united. On the other hand, the government had also received the resignations of Itō Miyoji, Gotō Shimpei and Inukai Ki from the Gaikō Chōsakai. Takahashi, therefore, appealed to both sides for a co-ordinated effort to reach a sensible solution. In a new formula for Article XIX, Japan named the islands that she would not fortify: the Ryukyus, Bonins, Amami-Oshima, Formosa and the Pescadores. Tokyo and the Advisory Council climbed down. But it was only after delivering a civilian broadside against Plenipotentiary Katō: 'the delegates have arbitrarily decided in the negative without trying to put their instructions into practice, thinking only of themselves, and without in the least considering the situation in Tokyo.' The Japanese government agreed to 'endure the unendurable' and accept the new formula, the Gaikō Chōsakai insisting only on the United States including the Aleutian islands in return for the Japanese including the Kuriles.[33] This was notified to the other plenipotentiaries on 30 January and incorporated in the five-power naval agreement which was signed on 6 February.

The Washington naval treaty was the most important disarmament treaty of the inter-war period. Yet in Japan the settlement was rather fragile. It was only accepted in the teeth of great opposition: the hostility of the Gaikō Chōsakai; division within the naval delegation; and dissension within the navy. In the course of time, some of this rancour was dissolved. The Gaikō Chōsakai, the fifth wheel on the chariot of Japan's decision-making for much of the Taishō period, was abolished on 16 September 1922. Admiral Katō Tomosaburō with his pragmatic, worldly approach to affairs was appointed prime minister in June 1922 and was thus able to engineer a broad-based acceptance of the Washington proposals. But his cabinet was short-lived, ending with his death in August 1923.

Within the navy, however, opposition to Washington continued and grew. Admiral Katō Kanji, partly because of ill health and partly because of his distaste for the settlement, returned in advance of the main naval delegation. His attitude to the treaty was hostile; and he was to draw up a detailed memorandum, attacking the whole idea of naval limitation as 'irrational' and showing that any formula of limitation based on naval ratios would not suit Japan's interest.[34] These were sober and persuasive views which began to attract wide support as Katō was promoted to Commander-in-Chief (1926–9) and chief of the naval general staff (1929–30). In this capacity he built up a group of protégés who espoused his views and came to be known as the Kantai-ha, or Fleet group, and gained influence in the navy after 1930. Meanwhile the cause of Katō Tomosaburō was upheld after his death by his two adjutants at Washington, Captains Hōri Teikichi and Nomura Kichisaburō, and by such senior figures as Admiral Okada Keisuke. But, despite the readiness of the navy ministry to operate within the restrictions of the treaty, the anti-treaty group with its strength in the naval general staff had gained much ground by 1930. The dispute which had come out into the open at Washington in 1921 was never resolved and was one of the causes of division within the navy in the 1930s.

The Washington naval settlement was later branded by the Japanese as 'humiliating' and by critics from the other naval powers as 'a gift to Japan'. It was humiliating in so far as Japan accepted a tonnage ratio inferior to Britain's and America's. From the stand-point of the 1930s, this seemed to many Japanese to be objectionable and became an obsession with Katō Kanji. At the time, there were, as we have seen from the writings of Baron Katō, many arguments in its favour in terms of national self-interest. Moreover it was part of a bargain. Japan accepted 10 : 10 : 6 in return for the guarantee that the Philippines and Guam *inter alia* would not be fortified by the United States. It appears from subsequent researches that the United States did not intend in 1921 to fortify Manila or Guam. The guarantee did not, therefore, entail much sacrifice for the Americans. By the same token, it was not too much of a gift for Japan. In 1921 the bargain seemed to offer a fair *quid pro quo*: and it was not naïve for Admiral Katō to lay so much stress on what he regarded as rather a scoop. For the Americans it was not an act of criminal folly to subscribe to the non-fortification agreement: it was a calculated concession which in the short term was inexpensive to offer and, until the full development of naval airpower took place, was not likely to be too disastrous. The historian, who always claims some degree of professional omniscience, may therefore conclude that the Washington naval settlement for Japan and the Pacific was not unfair to all concerned.

4

MYTH AND REALITY IN JAPAN OF THE 1930s

BEN-AMI SHILLONY

There is hardly another decade in modern Japanese history about which so much has been written as the 1930s. This was the decade in which Japan terminated its long policy of co-operation with the Anglo-Saxon powers and embarked on a course of confrontation with them. This was also the decade in which the promising trend towards democratisation was reversed and the military assumed increasing influence in the affairs of state.

To post-war Japanese intellectuals, the 1930s present an embarrassing reminder: it was in those years that many of them embraced a vision of a national mission which they later repudiated. To Western observers the decade was a shocking experience, shattering their sympathies for Japan and obliging them to treat that country as their mortal foe. The allied occupation of Japan, the trials of the wartime leaders and the vast reforms of the late 1940s and early 1950s assumed the existence, in the 1930s, of an evil turning-point, a tremendous fall from bliss, perpetrated by villains or necessitated by original sin. No wonder many books treat this period as a breakdown of modernisation and a setback in the general progress of Japan.[1]

Like any dogmatic approach, this one too prompted its antithesis. In Japan a new sense of self-confidence produced a romantic and heroic image of the pre-war and war years.[2] In the West the diminishing memory of the war excitement and the spectacular rise of Japan as a peaceful, democratic, industrial power, inspired a revisionist approach, which restored to the Japanese pre-war and wartime leaders the image of responsible people, reacting rationally to changing circumstance.[3]

It is the duty of historians to check the myths against the facts. The purpose of this paper is to examine in this way two popular myths about the 1930s, that of 'government by assassination' and that of 'the romantic samurai'.

81

THE MYTH OF GOVERNMENT BY ASSASSINATION

Many people regard the 1930s in Japan as a period of terror, in which ultra-patriotic assassins eliminated the liberal leadership of the country and enabled a group of military fanatics to suppress democracy and drive Japan into war.

In 1942 Hugh Byas, the well-known English correspondent who had spent ten years in Japan before the Pacific War, published *The Japanese Enemy, His Power and His Vulnerability*. In the introduction to that book he wrote:

'Japan is not a nation of individuals but a hive of bees working, buzzing and fighting collectively in defence of the hive. Latterly I never used the term "public opinion" in messages from Japan. . . . These things have been but the instinctive buzzing of the swarm. Behind the façade in modern style the Japanese system of government is still a Japanese structure . . . always the patriotic societies lurking in the darkness with dagger and bomb.'[4]

That same year Byas published his famous book *Government by Assassination*, which described his experiences in Japan. In that book he wrote: 'In Japan professional patriotism and professional crime drew together and blended in a way that made patriotism a stink in the nostrils. The big patriotic societies were only the one-third of the iceberg that shows above water; below, in the depths, a whole underworld of criminals hunted their prey under a mask of patriotism.' The young officers, according to Byas, were the strongest force in Japan and their agitation for a Shōwa Restoration had driven Japan to the Pacific War.[5]

Though other writers were less sanguine, the image of a 'government by assassination' haunted many of them. Even Fairbank, Reischauer and Craig in their *East Asia, the Modern Transformation*, published in 1965, describe the ultra-nationalist organisations of the 1930s as the most effective pressure group of their time, which drove the conservative government to its extreme and jingoistic position.[6] Yet, six years later Reischauer himself, in his article 'What Went Wrong?', admits that the assassinations and putsch attempts of the 1930s fell ridiculously short of success, were ruthlessly suppressed, and never amounted to a real threat to the system. All they did was to merge into the general sense of malaise and confusion of that time 'which obviously drew more strongly from other sources'.[7]

The 1930s witnessed the greatest number of political assassinations and attempted *coups d'état* that Japan had known since the early years of the Meiji period. The victims were Prime Minister Hamaguchi in 1930, Dan Takuma, Inoue Junnosuke and Prime Minister Inukai in 1932, General Nagata in 1935, and finally the 26 February

1936 rebellion, in which Lord Keeper Saitō, Finance Minister Takahashi and General Watanabe were killed, while several others, including Prime Minister Okada, barely escaped death. It was this series of spectacular assassinations which foisted upon Japan the image of a terror-ridden country.

Yet, if we compare Japan to other countries where political terror was in use, either by government or by rival political groups, we find that in Japan the actual number of acts of violence was relatively small. There was no mass terror in Japan as there was in Germany of the 1930s. Political rivals in Japan did not assassinate each other, nor did the government liquidate its opponents. Except for communists, who were jailed, most dissenters remained free. The worst that happened to people who disagreed with the government was usually that they had to renounce public office. Unlike Nazi Germany, Communist Russia or Kuomintang China of that decade, people did not disappear in Japan. No liberal lost his life because of his opinions. Liberal writers and politicians like Ozaki Yukio, Abe Isō, Baba Tsunego and Minobe Tatsukichi were restricted in their public utterances, but they were neither arrested not exiled. Despite the denunciations of the West, no Westerner was assassinated in Japan in the 1930s. The 26 February 1936 rebels were ostensibly courteous to the foreigners in the area under their occupation.[8]

Despite the great political and social unrest, Japan in the 1930s remained a country of law and order. William Chamberlin of the *Christian Science Monitor*, who stayed in Tokyo during the 26 February rebellion, in the course of which 1,400 rebel troops seized the centre of Tokyo for four days, was surprised by the orderliness which characterised the outburst. He wrote of 'The greatest political crisis in Japan . . . passing off without a sign of rioting or disorder and without any loss of life, except for the murdered officials and a few men especially engaged in guarding them.'[9] Ambassador Grew was astonished to learn that the rebels burned incense beside the bodies of their victims, as a token of respect.[10] We also know that one of the rebel officers, Captain Andō Teruzō, apologised to the wife of his assumed victim for what his soldiers had to do 'for the sake of Japan'.[11]

Were the people in power intimidated by these acts of violence? The evidence does not bear it out. All the attempts at a *coup d'état* failed and the terrorists were apprehended and punished. Some history books claim that the punishment was lenient, but that was hardly the case. The killers of Inoue, Inukai and Dan were sentenced to life imprisonment, the 26 February rebel officers were sentenced to death and executed, so was the killer of Nagata. The assassin of Hamaguchi was sentenced to death but his sentence was later commuted to life imprisonment. By no Western standards can these sentences be considered as lenient.

No politician, not even a Japanese prime minister, wants to be assassinated. Senior Japanese officials and politicians in the 1930s were apprehensive about the probability of physical attack. But their chances of being killed were hardly greater than those of many world leaders today. It has not been proven that any prime minister in Japan changed his policy because of intimidation by terrorists. As James Crowley has put it: 'If the fear of assassination or army *coups* influenced policy-making in the cabinet—*and it remains to be shown how it did*—the conspirational whispers and abortive escapades of the field-grade officers in army headquarters did not determine the perspectives governing basic army policies.'[12]

The setback that Japanese democracy suffered in the 1930s was not the result of terrorist acts. The purpose of the terrorists was a total change of the regime: suspension of the constitution, direct Imperial rule, limits on private property, a guided economy, a return to simpler ways of life, rejection of Western culture, and similar broad reforms. None of these objectives was achieved. The Shōwa Restoration, that loosely defined national renovation advocated by all the ultra-nationalists, was never proclaimed. The constitution was neither abrogated nor suspended, and the Diet continued to function throughout the decade. In the latter half of the 1930s the army wielded a great amount of power in both internal and external affairs. But this power was not total. In 1938 and 1939 the army wanted Japan to conclude a military pact with Germany, yet the objections of civilian politicians and bureaucrats to such a pact overrode the army's pressure. The influence of the political parties declined, but it was not eliminated. Prime Minister Hirota resigned in 1937 after being criticised in the Diet. His successor, General Hayashi, resigned after failing in the general elections. Nor was there a cultural break with the past. The *Kokutai no hongi* of 1937, which specified the fundamentals of national ideology, rejected both liberalism and fascism, and called for the creation of a new culture, based on the positive elements of Japan and the West.

It was war rather than the putschist attempts of the 1930s that suppressed democracy in Japan. Firstly, the Manchurian Incident of 1931 and its international repercussions created a highly nationalistic atmosphere. Then, the China War, which broke out in 1937, brought about further government controls and a stricter censorship. Yet the China War was not perpetrated by putschists, but was the result of miscalculations on the part of a civilian prime minister, Prince Konoe, and his military advisers. The war against the United States and Britain in 1941 was decided by the highest organs of state after long deliberations. Whether this was a right or wrong decision, there is no question about the fact that it was a legal one. The 'conspiracy theory' advanced by the International Military Tribunal for the Far East in its Judgement of 1948 rested on very shaky grounds from the start, and has since then been refuted by historians.[13]

THE MYTH OF THE ROMANTIC SAMURAI

Diametrically opposed to the myth of government by assassination is another myth, that of the romantic, idealistic, even pacifist samurai of modern times. Whereas the former myth viewed the terrorists and rebels of the 1930s as the scum of the earth, the latter treated them as the flower of Japan, the noblest, most sincere and most patriotic heroes between the *shishi* (the 'men of spirit' of the Meiji Restoration movement) and the *kamikaze* (the suicide pilots of the Second World War).

Already in the 1930s, the young officers, who perpetrated most of the assassinations and attempted *coups d'état*, were regarded by contemporaries as misguided idealists. It was obvious that they did not seek personal gain and were ready to die for the cause of Japan as they understood it. Even Hugh Byas admits that when the 15 May 1932 rebels went on trial for killing Prime Minister Inukai, there was immense public support for them.[14] The trials of the 26 February 1936 rebels were secret, so there was less public support evident for them. Yet even an opponent of the rebellion, like Colonel Imamura Hitoshi, writes that at the time he thought that the rebels, like the *shishi* before them, could have saved Japan.[15] Following the rebellion, the English-language newspaper *The Osaka Mainichi and the Tokyo Nichi Nichi* asked in an editorial: 'Wherein were the causes and reasons for the sincere young officers being driven to action by their sense of patriotism?'[16]

During the war and occupation years, the rebels were scarcely mentioned. After Japan regained its independence, a new myth started to develop around them. Former friends and sympathisers described them not only as sincere idealists, but also as opponents to the war regime, and therefore opponents to the war. It was pointed out that the *Kōdō* (Imperial Way) faction in the army, with which the rebels were closely connected, advocated war against Russia instead of war against China. Therefore, had the young officers had their way there would have been no Pearl Harbor.[17]

In recent years popular Western writers have embraced this view and even gone further, describing the rebels as pacifists. John Toland, in *The Rising Sun*, maintains that the main principle of the Imperial Way officers was the end of expansion. David Bergamini, in *Japan's*

Imperial Conspiracy, describes the Young Officers as 'anti-fascistic captains and lieutenants . . . not really interested in any strategic concept abroad'.[18]

While it is possible to conceive of the Young Officers as idealists and patriots, their image as pacifists can easily be refuted. Their ideological leader, Kita Ikki, wrote enthusiastically about the need for an expanded Japanese empire, including, in addition to Japan and Korea, Eastern Siberia and Australia. Their charismatic patron, General Araki Sadao, was the most eloquent spokesman for 'Japan's mission' to spread the Imperial Way in Asia, by force if necessary. The Young Officers themselves criticised the government for being too soft *vis-à-vis* the Powers and China. One of the reasons for Prime Minister Inukai's assassination was that he had planned to reach a compromise with Chiang K'ai-shek. It is true that some of the Young Officers preferred a war against Russia, but this hardly makes them pacifists.

One of the rebels' greatest sympathisers in recent years was the famous novelist Mishima Yukio. Looking for the manly and heroic virtues in Japan's recent past and anxious to 'restore the sword' to Japanese culture, Mishima found in the Young Officers all that he admired: youth, idealism, courage, violence and a tragic end. In his *Eirei no koe* (*Voices of the Illustrious Spirits*) he wrote: 'The collapse of the 26 February rebellion was for me like the death of a great god. . . . I admired the heroic posture of the rebels, their unmatched purity, their determination, their youth and their death. They seemed to be mythological heroes. . . . It was always my wish to clear them of the accusation that they were traitors.'[19] In a magazine article, Mishima defined the 26 February rebellion as the greatest clash between spirit and politics in modern Japan, a clash in which 'politics won and the spirit lost'.[20]

Mishima's best known work about the 26 February rebellion is his short story *Yūkoku* (*Patriotism*), which he made into a film, himself playing the main part. It tells the story of a young lieutenant, Takeyama Shinji, whose friends have staged the rebellion and are to be suppressed by force. Unable to bear the shame of his friends being branded as traitors and chagrined by the idea that he may be ordered to shoot them, Takeyama and his newly wed wife decide to commit suicide. They make love all night, and then before dawn he commits *seppuku* (ritual suicide) and she stabs herself to death in a long and gory scene.[21]

This story is based on fact. On the night of 28 February 1936, in the midst of the rebellion, Lieutenant Aoshima Kenkichi of the Imperial Guards Division's transport corps committed suicide by *seppuku* with his young wife in Tokyo. Aoshima was far from being handsome or gallant. According to his former friends, he was bulky and clumsy. He had known some of the rebel officers, but was not connected with the rebellion at all. The reason for his suicide is not known. He had previously suffered from a nervous breakdown and might have been depressed by the rebellion and its collapse to the point of killing himself and his wife.

Is the fictional Takeyama a representative of the Young Officers? To Mishima he is. He is young and handsome, loyal to the Emperor and to his friends, and he dies in the most beautiful way: by disembowelment and after a night of love-making. The combination of sex and death, so dear to Mishima, reaches here its climax. Yet this mixture of hedonism and masochism, this craving for an exciting life and a beautiful death, were apparently not shared by the Young Officers.

Three months after Mishima's own spectacular *seppuku*, Kōno Tsukasa, brother of one of the 26 February rebels and head of their memorial society (*Busshinkai*), published a booklet called *The 26 February Incident and Mishima Yukio*. Kōno praises Mishima for his keen interest in the rebels and his outstanding support of their ideals. But he also chides Mishima for having distorted the picture of the Young Officers in *Yūkoku*. In this story, Kōno says, sex and suicide out of patriotic motives are elevated to the same level. This does not fit Japanese tradition, which regards *seppuku* very highly, but keeps sex in the domain of concealed privacy. The mixture of sex with patriotism in this work of fiction, according to Kōno, is an imitation of Western literature and does not reflect the attitudes of former samurai or latter-day Young Officers.[22] Indeed, women hardly played any role in the rebellion. Most of the rebel officers were married and some were even newly wed, but none of them had informed his wife in advance about what was going to happen. The rebels' devotion to the uprising far outweighed their affection for women.

If sex played no part in the rebellion, what about the craving for a beautiful death? The Forty Seven Rōnin committed *seppuku* and went down in history as heroes; so did the Great Saigō; so did Mishima himself. Did the Young Officers seek a similar death? It does not seem to me that this was their overriding concern. None of the 15 May 1932 rebels committed suicide, though they had murdered a prime minister. Nor did Aizawa, who murdered a superior officer, kill himself after his deed. Out of more than twenty officers and ex-officers who led the 26 February 1936 rebellion, only two committed suicide. One of them, Captain Nonaka Shirō, shot himself, but the circumstances of his death are still unclear. He was probably compelled to do so by his commander.[23] The other one was Captain

Kōno Hisashi, who cut himself with a knife at the hospital, where he was recuperating from his wounds. Only Kōno's suicide can be regarded as *seppuku*. The other rebel officers were court martialled and most of them were sentenced to death and executed by a firing squad.

The rebels' failure to commit suicide was a clear departure from Bushidō and drew criticism, as such, from several quarters.[24] On the other hand, it shows the Young Officers caring more for the reforms they wanted to carry out, than about the beauty of their death. Japan, her glory and well-being interested them more than the code of the samurai.

CONCLUSION

Refuting two opposing myths leaves one in the uninspiring middle. Japan in the 1930s was not as bad as Hugh Byas portrayed it, neither was it as romantic as Mishima would like us to believe. It was a decade of many changes and much bewilderment. Yet, unlike some European countries experiencing a similar upheaval, the Japanese social and political fabric did not come apart.

Throughout the decade Japan remained a land of law and order, despite the eruption of occasional 'incidents'. It was governed by its constitutional institutions: the Emperor, the cabinet, the civilian bureaucracy and the military high command. There were constant frictions among them and periodic outbursts from below, but the system did not break. *Gekokujō*, or the rule of the higher by the lower, was a popular phrase with writers, but it very rarely materialised in reality. The special blend of pragmatism and fanaticism, which had characterised Japan in former times, continued to characterise her in the 1930s.

5

NATIONAL ELECTIONS AND ELECTIONEERING IN AKITA KEN, 1930–1942

R. L. SIMS

What exactly do we mean when we speak of the eclipse of the political parties in Japan during the 1930s? Does the phrase refer solely to their loss of ability, signified by the ending of party cabinets in 1931–2, to aspire to control of the central government? Or does it also imply a general decline in party activity? One reason for looking at elections in a particular prefecture is to find out whether there was an eclipse of the parties in this broader sense. Were the established parties so discredited and demoralised, in fact, that they could not thereafter have presented a challenge to military-bureaucratic control? Alternatively, is there any evidence which might support the theory that the parties lost their central role because the agrarian crisis split the party leaderships and their *zaibatsu* backers on the one hand from the prefectural branches, dominated by big landlords and local businessmen, on the other? These are but two of the important questions about pre-war Japan which cannot be answered from Tokyo alone. While this paper represents no more than an initial approach to them, it seems worthwhile to take the opportunity to draw attention to the need for greater exploration of the local dimension in modern Japanese history, especially in view of the vigour and enthusiasm of Japanese local historians.[1]

By way of further introduction, something should be said about the choice of Akita as an area of study. A principal factor was its geographical location in the Tōhoku region. The degree of rural distress which that area suffered in the 1930s suggested that any changes in the nature or role of local parties would be magnified there. Akita was as hard hit as any prefecture. Rice cultivation, which represented about 40 per cent of the production of the prefecture by value, was assailed repeatedly by bad weather. Wetland rice production dropped to 1·629 *koku* per tan in 1932, compared with the average of 2 *koku*, and was well below standard again in

1932, 1934 and 1935.[2] Partly as a result of governmental policy, however, rice prices did not rise in inverse proportion. The inevitable hardship caused when farming revenues failed even to repay costs was magnified by the high level of tenancy. Already by 1930, the proportion of tenant land in Akita had crept up to 61·67 per cent for paddy and 35·76 per cent for upland.[3] Despite this, the number of tenant disputes had remained low until the late 1920s, making it possible for it to be described as a landlords' paradise.[4] After 1928 the opposite term became increasingly appropriate. From 10 tenant disputes in 1926, the figure rose to 226 in 1931, finally reaching a peak of 487 in 1934, by which time Akita had established itself as the 'leading' prefecture in this respect.[5]

The situation of agriculture was extreme, but its plight was not unique, for at the same time Akita's other industries were experiencing the effects of the depression. Overall production in the prefecture dropped drastically. Its yen value in 1931 was less than half of that of 1925, which even allowing for a drop in price levels amounted to disaster.[6] Unemployment was very high. In 1933, the peak year, it was recorded as 6,312, nearly a thousand higher than the number of factory workers in Akita.[7] Official unemployment figures tell only part of the story, however. They could have taken little account of those who lost employment in the cities and returned to their native villages. Conversely, they do not include the number of workers who had to leave the prefecture either permanently or for seasonal work. According to one survey, in 1930 over 17,000 men and 3,000 women were compelled to leave Akita for this reason.[8] Until 1936 this desperate situation witnessed very little improvement.

The economic depression could not but affect the class which was most closely involved in political activity, the landlords. In 1930 there were 188 of these owning more than 50 *chō* of arable land, 1,252 with more than 10 *chō*, and another 7,349 who owned more than 3 *chō*.[9] These men too were intimately concerned with the effects of low rice prices and bad harvests. As early as 10 January 1930 the leading Akita newspaper, the *Akita Sakigake Shimpō*, stated that many landlords had borrowed money to engage in politics, often ruining themselves, and on 14 January 1936 it gave a figure of 104,000,000 yen for landlord loans in Akita.

Problems of this magnitude were bound to have repercussions on political attitudes. Whether they undermined the existing political system, however, is another matter. It may well be argued that public opinion became alienated from or disillusioned with the parties; nevertheless the electorate did not desert the polling booths in large numbers. There was, it is true, a drop from the voting rate reached in the 1930 and 1932 elections, but with a 90 per cent turnout, these must be considered exceptional years. In 1936 the figure was still a respectable 80·7 per cent, and in 1937 78·3 per cent. Moreover, the criticisms which were levelled against the parties by the *Akita Sakigake Shimpō* were consistently directed towards the parties in general, not the politicians who represented Akita. In 1936 and 1937, too, these criticisms were often matched by condemnations of bureaucratism or fascism, as threats to the normal course of constitutional government and contrary to the great principle of government by the people, for the people and of the people.[10] Local politicians seem to have been able to convince the public of the genuineness of their concern for the people's livelihood and the improvement of prefectural conditions. On 29 January 1930, the *Sakigake* even published an editorial implying that Akita politicians were less self-seeking than those elsewhere, under the heading 'The Feeling of Superiority of the People of the Prefecture about which they can Boast to the Whole Country'. In the view of the newspaper's distinguished editor, Andō Wafū, what Japanese politics required was moral, not institutional, change. When he advocated a Shōwa Restoration, and he did so repeatedly, it was not intended to be subversive.

One of the interesting features of elections in Akita in the 1930s is that the prefecture was among the relatively few areas in which either of the two main established parties could hope to gain a majority of the seats. This might not appear so at first sight. If one includes the first manhood suffrage election of 1928 as well as those of 1930, 1932, 1936 and 1937, one finds that the first of its two electoral districts (*ku*) returned thirteen Minseitō members to seven Seiyūkai; while in the second electoral district, in the southern half of the prefecture, the Seiyūkai had a slight advantage of seven to six over the Minseitō, with a proletarian party candidate breaking the established parties' monopoly by securing election twice, in 1936 and 1937. These figures may suggest an overall Minseitō dominance, but as the prefectural assembly elections show, there was an underlying near-equality which was reflected in the parties' keen, sometimes over-keen, rivalry.[11] In 1927 the Minseitō won only thirteen of the thirty-five prefectural assembly seats, compared with the Seiyūkai's twenty-one. One was gained by a proletarian candidate. Four years later the position was reversed when the Minseitō captured twenty-two seats to the Seiyūkai's thirteen. In 1935, the Minseitō's superiority became less clear-cut when it elected nineteen candidates against the Seiyūkai's continuing thirteen, the other three seats going to two independents and one proletarian candidate. Finally, in the last pre-war election the Minseitō lost a further three seats while the Seiyūkai remained constant. Voting rates, it may be added, shadowed those for national elections: 81 % in 1927, 88·9 % in 1931, 81·1 % in 1935 and 77 % in 1939.

One reason, of an accidental nature, why the Minseitō generally had an edge over the Seiyūkai in the first electoral district was the influence of Machida Chūji, a minister in the Wakatsuki, Hamaguchi and Okada cabinets and president of the Minseitō from 1935 until its dissolution in 1940. His prestige undoubtedly assisted the Minseitō and to some extent rose above party divisions; in 1932, a bad year for the Minseitō, he was elected (though in fourth place) without even returning to Akita to campaign in person, a distinction shared by only three others in that year.[12] However, there were other reasons for the Seiyūkai's unsatisfactory showing in the first electoral district, not the least of which were those which stemmed from the candidate selection process.

Candidate selection was a crucial problem for the parties in Akita in the 1930s and the process was frequently long drawn-out and bitter, overshadowing the election campaign itself. The difficulties arose mainly out of the two connected problems of tactics and personal or local rivalry. These problems were similar in some respects to those which face the Liberal Democratic party in present-day Japan—hardly surprisingly, since the present electoral system of three to five member constituencies is almost identical to the pre-war one. Pre-war politicians seem to have been less troubled by factional rivalry; but against this they had to cope with the difficulties resulting from the lesser degree of central party control, the lesser cost (one cannot say cheapness) of securing election, and the less distinct line between the main contending parties. This last fact, in particular, made it difficult to estimate the total vote a party could get in a particular electoral district. Much depended on the number of candidates who stood, and to what extent their *jiban* (areas of strong and dependable support) overlapped.

With respect to the number of candidates they endorsed, it is difficult to fault the tactics of the two parties in Akita. In the first electoral district, which returned four members to the Diet, the Minseitō consistently recognised three candidates, and only once was there any question of the party losing a chance of an extra seat, that is in 1930, when the three candidates accumulated over 62,000 votes while the top Seiyūkai candidate, Suzuki Ankō, only secured 12,691. Mathematically it seems possible that careful co-operation among four candidates might have brought additional success. However, this is to assume that some of the excess Minseitō votes could have been redistributed, which is far from certain. Even if it had been possible, it would have left some dangerously narrow margins. Perhaps worse, it would have put at risk one of the usual two or three Minseitō seats in future elections, not only because *jiban* needed constant nursing and protection, but also because it would make it more difficult to keep out a disruptive fourth candidate in years when the party's prospects were less rosy than when it was the government party. Few Diet men retired gracefully, unless they were at the end of a distinguished career or wanted to give their whole attention to business activities.

There was also one election when the Minseitō might have lost a seat through running three candidates in the first electoral district. In 1932, when the Inukai cabinet was in power, the two top places went to the two Seiyūkai candidates, Suzuki Ankō and Sugimoto Kunitarō. Between them they amassed 45,753 votes, while the fourth-placed Machida Chūji, absent in Tokyo, won only 15,294. Had there been another Seiyūkai candidate, Machida, the chief national campaign director for the Minseitō, might conceivably have suffered the indignity of defeat. But in all the elections between 1928 and 1937 the Seiyūkai preferred to play safe by permitting no more than two candidates.

The danger of having too many candidates was seen most clearly in the second electoral district in 1936. There the Minseitō branch was disturbed by a mixture of local rivalry and individual ambition comparable to that experienced by the Seiyūkai in the first district. In this particular case, two hopeful candidates refused to accept party control after failing to secure endorsement, and ran without party support. The resulting confusion was sharply criticised by the *Akita Sakigake Shimpō* (for example on 4 February 1936) as the worst in the country and particularly painful to those who placed their hopes for a Shōwa Restoration on the Minseitō. In an electoral district which returned only three members, two of whom had been Seiyūkai men in the previous election, the Minseitō now had not only its usual two official candidates but also two dangerous unendorsed members. The district contained four *gun* (counties) and each candidate had a *jiban* in a different one. It seemed highly likely that, confined within their own bases, none would secure election and that the field would be gained by the two Seiyūkai candidates and the up-and-coming proletarian leader, Kawamata Seion. In normal circumstances the two candidates without party backing would have eventually backed down, but in this case one, Inomata Kenjirō, was the sitting Minseitō member,[13] and the other was a previous member, Soeda Hiyutarō, a stalwart old businessman/politician who was anxious to revenge his defeat in 1932. The two endorsed candidates, on the other hand, were both newcomers as far as national elections were concerned. One, Tsuchida Sōsuke, was the son of one of Akita's most famous landlord/politicians, and a previous deputy leader of the prefectural assembly. His family had recently distinguished itself by winning the Japan Derby. In 1932, the prefectural branch of the party had been enthusiastic for Tsuchida Sōsuke to stand, but his 'stern father', as the *Sakigake* described Tsuchida Mansuke, refused to agree, although more than one delegation visited his residence.[14] Once endorsed it was most unlikely that a Tsuchida would stand down, so it was left to his less eminent running mate, Fujihi Ryōji (the current head of the Akita branch of the Minseitō) to ease the situation by withdrawing. Even then the Minseitō only just managed to elect one member—Tsuchida —and the poll was headed by Kawamata, the proletarian candidate. The irony was that 1936 was a good year for the Minseitō and if only Tsuchida and Fujihi had stood there would have been a chance of keeping out the successful Seiyūkai candidate, Oyamada, whose support was overwhelmingly based on the important Semboku *gun*, where Fujihi was also strong.

As some of these observations may have suggested, the number of candidates was not the only tactical problem. Equally crucial was the location of the candidates' *jiban*. A few prominent senior politicians, like Machida and Tanaka Ryūzō, minister of education in the 1929–31 Minseitō cabinet, who also stood in Akita's first electoral district, had in the course of time acquired a broad and highly dependable base of support. It is not easy to generalise, but this sort of *jiban*, which was based on a long-established connection between local *yūryokusha* (men of influence) and a particular local politician, was more durable and personal than the typical *jiban*. Its personal character was shown in that it could be handed down to a chosen successor, but when this happened there was no certainty that the *jiban* would not disintegrate rather than consolidate itself as time passed. Such a tendency was clearly evident in the case of Inomata Kenjirō, who, as the protégé of the well-known Sakakida Sebei, inherited the latter's *jiban* in Semboku *gun* in 1930. He then secured 8,307 votes, a very large number considering that he himself came from Yuri *gun*. In 1932 the figure dropped to 5,204, then in 1936 to 1,908. Finally, in 1942 he could tally no more than 956.[15]

The more typical type of *jiban* in Akita was that constituted by a group of *yūryokusha*, organised in a club or association at the *gun* level, without a fixed attachment to any particular politician. Their influence would usually be mustered in support of a candidate drawn from their own ranks, almost invariably a prefectural assembly member, but it would not necessarily be committed to him permanently, particularly if he should fail to gain election. In 1936, especially, there was strong pressure within some of these groups to jettison their previous candidate and give someone else a chance to sit in

Hibiya.[16] If no candidate from their ranks was endorsed by the party, some of the *gun yūryokusha* would not campaign enthusiastically or might refuse to support the particular endorsed candidate who seemed to have blocked the way of their own favourite. Part of Suzuki Ankō's striking drop in support from Kita Akita *gun* in 1932 was due to the fact that he, as branch head, had argued against endorsement of Nakada Gichoku, whom that *gun* had put forward.

The typical candidate, therefore, was one who enjoyed outstandingly strong backing in one particular *gun*, but who expected to get no more than 4,000 votes in a neighbouring *gun* with no candidate of its own from the same party, and considerably fewer in more distant areas, where his campaigning would be frowned on by his co-runner(s) as a breach of party campaign policy. The Seiyūkai's Oyamada provides a striking example. In 1932, he received 17,502 votes in Semboku *gun*, but only 3,056 in Yuri *gun*, 441 in Hiraka *gun*, and 251 in Ogachi *gun*. In 1936 the pattern was repeated with 12,781 votes in Semboku, and only 2,280 in the other three *gun* put together (see Appendix, pp. 111–12). Despite this imbalance, Oyamada was consistently successful in every election between 1932 and 1942, and even though he did not top the poll was always considered the one certainty in newspaper reports from the start of the campaign. Less successful, because he came from a smaller *gun* and faced an opponent who also had a *jiban* there, was Hirukawa Yasuhiko, an old Seiyūkai notable, who was pushed forward in order to stop the Minseitō's Inomata Kenjirō from dominating Yuri *gun*. Hirukawa managed to secure 8,409 votes in his home area, but in the three other *gun* could only accumulate 645 in all. No one on the Minseitō side was quite as unbalanced in his support as these two, with the exception of Kuroda Toshinari, a doctor from Yuri, who, on the only occasion on which he stood, in 1937, secured 12,015 votes in that *gun* and 1,915 from the other three. It was not unusual, however, in both electoral districts, for a candidate to get more than 50 per cent of his total votes from a single *gun*.

The fact that there were more *gun* in both electoral districts than the number of candidates either party could afford to put forward led to intense intra-party rivalry between *gun* branches at the start of every election campaign.[17] Because the larger *gun* always produced one endorsed candidate from either the Minseitō or the Seiyūkai the leaders of the other party in that *gun* tended to press particularly strongly for one of their own members to be chosen as a candidate too. If this did not happen, there was a real danger that the strength of the opposing candidate's local appeal might allow him to establish ties with the less committed *yūryokusha* of that *gun*, which might affect local elections also.

95

In Akita this concern for *jiban* protection disturbed the selection procedure of the Seiyūkai more than that of the Minseitō, possibly because the latter had more established representatives whom it would be fruitless and unwise for fellow party men to challenge. Intra-party rivalry reached its highest point within the Seiyūkai in 1932, when the prospect of fighting a campaign under the auspices of a Seiyūkai cabinet must have seemed particularly tempting. Following the announcement of the dissolution of the Diet on 21 January came a flurry of reports of political candidates being canvassed. In Kita Akita, one of the three important *gun* in the first electoral district, where the Minseitō's Machida had secured more than 50 per cent of the votes cast in the 1930 election, one of the biggest Seiyūkai landlords, Shōji Yasugorō, announced almost at once that he was going to Tokyo to try to persuade Kawamura Takeji to stand.[18] Kawamura, an ex-governor of Taiwan and an appointed member of the House of Peers, was known as the *ōgosho* (retired shogun) of the Akita Seiyūkai. Not even the prediction which Shōji made publicly that Kawamura was certain to become a minister if he won was sufficient to bring him down to the arena of competitive politics.[19] Other possible candidates of lesser eminence quickly emerged, however. A previous chief editor of the *Jiji Shimpō*, Akashi Tokuichirō, was mentioned, but only briefly.[20] More significantly, rumour circulated (*Sakigake*, 24 January 1932) that one of the sitting members, Suzuki Ankō, who was also the Ken branch leader (*Shibu-chō*), had lost support. He was particularly opposed by the Seiyūkai organisation in Yamamoto, which in the previous election had seen the Minseitō's Shida Giyuemon make a big step towards establishing an impregnable *jiban* in that important *gun*. No fewer than two possibles from Yamamoto were now canvassed, Sugimoto Kunitarō and Nakanishi Tokugorō, both of whom had been members of the prefectural assembly. From the city of Akita itself the name of Matsuzaki Ryōshirō was brought forward as an alternative to Suzuki. And despite his dismal showing in the 1930 election, Ishikawa Teishin, a protégé of Inukai Ki, was also eager to enter the lists again to secure revenge. He seemed to the *Sakigake* (26 January 1932) likely to partner Suzuki once more, even though his supporting *jiban* in Kita Akita and Minami Akita *gun* overlapped with Suzuki's. This still did not exhaust all the possibilities, for a number of *yūryokusha* in Kita Akita and Minami Akita, including Shōji Yasugorō, began to show an interest in importing Ikeda Kameji from the second electoral district, where many of his previous supporters were dissatisfied with him.[21] How serious this plan was is hard to judge. Ikeda had a considerable reputation in Akita as a result of his efforts to establish a rice-marketing organisation in

Ikebukuro which would get Akita producers a better price; and in 1920, when there had been a single-member electoral system, he had actually been returned for the Minami Akita constituency. However, in 1932, the suggestion that he might stand in the first electoral district may have been only a ploy to ease his replacement in Semboku by the young Oyamada Gikō, who was wealthy and promising but could not bring himself to turn his back on Ikeda because of the sense of loyalty and obligation he felt towards him.[22]

The idea of switching Ikeda was put forward at a meeting of Akita Seiyūkai leaders and advisers in Tokyo on 28 January, when several sympathisers suggested that he should stand together with Suzuki and Sugimoto, on whom there had been fairly general agreement.[23] However, the wrangling had scarcely begun. On 30 January the Odate Bokudōkai, the club which dominated the Seiyūkai in Kita Akita gun, wanting a candidate from its own ranks, put forward Nakada Gichoku, a local landlord and branch leader of the Zaigō Gunjinkai (Reservists Association), who also had the support of the Seiyūkai group in Katsuno gun. Nakada's bid became even stronger when it was reported that Sugimoto, who had gone to Tokyo on 29 January, had told Kawamura, the head of the Seiyūkai branch committee, that he would have to withdraw on account of insufficient campaign funds. Kawamura, however, was anxious not to upset the arrangement which had been reached. He phoned Akita to try to enlist support for Sugimoto, and, at a meeting which included Nakada and Matsuzaki, it was agreed, so the Sakigake reported, that they could not alter the selection because it would lead to chaotic competition among ambitious families. There would be such a swarm, it was said, that they would be unable to lift their fans.[24]

This agreement was reported to Tokyo on 2 February by Matsuzaki, but it failed to overcome Sugimoto's newly discovered reluctance. Seiyūkai branch leaders in Tokyo briefly reconsidered Nakanishi, but it was felt that he would not gain acceptance outside Yamamoto gun, and there was a movement of opinion towards Ikeda. However, the Yamamoto Seiyūkai group was unwilling to lose Sugimoto as a candidate, and a prefectural assembly member was dispatched to Tokyo. Presumably he carried with him the promise of financial support, since the Sakigake reported that his mission was expected to be successful. Its reading of the situation proved correct. On 4 February, after an extended selection meeting at Kawamura's residence in Tokyo, the branch committee confirmed its original decision.

Even after this meeting not all the disappointed candidates gave up hope. The Odate Bokudōkai made known that it had received a telegram report that Kojima Kazuo, a prominent supporter of

Inukai, was working strenuously to get Nakada endorsed by party headquarters, and it was argued that this time the Seiyūkai could afford to risk three candidates in the first electoral district. An indication that it might be dangerous to ignore Nakada soon followed, when a prominent Seiyūkai figure in Kita Akita was reported to be considering switching his support to the Minseitō's Tanaka Ryūzō. Yet further complications arose when Suzuki, returning from Tokyo, brought the news that Sugimoto had persisted in his refusal to run, and that Nakanishi was now regarded as the best alternative. To reach a firm decision, however, it was felt necessary to call another branch meeting, this time in Akita, on the 7th. Yet far from clarifying the situation, this meeting of local leaders put it back almost to square one. There was support from Minami Akita for Ikeda; Kita Akita would not back down over Nakada; and a telegram was received from Kawamura advocating Matsuzaki. With less than a fortnight until polling day, the Akita Seiyūkai was deadlocked.

Fortunately for the party, order was finally restored on 8 February following a general meeting of the Seiyūkai in Yamamoto *gun*. After the 550 members present had unanimously resolved again in favour of Sugimoto, they sent him a telegram in Tokyo and received a telegram of acceptance in return. Approval was given by party headquarters on 9 February. The Odate Bokudōkai, apparently relieved that Nakanishi had been avoided, accepted Sugimoto, and Nakada, who had gone to Tokyo to enlist support, gave up his campaign.[25] By way of postscript it should be added that Sugimoto and Suzuki succeeded in agreeing on a *jiban* division which allowed the former to campaign in Yamamoto and Kita Akita, while the latter concentrated on Minami Akita, Katsuno and Kawabe *gun*, and Akita city. Their late start had no adverse effects. Sugimoto topped the poll with 23,086 votes, closely followed by Suzuki. The two Minseitō ex-ministers were left far behind.

The Seiyūkai record in Akita in 1932 provides an excellent illustration of the fact that a sustained campaign was not the most vital ingredient in a candidate's success. More important were the determined backing of most local *yūryokusha*;[26] the support, either direct or indirect, of the prefectural governor and his officials; and agreement between running mates not to encroach on each other's *jiban*. It is noteworthy that in the second electoral district the Seiyūkai did unusually badly in 1930 when Katano Jūshun and Ikeda Kameji were unable to reach an agreement on strategy, whereas in 1932 the party scored a great success when Katano and Oyamada came to a precise understanding not only about *gun* but also, in Yuri *gun*, about certain towns and villages.[27]

Because the strength of a candidate's support and the prospect of campaign co-ordination usually became clear during the process of party selection, it might well be argued that this was the decisive stage in elections, rather than the campaign proper. The tendency to make such an assumption may, perhaps, be an indication of the limitations of newspaper coverage of elections. It is abundantly clear that much of the real campaign went on behind the scenes, out of the eye of reporters and police alike. Like the central fund-raising of the parties, the details of vote-raising remained a secret among secrets, confided by campaign managers to as few people as possible. At the same time, the actual existence of various illegal methods was very much an open secret. The *Sakigake* could report in 1932 that the parties were believed to have budgeted on a basis of 30,000 yen per candidate, a figure considerably at odds with the approximately 11,000 yen officially allowed.[28] Candidates' total expenditures were likely to be even higher. Katano Jūshun, who was convicted of election offences in 1930 and who somewhat ironically became election chief of the Taisei Yokusankai (Imperial Rule Assistance Association) in Akita in 1942, recalled that elections cost him about 70,000 yen, almost all of which he supplied himself.[29] In 1935, writing in the Home Ministry journal, *Shimin*, ex-minister Mizuno Rentarō, a long-time adviser (*komon*) of the Akita branch of the Seiyūkai, stated that election expenses ranged from 30,000 yen to 200,000 yen per candidate.[30] He made no special reference to Akita, but on at least one occasion the *Sakigake* (25 February 1932) implied that elections there were as expensive as anywhere. The allegation was borne out by the Seiyūkai general secretary in Akita, Iizuka Sadasuke, during the 1936 campaign, when he remarked to a reporter that in earlier elections Sakakida Sebei and others had spent up to 150,000 yen (*Sakigake*, 2 February 1936). Information on the Minseitō side is more scarce, but in 1968, Shida Giyuemon, who stood in every election between 1928 and 1942, recalled that 'elections were decided by the support of the bosses' and that the cost of a vote was 50 yen.[31] It may be that he had converted this into contemporary terms since it contrasts very sharply with Katano's recollection (above) of 1 to 3 yen. Probably, however, the price of a vote was very dependent on circumstances. For instance, at the admittedly rather lower level of village assembly elections, there appeared in the 6 April 1937 edition of the *Akita Sakigake* a report of an election offence of vote-buying near Akita city at 3 to 5 yen. Next to it was another report of alleged vote-buying, this time in Ogachi *gun* for only 50 sen. It would be surprising if similar discrepancies or injustices did not occur in general elections.

Despite the many indications of the power of financial manipulation, it would be a mistake to ignore the public election campaign (*genron-sen*) completely. Its three main dimensions were the distribution of duplicated letters or leaflets (*bunsho-sen*), the holding of public speech meetings (*enzetsukai*), and securing the endorsement of groups such as young men's associations (*seinendan*). In 1937, for instance, Machida Chūji's campaign manager had 80,000 duplicated letters sent to electors, and his rival, Nakada Gichoku, no less than 110,000.[32] Such a relatively impersonal method was probably much less valuable than speech meetings. Since the elections of 1930, 1932 and 1936 were all held on 20 February, during the season of heavy snow in Tōhoku, such meetings must have been considered fairly important for candidates and their spokesmen to have braved the hazards of trips to the outlying villages. In 1930 no candidate's election office arranged fewer than 40 meetings; while the two proletarian party candidates easily topped the list with 205 meetings between them, although their total attendance figures were below those of most established-party candidates.[33] In 1937, however, they headed the list for attendance as well as for number of meetings.[34] Perhaps because this election was held in May, perhaps because there was closer surveillance over illicit activities, all candidates held more meetings, in most cases over eighty. If one may judge by the reduced attendances, however—on average about seventy—their effectiveness had diminished rather than increased.

It is not easy to assess the significance of the more open campaigning activities. The content of speeches was rarely reported. However, in 1930 at least, meetings appear to have generated some enthusiasm, particularly at the Minseitō gatherings when a Hamaguchi recording was played. It was thought worthwhile by several candidates, not only in 1930 but in later elections, to invite outside speakers of national reputation. According to Katano Jūshun's retrospective assessment (above), speech meetings brought between 50 and 60 per cent of the number of votes acquired by vote-buying. However, the effectiveness of the *genron-sen* may have been greater in some areas than in others. An anonymous observer was quoted in the *Sakigake* on 13 February 1930 as saying that whereas the three northern-most *gun* (Yamamoto, Kita Akita and Katsuno) were still manipulated by election brokers, the three lower *gun* (presumably Ogachi, Hiraka and Yuri) had become politically self-aware. If such was really the case, it might be explained by the more purely agricultural character of the second electoral district in a time of great rural distress, and it would help to account for the unexpected success of the Shakai Taishūtō candidate, Kawamata, who topped the poll in 1936, 1937 and 1942. Lacking money, Kawamata's campaign rested on the two props of tenant organisations and speech meetings. His twenty campaign workers, almost all true peasants, thought nothing, it was reported during the 1936 campaign, of walking twenty-five miles for him, and arranged speech meetings in every town and village in the second district.[35] In 1936 he thought it worthwhile to invite all the other candidates to a joint speech meeting and the *Sakigake* (10 February) commented that such an occurrence would arouse 100 per cent interest on the part of the electors. Needless to say, nothing came of his proposal.

Genron-sen was also regarded as important in the city of Akita, which was characterised by a *Sakigake* commentator on 10 February 1930 as a place of intellectual independence where the influence of the *yūryokusha* was less dominant, unlike villages 'where the attitude of one powerful family sways tens of votes'. Occasionally, too, there were reports of candidates gaining sectional or interest-group support. Shida Giyuemon of the Minseitō, for example, was said in 1930 to have gained popularity among teachers, doctors, salarymen, literary people, sportsmen and, though this last group is of uncertain importance, women.[36]

This brief discussion of the main features of election campaigns can have conveyed nothing of their spirit. Contemporary newspaper reports give an impression of great vigour and activity. As election day approached, or at an earlier stage if there were two opposing candidates with overlapping *jiban*, the *Sakigake* would frequently describe the campaign as 'white-hot'. Most of the paper's reporting, however, used more traditional metaphors, giving almost a *Sengoku* period flavour. Reports from the election front often spoke of a candidate possessing an impregnable castle or being pressed hard in his great rock stronghold.[37] When Shida Giyuemon held a successful meeting in 1930 in the village where Suzuki Ankō's campaign organiser lived, the *Sakigake* described the event (17 February 1930) as the fall of the Seiyūkai's stronghold in Yamamoto *gun*. Candidates were said sometimes to be encroaching on another's border, and when Oyamada Gikō was hoping to pick up some uncommitted votes in Yuri in 1932 he was described (*Sekigake*, 15 February) as planning to gallop round the *gun*.

One major, perhaps decisive, factor in election campaigns remains to be discussed. Both the 1930 and 1932 elections were fought under party cabinets, and on both occasions the party in power, as was customary, won a sweeping victory. How much these successes were due to official interference is impossible to judge. But it is clear from a variety of evidence that the prefectural governor and his officials could exert influence in a good many ways. By the early 1930s it had come to be expected, though deplored, that a change of cabinet would result in a change of governor in up to half the prefectures, and that just before an election there would be a reshuffle of bureaux heads in the prefectural government. The police chief, in particular, was likely to find himself posted elsewhere, but neither the public works head nor the chief education officer was considered immune. In Akita in 1932 both the first two were replaced, and the previous governor would undoubtedly have been retired had he not anticipated the event by resigning (*Sakigake*, 21 January).

The most obvious way in which a governor could influence the campaign was by turning a blind eye to the activities of his own party's candidates while establishing a close surveillance over those of its opponents.[38] At a time when much of what a politician's campaign manager did infringed against the election regulations, official partiality of this kind could be a major hindrance. It could also have an additional deterrent effect in that prosecution, with the possibility of imprisonment or, more frequently, loss of electoral status, was more likely in the case of the opposition candidate than in that of the government party candidate, who would probably only receive a warning.[39] Just how effective police surveillance was can never be assessed precisely. One landlord/politician family—that of Tsuchida—tells of the police establishing themselves outside their gates and training binoculars on the reception room to see if any visitor received money;[40] and another Minseitō candidate, Shida Giyuemon, recalled in later life that his campaign activity in 1932 was so closely watched that he was unable to step outside his house.[41] Personal accounts of this kind lend a certain versimilitude to the criticism levelled by the *Sakigake* on 19 June 1930 that although the police had failed to halt the rise in serious crime they were so enthusiastic about preventing election offences that they would attach from three to five observers to a single *yūryokusha* to maintain watch by both day and night. Against this, commonsense suggests that only a massive police force or public co-operation could have stamped out illicit activities; and according to one report in 1930 (*Sakigake*, 16 February) no more than forty-five policemen, plus some special mobile units, had been allocated to hunt for election brokers. Still, their haul of 778 offenders bears out the *Sakigake's* comment on their enthusiasm.

Use of the police was the main way a governor could interfere, but some went further. Since the *Akita Sakigake Shimpō* favoured the Minseitō one must treat its allegations with caution, but its pages give a vivid picture of the machinations of Uchida Takashi, the pro-Seiyūkai governor of Akita in 1932.[42] A week before election day he promised a start of work on the railway planned in Kita Akita, solely, it was suggested, in order to win favour for the Seiyūkai and to destroy Machida's *jiban* there. On a lesser scale, in

Katsuno *gun* he had a polling booth removed from a *buraku* where twenty-five of the twenty-eight electors were believed to support the Minseitō. To register their votes the residents were suddenly faced with the prospect of traversing seven miles of difficult terrain in winter conditions.

The governor also involved himself personally in the party selection and campaign planning process, according to the *Sakigake*, which went so far as to describe him as the 'running dog' of the Seiyūkai. He was said to have advised the branch on how many candidates it should run and to have allowed his official residence to be used as a party office.[43] He several times visited Tokyo during the election period, supposedly either to consult with party head-quarters or to discover whether campaign funds could be found for Nakada Gichoku. All this might perhaps be explained away. But Uchida's efforts to secure the strongest possible Seiyūkai candidate in the second electoral district were exposed in a way which could not be denied. The party branch in Semboku *gun* were dissatisfied with Ikeda Kameji, who had lost the previous election and much of his campaigning zest, and had in the fairly recent past been briefly a member of the Minseitō. As was mentioned earlier, it was generally felt that Oyamada Gikō, a man 'from a famous gate', would attract enormous support in Semboku if only he could overcome his sense of obligation to Ikeda. To this end he was surreptitiously visited by Uchida by car, immediately after his return from Tokyo on 30 January. When questioned by a reporter, the governor stated that he did not know where he was going, but the possibility of such a coincidence seemed even less likely when he visited the still reluctant Oyamada again on 3 February, while nominally on an inspection. Oyamada, however, was troubled by new difficulties. On 4 February he denied newspaper reports that he had agreed to stand, explaining that at a time of national hardship he wanted to maintain his family just as it was rather than throw a shadow on its future. Uchida, however, still did not give up. Knowing that the main opposition came from Oyamada's family he invited Oyamada himself to the governor's residence, taking advantage of the absence of Oyamada's younger brother, Shirō. The reluctant candidate remained there from the evening of the 5th till the next night, being treated, the *Sakigake* put it, like canned goods. This time the governor met with success. It was, however, at the cost of Oyamada's younger brother visiting the *Sakigake* office and making a statement condemning the deprav-ity of party politics and the abuse of official power. The party had, he declared, taken advantage of his brother's weak nature, putting him in a position where he could not refuse and thus risking the ruin of the Oyamada family.

103

I have recounted this episode not only because of the light it throws on the question of official interference, but also because it touches on the question of finance. As has been seen, the cost of election was extremely high, even for a big landlord family like the Oyamada which had, according to a list of 1918, been the fourteenth highest taxpayer in the prefecture, paying nearly 4,000 yen at that time, mostly in land tax.[44] It is not surprising that Nakada Gichoku and Sugimoto Kunitarō also had financial problems and that the latter did not stand again, despite his victory in 1932 and his success as a businessman.[45] No doubt financial considerations also played some part in the family opposition to the Minseitō's Shioda Dampei and the Seiyūkai's Nakanishi Tokugorō when they wished to run for the Diet. It would be going too far to say that it was impossible for any but a wealthy landowner or businessman to secure election. But a politician of moderate means was unusual and would have to rely heavily on outside help. This would usually come, according to Katano, from party headquarters, associates and well-wishers, hardly at all from the prefectural branch.[46] Obviously, however, there was a tendency for the party to endorse candidates who would be able to draw on their own resources, and in Akita, as elsewhere, this gave rise to persistent criticism that money had perverted the meaning of elections and had pushed character and ability into the background.

There was widespread support, therefore, for the election purification (*shukusei senkyo*) campaign which began under the Saitō and Okada cabinets and resulted in stricter regulations and tighter surveillance, by special local committees as well as the police, from the prefectural assembly election of 1935 onwards.[47] That the *shukusei undō* (purification movement) made a considerable impact is clear. The reports and comments of the *Sakigake* (for example, 13 February 1936) indicate a diminution of the frantic activity of the campaign offices of the candidates, and the number of election offences went down to fifty-four in 1936.[48] Moreover, elections were purified in another important sense, in that there was, in 1936 and 1937, no government party to be favoured by official interference. Even though the Minseitō was regarded as a quasi-government party under the Okada cabinet and Machida Chūji was a minister, it does not seem to have received special treatment in Akita. The purification movement was, of course, accompanied by growing central control and military-bureaucratic domination, and did not therefore satisfy those liberals, who, like Andō Wafū, had hoped that it would lead to a political renovation in which the parties would play the leading role. What impact it would have had on party organisation had not the China Incident developed in 1937 is uncertain. The fact that it was now cheaper to engage in active politics might have been expected to tempt a greater number of ambitious candidates and reduce the role of the prefectural branch.[49] This did not happen to a significant extent in Akita in 1936 and 1937, perhaps because a major object of regional politicians was to get central government support for local projects such as ports and railways, and it was recognised that this was most likely to be achieved through strong parties.[50] After the main parties had been swallowed up in the Taisei Yokusankai in 1940, however, such a consideration disappeared, and one of the most striking features of the one wartime election (30 April 1942) was the proliferation of candidates.

The large number of candidates was a feature not only of Akita but of the whole country: 1,079 competed for 466 seats, 645 of them being new candidates.[51] Akita itself had 17. The pattern was rather as might be expected. In the first electoral district were Machida, Shida and Nakagawa, the established Minseitō figures, based respectively on Kita Akita, Yamamoto and Minami Akita, the three major *gun*. Out of the old Seiyūkai ranks came Nakada from Kita Akita, Futada from Minami Akita and Kagaya Yasukichi, a wealthy landlord, from Akita city.[52] In the second district, the two most populated *gun* each produced two candidates who had been prominent members of the established parties: from Semboku, Oyamada and Fujihi; and from Yuri, Inomata and Saitō Kenzō. In Hiraka, Tsuchida was not confronted by an ex-Seiyūkai candidate, although he did have to face the formidable Kawamata and a newcomer, Suzuki Yagorō, who had been born there but had been living in Manchuria. Only Ogachi had to be content with a single native son, Iizuka Sadasuke, an ex-Seiyūkai official.

This situation was an almost inevitable result of the extinction of the parties. With the government adopting a 'pure election' policy, the new local branch of the Taisei Yokusankai was in no position to exert control over the various competing *gun yūryokusha*. Official endorsement meant little in such circumstances; indeed, two of the endorsed candidates, Nakada and Fujihi, were beaten by Nakagawa and Kawamata. Of course, if there had been official interference with the campaign in such a way as to favour the endorsed candidates, this might not have been so. However, I have come across no allegation of preferential treatment, and the Taisei Yokusankai instructions of March 1942 emphasised that the campaign must be conducted with complete propriety. Not only was there to be no intimidation, house-visiting or vote-buying (which included promises of future benefits such as an improvement of the water supply or reduction of rents), but 'rest-rooms' (*kyūkeijo*) were not to be set up and candidates were advised not to establish election

offices in inns or restaurants.[53] The strongest evidence, however, that
the 1942 election was a 'pure' election, free not only from election
brokers but also from official favouritism or manipulation, is the
fact that an unendorsed candidate headed the poll in one district.
Significantly, the voting figures generally followed the pre-war
pattern. Local loyalties and established *jiban* survived, even though
competition was increased and corruption curtailed.

Perhaps, although this seems doubtful, the situation might have
been different if the official endorsements had been better publicised. An elector who relied solely on the campaign reports of the
Sakigake would not have known until after the election who actually
were the Taisei Yokusankai candidates. This may represent a stand
against totalitarian government; or it may be that the whole question
was an unreal one. There is a certain mystery here. According to
Shida's later recollection, selection took place on 26 March.[54]
However, the *Sakigake* reported (30 March) that the selection
meeting had been held on 28 March, but that after seven and a half
hours' discussion agreement could not be reached. Katano Jūshun,
the Akita branch head of the Taisei Yokusankai, had gone up to
Tokyo on the 30th and the line-up of candidates, it was reported,
would remain secret until it was published by central headquarters.
Nothing more was heard about endorsement by the *Sakigake's*
readers. It would seem that when it was finally bestowed, there was
some attempt to balance the previous parties, with a slight weighting
towards ex-Seiyūkai men in the second district. But endorsement
must have been nominal, since there was apparently no attempt to
reach agreement over *jiban* boundaries, and in the second district
two men—Oyamada and Fujihi—were chosen from the same *gun*, a
decision which spelled almost certain failure for one of them.

The 1942 election is not without value in attempting an assessment
of general trends in Akita politics in the pre-war period. It confirmed
the advance made by the proletarian movement in 1936 and 1937 in
that Kawamata Seion topped the second district poll for the third
time running. At the same time it showed that no other new party
had made any strong impression on the public. Even Kon Sakunosuke, of the Nichiren-influenced Rikken Yōseikai, who had many
contacts in educational circles and among young men's groups, did
little better in 1942 than in 1937. Nor, incidentally, did Nakada, an
ex-lieutenant, profit from his close connection with the Zaigō
Gunjinkai—perhaps not surprisingly, since, although it had 15,000
members in Akita, its official pronouncements seem usually to have
been of such a general and elevated nature that they could have provided no real voting guidance for its members.[55]

Above all, the 1942 election confirmed the strength and continuity' of local political organisation in Akita, notably at the *gun* level. This strength had been evident in the early 1930s, when, for instance, occasional thoughts of adopting candidates who had not served an apprenticeship in local politics made no headway, and in 1936 and 1937 were scarcely voiced at all.[56] Financially the landlords and landlord/businessmen who dominated prefectural politics appear to have enjoyed considerable autonomy; prefectural leaders may have found it advisable to consult party headquarters before each election, but there were no rejections by Tokyo of local party candidate proposals. If there was conflict within the parties, it was apparent not so much between Tokyo and the prefectures as between the prefectural branch and the *gun* associations. This is not to say that there was a clear-cut organisation or leadership in every *gun*.[57] Some of them contained both a mainstream and an anti-mainstream faction, or an area, such as Kameda-bu in Yuri *gun*, which had a tradition of local independence. Nevertheless, geographical conditions, the size of party membership (apparently between 300 and 550 in each party in such large *gun* as Hiraka and Yamamoto),[58] and the fact that even after having been abolished in 1921 as a unit of government they remained constituencies for the prefectural assembly, seem to have made them the effective unit in terms of vote-raising.

In stressing the importance of the local element in Akita's electoral politics, certain qualifications need to be made. Some Akita representatives, such as Machida and Tanaka, had direct connections with the central government. Others had close contacts with leading party politicians and were concerned with national problems even though they gave their chief attention to local development.[59] A considerable number had been educated at university level in Tokyo. On the Minseitō side, Machida and Kuroda had studied at Tokyo University, Nakagawa Jūshun and Shida at Waseda, Shioda Dampei at Tokyo Higher Commercial School, Tsuchida at a private university in Tokyo, while Soeda had gone to Germany for six years. Among Seiyūkai politicians, Katano had been at Tokyo University, Oyamada and Satō Yūshū at Waseda, Suzuki at the Franco-Japanese Law School, and Hirukawa at a training college in Tokyo. For the Shakai Taishūtō, Kawamata had attended Waseda and Furusawa Tokyo University. Candidates with business interests also had ties with the centre. Nakagawa had established his steamship company with assistance from the Mitsubishi and Asano *zaibatsu*, through his connection, apparently, with Katō Kōmei.[60] Links such as these were probably valued because they represented a major channel for seeking development funds which the region badly needed.

To conclude from this inevitably sketchy description of the workings of Akita politics that the only threat to the established pattern came from the totalitarian inclinations of central government would clearly be going too far. Already by the mid-1930s the challenge from the proletarian movement had made inroads on the position of the *yūryokusha*. In 1936 the *Sakigake* (10 and 13 January) contrasted the 'traditional *jiban*' of Tsuchida Sōsuke with the 'first organisation zone within the *ken*' of Kawamata, and further commented that to get elected it was necessary to have not only a *jiban* but also a *jinban*, by which term it seemed to imply something like popular appeal. It was significant that by 1942 Kawamata had left Tsuchida far behind in terms of electoral support. There was also, as has been noted, some pressure for new men to be chosen as candidates, a tendency supported occasionally by readers' letters and frequently, though indirectly, by editorials in the *Sakigake* which called for the selection of men of character and proclaimed that the salvation of Japan lay in its youth.[61] Even among local politicians there were some signs of dissatisfaction with the party system as it existed. When Tanaka Ryūzō retired in 1935 he sharply criticised the corruption and self-seeking of the parties, and let it be known that he did not wish his son to follow in his footsteps.[62] Finally, it would be impossible to ignore the numerous newspaper reports which indicated that public interest in national elections never again reached the peak which had been attained in 1930.[63]

Against all this, however, it must be recalled that criticism of political parties was far from peculiar to the 1930s. Moreover, the rise of new parties and the call for new men were natural developments which could equally well have stimulated the established parties as undermined them. Certainly the Minseitō-oriented *Akita Sakigake Shimpō* regarded the rise of the proletarian movement with sympathetic interest. The development which did most to change the character of elections, however, was neither of these, but the officially inspired purification campaign of the middle 1930s. Even this, though, need not necessarily have harmed the parties. The *Sakigake*, for instance, supported the objectives of the campaign because it believed the ending of corruption and official interference to be necessary to the restoration of popular faith in politicians.[64] As it turned out, the weakening of financial restraints on candidates did lead to a reduction in the influence of the party organisation, but this tendency was scarcely in evidence during the 1936 and 1937 elections, and became marked only in the prefectural elections of 1939, after the escalation of the China Incident and the launching of the movement for national spiritual unity. Even thereafter, however, the 1942 election revealed that at the local level *jiban* and *gun* loyalties still survived largely intact.

To return to the questions posed at the beginning, manifestations of resentment by local landlord/politicians against the party leaders and their business connections are not easily discernible. Lack of evidence can hardly be conclusive in this case, but it receives some confirmation from the surprising absence of anything more than occasional insignificant criticism of the *zaibatsu* in either the editorial columns of the *Sakigake* or its readers' letters, even when such topics as rural distress, unemployment or the dire need for regional investment were discussed. The presence of Machida Chūji and, after 1936, the initial implementation of a major scheme for the revival of Tōhoku, might have helped to reduce such antagonisms, but could hardly have cloaked them to this extent. It is significant, too, that relations between party headquarters and prefectural branch remained harmonious in every election. If one answers the other question about party demoralisation by pointing to the fierce competition for party endorsement in 1930, 1932 and 1936, it becomes difficult to argue that the eclipse of the parties' influence over government was facilitated or matched by a decline of political activity at the prefectural level.

This conclusion notwithstanding, local politics should not be dismissed entirely as a factor in the parties' eclipse. Relations between headquarters and prefectural branch may well have been harmonious only because the former found it expedient not to challenge the autonomy of the latter. The very vitality of prefectural politics, in fact, may have weakened the parties by limiting the latter's role. In the case of Akita, aspects of the 'dual structure' which Masumi Junnosuke describes in his study of political organisation in the early Taishō period[65] were still to be seen in the selection of candidates primarily by the local branch[66] and the fact that local politicians did not hold rigidly to party policies which ran counter to prefectural interests. It is significant that in 1937, when it was reported that party headquarters intended to co-operate to ensure the return of the sitting members,[67] local rivalries ensured that the struggle was no less fierce. Such occurrences suggest that the personalities and *jiban* of local politicians stood between the parties and the electorate. As long as elections remained to a considerable extent contests between the *gun yūryokusha*, on whom voting loyalties were focused, the ground was lacking for a firm public attachment to grow up towards the parties.[68]

From this viewpoint it would appear that the strength of local loyalties operated as a barrier to the development of modern political parties.[69] This is only one side of the coin, however. The other is the resistance in practice of local politicians and electors to the Tōjō government's efforts at single-party domination in 1942.[70]

While there seems no reason to suppose that local politicians would
have spearheaded a revival of party politics, their continued vitality,
in the face of all the changes of the 1930s, suggests that a revival at
the centre would probably have found a ready response and an
effective political network at the prefectural level. In Akita, certainly,
the eclipse of the political parties was far from total.

APPENDIX: VOTING FIGURES IN NATIONAL ELECTIONS IN AKITA PREFECTURE, 1928–1942

A. FIRST ELECTORAL DISTRICT (4 MEMBERS)

		MINAMI AKITA	KITA AKITA	YAMA- MOTO	KAT- SUNO	AKITA CITY	KAWABE	TOTAL
1928								
MACHIDA	(M)	2,484	10,269	377	4,234	779	209	18,352
IKEUCHI	(S)	6,387	338	7,567	61	168	2,873	17,394
TANAKA	(M)	6,505	2,598	198	2,318	2,467	3,135	17,221
SUZUKI	(S)	4,317	6,652	219	2,055	2,533	926	16,702
SHIDA	(M)	3,477	507	8,678	106	659	157	13,584
HATAKEYAMA	(P)	1,677	300	510	145	24	21	2,995
1930								
TANAKA	(M)	7,769	2,695	565	3,717	2,376	3,677	20,799
MACHIDA	(M)	3,073	11,132	759	3,898	958	970	20,790
SHIDA	(M)	5,801	1,094	11,057	225	1,598	802	20,577
SUZUKI	(S)	1,998	3,253	5,040	195	1,330	875	12,691
ISHIKAWA	(S)	4,078	1,838	239	722	370	732	7,979
KANEKO	(P)	1,954	773	333	538	484	324	4,406
KON	(RY)	61	671	49	49	108	51	989
1932								
SUGIMOTO	(S)	675	10,591	10,625	326	343	526	23,086
SUZUKI	(S)	12,161	674	244	3,447	2,424	3,717	22,667
TANAKA	(M)	6,506	1,916	131	2,695	2,426	2,490	16,164
MACHIDA	(M)	2,993	7,964	131	2,835	874	497	15,294
SHIDA	(M)	3,012	687	7,685	351	1,504	297	13,536
1936								
MACHIDA	(M)	5,104	9,150	887	5,198	3,988	2,099	26,426
SHIDA	(M)	2,787	457	12,008	175	999	769	17,195
NAKAGAWA	(M)	9,200	316	165	879	1,553	1,468	13,581
NAKADA	(S)	145	7,016	2,483	793	589	119	11,145
ISHIKAWA	(S)	5,123	113	1,628	1,001	1,190	2,089	11,144
KON	(RY)	1,069	2,902	686	473	466	530	6,126

		MINAMI AKITA	KITA AKITA	YAMA-MOTO	KAT-SUNO	AKITA CITY	KAWABE	TOTAL
1937								
MACHIDA	(M)	3,920	6,218	313	3,740	2,816	1,422	18,429
SHIDA	(M)	2,020	396	10,155	71	754	538	13,934
NAKADA	(S)	859	8,110	2,404	1,039	656	156	13,224
NAKAGAWA	(M)	7,378	306	82	643	2,183	1,684	12,276
FURUSAWA	(P)	2,862	1,394	1,500	1,363	1,018	980	9,117
ISHIKAWA	(S)	3,172	565	1,568	617	961	1,445	8,328
KON	(RY)	722	3,096	574	241	412	458	5,503
NAKAMURA	(I)	125	175	46	1,072	55	39	1 512
1942								
MACHIDA	(TY)	1,401	4,509	1,095	4,569	5,400	1,637	18,611
SHIDA	(TY)	919	354	9,358	69	441	155	11,296
FUTADA	(TY)	6,589	89	1,320	208	1,243	1,671	11,120
NAKAGAWA		4,488	811	1,127	1,113	1,868	1,065	10,471
NAKADA	(TY)	78	7,759	972	1,049	414	65	10,337
KON		407	4,553	726	580	384	238	6,888
FURUSAWA	(T)	1,335	618	1,198	1,184	1,545	661	6,540
KAGAYA		1,714	125	737	81	2,968	367	5,992
HATAKEYAMA		107	2,070	111	444	73	180	2,985

B. SECOND ELECTORAL DISTRICT (3 MEMBERS)

		SEMBOKU	YURI	HIRAKA	OGACHI	TOTAL
1928						
SAKAKIDA	(M)	14,748	4,259	576	524	20,107
IDE	(S)	227	11,622	866	6,977	19,695
IKEDA	(S)	10,097	48	7,216	95	17,456
SHIODA	(M)	192	3,765	7,032	5,145	16,134
SAWADA	(P)	1,395	296	3,364	883	5,938
SOEDA	(K)	468	355	450	2,286	3,559
1930						
SHIODA	(M)	5,821	998	10,621	8,943	26,383
INOMATA	(M)	8,307	12,336	91	986	21,720
KATANO	(S)	787	5,688	7,733	5,315	19,523
IKEDA	(S)	10,531	1,554	160	517	12,762
KAWAMATA	(P)	1,982	511	1,679	881	5,902
1932						
KATANO	(S)	3,797	78	13,800	8,690	26,365
OYAMADA	(S)	17,502	3,056	441	251	21,250
INOMATA	(M)	5,204	7,164	283	1,936	14,587
SOEDA	(M)	1,528	628	5,138	6,092	13,386
HIRUKAWA	(S)	219	8,409	236	90	8,954

		SEMBOKU	YURI	HIRAKA	OGACHI	TOTAL
1936						
KAWAMATA	(P)	5,872	2,972	5,943	2,628	17,415
OYAMADA	(S)	12,781	2,076	150	54	15,061
TSUCHIDA	(M)	4,221	1,033	7,178	1,245	13,677
SOEDA	(M*)	603	2,887	1,513	7,614	12,617
SATO	(S)	350	3,577	4,706	3,848	12,482
INOMATA	(M*)	1,908	6,612	84	396	9,000
1937						
KAWAMATA	(P)	6,202	2,931	6,226	4,364	19,723
OYAMADA	(S)	13,300	2,108	182	76	15,666
TSUCHIDA	(M)	4,668	872	7,671	1,507	14,718
SATO	(S)	334	1,965	4,689	7,404	14,392
KURODA	(M)	474	12,015	264	1,177	13,930
1942						
KAWAMATA		4,673	1,380	7,216	3,807	17,076
OYAMADA	(TY)	11,295	1,598	1,898	1,614	16,405
SAITO	(TY)	181	9,542	610	2,433	12,766
TSUCHIDA		1,256	183	5,601	1,499	8,539
FUJIHI	(TY)	6,451	73	893	102	7,519
INOMATA		956	5,913	304	213	7,386
IIZUKA		295	23	277	5,618	6,213
SUZUKI		186	110	1,318	335	1,949

Note: The Yamamoto figures for 1942 include those for Noshiro city, which had been made a separate electoral sub-division.

(M) = MINSEITŌ: (S) = SEIYŪKAI: (P) = PROLETARIAN:
(RY) = RIKKEN YŌSEIKAI: (I) = INDEPENDENT:
(T) = TŌHŌKAI: (TY) = ENDORSED BY TAISEI YOKUSANKAI

* Indicates candidates who did not have official party endorsement.

6

THE GREAT TOKYO AIR RAID, 9–10 MARCH 1945

GORDON DANIELS

If curiosity drives the historian to investigate the Great Tokyo Air Raid he is soon aware of the destructive power of his fellow scholars. It is inevitable that researchers omit and discard much of the human past when transmitting a serviceable version of events to the next generation; but in this instance one is drawn to analyse the process of selection which has almost removed this incident from historical consciousness. Such an analysis may not only spotlight the event itself but also amplify the rhythms and dissonances of a whole period. Furthermore, this investigation may further clarify the prejudices and priorities of important and influential historians.

If one consults the six most widely used histories of Japan written in English one finds scant information on the Tokyo Air Raid. The fullest treatment swells to some four sentences, but three of the works condense their account into a single sentence or dismiss it without mention.

Similarly, if one searches for factual or statistical material the results are even more disappointing. Three books provide no indication of the fatalities involved and those books which do give somewhat different estimates.[1] It may be tasteless and almost inhuman to discuss the measurement of what is psychologically and emotionally immeasurable, but any attempt at sympathetic reconstruction must begin with a keel of fact, a due concern for documentary precision.

If the investigator then turns to the work of Japanese historians he will find them surprisingly similar in their treatment of the event. Professor Ishida Takeshi's *Hakyokyu to Heiwa* (1941–52), like Tōyama, Imai and Fujiwara's older *Shōwa shi*, makes no specific reference to the March raid, while Professor Inoue Kiyoshi's *Nihon no Rekishi* baldly states that 'Southern Tokyo received a heavy raid and became a burnt out area'.[2] The five authors of the Asahi Shinbun publication *Shōwa shi no Shunkan* omit 10 March from the incidents they describe in detail and only refer to its

'90,000 casualties' in the context of the quickening policy of evacuation.[3] As one might expect, Hayashi Shigeru's 500-page work, *Taiheiyō Sensō*, the twenty-fifth volume in the Chūō Kōron History of Japan series, gives more spacious coverage to the catastrophe. But this account only amounts to some five and a half illustrated pages entitled 'Air Raids' with the subtitle 'indiscriminate bombing'.[4] It outlines the stages of the bombing campaign, the inconsistencies in civil defence thinking, and popular superstitions of the time. Even this narrative is somewhat weak in military and social analysis and is less rewarding than the mosaic of documentary material assembled in the third volume of *Nihon no Hyakunen* by Tsurumi Shunsuke and his co-editors.[5] This account is of similar scale and scope to the section in *Taiheiyō Sensō* but gains special vividness from its extracts from official reports and diaries.

One obvious reaction to these threadbare descriptions and analyses is to question why important documents and the deaths of tens of thousands of people have received so little attention from historians on both sides of the Pacific Ocean. There are perhaps four tests one might apply in seeking an explanation of this flagrant case of historical negligence. Initially one may query whether the raid was in fact unique or remarkable in the sequence of air assaults on Japan. Despite all the casualties and destruction, if this was merely one of many similar strikes one may argue that it should be ignored. But this was clearly not the case. This was the first mass incendiary bombardment after some nine months of predominantly high explosive bombing. Other ambitious fire attacks followed, but this was undoubtedly the most efficacious.[6]

A further possibility is that this incident, for all its vast scale and well-recorded effectiveness, was overshadowed by other strikes against the Japanese mainland. This it was, for the nuclear attacks of August 1945 were more dramatically destructive and thus for scientific as well as political reasons have received much greater attention in academic and popular literature.

It is also true that the overwhelming majority of historians are more concerned with the history of politics and society than with the analysis of destruction, and these scholars may wish to know if this disaster had any important impact on the domestic policies of the Japanese government, or on Japan's ability to wage war. A dissection of the immediate aftermath of 10 March indicates that the attack was a momentous one in all these fields and any broad-ranging political analysis cannot justifiably ignore the effects of this one night's bombing on Japanese society.[7]

Finally, and most importantly, one must ask if the historiography of this single incendiary attack can be linked with the general assumptions of historians about the Pacific War. One view which unites virtually all the historians under discussion is antipathy or hatred for the men who ruled Japan in the years 1941–5. Japanese Marxists and American liberals can agree on this object of scorn though they may dislike each other and disagree in their diagnosis of Japanese military rule. Almost all these writers not only object to the authoritarian domestic policies of Prime Minister Tōjō and his successors, but they rejoiced in the total collapse of their expansionist foreign policies. As a result, all of them have consciously or unconsciously sought to detail the decline and demise of Imperial Japan and have concentrated attention upon events which best mark the process of irrational staggering to inevitable collapse. If defeat is to be the *leit-motiv*, then perhaps it is understandable if not wholly accurate to dwell upon certain military catastrophes rather than upon domestic policies or instances of American failure. Such an approach may well explain the neglect of this incident, which is directly linked to these elements in Japanese war history.[8]

If American writers lay most emphasis on allied victory and the gashes cut out through Japan's defences, Japanese scholars have a somewhat broader focus. They place more stress upon the deprivation and suffering endured by ordinary Japanese as the result of the stupid acts of their rulers. The *kamikaze* plane, the suicidal struggle for Saipan, falling rations and aerial bombardment are understandably presented as the outcome of irrational policies, but positive government policies are correspondingly ignored.[9]

Viewed from the 1950s, the 1960s or the 1970s, the final six months of the Pacific War appear as a time when Japan was straining towards inevitable defeat. But in March 1945 American soldiers, sailors and air crews were still suffering considerable casualties and they counted their losses more carefully than their enemies. To these men the irrationality of Japanese tactics was no consolation; if anything it added to their difficulties.

Despite costly and exhausting struggles, by March 1945 the United States had gained important bases in the Marianas. The Japanese air force had made its last attack on Saipan and B29s based in China had been attacking mainland Japan for almost nine months. Against this was the surprisingly costly battle for Iwojima, and until this was over there was no completely safe haven for American aircraft between their targets and their island bases 1,500 miles to the south. The vital battle for Okinawa still lay in the future. In China, Kuomintang forces had failed abysmally against Japan's Ichi-Go offensive of 1944.[10] At this point the outcome of the war may have been decided, but how long Japan would resist and how expensive victory would be were serious and depressing enigmas. The historians of Japan whom I have cited, correctly describe the ever increasing momentum of American heavy bombing of Japan which had begun with the Superfortress raid on the Yahata steel works on 16 June 1944, but the rising frequency of American raids should not be interpreted as a story of unqualified success. The first nine months of B29 action were marked by a series of technical problems which produced deep exasperation at the inability of this new, expensive plane to achieve what had been hoped. The fast, well-armed, high-flying Superfortress had been designed for un-escorted, daylight precision raids, and this had been its role in the first phase of its strikes against Japan.[11] Unfortunately, even in the summer of 1944 the plane's fuel system was causing repeated problems, and there were numerous losses due to mechanical faults.[12] Its radar system for bomb-aiming was also new and imperfect, while the technical novelties of this electronic equipment were further complicated by the vagaries of personnel policy in the United States air force. For several months radar operators were chosen from men who had been trained as gunners, a pool of airmen who had failed to pass aptitude tests for such skilled roles as navigators and radio operators.[13] In other words, advanced, delicate equipment was being handled rather clumsily and unsuccessfully by men with the least technical ability among flying crew personnel.

Weather conditions also contributed to a large number of abortive sorties against key military targets. Cloud over Yahata had foiled the first raid on Kita Kyūshū, and damage to the steel plant had been derisory.[14] High winds often blew bombs off course and added a further margin of inaccuracy to American attacks. It required some eight raids to inflict significant damage on the Nakajima aircraft factory on the western fringes of Tokyo, which seemed a poor return for all the research and resources which had been invested in America's most advanced bomber.[15] It was against this background that the 10 March raid on Tokyo was conceived, planned and executed.

Despite the trouble and failures which had thwarted daylight precision bombing it was not easy to embark upon a new policy. The original conception of the Superfortress's role was so deeply ingrained in official thinking that it was not a simple matter to reject it for some new strategy.[16] Perhaps more important was the view that the plane's unconvincing performance was due to its novelty and that to change tactics at this stage might create a new range of operating difficulties.

Although the idea of a large incendiary raid on Honshu was clearly the outcome of previous failures, the notion of fire raids on

Japanese cities had been discussed in the air force for some time.[17]
At first there were surprising doubts about the inflammability of
Japanese buildings and in 1943 an initial experiment was carried
out. Mock-ups of Japanese houses were constructed at Eglin air
base in Florida and then ignited with incendiary bombs. The results
were deemed to be satisfactory, but before the new weapon could be
employed with concentrated might a more realistic test was thought
necessary. The next step towards the use of incendiaries was taken
by General Curtis LeMay, who had recently replaced General
Hansell, the unsuccessful commander of the B29 fleet in the Marianas. On 25 February against considerable specialist opposition,
LeMay ordered 130 bombers to make a trial raid on Tokyo. Just
before 3 on a snowy afternoon incendiaries were dropped and large
fires were started. Perhaps because this was a daylight raid, casualties
amounted only to 640, but a record number of 25,000 buildings
were destroyed.[18] These results helped LeMay to overcome the
sceptics and attempt to repeat his successful Hamburg fire raid
over Tokyo.

At this point one is led to explore the results which this new
policy was expected to achieve in terms of the generalities of the
Pacific War. First, one might note that what was now proposed
was not a new method of attacking the exactly defined military
targets which had so far been the objectives of United States'
bombers. There seems no reason to doubt that aircraft factories
and munitions plants were still of great military importance, but now
a dramatic shift of target was envisaged. The destruction of special
factories was no longer seen as the overwhelming priority, and
attention was turned to the heavily populated areas of Japanese
cities. Here buildings were light, inflammable and tightly bunched
together. Inflammability was probably the chief qualification these
quarters had as targets for fire bombing, but one cannot deny that
these areas played at least some role in Japanese war production.
It is well known that the segregation of residential and industrial
areas in Japanese cities is unclear and often non-existent. And this
is particularly true of areas with large numbers of small- and
medium-scale firms making components for large and more sophisti-
cated companies. In view of this, the destruction of any thickly
peopled *shitamachi* area would destroy some of the tap-roots of
military output, besides leading to the permanent or temporary
absenteeism of workers living in the locality. If one was to destroy
and disrupt the activities of hundreds of small workshops and ware-
houses it was inevitable that residential areas would burn and
people die. If this was a military imperative perhaps it was unavoidable, but experts such as official historians, sympathetic to

Twentieth Air Force, never present the burning of civilians as a necessary evil, secondary to razing minor factories. Equally important in contemporary minds was the psychological impact of death and destruction. At a time when the Japanese were showing amazing success in gearing their forces to unprecedented self-sacrifice, it seemed important to unbalance Japanese morale by a spectacular exhibition of American power. A clear demonstration of the air superiority of the United States could well damage the weakening faith of the Japanese in their leaders and help make the austerities of war unacceptable. In short, aside from physical destruction and fear it was hoped that such a raid would make recent American victories clear to millions of Japanese people.[19] In a strange and macabre sense, it was to be an appeal to the people over the propaganda palisades which protected Japanese from news of American triumphs in the Pacific islands. Parallel to these broader objectives was probably a somewhat weaker hope that extensive damage to the Imperial capital might unsteady the resolve of the Japanese government to carry on the war.

If attention is turned to the domestic politics of the Twentieth Air Force it seems certain that the ineffective programme of precision raids had created a strong head of pressure for some redeeming act which would prove the worth of the B29 and remove any suspicion of ineffectiveness surrounding the higher command.[20] It was necessary to show that the Superfortress fleet was making a demonstrable contribution to shortening the war and reducing casualties. It is difficult to assess the various currents of motivation surrounding the decision to change the policy, but perhaps both service pride and military considerations played a part in producing the final verdict.

A new choice of target and a new weapon—the incendiary—were not the only innovations which were planned for the great attack. One arresting new feature was the scale of the force to be launched against Japan's most populous city. Although the numbers of aircraft involved are a matter of some controversy, it is clear that an unprecedented body of planes bombed Tokyo. On 11 March, *Asahi Shinbun* reported that '130 B29s carried out indiscriminate bombing of the Imperial capital last night'. But these figures were issued by the Imperial headquarters which probably sought to minimise the attack in information given to the public. The confused condition of Tokyo during the raid may also have made accurate estimates difficult. The Fire Defence Board (*Shōbōchō*) later published an estimate of 150.[21] This latter figure is frequently cited by Japanese historians, but it is difficult to accept.[22] The official history of the army air forces, written long before the raid became a matter of moral controversy, states that 334 planes made up the raiding force, and contemporary press accounts all claimed that 'over 300' machines had left their bases.[23]

The general tactics of the American aircraft could all be summarised under the heading 'surprise'. Whereas most previous raids had been carried out from high altitudes of up to 30,000 feet, in daylight, this was to be a low-level night attack. Apart from the obvious advantages of the cover of darkness, it was known that Japanese anti-aircraft defences were psychologically and technically unprepared for planes crossing the city at night at low altitudes. If aircraft flew low they could discard the fuel usually carried for climbing and operating at high altitudes and replace it with a much heavier bomb load. Weight-saving and the advantages of a surprise attack were valued so highly that the bombers apparently carried no ammunition for their ten defensive machine guns. This was also thought to have the added advantage of avoiding accidental damage to friendly planes.[24]

Surprise was also evident in the pattern of approach planned for the American aircraft. Rather than arriving over the target region in clearly structured formation, they were to come in small groups, bearing in from different directions. This would make their flight paths unpredictable to defensive forces and enable American crews to single out visually patches of the city which were still free from fire.

American commanders knew from trial raids and intelligence of the likely defensive armament which the Japanese would turn against them in such a raid. Japanese aircraft production had reached its peak in 1944, when 28,000 planes were produced, but now output was falling and fighters were in critically short supply.[25] In the spring of 1945 Japan had only two units of effective night fighters available for action and many interceptor aircraft were being held in reserve to defend Okinawa and the mainland from physical invasion. Japan's anti-aircraft batteries were also poorly equipped to repel a major onslaught on the capital. They lacked the effective radar-controlled gun-laying system which had been developed in Western Europe and America and gunners relied on search-lights when taking aim. Aircraft batteries were principally deployed around heavy industrial areas, and Tokyo had almost none of the 20 mm and 40 mm weapons needed for dealing with low-level raiders.[26]

In facing the superior population, productivity and resources of the United States and her allies, it is understandable that Japan's military defences were in the end inadequate. But this hardly explains the tardy and ineffectual nature of her civil defence preparations.

Air raids had originally been regarded by Japanese rulers as part of the new, modern scientific world of the inter-war years. The first recorded air raid drill took place in Osaka in June 1928.[27] This was primarily an exercise in extinguishing lights, but more serious and frequent demonstrations of interest soon followed. At this stage air-raid precautions were the exclusive concern of municipal not national government, and it is thus no coincidence that the reform of Tokyo administration in 1932 helped quicken interest in civilian defence. The reform of Tokyo's government system transformed the eighty-four suburban cities of Tokyo into twenty new wards with a population of three and a half million. These were added to the fifteen wards of the old city making a total population of 5,500,000. This new municipal authority sought to demonstrate its modernity in every possible respect; and air raids appeared to be the most up-to-date city problem that could confront a progressive administration.[28] Tokyo now redoubled its efforts to rouse its citizens to awareness of civilian defence. In August 1933 the first major blackout exercise was held in Tokyo and it subsequently became an annual event. Exhibitions of model planes, First World War bombs and model shelters were often held in department stores to accompany blackout week, but there was no large expenditure of money or public commitment to the programme.

The first government legislation as opposed to municipal action came in April 1937 with the enactment of the National Civilian Air Defence Law, which transferred responsibilities in this field to national and prefectural authorities. Tokyo's air-raid measures were to be the model for other large cities. Unfortunately, the effect of the new law was to create confusion, time wasting and conflict. At the national level individual ministries were empowered to construct their own regulations with no clear provisions for co-ordination. Rules were drafted with little thought to consistency and often produced contradictory provisions. In Tokyo this administrative cocktail was even more piquant as the Tokyo Municipal office which had created the original programme came into conflict with the prefectural government. The latter had the legal powers to manage civil defence but was resisted by the older authority. If this administrative jostling was not enough there was always the Metropolitan Police Board, which considered itself quite independent of the rest of the city's administration and refused instructions from any body but the Home Ministry. Such kaleidoscopic rivalry diverted much energy from civil defence to manhandling rival bodies. The end result was delay and maladministration.

Above the internecine strife of administrators the national government dictated the broad strategy of all aspects of defence. From the beginning civil defence thinking was swathed in ambiguity and misunderstanding. In the early stages of the war military successes and economic needs combined to produce considerable complacency. At first, warnings of American aircraft near Wake island were transmitted to Tokyo, frequent siren warnings were sounded and workers left their desks and lathes. This soon proved economically disastrous and Tokyo's population were subjected to less frequent sirens and a feeling of security.[29]

In some senses the ambiguity of policy was deepened by the Doolittle raid of sixteen B25s on Tokyo in April 1942. Due to mistakes by Japanese observer ships, which believed that the bombers' carrier *USS Hornet* was too far from Tokyo for an attack to be possible, the attack was a complete surprise. Sirens only sounded after bombs had fallen. Yet losses were light. Fifty people were killed, a hundred houses destroyed, fires were easily extinguished, and existing provisions seemed adequate if not totally satisfactory. The basic premise of the Japanese government was that enemy planes would rarely reach Japan and that those that did would be few in number, seeking out individual buildings. Nets were later used to camouflage the Diet building, but 90 per cent of office buildings were never camouflaged in any way. The Japanese government felt that their image of omniscience had been damaged by the Doolittle raid. Three captured pilots were executed, but there was no important change in civil defence.[30]

Between April 1942 and Spring 1945 Japan experienced a depressing series of military reverses and the realities of air power became unpleasantly apparent. From November 1944 B29s raided factories in the Kanto, and Tokyo citizens referred to the frequent visitors as 'Lord B', '*okyakusama*' (visitors), and 'regular mail'.[31]

In response to these developments air-raid counter-policies became more serious and new lines of action were initiated. In view of Japan's early interest in civil defence and her own bombing activities in China it is surprising that these measures were so slow to gather impetus and so inefficient in execution. Whatever the chronology of official action, its inconsistencies were so great that it is impossible to determine at what point most leaders felt genuinely certain that Tokyo was secure and when their statements were made to prevent the corrosion of morale.

Even as early as 1940 there were already deep contradictions in official statements. At this point most officials with civil defence responsibilities believed, on the basis of government statements, that Tokyo was in little serious danger from air bombing. In contrast, the undertakers of Tokyo became concerned at their likely role in any possible air raid. In the event of such an attack they were to co-operate with the police in gathering bodies and disposing of them in an orderly manner. In order to make appropriate plans they asked the army headquarters to estimate the likely number of extra deaths in one year, in the event of an air war. The official answer to this inquiry was the figure of 30,000.[32] This statistic was easily surpassed on 10 March, but that it was presented before Pearl Harbor shows that some military men were hardly confident of Tokyo's invulnerability.

By the spring of 1945 Tokyo had undergone yet another administrative transformation. In July 1943 the prefectural and municipal governments were combined into Tokyo-to, which helped to improve co-ordination in air defence.[33] Parallel with this were three main areas of renewed government activity. The first of these was instruction. By now the 2·75 million citizens organised in a hierarchy of organisations were receiving increasing training in civil defence. Some 2·5 million people were embraced in the *tonari-gumi* system, while a further 32,000 professional and volunteer workers including the police, fire department and an emergency public works construction unit were undergoing more intense instruction on defence against raids.

The second main sphere of central government activity lay in the dispersal of buildings, institutions and people. In comparison with the preliminary evacuation of children in Britain at the opening of the European war this policy was discussed and decided at a very late stage in Japan. It was not until after the lions in the Ueno Zoo had been destroyed for fear of them escaping in an air raid that the evacuation of government offices was decided in September 1943.[34] Plans for evacuating important sections of the community were not published until November and no orders were issued until January 1944. By this time from 10,000 to 20,000 people had already left Tokyo voluntarily, but the future pattern of evacuation was determined by military defeats rather than by an organised plan. With the invasion of Saipan in June 1944 there were efforts to reach a total of one million evacuees by September. These were primarily people not essential for industry. It was not until August that primary school children in the third to sixth forms were moved in groups to country areas. By March 1945 over 1·7 million people had left Tokyo, including over 20,000 citizens whose homes had been demolished to create fire breaks. This still left over 6 million people in the city and there was no compulsory evacuation of any groups apart from part of the primary school population. In view of the very close ties most Tokyo dwellers had with relatives in safe rural areas it is surprising that no more ambitious evacuation policy was enforced after November 1944.[35] This somewhat cautious line of action is particularly strange as evacuation is relatively inexpensive in comparison with most other aspects of civil defence and had been widely employed in Western Europe.

The third main sphere of civil defence provision was that designed to provide physical protection for people living and working in the city. The most ambitious aspect of these activities was the provision of shelters of varying types and sizes for Tokyo residents. This policy, like evacuation, was begun late, and this not only restricted time for shelter construction but also meant that building materials were required when resources were short and could not be spared for such 'non-essential' construction. It is true that by the spring of 1945 every Tokyo citizen was supposed to have a shelter in which to seek refuge, but their location and quality left much to be desired. As Tokyo's underground was shallow and her soil relatively unstable they were unsuitable for shelters. Thus the most effective ready-made shelters were in the basements of modern Western-style buildings, many of which had been designed to resist possible earthquakes. Whatever the structural merits of these underground shelters they were mostly to be found in the business centre, far from the homes of people allocated to use them. Equally effective structurally were concrete shelters planned by the authorities, but cement was so scarce that only eighteen were built by the spring of 1945 and their total capacity was less than 5,000.[36]

In other words, the shelter provision for most of Tokyo's population was highly inadequate. Trenches, at best covered with a concrete roof but without seating, heating or sanitation, were provided for some 2 million people, but they provided little protection. Space between houses was often so restricted that garden shelters provided little more safety than following the government's first instruction, to hide in the clothes cupboard of one's own home.[37] The next most prevalent shelter was the tunnel variety, often driven into hill-sides, frequently at a distance from residential areas. These were often provided with equipment and food, but in the case of sudden attacks they were difficult to reach. In the case of smaller tunnel shelters, the occupants were likely to be suffocated if large-scale fires broke out in the immediate area.

Overall it is clear that the statistical balance between citizens and shelter space in Tokyo was sickeningly deceptive. Modern accessible shelters were negligible and the distribution of all types of shelters was tragically unsatisfactory. The main control centre of civil and military air-raid action was in the basement of an ordinary Western-style building, and hospitals had inadequate shelter provision in their immediate areas.

To complement their developing shelter policy the Japanese

authorities recognised that special measures were needed to protect the densely populated warrens of narrow streets and wooden buildings which made up much of the poorer areas of Tokyo. The main defensive action announced in late 1943 and acted upon the following year was the destruction of lines of buildings to provide fire breaks. Had this policy been carried out speedily on a vast enough scale it may well have done something to contain spreading flames, but this was not the case. Shortages of men and equipment prevented the fire breaks being developed on a sufficient scale to fulfil their purpose. In many cases houses were evacuated and demolished but piles of timber were left where the buildings had stood so that the whole object of demolition was vitiated.[38]

It was thus against fragile and depleted civilian and military defences that the unprecedented force of B29s was launched on 9 March. Units from the 314th Wings 19th and 29th groups took off from Guam, and soon after more aircraft left Saipan and Tinian. It took some two and a half hours for all the planes to take off with their maximum load of six tons of incendiaries. Oil, phosphorous and M69 napalm bombs were carried, the latter being used by the first group of planes to start fires and illuminate the target. This was the Asakusa ward, to the east of the Imperial Palace (which was clearly designated as outside the target zone). Besides being a flat area of narrow streets and flimsy structures, it was characterised by a very high roof density.[39] Its population density was 103,000 per square mile. It was approximately 12 square miles in area and some 2,000 tons of incendiaries were used for its destruction.

Japanese radar stations in the Bonin islands and observer ships patrolling off the mainland detected the aircraft before they reached the Japanese coast, but no warning was broadcast until 10.30 p.m. when the first planes appeared over the Bōsō peninsula. Early warnings explained that the bombers were turning away to the sea but these may well have been decoy aircraft. By 12.08 hundreds of incendiaries were falling over large areas on both sides of the Sumida river. The attack warning was not broadcast until 12.15, and the raid continued for two hours.[40] During this time fighter planes, anti-aircraft batteries, and over 300 fire engines sought to resist the American planes and the conflagration which they created. Some American aircraft reported 'flak moderate, fighter opposition nil', but fighter interception developed during the two hours of the attack. Some forty-three sightings of fighters were reported and though American press reports spoke of two or no planes lost the *Asahi Shinbun* and the official *Air Force History* report fourteen and fifteen planes brought down by interceptors and anti-aircraft fire.[41] Numbers of Japanese fighters were small, there was no low-level anti-aircraft fire and many gun emplacements were overcome by the webs of flame which stretched over large tracts of the city. As a result, no military action could divert or interrupt the execution of the raid. Tokyo was defenceless.

The technical and military superiority of the United States Air Force combined with the tinderlike character of Japanese buildings was sufficient to ensure a vast destructive fire, with thousands of deaths. But topography and weather conditions transformed the scene into an almost surrealist masterpiece of flame and agony reminiscent of Bosch, Bacon or Goya in their most tormented works. Through the two hours of falling bombs a high wind cut through the city at over forty miles per hour, spurring on the fire and pressing it well beyond the predicted target area.[42]

For residents hoping to flee from the vast red dome which enclosed them the very rivers and canals which gave commercial vitality to *shitamachi* Tokyo became barriers to escape, and many flung themselves into waterways to sidestep the stampeding fire. Hundreds were drowned as thicker and thicker crowds sought refuge in narrow channels. To hold one's head above the surface for a moment was often to be choked or burnt to death by smoke and barbs of flame.[43]

Besides the invincible combination of wind and fire, Tokyo's citizens were also threatened by the unscientific instructions propounded in government manuals on air-raid precautions. People had repeatedly been told to keep sand bags and buckets in each *genkan*, and place sticky tape over glass doors; but more important than all these had been the emphasis placed on communal effort, resolve and courage. The Air Defence Law forbade essential workers escaping from the city during a period of raids, and training had instilled a willingness to fight fires with simple bucket chains and bags of sand.[44] The avoidance of panic which was often preached was certainly an important virtue, but vain unscientific attempts to fight uncontrollable fires probably caused far more deaths than they prevented. Tokyo's fire brigades were hardly well equipped in comparison with metropolitan forces in North America and Europe, but they received notable help from the forces of nearby Kanagawa, Chiba and Saitama prefectures, and tried courageously to limit the spreading fires. The experiences of the head of the Tokyo fire brigade vividly illustrate the impossibility of quenching the fires and the worsening situation during the first two hours of 10 March. After hearing of the fires, Fire Chief Shinoda went by car to Kanda where there were huge fires. At Shitaya his car caught fire, and after this had been extinguished he proceeded to Ueno and Honjo where flames again spread to his vehicle. After seeing the road at Fukugawa blocked with corpses and encouraging some of his men, he returned to his headquarters, lucky to have survived the twisting course of the conflagration.[45] For the thousands of people who were fleeing from the blaze the only substantial buildings which might afford shelter were schools and theatres. It was in these places that tightly packed masses of people gathered and were caught by the uncontrollable flames.

Almost every relief service collapsed under the immediate impact of the raid. Of over 250 medical stations operated by the government and Red Cross, 100 were destroyed by fire. Already medicine and other supplies were in extremely short supply as no one had envisaged such enormous hordes of casualties. In some cases, doctors were driven to using soiled dressings and the maintenance of minimum standards of hygiene became almost impossible.[46]

Perhaps the scale of the fires, which spread far outside the original target area, can best be gauged by the eye-witness accounts of pilots and journalists travelling in B29s participating in the attack. They reported that Tokyo's fires could be seen 150 miles out in the Pacific and aircraft over the city were permeated by smoke rising from the blaze. 'The plane smelt like the interior of a long burnt building' remarked one journalist,[47] and on returning to their bases in the Marianas the fuselages of the planes were covered with soot which had risen from the inferno. Hot air rising from the devastated area created thrusting air turbulence which spun the 90 feet long aircraft 2,000 feet skyward. Pilots had been asked to evaluate their results on a four-point scale—none, small, large and conflagration, and unanimously they reported Tokyo in a state of conflagration.[48]

The original target area of ten square miles had been easily exceeded by the spreading blaze. The total devastated area was some fourteen square miles in which 60 per cent of all buildings were destroyed. The original target had been astride the Sumidagawa; one-third being to the east and two-thirds to the west. The areas of Asakusa, Honjo, Fukugawa, Jōtō and Edogawa had all been devastated. The stables of the Imperial Palace caught fire and according to Japanese broadcasts blazed until 3.00 a.m. Many other fires continued to blaze and smoulder for twelve hours after the raid had commenced. The scale of devastation was made graphic for Americans in the following description in the *New York Times*:

'Imagine Manhattan from Washington Square northward to Sixtieth Street plus the Borough Hall, Bay Ridge, Greenpoint, Williamsburg and Fulton Street, sections of Brooklyn, add Long Island City and Astoria and Staten Island burned out so not a roof

126

top is visible and the picture becomes clearer of the area burned
out by the American bombers yesterday morning.'[49]

This was confirmed later by statements by the Tokyo fire chief, who
listed over forty-three factories damaged by this single raid.[50]
  Whatever the failures of policy, politics and imagination which
had characterised government action before this raid, this overwhelming catastrophe, which was clear to everyone in responsible
positions, compelled drastic changes in a whole range of policies.
Perhaps equally significant was the great change in public mood
which accompanied the sight of over a million homeless people, in
desperate need of temporary shelter and emergency provisions.
Citizens who had survived the fire in Tokyo and residents in nearby
prefectures immediately threw open temples, schools and theatres
to accommodate and provide free meals for survivors. Several
communities even offered survivors free use of their bath-houses
until the emergency was over.[51]
  Perhaps as striking as cabinet discussions on relief policy was the
manner in which the customary cobwebs of Japanese bureaucracy
were torn away to allow rapid action. After previous air raids
certificates had been necessary to obtain meals or emergency
accommodation. Even more important, they had been demanded
when an air-raid victim wished to travel on trains reserved for
evacuees. In the crisis after 10 March all requirements regarding
documents were waived in an all-out effort to relieve suffering.[52]
Although this implied a sharp reversal of official practice it is
doubtful if it led to any widespread abuses. Apart from the communal
spirit which was fortified by adversity, the highly organised and
integrated character of Japanese society, with its hierarchy of
citizens' organisations, made it extremely difficult to pose falsely
as a victim without being discovered. Within five days, when the
immediate wave of disaster had passed, certificates were again
demanded and a frail element of normality returned to the situation.
Over a million people left Tokyo as a result of the air raid and
evacuation took on a solid urgency which had never motivated
government policy in earlier years.
  While the survival and evacuation of survivors was the first
priority after this catastrophe, the disposal of the dead and the
restoration of disrupted water supplies and other public services
was also of pressing importance. In both these fields existing plans
and arrangements proved completely inadequate to deal with the
task at hand. Previous plans provided for the orderly collection of
bodies, their identification by relatives or the authorities, and burial
or cremation in individual graves. Faced by vast numbers of dead

and the lack of means of identification of heavily charred corpses, it was decided to bury many in mass graves, with the intention of exhuming them three years later for more orderly burial. All the remains were not cleared for some twenty days after the raid.

After earlier air raids public authorities had usually been able to repair roads, railways and water supplies with reasonable efficiency and speed. After the raid of 10 March bomb-gouged roads, torn pipes and twisted tram lines took much longer to repair and in some cases attempts at reconstruction were abandoned. In the immediate aftermath of the raid thousands of soldiers combined with volunteers to clear away wreckage and retrieve corpses, but morale was so shaken and numbers were so great that there was very little co-ordination between repair crews from water, gas and electricity companies, and work often had to be repeated. Perhaps the best indication of the trauma suffered by Tokyo people lay in the fields of electricity and public transport. In Japan earthquakes were usually followed by energetic reconstruction, but after 10 March pessimism halted some activity. Tramway managers refused to repair tracks in some areas as people no longer lived there, and electricity supplies were similarly not restored where the homes of consumers had been destroyed. This temporary despair in private and municipal organs was also found in high circles of civil defence administration. Here there was a recognition that all previous programmes had been quite inadequate.[53] Up to this date the police and auxiliary services had operated civil defence schools for training organisers, but following the great air raid virtually all activities in these schools were abandoned, and training ceased.[54]

Despite dismay on the part of civil defence planners, the government began unprecedented action to relieve suffering and to minimise further casualties. The cabinet created two special committees to co-ordinate relief operations. Emergency stocks of dried tuna fish were distributed as emergency rations to citizens in large cities, while important industrialists attempted to raise fifty million yen for rehousing and relief operations. The Emperor made a personal contribution of fifteen million yen to this fund and government and private relief was co-ordinated.[55] Perhaps the most important measures taken in the aftermath of the incendiary raid were redoubled efforts to accelerate evacuation and the closing of virtually all schools to allow pupils to work in farms and factories.

The dramatic impact of the raid on government policy is clear from one of the most ambitious schemes mooted in these gloomy days. It was proposed that some of the million homeless people of Tokyo should be evacuated to Hokkaido to bring land back into cultivation. In a time of increasing food shortage there was an attractive if superficial logic in the scheme, but one is tempted to think that the Japanese state machine was too disheartened, exhausted and uncoordinated to carry out any major complex piece of social planning at this time. Even ignoring such general hypotheses for the failure of the scheme, it should be noted that the bulk of the people who were to make up this new work force had no agricultural training and were unwilling to move away from all relatives and friends.[56]

The success of the expanded evacuation scheme was based upon the obvious tensions and strengths of Japanese society as much as upon decisive government action. Not only did the destruction of lives and homes create immediate needs, but the obvious inability of the government to protect the capital had been dramatised in an unprecedented way. The spontaneity of the desire to leave Tokyo is clear not only from the vast numbers who co-operated with government policy, but in the flight of many essential members of Tokyo's medical services from the city. The number of nurses and doctors fell drastically immediately after 10 March and this was attributed to flight rather than to casualties. Besides fear and need, the rural roots of Tokyo's population made evacuation succeed without complex arrangements in the provinces. Over 90 per cent of refugees found homes with relatives in nearby prefectures so that the unwilling acceptance of refugees as a result of government order was almost unknown.[57]

The casualties of the air raid were clearly vast, but the precise statistics are extremely difficult to establish. The Tokyo municipality estimated that over 76,056 people had died as a result of the bombing, while the fire department estimated some 82,790 lost. Although American researchers accepted the higher of these figures, it seems likely that they may be inadequate. When unfound corpses and information from relatives is taken into account it may well be that over 90,000 people may have perished in the two hours of the raid.[58] At least 40,000 injured were reported to the authorities and the margin between these figures indicates the impossibility of escaping from the blaze.[59]

The casualties inflicted in the raid were probably greater than those resulting from the great earthquake of 1923 for which the estimated losses in Tokyo were 73,000. The casualties were approximately half of those suffered by Hiroshima in the attack of 6 August, but possibly higher than those inflicted on Nagasaki three days later.[60] This destruction of life on a scale similar to that of the second atomic bomb clearly had a deep impact on Japanese morale and diverted energy and resources from military activities.

For the United States Air Force the raid provided the spectacular success that it had hoped for. The conflagration and damage had exceeded all expectations and the planes lost were a mere 4 per cent of the total, lower losses than those suffered on most earlier strikes. General Le May's tactics had been justified, and his reputation and that of the B29 were, in a sense, secure.

Some would argue that the element of surprise was so important to the success of this raid that it would have been quite impossible to warn the population of Tokyo by leaflet or broadcast of the coming attack. But one's analysis of the raid makes this a dubious if not invalid argument. Japanese resistance may have been unexpectedly light. The United States air force may have lacked perfect intelligence on aspects of Japanese anti-aircraft batteries, but there must have been a high degree of confidence in Japan's inability to resist for the bombers to have carried no ammunition and for so many aircraft to have been risked in the enterprise. Furthermore, test raids had already been carried out which exposed the vulnerability of central Tokyo to enemy attacks. Perhaps two factors were uppermost in impelling the Twentieth Air Force to use this tactic in the closing months of the war. Vast amounts of money had been invested in the B29 fleet. It existed to be used, not to be kept inactive while marginal considerations of morality were debated among army, military and civilian leaders. In addition, the whole character of Japanese warfare, with defiance of international conventions and suicidal resistance, had blunted moral sensibilities, so that civilian losses were no longer a serious consideration in a total war where all adults played some role in military production. Military leaders facing governments who did not evaluate defeat in the restricted conventional terms of the nineteenth century perhaps had little choice but to attack the general morale of an enemy, and in most situations this involved attacks on the civilian section of the population. Japanese writers refer to non-combatants suffering at the hands of American bombers,[61] but in a sense it was the Japanese government more than any other which had developed the concept of a samurai nation devoted totally to supporting military success. One cannot escape the further speculation that in a war in which both parties had at various times declared the enemy to be inferior or subhuman, it became reasonable to value one's own nationals more highly than those of one's enemy and to seek any possible way to abbreviate the war and restrict one's own casualties. One further charge which demands examination is the Japanese accusation that this attack was immoral because it was indiscriminate. It clearly made no attempt to discriminate between civilian and military targets absolutely, but Japanese bombers had bombed civilian targets in China with equal lack of moral fastidiousness. Some might respond, with justice, that the West which claimed a superior morality should have made at least slightly greater efforts to avoid the excessive civilian losses of the Tokyo attack.

Japanese charges have recently tended to move away from the generalities of the raid to particular excesses of action against the civilian population. One eye-witness claims that gasoline was dropped like rain upon the blazing city, but this seems unlikely as the napalm bombs used would seem to be an even more effective weapon.[62] A more serious allegation is that Superfortresses machine-gunned civilians escaping from their fire-stricken homes.[63] If as American writers claim the bombers were carrying no ammunition this was clearly impossible, but one cannot evaluate rival evidence on this point without access to confidential United States documents.

If one is to venture to pass judgement on military policy towards civilian populations in the Pacific War it is impossible to refrain from some mention of the policy of the Japanese towards their own civilians. The time and effort they directed towards air-raid prevention was surely wholly inadequate and the failure to evacuate Tokyo with more urgency, and to devote more resources—when they were still available—to shelters, seems to show culpability of a high order. That rulers chose their own prestige before the welfare of their own citizens is perhaps more culpable than the lack of concern of an air commander with enemy casualties.

Whatever the findings of future researches it is certain that the raid of 10 March was a crucial event in the war experience of the Japanese people. The almost total closing of schools, the mass evacuation and the abandonment of civil defence training are but a few examples of the vital impact it had on the policies of a government drawn irresistibly towards disaster.

PART II
LITERATURE

7

MATSUI SUMAKO:
ACTRESS AND WOMAN

BRIAN POWELL

Matsui Sumako was born in December 1886, the nineteenth year of the Meiji period.[1] Her place of birth was a village called Matsushiro in the old province of Shinshū. Shinshū people are said to have a positive attitude towards life and to be progressive in their thinking. Matsui Sumako's family seems to have conformed to the Shinshū type. Her parents were from the old samurai class. Her father had been involved enough in the issues of the Restoration to go to Edo and fight against the Imperial forces. He returned to Yamashiro and became a vigorous business man who had no patience with traditional methods if they were not efficient.[2]

Matsui Sumako was the youngest of eight children and the fifth daughter, not a happy birthright for any Japanese child. Ten years ago there were still villagers who remembered her as unruly and lazy.[3] She was constantly fighting with her brothers and is said never to have given in. Possibly because of the size of the family the young Masako (Kobayashi Masako was her real name) was sent at the age of 6 to an aunt's as an adoptive daughter. This was a common practice at the time. It could have meant much unhappiness, as a kind of inferior *au pair* with no rights, but it seems that her uncle and aunt were kind to her. Her uncle died suddenly, however, and the family broke up. Masako returned to her parents' house.

One of Masako's sisters married and began running a family business, a cake shop, with her husband in Tokyo. At the age of 16 (in 1902) Masako went to live with them. In her spare time she was expected to serve in the shop, an occupation which she disliked and at which she was rather unsuccessful. Not only did she spend her time behind the counter buried in a novel or a light romance, she was also quite incapable of tying up the simplest packet, as she graphically describes in her autobiography.[4]

There was soon an offer of marriage, as might have been expected in the circumstances, and Masako went to be mistress of a country inn in Chiba prefecture. The marriage failed within a year and

Masako was sent home. It appears that she was not physically strong enough for the life, and this would have been adequate reason for the husband's family sending her back. From her autobiography, written in 1913, she seems not to have been unhappy and to have felt rather bewildered, even bitter, when the marriage ended so suddenly.[5]

On her return to Tokyo it was discovered that she had contracted a disease that required a period in hospital. Biographical sources are reticent about naming the illness, but it appears that it was caught from her husband and may well have been a form of venereal disease.[6] Masako had certainly experienced the indignities to which women of her time were subject.[7]

A contemporary acquaintance noticed a change in her attitude at this time; an introspection, and a conviction that she could rely on no one except herself.[8] She also began to read more serious books during her three weeks in hospital and this continued during a convalescent period in this same acquaintance's home. The latter was a student, who was receiving extra tuition at home from a young teacher named Maezawa. Maezawa was later to become Masako's second husband.

Maezawa was on the fringe of the Meiji theatrical world and had connections with a group of traditional story-tellers who were experimenting with dramatisations of children's stories. Masako went to see one of these productions and it seems this was a turning-point in her life. From that moment on she wanted to be an actress. The authoress of the novel on her life (Nangō Terumi) speculates that Masako saw on the stage a truth between human personalities that she had missed in her unhappy past (which, it must be said, was a common form of past for Japanese girls at the time).[9] Masako herself did not mention this episode in her autobiography and it is suggested that she was ashamed of her later association with the group.[10] She only makes general comments on the attraction which the theatre held for her, in that life on the stage was lived at a more intense level. There she could express her emotions freely, could cry as she wished. One day she would play a part which was close to the unhappiness of her own life, and then she would be able to react naturally and fully.[11]

Masako now, in 1907, had an ambition and from this time she acts with the ruthless pertinacity for which she has been either admired or reviled by later commentators. Her first instinct was to rely on her own efforts. She went to the place where the children's plays were being rehearsed and, without introduction (highly unusual for a man, unheard of for a woman, at the time), requested an interview with the leader of the group. She begged to be allowed to join the group, was refused, but persisted and was finally admitted.

In the autumn of 1908 she married Maezawa and there began a tempestuous marriage (tempestuous mainly on Masako's side) which lasted three years.[12] Masako had not been a great success as a shop girl, as a housewife she seems to have been abominable. Maezawa could never expect to find a dinner waiting for him on his return, tired and hungry, from a day's work. Masako hardly bothered to cook for herself. It is said that her culinary efforts were confined mainly to *nattō*, beans in a strong smelling fermented paste, that may be compared in their effect on the domestic atmosphere to pickled onions or an over-enthusiasm for garlic. Undoubtedly Maezawa suffered, but he was in love with Masako, whose strong sensuality was to disturb many a Japanese man's superior dignity over the subsequent decade.

Maezawa was not only a husband; he was also a possible medium to an acting career. From November 1907 he was associated in the first Japanese school of acting.[13] Masako was determined to enter this school and Maezawa placed the proposition before two of the senior teachers. They visited the Maezawa home and were not impressed with Masako. She was not capable even of greeting her guests with the expected civility. One can imagine also that the flat was in a considerable mess. In their eyes a woman who could not fulfil even the simplest functions required of a Japanese housewife was hardly likely to be equal to the more complicated demands of a stage career. Two physical features were noticed by them, one damning and one commendatory. Masako had a snub nose that was unusual even by Japanese standards and she had a body of ample proportions.[14] The first was capable of being corrected; Masako had plastic surgery and it may be significant that the only photographs of her which survive were taken after this operation. It must be said that this was an unusual and painful operation at the time and it is further evidence of Masako's determination that she went through with it. The second physical characteristic, her large body, needed no correcting and may have contributed greatly to her acceptance as a student-actor in a new organisation that is acknowledged as having laid the foundations of a modern Japanese drama.

The year was 1909. Japan is said to have begun her 'modern' period in 1868. Forty-one years had therefore elapsed. The question arises why the foundations of a modern Japanese drama should not have been laid many years before. Perhaps in the sense of drama as literature, they had. Writers were beginning to free themselves from the shackles of Tokugawa literary tradition as early as the 1880s. Although some writers, in different ways and varying degrees, looked back to the earlier period, a break was made and new styles and content began appearing in literary works. In drama the stereotyped plots and obsequious principles of dramatic composition gave way to the attacks of scholars and 'modern' novelists. A new attention to realistic detail and to the psychology of the characters, and a desire to incorporate new themes were both well established by the first decade of the twentieth century. There was an Ibsen boom around the turn of the century and a general boom in playwriting soon afterwards. It seemed that no novelist could refrain from writing plays. There were ample opportunities for publication in the various coterie magazines, and from this period Japan has a large corpus of published but unperformed, even unperformable, dramatic literature.

Even if these plays had been performable, who was to perform them? Public performances of plays at the end of the Tokugawa period had been virtually monopolised by Kabuki. Kabuki in its history had achieved very high standards of technical accomplishment and had also acquired a comprehensive and rigid artistic tradition. Kabuki drew large audiences throughout almost the entire Meiji period and does so today. But its artistic traditions were not suitable to the new drama with which Meiji writers were experimenting, and especially not to the Western drama that was being translated. A new type of actor was crucial to the development of a new drama in Japan, and such was the thoroughness with which Japanese theatre designers, sponsors, managers and the audiences themselves had been conditioned to accept Kabuki tradition that little progress had been made even forty years after the Meiji Restoration.

1909 saw the start of activities on the part of two groups aiming to overcome this problem.[15] The difference in their approaches to the problem of acting is quoted in every book on Japanese theatre. One group, called Jiyū Gekijō (Free Theatre), was composed mainly of professional, that is Kabuki, actors, who were expected to develop a different style of acting, to become amateurs. The other group, Bungei Kyōkai (Literary Arts Association), had as actors young students with no previous theatrical experience—amateurs—who were to train to become 'professional' actors of a new type.

Jiyū Gekijō, using only male actors, opened with *John Gabriel Borkman*, and was soon performing *The Lower Depths*. The actor playing Kletsch in the latter was simultaneously appearing as a swashbuckling samurai in a Kabuki play. That there were serious weaknesses in this situation was certainly recognised by the leaders. One of them, Osanai Kaoru (who had been a teacher at the acting school with which Maezawa had been associated), came back from a trip to Moscow convinced that female parts in Western plays could never successfully be performed by male Kabuki actors. A revival of *The Lower Depths* after Osanai's return was planned to be a mixed production. In the end only one actress could be found and the other female parts were played by men as before.

Bungei Kyōkai was quite a different type of venture. It was not even intended to be a drama group. As the name suggests, it was a kind of literary club. It was attached to Waseda University and headed by Tsubouchi Shōyō, the great translator of Shakespeare. The original Bungei Kyōkai had been founded three years before, but its activities had been desultory. The members, mainly students from Waseda, pressed Tsubouchi to expand the drama section, but this he was unwilling to do. He was finally persuaded to reorganise Bungei Kyōkai into virtually a drama group by a young lecturer at Waseda, his own disciple, Shimamura Hōgetsu.

In fact Bungei Kyōkai never lost its character as an educational institution. Although productions of plays began in 1911, a regular time-table of lectures continued for three hours per day throughout its existence. The students were mixed. The female students were mostly graduates of the newly established women's colleges and universities. It is important to realise that Bungei Kyōkai was one of the first co-educational establishments of its kind in Japan. Tsubouchi was a man of high social standing, close to Ōkuma Shigenobu, president of Waseda and one-time prime minister of Japan. He was determined that the strictest discipline should be maintained within the group and the slightest misdemeanour was punished with immediate expulsion. Simply being seen sharing an umbrella on a rainy day was a sufficient reason for Tsubouchi to expel the offenders.[16]

Into this situation came the twice married, sensual and determined Masako. Tsubouchi had been unwilling to launch Bungei Kyōkai on ambitious theatrical undertakings. How much he must have later regretted ever admitting Masako. But admit her he did, in 1909. Again it seems that Maezawa was instrumental in securing her admission through a superior colleague who had the ear of Tsubouchi.[17] And again Masako's physical appearance was to her advantage. Tsubouchi noticed her full, robust figure and it was what he wanted for his Shakespeare heroines. It may sound odd to want a strapping Ophelia, but one should remember that in general Japanese girls did not have the positive feminine physiques which were regarded as normal in the West. Tsubouchi admitted Masako and gave her the part of Ophelia in the group's first production.

Now that real opportunity to achieve her ambition had presented itself Masako redoubled her determination. She learnt the whole of *Hamlet* off by heart. She became known inside Bungei Kyōkai for her great application and she was always to be found reading translations of Western plays. There was a fierce competitiveness in her attitude towards the other actresses, all of whom had received a respectable middle-class education which had included courses on Western literature. Masako was not going to be outdone by any other woman, and in all productions after *Hamlet* she was given the female lead.

Her personality also impinged on the men in the group. The number of men who have been mentioned as having been attracted to her is remarkable. One distinguished theatre man even suggested in his diary that Tsubouchi himself fell in love with her. Other students of Bungei Kyōkai would suggest the same of their fellows, deny it of themselves, then admit there was an earthiness about Masako that would have attracted anyone.[18] One must remember the impressionability of the young actors, who would not have been accustomed to being on what we would regard as normal terms with girls. Masako was continually asking them to rehearse this or that scene or this or that dance with her, even pulling them onto the stage. However innocent the intent, Masako's behaviour could only have been regarded as provocative.

On balance it seems that during these first two years Masako was an unusually determined and devoted student-actress, who happened to attract men. Even her critics testified to her determination. In 1912 a popular magazine published a frivolous list of her qualities and even here one can sense the seriousness of her purpose: favourite food—sweet potatoes; favourite reading matter—theatrical journals; hobbies—saving money; religion—Tsubouchi Shōyō . . . character—indomitable will to win.[19]

Hamlet was performed for seven days in the vast Imperial Theatre in May 1911. It was not an unqualified success, but it established Bungei Kyōkai as an important force in Japanese theatre and sponsors were not difficult to find thereafter. Indeed, the next production was moved to the Imperial Theatre only two months after opening in Bungei Kyōkai's own small auditorium. The programme consisted of three plays, of which the first was Ibsen's *A Doll's House*. It began a seven-day run in the Imperial Theatre in November 1911. The part of Nora was played by an actress called Matsui Sumako, the stage name of Kobayashi Masako.

A Doll's House was a sensation, and mainly because of Matsui Sumako's acting. For a time everyone was talking of Nora—the play itself was known by this title, as it was also in Europe. Reviews were ecstatic. 'As the play progressed, I began to feel more and more happiness that for the first time I was hearing lines delivered naturally by an actress born in Japan. . . .' In the *Yomiuri Shinbun:* 'It is no exaggeration to say that the Nora of this actress will long be remembered as having solved for the first time Japan's actress problem and as having liberated women on the stage for the first time.' Even a veteran Kabuki critic who had started writing reviews of Kabuki thirty-eight years before was moved by the performance.[20]

The reviews did not confine themselves to Matsui Sumako's acting. This was the first time an Ibsen play had been seen at the Imperial Theatre and the content also caused comment. One word appeared frequently in the reviews—*jikaku*, 'self-awakening'—a reference to the process of Nora's development in the play. It was because there was this element in the play's subject matter that one magazine added a special *Nora* supplement to one of its issues. This magazine was called *Seitō* (*Blue Stocking*) and it was a literary magazine run by women.

After their Heian glories women had gradually lost many of their rights during Japan's long feudal period. The officially adopted Confucian code of the Tokugawa period confirmed their subservient position. Their status did not improve with the political and legal changes of the Meiji period. The framers of the Meiji Constitution denied women the right to join political parties or to take any active part in political activities, even to attend political meetings.[21] Their role in society was summed up in the phrase *ryōsai kenbo*, 'good wife and wise mother'.

Nevertheless there were forthright women who were not satisfied with this state of affairs, and institutes of higher education for women began to be established. The famous Tsuda Women's College was founded in 1900 and others soon followed. It must be said that the students were almost all from well-to-do families, but they encouraged the spread of women's education at all levels. There was thus created a potential readership for women's magazines and several were published between 1905 and 1910.

No matter how educated these middle-class women might become, however, they had no scope in society to use their education in any effective way. The only woman to engage in active politics was an anarchist called Kappo Suga, who was implicated in the High Treason Incident of 1910 (when a group of socialists and anarchists were sentenced for complicity in an abortive plot to assassinate the Meiji Emperor). Charitable work was open to them, but this could give little intellectual satisfaction. Literature seemed to offer the only opportunity for women to fulfil themselves in what seemed a meaningful way. Already by the end of the first decade of the twentieth century two women writers had distinguished themselves in the literary world—Higuchi Ichiyō and Yosano Akiko. The magazine *Seitō*, staffed entirely by women, was intended to provide a forum for the discussion of women's problems and space for the publication of their literary works. As its manifesto stated, women had once been the sun, but were now the moon. The time had come for them to regain their rightful status. *Seitō* was first published in September 1911, two months before the performances of *A Doll's House*. It continued until 1916.[22]

Seitō's reaction to Nora was perhaps predictable. None of the writers of the various articles in the supplement put any high value on Nora's character or the motives for her action. She had acted instinctively; she was not really a self-awakened woman at all. She may have slammed the door on her husband, but what did she think she was going to do in the dark, outside world? What was her future? One contributor thought she would simply return and serve her husband faithfully as before. Another criticised her obstinacy in not accepting Helmer's submission; she had lived in a small subjective world and she could not escape from it. There was no real self-assertion in Nora; this could only come later.[23]

The typical reaction of ordinary women to Nora was shock that any woman should contemplate such an act as leaving her husband and home. In a later issue of *Seitō*, the comments of women in the audience of one of the Osaka performances of *A Doll's House* are recorded. All were scandalised and felt sorry for Helmer having such a wife. Where was the beauty—*bi*—of personality that was every Japanese woman's goal? To them, being treated like a doll by one's husband was on the contrary a highly desirable state of affairs. If only their own husbands had shown their love in this way.[24]

Sumako's own ideas of Nora come about half-way between these two poles. During rehearsal she says she had no time to think about the rights and wrongs of Nora's actions. Perhaps she might never have done so if the production had not provoked so much public debate about the 'woman problem'. She decided for the time being that it was difficult to sympathise with the way in which Nora sacrificed the love of her three children. On the other hand, she was doubtful of the outcome if Nora had stayed at home because of the children and tried to educate herself to the world there.[25]

The sensation of *A Doll's House* was quickly followed by the sensation of *Die Heimat*, known in the West as *Magda* after the name of the principal character. Needless to say, Matsui Sumako played Magda. The production, again in the Imperial Theatre, was a great success and the house was always full. By this time, however, the authorities had become very worried about the widespread discussion of women's rights that these two productions had provoked. The police stopped the performances of *Die Heimat*. The reasons given by the Home Ministry were indicative of the official policy towards women. The Ministry was responsible for the control of books and other publications and it based its policy on the Education

Rescript of 1890. Loyalty and filial duty—*chūkō*—were the basic principles of the Rescript; Magda clearly offended against this code, but the play contained no refutation of her conduct; therefore it was not something which should be seen by the public at large. Shimamura, who had both translated and directed the play, appealed against the decision. He finally brought himself to write an extra scene to be added at the end of the play. Magda kneels before God and confesses she was to blame for everything. The Ministry accepted the emendation and the play proceeded.[26]

Die Heimat was performed in May 1912. It confirmed Matsui Sumako as an unrivalled star in the modern drama movement—the first star. From being accepted as an acting student only after using connections, she had attained heights of popularity that few modern drama actors have equalled since. There had also been a change in her personal circumstances. Her marriage had broken down and she and Maezawa parted. By the time of *Die Heimat* or soon afterwards Matsui Sumako had a lover.

During 1910 and 1911 Shimamura, the stern Tsubouchi's favourite disciple and acknowledged as joint artistic leader of Bungei Kyōkai, had lapsed into a period of gloom and *ennui*. His marriage had not been successful and he had been seriously ill. Although he had been chosen to direct *A Doll's House*, he had shown little interest in the rehearsals at the early stages. As they progressed, however, he became more and more excited, apparently inspired by Matsui Sumako's 'life force', as one contemporary described it. Another contemporary suggests that Shimamura began to exert a direct influence over her at the time of *A Doll's House* and that by the time of *Die Heimat* special feelings existed between them.[27] In the October issue of the Waseda literary magazine, in the time-honoured way, Shimamura wrote a series of short love poems to her, thus publicising the fact that they were now lovers.[28] Tsubouchi had known about the relationship that was developing and in other similar cases he had immediately expelled the offenders (more than twenty of them). He hesitated several months when one of the parties was his trusted disciple, but finally his patience was exhausted and Matsui Sumako was expelled on 31 May 1913. Soon afterwards, in July 1913, with this affair as a contributory factor, Bungei Kyōkai disbanded.

Sumako was writing her autobiography probably during the early months of 1913. It was published in July. By this time her views on Nora had changed and she was outspoken in stating her opinions on the position of women. She now approved of Nora's determination to fulfil her sacred duty to herself and to be prepared to sacrifice other socially required duties to do so. Nora's action, however, was only a first step. She would need a much stronger self-awakening to be able to smash the doll's house and replace it with a house of human beings.[29]

Sumako's new thoughts on Nora show some move in the direction of the position taken by the *Seitō* group. Their views differed greatly, however, in the case of Magda. Sumako saw a wide gap between the two characters; for her Magda's actions were based on a much stronger self-conviction, an independence of spirit formed in the turbulent waters of the real world.[30] Hiratsuka Raichō, the *Seitō* leader, however, denied that Magda was a new woman in any sense or that her actions sprang from the self-assertiveness essential to a liberated woman.[31]

Seitō has been generally criticised for its reaction to these two plays. The magazine is judged as having been out of touch with the reality of Japanese women. There was, for example, no mention of the Home Ministry incident in its pages. *Seitō* was not trying to be anything other than it had set out to be—a journal through which women of education and literary aspirations could fulfil their ambitions—but its strictly non-practical attitude at a time when Sumako's performances were provoking discussion at all levels, lay it open to criticism.

By contrast Sumako now had complete confidence in herself as an actress and perhaps also as a woman. Her autobiography contains passages which frankly describe the humiliations of a women in the artistic world. She tells how in rehearsals any idea of her own or disagreement with other actors was greeted with 'How conceited she is—just like a woman'. Why, when she had been taught the suitable body movements for Salomé by an Italian instructor, should she later have to agree with a Japanese man who knew nothing about it? 'If women had any spirit, they would not put up with this for ever. I would rather die than be separated from my art. I hope that in the artistic world the word "woman" will be banished for ever, because use of it immediately puts one at a 30 per cent disadvantage.'[32]

Sumako knew of women's problems in Japanese society from her own varied and hard experience. In 1913 she was perhaps uniquely placed to offer some leadership in the cause of women's rights. But it seems that either success or the difficulties of her passionate love affair with Shimamura (on whom she depended utterly) turned her head. She achieved another huge success in 1914 in the part of Katusha, the heroine of Tolstoy's *Resurrection*. This was a Japanese dramatisation of the novel—with music; in particular, with a song sung by Katusha. The record of this song became Japan's first popular hit. Thereafter Sumako sought more and more for the cheap popularity of such productions. She clashed constantly with the actors around her and she made impossible demands on Shimamura.

Contemporaries who defended her behaviour during the Bungei Kyōkai period are generally critical of her *prima donna* qualities afterwards.

Matsui Sumako's life ended in a blaze of publicity at least the equal of her greatest successes. Shimamura caught influenza from her in the winter of 1918 and he died in November. Sumako's world collapsed. She committed suicide by hanging herself on 5 January 1919, almost to the minute two months after Shimamura's death. She had taken the trouble beforehand to ensure that her make-up was perfect.[33]

It is impossible to assess the quality of Matsui Sumako's acting with any confidence. The audiences who filled the Imperial Theatre night after night certainly went with the purpose of watching the actress, Matsui Sumako. But actresses were still almost unknown on the Japanese stage and these audiences could rarely have decided to see Matsui Sumako in preference to others. The reviews of her performances and comments by some who saw her are very varied and reflect the lack of any standards by which to judge a modern Japanese drama.

It is more in Matsui Sumako's career as an actress than in the roles she created that her significance lies. There had been a few actresses before her, but none had achieved her immense popularity. Men had been predominant in Japanese theatre and the special characteristics of the theatre as an art form needing considerable organisation had been unfavourable to any attempts to break that dominance. Matsui Sumako had proved that a woman could achieve fame in this world. Her example undoubtedly encouraged other aspiring actresses to make the sacrifices necessary for success and since the 1910s a series of distinguished actresses has appeared on the Japanese stage. To this extent Matsui Sumako has performed a great service in the cause of modern theatre in Japan.

It is even more difficult to be precise about her importance as a woman in modern Japan. She was outspoken on discrimination against women and her fame was such that her views would have been widely disseminated, at least in Tokyo. Her own personality and the roles she played caused more discussion of the issue of female emancipation in 1911 and 1912 than the only women's organisation of the time, Seitōsha. However, once her fame was established on a national scale (with *Resurrection* and Katusha's song), the only comment she provoked was of the scandal-sheet variety. Although Seitōsha members were also involved in much publicised love affairs, none approached the notoriety of that between Matsui Sumako and Shimamura Hōgetsu. After *A Doll's House* and *Die Heimat* Matsui Sumako by her behaviour only confirmed the prejudices both of those who opposed female emancipation and those who regarded theatre artists in general as moral reprobates.

But she has represented something to succeeding generations of Japanese women. Most women of over 30 in contemporary Japan will know of her and many younger women and girls will at least have heard her name. To some she represents a freedom in following one's own heart that is not always achieved even today by Japanese women. To others she is known as a famous actress of the past. Films have been made of her life and plays have been written about her. Many disapprove of her and what she did; many have envied her. To both sides, however, Matsui Sumako set a positive standard by which to measure their own views on women, and she is therefore not without importance in the shaping of popular attitudes in modern Japan.

8

MODERNISATION OF THE JAPANESE
THEATRE: THE SHINGEKI
MOVEMENT

A. HORIE-WEBBER

Among the diverse activities of the contemporary Japanese theatre, which range from commercial theatres of the musical comedy type to bizarre presentations of contemporary themes by underground troups, our attention is invariably called to a most remarkable feature: the insurmountable gulf between the two leading theatres, Kabuki, representing tradition, and Shingeki (New Theatre) representing a Japanese accommodation to modern (that is, Western) forms. These theatres stand as totally independent entities, each possessing its own orthodoxy, without association with the other.

The gulf between these two theatres is indeed complete. Neither in craft nor in function do they resemble one another; no artistic communication exists between the two; nor do they share an audience. The majority of the Kabuki audience will perhaps never go to a Shingeki production, while a similar fraction of the Shingeki audience may manage without going once to the Kabuki theatre. Moreover, it would not be surprising to find Kabuki actors who have never seen a Shingeki production, and vice versa.

This characteristic division between Kabuki and Shingeki is indicated further in the activities of Japanese critics, scholars, playwrights and directors. A critic who reviews a production of Arnold Wesker or Friedrich Durrenmatt is unlikely to enjoy sitting through a five-hour Kabuki performance. Likewise, a scholar involved in the study of modern subjects such as Antonin Artaud or Samuel Beckett is unlikely to be familiar with Chikamatsu's dramaturgy, or to be enthusiastic about investigating the nature of the traditional theatre. And the attitude of a budding playwright is so conditioned that, unless he is eccentric or exceptionally original, he naturally looks for guidance to Ibsen, Brecht or Shakespeare, before considering the possibility of learning from the unique form of the Maruhon Kabuki plays. I have yet to hear of a Shingeki production in which a director has successfully incorporated features of Kabuki

147

aesthetics, even though Shingeki directors travel all the way to Europe to study the directorial techniques of Peter Brook's productions or the theatre of Jerzy Grotowski.

This division in the Japanese theatre is a consequence of the manner in which modernisation swept Japan during the Meiji period. More precisely, it is a reflection of the problem manifest in the Shingeki or the New Theatre movement, which was initiated in Meiji as an effort to modernise the Japanese theatre. In my view, the Shingeki movement symbolises some of the problems caused by the modernisation of Japan. Thus by examining the problems inherent in this movement, I hope to illuminate some aspects and consequences of Japanese modernisation.

To this end, my paper will examine the two contrasting faces of Shingeki, its present one and its earliest one. First, I shall review the present condition of Shingeki, basing my account on the incidents that assailed it in 1971, and then, going back to the beginning of the Shingeki movement, I shall examine the process of its origin, in the hope of illustrating some factors that may have contributed to its present problems.

Towards the end of the 1960s, the Shingeki movement, which had been subjected to artistic and financial difficulties ever since the days of its origin, seemed from all appearances to have finally reached its prime. What had been originated by a handful of artists and reduced practically to nil during the last war had now expanded into numerous theatre companies (*gekidan*), some of which contained over a hundred members, performing continuous repertoires throughout the year. With the withdrawal of Kabuki theatre from the forefront to a back-bench position of classicism in the post-war scene, Shingeki had emerged at last as the champion of the Japanese modern theatre that was supposedly in tune with the sentiment of contemporary Japanese.

To give some idea of the extraordinary expansion of the post-war Shingeki, I shall quote some figures concerning Gekidan Mingei, one of the five major theatre companies in Tokyo. In 1950, when the present Mingei was formed, it consisted only of 12 members: 11 actors and 1 director.[1] By 1960, this small group had expanded into a company of 119 members: 51 actors, 13 directorial members, 16 management workers, plus 39 apprentices, producing 6 plays a year, performing 240 nights.[2] In the next ten years, however, that is by 1970, Gekidan Mingei grew into an organisation of 250 members, producing 10 plays a year, with performances on 600 nights.[3] To understand the enormous scale of this expansion, we can compare these figures to those of the two leading companies in England, the

National Theatre and the Royal Shakespeare Company. In both cases the number of acting members of the companies is kept at around forty. By the end of the 1960s, the Japanese Shingeki-kai had no less than five Mingei-size *gekidan*, about fifteen medium-size *gekidan* (fifty to ninety members), and numerous small theatre groups, including semi-professional underground theatres.

Similar expansion may be seen in the growth of Shingeki's business. The greatest problem of Shingeki was well known to be its finances, due to its inability to mobilise a sufficient audience for *omoshirokunai* (uninteresting) productions. However, to overcome this persistent financial instability, most Shingeki *gekidan* resorted to dependence upon two compensatory methods of financing. First, by organising a membership-audience through clubs and unions of working men and women, they secured approximately one-half of a capacity audience for any production. Then, to offset further prospective losses, they employed the so-called 'percentage system', an ingenious method of leasing the member actors to mass-media such as television or film industries and thereby diverting from 20 per cent to 30 per cent of their pay to the reserve of *gekidan* capital.[4] By these means, by the end of the 1960s the Shingeki *gekidan* had grown to be huge business enterprises. For example, to quote figures from the case of Mingei again, its gross income for 1970 is reported to have been 300 million yen, two-thirds of this coming from theatre performances and one-third from the percentage system.[5] It is also said that each major *gekidan* has four to five actors who earn at least 10 million yen a year from their work in the mass-media alone.[6] Thus, as a senior Shingeki actor can now draw a salary of 2 million yen for a production which usually takes three months,[7] we can no longer apply the old epithet *binbōna* (poor) to the flourishing Shingeki of the present day.

Of course, such an expansion in the scale and business of Shingeki was accompanied by an increase in the variety of their repertoire. The plays produced ranged from Shakespeare to Samuel Beckett, from Maxim Gorki to Arnold Wesker, not to mention a range represented by Ariyoshi Sawako and Abe Kōbō. Furthermore, every new trend of the world theatre, from *Hair* to *Marat/Sade*, was soon to be reproduced in Japan. Indeed, it has been said that there is nothing one cannot see in Japan that is happening in any other part of the world. Thus, although murmurs about *omoshirokunai* Shingeki were still heard in the distance, the appearance of the contemporary Japanese theatre had come to acquire all the signs of success.

However, the coming of 1971 shattered this appearance. Waves of internal revolt spread from one *gekidan* to another, exposing the true state of affairs in each *gekidan*, splitting and dissolving many, including major ones like Bungaku-za, Haiyū-za and Mingei, which hitherto had seemed to be capitalising on their group solidarity. The epidemic force of these disturbances was so considerable that the tumultuous year inevitably left a growing apprehension among those concerned of some fundamental problems inherent in the Shingeki movement. Thus Shingeki was brought in 1971 under the light of renewed criticism.

At first sight, the incidents that triggered the 1971 upheaval seemed trivial. For example, in the case of Gekidan Mingei, it was started by a questionnaire which asked each member of the company to evaluate himself in relation to the *gekidan*, according to five categories printed on the paper.[8] This high-handed action on the part of the leadership was immediately met by loud cries of dissent. For those who had worked for the company for ten to fifteen years (most of them well over forty), this sheet of paper came as a personal insult and as an ultimate symbol of the distrustful and autocratic mentality of their company's leader. Refusing to submit to the questionnaire, thirty of the most able members eventually left Mingei.[9] The case of Haiyū-za was an ideological collision: for some time the company had been divided into two factions of left-wing ideology; the Yoyogi-ha, representing the older generation, and the anti-Yoyogi-ha, consisting of the young members of the company. The tension between these two camps rose to a climax over a dispute about whether or not to choose a play, *Hanran Kyōsōkyoku* by Suga Takayuki, for the repertoire. The rejection of the play by the majority, led by the leader, was followed by a revolt by the supporters of the play, leading to the defection of eleven gifted young members from the company.[10] The troubles of Bungaku-za, which, it was revealed, had been torn by internal discord over the management and the choice of repertoire, were brought to the surface in the selection of the working committee. In this event, five out of seven candidates appointed by the Kanji-kai (the executive committee consisting of a few original members of the company), including the leader herself, failed to obtain a vote of confidence from a majority; thus the authority and the power of the Kanji-kai were embarrassingly undermined by the rebellious company.[11] Haiyū Shōgekijō, a medium-sized *gekidan*, was simply dissolved owing to managerial difficulties arising from its inflated size. In eleven years, this *gekidan* had grown from seven to eighty-three members.[12] A similar end befell Waseda Shōgekijō, a progressive small theatre group, when nine of its thirty-six members broke out in revolt on the grounds of artistic indoctrination by the leader and the leading actress of the company.[13]

The assessments of these and other 1971 incidents by those

involved differed inevitably depending on which side of the fence they stood. The leaders of major *gekidan*, to whom the blow was greatest, invariably took them emotionally, simply as unjustifiable personal vendettas against them by the malcontents. By attributing these revolts to such general factors as a communication gap or a generation gap, they ignored the significance of the events or their true causes, dismissing the rebels as ingrates.[14] On the other hand, for the rebels, who sacrificed their artistic and financial security by breaking away from the *gekidan*, the issues involved were more essential: they defended their cases by attacking the autocracy of their leaders or their paternalistic denial of artistic and ideological freedom, but above all by professing their sincere anxiety for the future of the Shingeki *gekidan*, which they saw had now become a monstrous establishment that undermined the ideals of the original movement.[15]

The drama critics, however, reviewed the 1971 upheaval in more general terms. Their assessments reflected two basic viewpoints. First was a view that attributed the causes of the 1971 revolts solely to the problems inherent in the system of *gekidan*, that is to say the operational difficulties of carrying out artistic activities in such large organisations which simultaneously aimed at financial success.[16] The second view related the causes of the incidents to the old Shingeki question: *Dōshite Shingeki wa omoshirokunai ka?* (why is Shingeki uninteresting?). These critics suggested that the 1971 revolts were the ultimate manifestations of age-old Shingeki problems such as its inertia and lack of strong motivation in the choice of repertoire, its deficiency in the spirit of confrontation with society and tradition, and its lack of direction.[17]

These causes to which the 1971 revolts were attributed by the various parties can in my view be reduced to a single fundamental point: the paradoxical nature of the present Shingeki, that is, the contradiction between its ideals and its actual condition. Traditionally, the Shingeki movement has adopted the progressive ideologies of each period of its development, starting with modernism, then anti-capitalism, socialism, communism and, most recently, democracy, and has aimed at enlightening the public with whatever was implied by these labels. But from what we can see, the movement itself seems to have remained unaffected by these principles. For example, the movement has advocated the ideals of anti-capitalism and socialism, and yet most *gekidan* are now run according to totally capitalistic principles. The movement has advocated the ideals of democracy and equal rights, yet paternalistic autocracy is the rule in most *gekidan*, demanding the loyalty and obedience of members. The movement has adhered to the new ideologies of each period, yet most *gekidan* today are themselves anachronistic and doctrinaire, tending towards the regimentation of individuals and suppression of progressive or original inclinations.

This tendency is seen particularly strongly in the major *gekidan*. For instance, in Gekidan Mingei, which aims at the theatre of 'Social Realism', a school of theatre that was initiated in the U.S.S.R. about forty years ago, ideologies that are not 'Social' and creativity that is not 'Realism' are likely to be slighted or neglected by the authorities. Less repressive but similar is the situation of Haiyū-za. The speciality of this *gekidan* at present is 'Brechtian' theatre, owing to the leader's personal penchant. Again, whatever does not agree with the didactic, rational approach of Brechtian epic theatre is likely to be subjected to paternalistic pressure from the authorities. Of course, there is nothing illegitimate about the theatre of 'Social Realism' which functions to revolutionise society, or the application of the Brechtian technique of 'alienation' in a production. But problems arise when these jargons become the exclusive doctrine of a theatre.

Furthermore, to continue with the paradox, the movement has come to boast of its thriving activities, and yet the spectre of *omoshirokunai* Shingeki still lurks in the wings. Above all, it was the spirit of modernism that initiated the movement, and yet most *gekidan* remain today permeated by feudalistic principles. In my view, it was these paradoxical features of the present Shingeki that were at the very root of the discontent which led to the 1971 revolts. In these circumstances, perhaps it was only natural that the Shingeki *gekidan* should start breaking up from within. The flourishing of Shingeki towards the end of the 1960s was merely the outward appearance of what was in fact an insubstantial and unstable condition.

The question that arises next is why—why must Shingeki suffer from these syndromes? Why did the movement fail to live up to the intrinsic values of its own ideals, becoming itself the antithesis of everything it upheld? To find the answers to these questions, one should consider various factors—social, historical and political circumstances, as well as the characteristically Japanese temperament of the people involved—throughout its sixty-four years of development. However, it is my contention that the fundamental flaws, those that determined the course of Shingeki and undoubtedly contributed to its present condition, had already been sown at the time of its origin, in the process of modernising the Japanese theatre. Therefore, in this chapter I shall focus my examination on this period, the genesis of the Shingeki movement, in order to clarify the root of the problems that undermine Shingeki today.

The process of modernising the Japanese theatre began in early Meiji, following the general mood of the period. It evolved chiefly through three separate movements: the Kabuki reform movement (1873–c. 1890), the Bungei Kyōkai movement (1906–13), and the Jiyū Gekijō movement (1909–19). Since the foundation had been laid for the future of Shingeki by early Taishō, when the last of these three was dissolving, our attention should be concentrated on the nature of the contributions made by these movements.

The attempt at Kabuki reform was perhaps the most crucial event in the history of the Japanese theatre, particularly for the development of the Shingeki movement, because it was the controversy about Kabuki reform that first introduced to Japan the modern (or Western) concept of the theatre, and thus prepared the ground for the advent of Shingeki. It is common knowledge that the opening of the country at the Meiji Restoration was followed by a period characterised as Bunmei Kaika (cultural enlightenment). The significant factor in this transition of Japan from a pre-modern to a modern nation was that the imposition of modernisation meant simultaneously 'Westernisation', an awakening not only to the new or modern, but also to the entirely different occidental culture. With the encouragement of the governments of the time, who were eager to establish Japan as a respectable modern nation among her Western competitors, a hasty Westernisation of many aspects of the traditional culture was carried out in the name of modernisation. The mood of the day is epitomised by a popular song of the period: 'If you hit *Chonmage atama*, you can hear the sound of anachronism; if you hit *Zangiri atama*, you can hear the sound of Bunmei Kaika.'[18]

In these historical circumstances, it was inevitable that Kabuki, a product of the feudal society, should also come to be subjected to modernisation. As early as 1873, the government issued a notice to the Kabuki troups in Tokyo to the effect that in order to participate in enlightening society, Kabuki should be reformed into a refined theatre suitable for an enlightened audience and for the taste of foreign visitors.[19] However, what took place in Kabuki theatre during the first decade or so of Meiji was simply a superficial adjustment to and adoption of the fashions of the Bunmei Kaika period. For example, in a representative play of this period, *Shimachidori Tsukino Shiranami* (1881),[20] the characters with *Zangiri atama* appear on stage attired in presumably the most fashionable (*haikara na*) mode of the day: although in kimono, they wear straw hats and short boots, carrying brief-cases and umbrellas, one with a conspicuously large watch attached to his *obi*. When they speak, their dialogues are peppered with new terms such as *gakkō* (school), *keisatsukan* (police officer), *shinbun* (newspaper), *yūbin* (mail), *saibansho* (court), *ginkō* (bank), and so forth. Furthermore, the play employs the new methods of counting time and money, while still maintaining such traditional features as Kabuki music and acting as Chobo, Aikata and Mie.[21] Similarly, Kabuki actors prepared chairs in the best locations in the theatre to receive foreign guests,[22] and wore frock coats on ceremonial occasions to greet distinguished members of society.[23] The effort of Kabuki to respond to the new age is sadly and incongruously summarised by the case of a Kabuki actor, who not only ventured to produce a Kabuki play, *Hyōryū Kidan Seiyō Kabuki* (1879), with foreign actors, but 'reformed his living entirely to the Western style, refused to take *shōyu* [soya sauce] or *miso* [bean paste] on the grounds that they would harm his health, refused to drink *saké* [rice wine] in favour of beer, and would not eat *sashimi* [raw fish] unless it were baked first'.[24]

It was the coming of the Itō government in 1885 that finally gave official status to the movement of Kabuki reform. In 1887, at the peak of the Rokumei-kan period, the Engeki Kairyō-kai (Kabuki Reform Committee) was formed. It was headed by Itō's son-in-law, Suematsu Norizumi, a scholar of English law who had just returned from a stay in Europe, and supported by the names of forty-six celebrities representing the political, industrial and academic fields of the time, including Itō Hirobumi, the prime-minister himself.[25]

The basic aims of the Engeki Kairyō-kai, as proclaimed in its manifesto, were to transform 'vulgar' and 'low-bred' Kabuki into a high-brow theatre suitable for the audience of high society and for the liking of gracious foreign guests, to entrust the task of playwriting to enlightened scholars in order to elevate the subject matter, and to build a new theatre fit for the performances of the new, presumably reformed, national drama.[26]

To implement this reform, the chairman of the committee, Suematsu, proposed several points. First, was the building of a new theatre. His models being the Théâtre Française and the Théâtre de l'Opéra, Suematsu recommended that the new theatre should be made of brick or stone, with two or three storeys, and dismissed such traditional structural features of the Japanese stage as *Hanamichi* and *Seridashi* as redundant tricks serving only the purpose of attracting the audience's attention.[27] Secondly, pointing out the banality of extant Kabuki plays, Suematsu stressed the need for promoting new drama for *kōshō na* or 'refined' theatre.[28] This, according to him, could be achieved by aiming at what he called an artistic end. He argued: 'By mastering what is beautiful, we can ultimately influence our morality, for by upholding the beautiful, we shall refrain from seeking subject matter that involves violence, injustice, disloyalty or irrationality, because such elements do not truly satisfy our hearts: thus without trying we can naturally arrive at the morality of *kanzen chōaku* [rewarding the good and punishing the wicked].'[29] Suematsu's position here is that of a moralist, who would castrate the theatre for the good of society. What he called *kōshō na engeki* ('refined' theatre) is in fact none other than a beautifully camouflaged version of the theatre of *kanzen chōaku*. Also, as to the rules of playwriting, he recommended unity of action —reminiscent of the rules adhered to by the French neoclassicists of the seventeenth century—and dismissed as an ineffectual device the idea of mixing tragic and comic in a single play.[30]

Thirdly, as to the style of the theatre, he pronounced a preference for Realism. Measuring Kabuki according to the criteria he gathered from observing the nineteenth-century European theatre, and believing that language was the most important asset of the theatre, Suematsu stated: 'By comparison, Kabuki employs very little [language]; notwithstanding, the actors are reluctant to speak all of it, and instead, by handing it over mostly to the accompaniment [*chobo*], they resort only to gestures.'[31] Condemning this as sly negligence on the part of actors, he claimed further that their gestures were too dance-like and their speeches too exaggerated to convey sincere emotions. Thus he suggested the abolition of *chobo*, extravagant gestures, mannered speeches and the role of female impersonators (*onnagata*).[32]

As we have observed, what characterised the reform policy of Engeki Kairyō-kai, represented by Suematsu's proposals, was its attempt to remodel Kabuki as a pseudo nineteenth-century European theatre of Realism, as well as to emasculate Kabuki, so that it could not only suit the taste of the upper-class audience, but also serve the moral purposes desired by the government. The opinions contributed by others were very much on the same lines. Another member of Kairyō-kai, Sotoyama Shōichi, added to Suematsu's proposals: the omission of Kabuki plays that dealt with *yūri* (the licensed brothel quarters), cruelty or vulgarity; the abolition of *kōken* (assistants); and the reformation of actors' personal conduct.[33] One blatant reformer even claimed that the Kabuki hero ought to fight for the independence of the country, instead of committing *seppuku* (ritual suicide) for trivial reasons like loyalty to his feudal lord.[34]

However, there were some critics, like Tsubouchi Shōyō and Mori Ōgai, who were apprehensive about the simplistic, pro-Western and moralistic approach taken by the Kairyō-kai. Tsubouchi (who later became a leader in the Shingeki movement) disputed Suematsu's art-morality theory, insisting that art must not become a slave to morality.[35] Mori, on the other hand, castigated the superficiality of the Kairyō-kai's proposals, and stressed the importance of promoting the rise of good new drama above all else.[36] But by and large, concerning Kabuki, they uniformly shared the opinion of the Kairyō-kai, that it was indeed unfit for the modern age.

The climax of this reform movement came in 1888 in the form of Tenran-geki, a four-day performance of Kabuki before the Imperial family and distinguished foreign and native guests. Considering the practically non-existent social status of Kabuki actors only twenty years before, as indicated by the old epithet applied to them, *Kawara Kojiki* (beggars, outcasts), this was an epoch-making occasion in Kabuki history. But what concerns us here is the fact that this event was organised by Suematsu as a sort of model performance of the reformed Kabuki and that it provides us with some idea of the practical extent of the reform.[37]

The most distinctive feature of this project was the exclusion from its programme of *sewa-mono* (portrayals of the lives of common people). Instead, the programme consisted entirely of dance pieces and *jidai-mono* (tales of historical heroes) such as the Soga story, *Teragoya, Kanjinchō, Takatoki* and *Chūshingura*, with revised texts.[38] This choice of plays not only reveals the moral and political intent of this reform movement, in that the themes of these *jidai-mono* concern the ideals of loyalty and self-sacrifice, but also reflects the crippling effect of the reform, in rejecting the most vital portion of Kabuki theatre, *sewa-mono*, which embodies the sentiments of the ordinary people at the root of society.

On the directorial level, the reforms displayed in the project amounted to superficial and insensitive manoeuvres over the aesthetics of Kabuki. It omitted the use of *hyōshigi* (the clapping of wooden blocks) at the beginning and end of the performances, and of *tsuke* (another kind of wood-clapping) which usually accompanies the climactic movement to heighten their dramatic effect. Also omitted was the appearance of *kōken* (assistants) on stage, while the use of *chobo, hayashi* and songs was reduced to the minimum possible.[39]

As we know from today's Kabuki with all its traditional aesthetics intact, Kabuki survived this difficult period of ingratiating Westernisation. The 250 years of its native tradition and the vigour of its boisterous audience proved to be stronger than the lashes of hasty criticism. The reviews that appeared in the opposition newspapers on the following morning, condemning Suematsu's 'reform' (*kairyō*) as *Kabuki shirazu no 'kaiaku'* ('a change for the worse', ignoring Kabuki),[40] were indicative of what was to follow. With the fall of the Itō government and with the rise of a nationalistic Japan in the next decade, the role of the Engeki Kairyō-kai diminished, and the people saw the flourishing of Meiji Kabuki with its great actors, Danjuro

9th and Kikugoro 5th. Nevertheless, during this period, the reform movement was continued by two successive groups, Engei Kyōhō-kai (1888) and Nihon Engei Kyōkai (1889); however, both took a conservative line, by promoting mainly good new Kabuki plays.[41]

For Kabuki it was better that the attempt at reform ended in failure. But for the development of the Japanese theatre, this episode left lasting scars, in the form of enduring prejudices that Kabuki was a low-bred entertainment for the uneducated masses, and that the contemporary Western counterpart was the ideal modern theatre. As a result, the advocates of modern theatre, having found the attempt at Kabuki reform futile, began looking to the West for material for the new theatre.

It was in these circumstances that the pioneering Shingeki movements, Bungei Kyōkai and Jiyū Gekijō, commenced their search for a new theatre at the turn of the century. The first of the two, Bungei Kyōkai, was formed in 1906 at Waseda University as a research association for dramatic arts, and then was reorganised in 1909 as an institution for advancing a new theatre by Tsubouchi Shōyō, a great literary scholar and a former participant in the Kabuki reform movement.[42]

In order to grasp the characteristics of the Bungei Kyōkai movement, we should refer first to its attitude to the traditional theatre, as represented by Tsubouchi's views. Twenty years after the reform movement, Kabuki was still the thriving theatre of the Japanese people. Perhaps because of this irrepressible vitality of *kyūgeki* (the old theatre), as they called it, the attitude of the Kabuki critics seems to have grown even harder. Tsubouchi, who himself had written several plays for the Kabuki theatre during his involvement in the reform movement, was considered a moderate by the majority of the Shingeki advocates. But his views on Kabuki were far from being moderate, as may be seen from the following quotation.

'If we liken the aesthetic experience of Kabuki to a dream, 70 per cent of that dream is for pleasure-hunting libertines or rakes. That is to say, the sensual pleasure Kabuki provides is like a fool's paradise. Visually it resembles the permutations of Nishiki pictures: colourful, gay and pretty, as if one is looking through five-coloured glasses. But it is usually frivolous, illogical, unnatural and stupid, like a fairy-tale. While on the one hand, it is painstakingly but superficially realistic about minor details, on the other hand, it is candid, pornographic, vulgar, idiotic and brutal without fail. Thus Kabuki is not at all a dream which sober, serious, healthy and intelligent men should have. Similarly, if we liken the aesthetic experience of theatre to a drunken state, we may be sure that what Kabuki provides is not like the mellow feeling obtained from the sacred wine prepared by a divine hermit, but rather it is like a physically drunken state, soaked in the cheap wine at gay festivities, at flower-viewing parties, or at a feast in the courtesan's quarters.'[43]

This passage clearly indicates Tsubouchi's unchanged view that Kabuki was an unsuitable theatre for what he called 'sober, serious, healthy and intelligent men' of the new age.

As a result of this opinion of the traditional theatre, Tsubouchi was determined to make a fresh start with Bungei Kyōkai. The aim of the movement was proclaimed to be 'to advance a new theatre suitable for the new age, which overcomes the ills of the traditional theatre and which indirectly, through providing aesthetic experiences, works to enlighten society'.[44] To achieve this objective, Tsubouchi specified further the policies of Bungei Kyōkai. Firstly, it would undertake the two-fold task of promoting new plays and educating enlightened, *shikiken aru*, Shingeki pioneers.[45] Secondly, he stated that in doing so 'we shall focus mainly on the feature of novelty, *zanshin*'.[46]

Thus, first of all, in selecting prospective Shingeki actors, Bungeki Kyōkai made it a rule not to hire anyone who had previously associated with either Kabuki or Shin-pa, taking instead amateurs, mostly students.[47] It should be noted that this was the first co-educational school ever to be founded in Japan. Then, to educate the pupils as *shikiken aru* Shingeki pioneers, it set up a curriculum that included all dimensions of theatre arts: not only the study of acting techniques and the plays of Shakespeare and Ibsen (who, Tsubouchi thought, represented respectively the Romantic and Modern theatre), but also such general subjects as psychology, history of theatre and philosophy of art. However, reflecting the *zanshin na* policy, the curriculum specifically excluded the study of any Kabuki or Jōruri plays, although employing for acting exercises some new native plays and the ingredients of the traditional theatres, such as Kyōgen, Yōkyoku, Joruri, Japanese dancing and sword-fighting. Tsubouchi believed, interestingly enough, that these assets of the traditional theatres would help actors to master vocal and gestural aspects of acting techniques.[48]

After two years of training, Bungei Kyōkai produced its first full-scale public performance, *Hamlet*, in 1911. In the following three years, it produced eight European plays and five experimental dance pieces written by Tsubouchi himself.[49] During the five-year span of its activities,[50] Bungei Kyōkai is said to have taken in eighty-one students, of whom twenty-one were dismissed on the grounds of misbehaviour.[51]

The contributions made by the Bungei Kyōkai movement were many: it set up the first drama academy in Japan that presented comprehensive programmes of education; it sent out the first famous Shingeki actress; it produced up-to-date plays like Ibsen's *A Doll's House* and Sudermann's *Magda*, which aroused controversy and social awareness among some Japanese. But, above all, what determined the character of the movement and must be paid a special tribute was its integrity in adhering to the objective of searching for a new 'national' theatre. While rejecting the traditional theatre as a possible candidate for a modern theatre and taking guidance from Western drama, Tsubouchi was not content with mere imitation of Western counterparts but was devoted to opening the way for the rise of a new Japanese theatre. This fact is underlined by his persistent preference for the universality of Shakespearian drama over the contemporary themes of the Ibsenian modern theatre (much to the dismay of young Ibsen admirers),[52] and reflected in the long-term programme set by Bungei Kyōkai, designed to educate legitimate pioneers of the Shingeki movement. This aspect was the most significant element of this movement, especially in view of what was to be advanced by Jiyū Gekijō.

And yet, in the final analysis, what was promoted by Bungei Kyōkai was a high-brow theatre, influenced by Tsubouchi's own scholarship. This point is epitomised by the following episode. The first production of Bungei Kyōkai, *Hamlet*, received an unfavourable review to the effect that the play was too difficult to be understood by the audience. To this criticism, Tsubouchi replied typically: 'It is not our function to perform for the purpose of business or for our own pleasure. Therefore, we cannot make it our aim to produce an easy sort of play which any common wit may grasp at first sight.'[53] He added that the audience ought to have read the play before they came to the theatre. Although Tsubouchi was adamantly opposed to a moralistic theatre of *kanzen chōaku* type or a didactic theatre that sought to teach controversial 'new' ideas, he nevertheless believed that the ultimate goal of the theatre was enlightening society (*shakai no fūka*).[54] Thus he was uncompromising in setting a standard of what, in his view, the ideal theatre ought to be. As this episode illuminates, it may be said that the project of Bungei Kyōkai was, to borrow his own words, 'a sacred wine prepared by a divine hermit',[55] perhaps too cultured and removed from the sentiment of the ordinary people of the time.

In the same year, 1909, that Tsubouchi's Bungei Kyōkai made a fresh start as an institute for advancing a new theatre, another

Shingeki movement was launched by a young man, supported by the *literati* of Naturalism. This movement was named Jiyū Gekijō, or Free Theatre, borrowing its title from André Antoine's Théâtre Libre (1887) in Paris and Otto Brahm's Freie Bühne (1889) in Berlin. The leader of the Jiyū Gekijō movement was Osanai Kaoru, a 29-year-old former student of literature at Tokyo University and an advocate of Modernism, and behind him was a company of Kabuki actors, led by Ichikawa Sadanji, who had just returned from an eye-opening tour of Europe. In comparison with the conservative integrity of Bungei Kyōkai, what determined the character of this movement was radicalism, precipitated by an adamant adherence to the ideals of Modernism, particularly Naturalism, and reinforced by youthful attraction to novelty and exoticism.

Shortly before the awakening of the Shingeki movement, during the late Meiji 30s, the Japanese literary world was at the peak of its enthusiasm for the latest literary trend, Naturalism. Apparently, the ideals of Naturalism—the honesty of fiction as a photographic copy of the reality of life and the social mission of the Naturalistic writer (as understood by its Japanese advocates)—must have had a great appeal to the writers of this period. It is said to have dominated the entire field. For example, illustrating the size of this boom, Tanizaki Junichirō, then a budding writer in his early twenties and one of the few anti-Naturalists, stated:

'Indeed, the tyranny of Naturalism was so fierce . . . that any common hack could obtain literary recognition just as long as he wrote a Naturalism story. Like the old saying, "You are not a man, if you are not of the Heike stock", the mood of the day was, "It is not literature, if it is not of the Naturalism stock".'[56]

In the atmosphere of the intolerant ferocity of this boom, it was inevitable that the Shingeki advocates, who were after all mostly *Bungaku Seinen* (the literary youth) or young belletrists, should also be influenced by the ideals of Naturalism. Among them, this latest trend of literature crystallised as a fervent devotion to a single writer, Henrik Ibsen, and subsequently to the Ibsenian modern theatre. For those who had been probing for a new form of theatre, Ibsen's realism, combined with the social implications of his contemporary themes, came as a god-sent model for what they sought as the ideal modern theatre. One of his themes in particular, the exposure of reality through the destruction of the illusory façade of life, seemed in their view to match the ideals of Naturalism. Also, it must have been gratifying to those young revolutionaries of the theatre to identify within themselves the romantic traits of Ibsen's self-assertive heroes. To commemorate Ibsen's death, the magazine *Waseda*

Bungaku issued a special edition on Ibsen (July 1906). The March 1907 edition of *Shin-Shōsetsu* published 'A New Study of Ibsen' by Ueda Toshi, and, in the same year, the Ibsen-kai (1907–13) was formed by his admirers, issuing its own journal, *Shin-Shichō*, which ran a special series of studies of Ibsen's plays. By the start of the Shingeki movement in 1909, Ibsen was enshrined as the champion of the modern theatre.

Characteristically, the enthusiasm for Ibsen and the Ibsenian modern theatre is said to gave grown to intolerable proportions, to the extent of castigating anything that did not conform with its principles. A former member of the Ibsen coterie stated that at their meetings 'for love of Ibsen, even Shakespeare was dismissed as a block-head', and that 'for producing Shakespeare, Tsubouchi's Bungei Kyōkai was a constant target of their sneers'.[57] The extremity of naïve devotion to novelty and Naturalism among the young Shingeki actors of the time is illustrated in the following remark by a former Bungei Kyōkai student:

'In those days, we were being tyrannised by the dogma that novelty was nobility, and the old-fashioned was ill-fashioned. . . . In producing plays, everything was geared towards a single principle— Naturalism—indeed so much so that we all felt that we would even die for this cause.'[58]

It seems that only senior figures like Tsubouchi Shōyō, Mori Ōgai and Natsume Sōseki stood above this wave of Naturalism.

Osanai, the young leader of Jiyū Gekijō, was an advocate of Modernism and an ardent member of the Ibsen-kai. Naturally, the character of the Jiyū Gekijō movement was to be influenced by his own radical inclination towards the Ibsenian modern theatre. His aim was to create a new theatre that was neither Kabuki nor Shinpa.[59] But like Tsubouchi, Osanai was faced with the immediate problem of the scarcity of native plays which met his criteria. While Tsubouchi nevertheless took the course of promoting a new national theatre, by resorting to the plays that had, in his view, universal appeal, Osanai believed that the situation could be improved only by disowning the traditional theatre and concentrating entirely upon the importation of Western models, at least for the time being. Thus, in order to achieve the ultimate goal of creating a modern theatre, he specified the immediate task of his movement to be 'promoting a true age of translation [*honyaku-jidai*] both in the area of drama and in the techniques of performance',[60] and proclaimed his famous slogan: 'Ignore tradition'.[61]

As a result, the activities of Jiyū Gekijō consisted mainly of importing the contemporary European plays and reproducing them

'faithfully' on the Japanese stage. Within ten months of its inauguration (in sharp contrast to the two years spent by Bungei Kyōkai in
training its students), Jiyū Gekijō mounted its first production,
Ibsen's *John Gabriel Borkman*. During the next ten years it produced
the latest in the European theatre, such as Wedekind's *The Tenor*,
Gorki's *The Lower Depths*, Hauptman's *Lonely Lives*, and Chekhov's
The Marriage Proposal.[62] To achieve the Western style of Realism in
the performances of these plays, Osanai characteristically adopted
several imported theories and techniques of the theatre. Firstly, he
borrowed a theory from G. Craig's *The Art of the Theatre* (1905),
that the ideal actor was to be a pure instrument (or 'super puppet')
of a text, working under the instruction of a master-mind, the
director. Then, to enable his Kabuki actors to perform in accordance
with these principles, he applied in rehearsals the eurhythmic method
of J. Dalcroze to liberate their bodies from the traditional movements, and employed the techniques of expression conceived by a
former French opera singer, F. Delsarte, to equip them with appropriate gestures.[63] The difficulties Osanai must have faced in directing
his Kabuki actors are explicit in a phrase he used repeatedly at
rehearsals: 'do not dance but move, do not sing but speak'.[64]

Although the promotion of *honyaku-jidai* was Osanai's immediate
aim, it should be remembered to his credit that he offered the first
opportunities to budding Shingeki writers to have their plays
produced. Unfortunately, however, this aspect of the work done by
Jiyū Gekijō failed to make much appeal to its audience, chiefly
because the overwhelming excitement caused by the imported plays
overshadowed the efforts of the native writers.[65]

The Jiyū Gekijō movement made a great impact upon the Shingeki
field at this impressionable stage: its radical enterprise commanded
enthusiastic support from young artists of the time;[66] the opening
night of its first production is recorded as the epoch-making and
most memorable moment of Shingeki history; its continuous
introduction of the latest Western plays no doubt opened the eyes of
native writers to new possibilities in the theatre; it provided some
native writers with their first chances to have their plays performed.
And yet, by adhering to the promotion of a true *honyaku-jidai* and
by catering for the inclination of progressive belletrists, what Jiyū
Gekijō promoted, in fact, was not so much the rise of a Japanese
modern theatre, but rather the transplantation of foreign plays to
the Japanese stage. This fact is confirmed even to the extent that the
majority of new native plays written during this period were no more
than imitations of specific Western plays, not only in terms of plot
and structure but also in adopting their dramatic ideas and themes,
even when they seem quite irrelevant to contemporary Japanese

society.[67] As a result, however unwittingly, the Jiyū Gekijō movement in effect deflected its goal from that of creating a modern
theatre to that of enlightenment, and gave a final push towards
planting the roots of Shingeki in foreign soil. This, I believe, was the
most significant consequence of this movement, which in due time
served to mark an irreparable break in the tradition of the Japanese
theatre.

Needless to say, for any theatre to function, it is essential that its
native tradition and culture, and the sentiment of the people, are
kept intact. After all, the modern European theatre, to which Osanai
and his supporters looked so trustingly, was the heir to its own
two-thousand-year tradition and a product of its immediate social
environment and historical circumstances. Without such a tradition
and social background, how could these modern European plays be
truly appreciated by the Japanese audience, who were still recovering
from the strains of radical changes imposed only fifty years earlier?
How could the ordinary Japanese of the time identify themselves
with the self-assertive and often destructively aggressive Ibsenian
heroes, or with the European life-style manifest in these plays? Of
course, these were the very elements that appealed to the young
belletrists who supported Jiyū Gekijō. But the sentiments of the
majority were still those ingrained in their immediate feudal past.
Their popular heroes were those who showed their virtue and strength
by persevering in their predicament, but not those who rebelled
against it. Their popular heroines were traditional types such as
those portrayed by Higuchi Ichiyō. Even the poet Yosano Akiko, a
most liberated woman of the time, is said to have condemned Ibsen's
Hedda Gabler as a manifestation of the evils of sex and a betrayal of
true womanhood.[68] In view of these considerations, we may well
question the legitimacy of the radicalism that characterised the Jiyū
Gekijō movement, and doubt the prospect of such an enterprise
becoming the forefather of a modern theatre for the Japanese people
at large.

Yet, as history stands, it was Jiyū Gekijō, not Bungei Kyōkai, that
became the main influence on the nature and direction of the Shingeki movement and the antecedent of the modern Japanese theatre.
This crucial turn of events was consolidated by several circumstances.
Firstly, the first sensational production of Jiyū Gekijō came two
years earlier than that of Bungei Kyōkai, and its activities continued
until 1919,[69] six years after the dissolution of Bungei Kyōkai.
Secondly, while the former students of Bungei Kyōkai were dispersed into small groups, eventually into commercial theatres, films
and academia, the thread of the Jiyū Gekijō movement was taken
up by Osanai himself in the second phase of the Shingeki movement,

at Tsukiji Shogekijō (1924–8). He then followed a policy similar to that which he had initiated with Jiyū Gekijō, and many of his disciples at Tsukiji Shogekijō later became the leaders of the post-war Shingeki.[70] But above all what helped to consolidate the influence of the Jiyū Gekijō movement was the tendency of the young belletrists and artists involved in the promotion of Shingeki, who had a somewhat confused notion of Modernism, to keep their minds turned abroad for the impetus for their own theatre.

Although Japanese writers began in the late 1920s to produce some competent plays in their own social context, and the need to assimilate traditional materials into Shingeki came to be realised then in some quarters,[71] the general course of the modern Japanese theatre had been irrevocably set by this time. Whatever was established by the Jiyū Gekijō movement had become the tradition of Shingeki.

I have tried in this discussion to present two faces of Shingeki: first, its present problems and condition; and then, in juxtaposition, the circumstances at the genesis of the movement.

What emerges as the most critical feature of Shingeki at the origin is its unnatural and forceful break with native dramatic tradition, and this, I believe, was the crucial flaw in its foundation, which in due time contributed to its present problems. That is, by adopting at its origin the foreign ideas and modes of living manifest in Western drama, rather than delving deeply into the native sentiments at the root of its own society, Shingeki deprived itself initially of native theatrical impetus and eventually of its organic native audience. Thus it prepared the ground for the extrinsic nature of present Shingeki, which is versatile in form, impressive in its stature, but lacking in appeal to the hearts of the audience. Furthermore, by adhering to the mission of introducing the new ideologies and styles of Western theatres, rather than concentrating on promoting a national theatre of its own, the movement at the origin deflected its function from an artistic direction to that of 'enlightenment', setting a precedent for an ideology-bound and artistically unsatisfying Shingeki. As a result, Shingeki today is saturated with worn-out and conflicting ideologies accumulated over its sixty-four-year history, which no longer have immediacy or true meaning either for the public or for those involved in the movement.

In view of these conditions, it is only natural that Shingeki should remain what has often been observed to be: *omoshirokunai* Shingeki. Its present paradoxical nature, represented by the immensity of its size and the scarcity of its substance, comes to us as a living proof of the inadequacy of this attempt at the modernisation of the Japanese theatre. If it were simply a matter of adopting the new ideas and technologies of the Western theatre, what was achieved by this movement might be called a success. But as a movement for creating a theatre, which demands the honest commitment of artists and the true sentiments of the people, this could only prove to be an insubstantial and ineffectual enterprise. When we consider the fact that the Shingeki movement has involved progressive artists and intellectuals of every period, its present condition and the problems underlined by the 1971 upheavals may constitute an ominous sign of the true state of modern Japan.

9

ABE KŌBŌ AND ŌE KENZABURŌ: THE SEARCH FOR IDENTITY IN CONTEMPORARY JAPANESE LITERATURE

HISAAKI YAMANOUCHI

The literary scene in Japan during the last five years or so has been eventful. The award to Kawabata Yasunari (1898–1972) of the Nobel Prize for Literature in 1968 brought Japanese literature into the international arena for the first time. Tanizaki Junichiro (1886–1965), who had been reputed to be a candidate for the Prize for many years, did not survive to witness the event. Kawabata himself ended his life by a rather anti-climactic suicide in 1972. This had been preceded eighteen months earlier by Mishima Yukio's (1925–70) more dramatic and ostentatious ritual suicide (*seppuku*). With the death of Shiga Naoya (1883–1972) we have scarcely any writer of importance left who began his career in the Taishō period (1912–26). Of the writers who started working before the Second World War, Ibuse Masuji (1897–) and Ishikawa Jun (1899–) deserve special mention, but the major roles in the contemporary literary scene are played by post-war writers. Among these, we choose for discussion here two men whose choice of themes and innovation in literary methods make them particularly relevant to an understanding of modern Japan: Abe Kōbō (1924–) and Ōe Kenzaburō (1935–). They are writers who have already produced important works and are likely to produce more in the years to come.

Despite the gap in their ages (Ōe being eleven years the younger), there are interesting similarities as well as differences between the two. Both are concerned with the solitude of men and women alienated from contemporary society and suffering from a loss of identity. Besides the thematic parallels in their works, Abe and Ōe agree in their deliberate deviation from the dominant trend of the pre-war Japanese novels. They are completely free from the sentimentality or self-commiseration characteristic of the 'I-novels'. Their prose style is also a mark of their deviation from the Japanese tradition. Abe's style is objective, logical and lucid. Ōe, on the other hand, deliberately distorts the traditional syntax, but is incomparable in his use of vivid imagery. Comparisons are often odious, but Abe's literary world has a closer kinship with that of Kafka and some contemporary European writers than that of his countrymen. It is also evident that Ōe is greatly indebted to and has absorbed much of Jean-Paul Sartre, Henry Miller and Norman Mailer.

Except for a collection of poems privately printed in 1947 Abe's first published work is *The Road Sign at the End of the Road* (*Owarishi michi no shirubeni*, 1948). This work is inferior to his major works, but its significance is borne out by his own words:

> 'On re-reading it I have come to feel that after all I must acknowledge this work as my point of departure. Although I do not like the view that a writer inevitably returns to his first piece of work, I cannot deny that this is the beginning of an important thread that even now runs through my work.'[1]

The protagonist of this novel is in self-imposed exile in Manchuria, captured by a bandit in a border village and suffering from tuberculosis and opium addiction. The setting is important not only because Abe spent the sensitive years of his boyhood in Manchuria but also because many of his characters are deracinated either voluntarily or involuntarily. In this novel the 'homeland' is used in a double sense. There is the homeland of Japan, where the protagonist was born; and another homeland to which he had escaped to find himself. But the ultimate consequence is his confinement and deprivation of freedom. Finally he becomes alienated from the external world and loses his identity completely. The novel thus embodies the themes of deracination, confinement, deprivation of freedom, alienation and lost identity.

From the point of view of literary technique Abe explored a new and unique possibility for prose fiction in his *The Crime of Mr Karuma* (*S. Karuma-shi no hanzai*, 1951), for which he was awarded the Akutagawa Prize in 1951. This story is concerned with the metamorphosis of human beings, a theme which he treats also in his other works such as *Dendrocacalia* (*Dendrorokariya* (1950), *The Red Cocoon* (*Akai mayu*, 1950), *A Badger in the Tower of Babel* (*Baberu no tō no tanuki*, 1951), *The Magic Chalk* (*Mahō no chōku*, 1951) and *A Stick* (*Bō*, 1955). These resemble in a way Kafka's *Metamorphosis*, where the technique is far removed from realism. From the thematic point of view, however, the author is still concerned with the problem of lost identity. The alternatives for Abe were whether to employ a realistic method or a method which one may call allegorical, symbolic and even surrealistic. The difficulty that the latter alternative involves lies in the extent to which the use of the irrational and absurd can be plausible in rationalistic terms. There was in this sense a limitation to the highly allegorical stories of metamorphosis. It was natural enough that instead of the purely surrealistic or absurd, Abe came to deal with the realistic situation while still charging it with implications that are above mere realism.

Of Abe's major themes, that of deracination is in the foreground of *The Beasts Go Homeward* (*Kemonotachi wa kokyō o mezasu*, 1957). The hero, a boy of 17, is left alone in Manchuria at the end of the war with all his relatives dead and abandoned by his countrymen. The Manchurian wilderness is the setting in which the lonely, disorientated boy·is left to wander, accompanied by a fraudulent half-caste, in search of his homeland and lost identity. Its symbolic effect prefigures that of the dunes in *The Woman in the Dunes* (*Suna no onna*, 1962). At the end of his futile journey the hero finds himself confined in the bowels of a smugglers' ship. The effect of the work depends so much on minute details that it does not yield itself to paraphrase, but its theme is eptomised by the hero's internal monologue in the concluding paragraph:

'Damn it! it is as if I were circling round and round in the same place . . . however far I go, I cannot get out of the wilderness . . . maybe there does not exist a Japan at all . . . as I walk along, the wilderness moves along with me. Japan runs farther and farther away. . . . For a moment I had the flash of a dream, a dream of my childhood in Bakhalin. Over a high wall my mother is washing clothes. Crouched beside her the child is amusing himself by squashing bubbles in the tub one after another with his fingers. . . . Timidly watching this scene from the other side of the wall is the other self, worn out and quite unable to cross the wall. . . . Do I have to be loitering like this outside the wall all my life? Outside the wall man is lonely and must live, baring his teeth like a monkey . . . one can live only like a beast. . . .'[2]

This passage is instructive in many ways. There is little to choose between the tantalising situation over the wall and loitering in a wilderness outside. In the dream episode, the wall divides the childhood self, which is protected by the maternal love in a paradisiacal garden encircled with a wall, from the mature self which is outside the wall. The divided self symbolises the loss of identity. The passage also clarifies the meaning of the title: in a state of deprivation man embodies beast-like instincts devoid of reason and confronts his fellowmen as enemies.

With Western audiences the film version of *The Woman in the Dunes* has become as popular as the novel itself. The novel represents all of Abe's major themes and reveals a highly ingenious technique. The protagonist is cut off from his home and society, and caught in the labyrinth of the dunes. In ordinary society he maintains his identity through his profession as a school-master and through his legal relationship with his wife. In the dunes his identity is completely lost. The dunes in their symbolic effect are equivalent to the wilderness in *The Beasts Go Homeward*. They function, in this case, as a setting for confinement, in which the protagonist is deprived of freedom. The novel is built up on a series of ironies and paradoxes. The protagonist is not aware of the similarity between the insects which he collects and himself. Furthermore, though he himself is not aware of it, his excessive curiosity about the insects might be a symptom of his social maladjustment. In fact, in the course of the development of the novel it becomes clear that there existed an unbridgeable gap between him and his wife. It is an irony that he wishes to return to society where his identity is only an illusory one and that he tries to threaten the villagers of the dunes with this illusory identity. A further irony is found in his gradual realisation of the futility of his attempt to escape. In his attempt he only finds himself caught in a worse trap of quick-sands. At the end of the novel he shows no wish to escape by means of a rope ladder to which he has now access.

What then emerges from *The Woman in the Dunes*? It exhibits Abe's penetrating view of such concepts as home, identity and freedom. In the first half of the novel the protagonist shares the conventional and illusory idea that he maintains his identity with his home and society, and that confinement in the dunes is the antithesis of freedom. But at the end of the novel he seems determined to stay in the dunes. His determination of course cannot be satisfactory in every respect. Certainly there exists a feeling of sympathy between him and the woman in the dunes and the latter becomes pregnant. This pregnancy, however, is extra-uterine and thus symbolic of abnormality in the relationship. The only positive sign of hope, though still faint, is his discovery of water accumulated from the sand by capillary action. In the terms which Abe uses in *The Road Sign at the End of the Road* the protagonist parts company from the homeland of his birth and finds himself in another homeland, the equivalent of Manchuria. His identity is not established in either. Abe seems to say that identity cannot be found anywhere, but consists in a continuous search in the new homeland, which in this case is symbolised by the dunes. Since the dunes never stay stable but move continuously, like the myth of

Sisyphus, man can never stop his effort, for then he ceases to exist at all.

The theme of alienation and lost identity is further elaborated in *The Face of Another* (*Tanin no kao*, 1964), which focuses on the relations of one individual with another and tries to define precisely the nature of individual identity. The protagonist, a chemist, has a face covered all over with a leech-like mass of keloid scars as a result of a laboratory explosion. The novel consists of his private notebook or diary in which he writes down the process of his making a mask and the subsequent psychological effect on both himself and his wife with whom he wants to re-establish a rapport by wearing the mask.

The protagonist's alienation derives from the assumption on the part of society that one's face is one's identity and that ugly disfigurement deprives a person of his claim to be a member of that society. One of the many ironies in this novel, however, is that the protagonist, as a result of his unfortunate disfigurement, discerns the falsity of this common assumption. He becomes aware that the normal face is as unreal as a mask and that it can conceal beneath it a self which is far uglier than a disfigured face. Another irony is that the initial success of the mask comes to nullify, or at least temper, the hero's fearful obsession with his keloid scars:

'. . . when I returned to my room, took off the mask, washed away the adhesive material, and again looked at my real face, the merciless scar webs seemed less real. The mask had already become just as real as the webs, and if the mask was a temporary form, so were the webs. . . . Apparently the mask was safely beginning to take root on my face.'[3]

On one occasion, to test the use of his mask, the protagonist tries it at a Korean restaurant. What matters is not so much his subconscious racism, in his conviction that he can easily dupe the Koreans, as the intensified realisation on his part of the extent of his hopeless alienation, which is comparable to that of the Koreans unjustly discriminated against in Japanese society.[4]

With the use of the mask the protagonist gains insight not only into other people but into himself. Once in a crowded train he is squashed close to a woman but his mask conceals his embarrassment. In his notebook, however, he confesses that his sexual desire was aroused on that occasion. The irony of the situation is that the mask conceals but does not change his real self. The problem has a deeper implication as developed in the protagonist's after-thought: it has to do with man's helpless solitude in contemporary society. The author seems to say that human beings are enemies of one another and that philanthropism is a fiction to disguise this very fact. The sexual desire that the protagonist feels towards the woman in a crowded train is a facet of such sterile human relationships in contemporary society.[5]

'Surely one may say that an aimless erotic act is a sexual tangent to the abstract human relationship. As long as the definition of "other people" is confined to abstract relationships, those people are merely something in abstract opposition, one against others, enemies; and their sexual opposition is, in short, the impersonal erotic act. For example, as long as the abstract idea of womanhood exists, free-floating masculine eroticism is an unavoidable necessity. Such eroticism indeed is not the enemy of women, as is usually thought; rather woman herself is the enemy of its impersonality. If that is true, an erotic existence is not deliberately distorted sex, but may be considered a typical form of sex as it exists today.

'Anyway, today the line of demarcation between enemy and fellow man, which in other times was easily and clearly distinguishable, has become blurred. When you get on a street-car, you have innumerable enemies around you rather than fellow men. Some enemies come into your house disguised as letters, and some, against which there is no defense, infiltrate into your very cells in the guise of radio waves. In such circumstances, enemy encirclement becomes custom to which we are already inured, and "fellow man" is as inconspicuous as a needle in a desert. We have coined concepts of succor, such as "All men are brothers", but where is such a vast, imaginary repository of "brothers"? Wouldn't it be more logical to reconcile oneself to the fact that others are enemies and abandon such highflown, misplaced hopes? Wouldn't it be safer to hurry up and produce some antibody for loneliness?

'And why shouldn't we men, surfeited with loneliness, become involved in impersonal eroticism even with our wives, not to mention other women? My own case cannot be exceptional. If, as a function of the mask, I acknowledge a considerable abstracting of the human relationship—indeed, I am probably addicted to empty fancies precisely because of this abstracting—I, who am trying to find some solution, had best shelve my own problems and shut up. Yes, no matter how clever I am, the very subject of my plans is perhaps merely erotic fancy.

'If that is so, the plans for the mask were not my own special desire alone, but merely the expression of a contemporary, detached man's common craving. Even though it seemed at first blush that I had again lost to the mask, in reality I had not at all.'[6]

171

From the protagonist's realisation that the use of a mask can allow free play of his libidinous impulse follows a generalisation that the mass production of masks would create an immoral as well as an amoral society. Abe's vivid imagination is employed in his fantastic picture of the world in which manufacturers of masks prosper by meeting the demands of people and in which one crime after another is committed.

'Some people would suddenly vanish. Others would be broken up into two or three people. Personal identification would be pointless, police photographs ineffective, and pictures of prospective marriage partners torn up and thrown away. Strangers would be confused with acquaintances, and the very idea of an alibi would collapse. Unable to suspect others, unable to believe in others, one would have to live in a suspended state, a state of bankrupt human relations, as if one were looking into a mirror that reflects nothing.

'And when it became common practice to constantly seek new masks, the word "stranger" would become obscene, scrawled in public toilets; and identification of strangers—like definitions of family, nation, rights, duties—would become obscure, incomprehensible without copious commentary.'[7]

Abe can also be humorously ironical about the possible plight of his own profession:

'On balance, of course, some things would be definitely negative. The popularity of detective stories would naturally decline to a shadow, and novels of family affairs dealing with double and triple personalities would be popular for a while; but since the purchasing of masks would occur at the rate of five or more different kinds per person, the resultant complexities of plot would exceed the limits of the readers' patience. For some the *raison d'être* of the novel, except for fulfilling the demands of lovers of historical fiction, would possibly disappear.'[8]

The ultimate end of the protagonist's plan to seduce his wife under a mask is partly to take vengeance on her because she has rejected him and partly to re-establish a relationship with someone other than himself, but the execution of his plan is bound to take the form of raping his wife. He can perceive this much, but cannot foresee the consequences it will entail. His wife's apparently unresisting acceptance of his seduction under the mask appals him, but the actual fact is that his wife is aware of his identity. The vulnerability of the mask is indeed hinted at by the irony that a mentally retarded girl easily identifies him under the mask. No wonder his wife, too, knows him. She overcomes her initial embarrassment by trying to see his scheme as being based on his consideration towards her. She is morally innocent so long as she knows that the mask is a mere fiction and that she is actually re-establishing a rapport with her husband. The protagonist, on the contrary, is testing her and fostering distrust of her, which proves not only tormenting to himself but also injurious to her good will towards him. It is inevitable that the gap between the two becomes more deeply felt. The ultimate irony is that the mask which the protagonist invents to restore a tie with his wife actually contributes to an irrevocable streak.

What *The Face of Another* amounts to may be summed up as follows: according to the common assumption, one's face represents one's identity and disfigurement means a damaged personality; the creation of a mask seemingly compensates for disfigurement and helps to restore one's identity, but, in actual fact, the mask is false and can be no more one's identity than can one's face; ironically enough, the mask helps the process of introspection and brings with it a realisation that, whether one wears a mask or not, the real self is ugly, helpless, lonely, and unable to commune with another individual; the search for one's lost identity inevitably leads to the recognition that the ideal self does not exist. *The Face of Another* was followed by *The Ruined Map* (*Moetsukita chizu*, 1967), which is another novel about a search for identity: a private detective, while engaged in looking for a man who has disappeared into thin air, loses his own identity. Thus Abe does not give any easy solution to the search for identity. However, this may not be so much a pessimistic philosophy as a realistic acceptance of the human condition. It reminds us that to dream of release from our impasse must prove illusory. The lost identity is not to be discovered, and yet life is meaningful only if the search is continued: the cessation of the search means death. If we use Abe's own metaphor, we are surrounded by desert or dunes, and there is no other place for us.

The link between Abe Kōbō and Ōe Kenzaburō is evident from the latter's remark in his introduction to the selected works of Abe:

'When I first started writing novels, there was nothing for me but to imitate Abe Kōbō. I tried my best to imitate his way of thinking, but naturally I never attained the clarity characteristic of the world he created. I soon gave up imitating him and wrote a short story. Its publication in the newspaper of the University of Tokyo marked the beginning of my literary career. Soon after that

I was asked for the first time to contribute a review of *The Beasts Go Homeward* to that newspaper.

'Abe Kōbō was thus very important for me to start my career as a writer. This is still true even now when I can talk face to face with him.'[9]

Between the two writers there are parallels in more ways than one. Abe's earliest work came to be published through a recommendation by Haniya Yutaka (1910–   ) who was then a member of the magazine *Kindai Bungaku* (*Modern Literature*). Practically the earliest of Ōe's short stories, *A Queer Job* (*Kimyō na shigoto*, 1957), was chosen for the University of Tokyo Newspaper Prize by Ara Masahito (1913–   ), who was also a founding member of *Kindai Bungaku*. Abe and Ōe thus share the qualities that must have appealed to the literary taste of their elders, who constituted one of the main forces of the post-war Japanese literature. But these circumstances are in a way incidental. The link between the two must be defined in more fundamental terms. In Ōe's earliest short stories such as *A Queer Job* and *The Extravagance of the Dead* (*Shisha no ogori*, 1957), the main characters are university students who are engaged in humiliating hack work for their livelihood. Unable to resort to political activities as their fellow students do, they find no way out from their present impasse. In this respect their condition may most appropriately be described as one of confinement, alienation and deprivation of freedom, which are all unmistakably Abe's major themes.

The Catch (*Shiiku*), for which Ōe was awarded the Akutagawa Prize for the first half of 1958, has many merits, and, despite its limitation as a short story, embodies in many ways the best of his literary talent. Instead of the baffled youths suffering from mental inertia and alienation in the metropolis, as in *A Queer Job* and *The Extravagance of the Dead*, the major characters are country boys. The story in fact owes its vigour to the vivid picture of the Japanese countryside. This is something genuinely inherent in Ōe himself, who is deeply rooted in his native province of Shikoku. In this respect he differs from Abe who, born in Tokyo but brought up in Manchuria, is essentially a déraciné. While the fact of deracination and solitude in the Manchurian wilderness is the framework of Abe's *The Beasts Go Homeward*, Ōe's story is built around the boys' sense of oneness with the natural surroundings of the Japanese countryside. It is also possible that Ōe might have obtained from Abe the idea of using the boy as the point of view. Furthermore, *The Beasts Go Homeward* and *The Catch* reflect the impact of wartime experience on the authors, one in his adolescence and the other in his boyhood.

The setting of the story is intriguing. From the common-sense point of view the captured Negro American pilot represents the enemy country. From another point of view, though this is not explicitly brought into the context of the story, the Negro belongs to a minority group alienated within American society and cannot be entirely identified with the enemy country. From yet another point of view, Ōe may anticipate a recently fashionable idea that black is beautiful. The first point of view is represented by the adults, while it is on the tacit understanding of the second and the third that the boys' actions are based. For them the captured Negro is the object of their admiration, for he embodies the life force of organic Nature which they also find in the natural surroundings of their native village.

What Ōe creates through the eyes of the boys is an almost paradisiacal state of innocence in which man and Nature are organically united.[10] Harmony seems to pervade the whole community, so that there no longer exists a barrier even between the adults and their captive. However, the harmonious state of the community proves vulnerable to the code of the external world: the Negro must be handed over to the local authorities. Ironically enough, when the protagonist discloses the news to the captive, he finds himself held as a hostage. The story ends tragically: the Negro is killed, and the boy's hand wounded by his father's axe, and thus the dream of innocence is completely shattered.

Ōe's first novel, *Plucking Buds and Shooting Lambs* (*Me-mushiri ko-uchi*, 1958), is an extended version of *The Catch*. In *The Catch* the antithesis between innocence and experience, juvenile spontaneity and social restraint, is only gradually realised in the course of the story, but in this novel the antithesis is presented from the outset in that the protagonist and his companions are stigmatised as juvenile delinquents. They are outsiders, unlike the boys in *The Catch*, who are natives of a local community. But in the course of the story it becomes evident that they are in fact variations of the boys of *The Catch*, and that in spite of their social stigma, paradoxically enough, they represent potential innocence, while the villagers embody malignity, hypocrisy and injustice.

Ōe succeeds to the fullest extent in bringing home the theme of confinement and alienation from the outside world, which he shares in common with Abe and with which he was concerned in his earliest short stories. The hero and his companions find themselves not only deserted by the villagers, who run away for fear of an epidemic, but also locked up in a shed from outside. One can also recognise here a caricature of wartime Japanese society: the juvenile delinquents share their lot with a Korean boy, the daughter of an evacuee and

175

an army deserter. Their initial animosity against one another changes to a sense of fellowship derived from their common lot.

The author's sympathy lies with the juvenile delinquents, but do they embody any positive value? They are certainly akin to the boys of *The Catch*, but the fact of their deracination and alienation makes their rapport with the external world weaker than in the case of their prototypes. The utmost they can achieve is reduced to a kind of primitivism: for instance, their curious affinity with animals. Another aspect of the potential good that they could embody is their uninhibited life force. But again there is an ambivalence about it: their uninhibited spontaneity can manifest itself, for instance, in sexual perversion as practised by one of the boys.[11] Perhaps the only positive moment of communion is achieved between the hero and the deserted girl. Only this act embodies genuine human solidarity and therefore a positive value.[12]

Both *The Catch* and *Plucking Buds and Shooting Lambs* reveal Ōe's wish-fulfilment for envisaging a universe pervaded with pantheistic harmony. Two approaches are therefore discernible in Ōe's work so far: those which directly treat confinement, alienation and lack of freedom against the background of urban society, and those which envisage an aspiration to the potential pastoral. These are in fact two sides of the same coin. Since the latter is not easy to achieve, as illustrated by *Plucking Buds and Shooting Lambs*, it was natural for Ōe to concentrate on the former in his subsequent writings, producing such works as *Leap before You Look* (*Miru mae ni tobe*, 1958), *Our Age* (*Warera no jidai*, 1959), and *The Youth Who Came Late* (*Okurete kita seinen*, 1962). All these are concerned with the theme of how to get out of a state of humiliation and restraint.

The sense of confinement in Ōe's earlier short stories and novels is an expression not only of an existential anxiety but also of an intuitive apprehension about the post-war political situation at large. When the Pacific War ended, Ōe was in the fifth form of a primary school. He listened to the Emperor's speech on the acceptance of the unconditional surrender, but he did not understand a word of it, nor the reaction of his elders. Unlike Mishima, for whom the end of the war was almost the end of the world, Ōe belonged to the generation that accepted the post-war 'democratisation' initiated by the American occupation. For him as well as Oda Makoto (1932–) the post-war 'democratisation' and the New Constitution which proclaimed the renunciation of war form the bases of their political views and activities. They are thus in a sense the best pupils of the post-war American policy; and yet the irony of the situation is that they came to feel at odds with many products of

176

the American presence in the Far East.[13] It is against this background that Ōe wrote the works which express his sense of helplessness and humiliation such as *The Human Sheep* (*Ningen no hitsuji*, 1958), *Today the Struggle* (*Tatakai no konnichi*, 1958) and *Our Age*.

Already in his earliest works Ōe's concern with sex is evident. In the early 1960s he wrote three novels in which sex occupies an important place: *Seventeen* (*Sevuntiin*, January 1961), *Outcries* (*Sakebigoe*, November 1962) and *The Sexual Man* (*Seiteki ningen*, May 1963). In his treatment of sex two features stand out clearly. The first is his complete freedom from any kind of inhibition. This reflects partly the change of attitude to sex in Japanese society at large. This freedom is also shared by Ishihara Shintarō (1932–), who was awarded the Akutagawa Prize for his *The Season of the Sun* (*Taiyō no kisetsu*) in the first half of 1956. But the parallel does not go very far. Ishihara treats sex as an end in itself and goes no further than the sensationalism of the Japanese naturalistic tradition. The detailed description of sexual scenes in Ōe's novels, however, is characterised by the author's callousness. Sex almost becomes an abstract object as is, to some extent, common in Abe's novels. In spite of full details, sexual description in Ōe's novels arouses no pornographic interest.

This is due to another feature of Ōe's treatment of sex: namely the sexual impulse in his novels matters not in its own right but as an equivalent of an unfulfilled, repressed social ego. In *Seventeen*, for instance, the protagonist's habitual masturbation is a compensation for his discontent with the external world. In criticising the political and social situation of Japan the protagonist appears to be a potential left-wing radical. Curiously enough, however, he becomes indoctrinated by the right wing instead of the left. The sequel to this novel, *The Death of a Political Boy* (*Seiji shōnen shisu*), which echoes the assassination of the chairman of the Japan Socialist Party by a right-wing youth, provoked threats to Ōe and his publisher by the right. Ōe's position in these novels is extremely complex. The process by which the protagonist's sexual impulse is sublimated into a political passion is an extension of the reaction of the juvenile delinquents to the hypocritical adults in *Plucking Buds and Shooting Lambs*. In drawing a parallel between the sexual impulse and right-wing fanaticism, *Seventeen* and its sequel resemble Mishima's story *Patriotism* (*Yūkoku*, 1959). And yet Ōe himself is no ally of the right wing. Ōe's works in question parallel Mishima's story only superficially and are at best a parody. Ōe wrote them with his tongue in his cheek and their effect is one of irony. He commits himself neither to the left nor to the right, but is concerned with the curious fact that the sexual impulse as an equivalent of a repressed social ego can reveal itself either as left-wing radicalism or as right-wing patriotism and that the two are interchangeable.

The theme of *Seventeen* is taken over with a slight variation in *Outcries*.[14] The four central characters, including the narrator, are all social misfits in one way or another but united by their common intention to build a yacht and run away from their present state of maladjustment. Their social inadaptability is presented in the form of lost identity due to their racial background. A half-caste, born of a black American and a Japanese–American, nick-names himself 'Tiger' as the colours black and yellow are mixed in his skin. As a misfit in Japanese society, his dream is to go to Africa in search of his lost identity. Another character, Takao, is born of a Korean father and a Japanese mother. An interesting feature of the characterisation of Tiger and Takao is the curious interlocking of the fact of their alienation with their sexual life. For instance, Takao, like the protagonist of *Seventeen*, finds self-sufficiency in the habit of masturbation. That he can be neither Japanese nor Korean is shown by the fact that he finds himself a stranger in a Korean ghetto. He writes down in his diary the French words '*l'homme authentique*', by which he means man secure within society, the exact antithesis of himself. After Tiger's death his previously self-sufficient masturbation proves inadequate and he fails to achieve a sense of mastery over the external world. As an alternative, he kills a female high school student, whom he sees as an example of '*l'homme authentique*', under the guise of raping her. Ōe models this on the actual murder of a female high school student by a Korean boy, which is known as 'the Komatsugawa Incident'. He transforms, as Mishima did in his *The Temple of the Golden Pavilion* (*Kinkakuji*), a criminal into a coherent character. Takao is an extension of the hero in *Seventeen* and represents a socially repressed and alienated ego whose release consists in either sexual activity or else an act of destroying a symbol of the established social order.

Preceded by *Seventeen* and *Outcries*, *The Sexual Man* looks like the final part of a trilogy dealing with the human condition in terms of sex. At the end of the novel the protagonist, who has had only a sterile relationship with his wife, tries to achieve a sense of presiding over society by means of his sexual misconduct in public. Here again we see the author's use of the sexual act as a means of revenge on the society from which one is alienated. This novel has little to add to *Seventeen* and *Outcries*, but one notable feature is the author's sense of the primitive, which is not unfamiliar in his earlier works such as *The Catch* and *Plucking Buds and Shooting Lambs* and which was to play a more important role in *The Football in the First Year of the Man'en Era* (*Man'en gannen no futtobōru*,

1967). In a fishing village where the protagonist and his company are staying to make a film entitled *Inferno*, the villagers happen to be suffering from poor catches, which they attribute to some supernatural cause. The village is thus a miniature of the waste land. In the meantime the protagonist and his company feel the presence of 'a pair of eyes' in the villa where they are staying. They turn out to be the eyes of a village boy who has been hiding in the villa and witnesses the protagonist's sterile intercourse with his wife. The boy runs away, passing through a window and crying in a local dialect, 'I've seen ogres'. There is an ironical effect that the protagonist and his company themselves have been playing both the real and fictitious roles of infernal characters. The villagers' attempt to regain fertility and the sterile sexual life of the city dwellers who are uprooted from the sources of life are starkly contrasted. This is another instance which suggests that except for the momentary synthesis of the primitive and life force in *The Catch* the sexual power in Ōe's novels is embodied only by the characters who are alienated from the root of life.

In the whole corpus of Ōe's works *The Football in the First Year of the Man'en Era*[15] is monumental in that it synthesises all the elements in his earlier works in a new and wider perspective. The major character suffers from the sense of being cut off from reality and the story opens with his sitting at the bottom of a hole, which is a symptom of his anxiety about existence itself. This has been partly caused by the birth of an abnormal and defective child, and the subsequent impotence of himself and frigidity of his wife. He is also haunted by the memory of his activist friend, who, after the failure of the 1960 campaign against the Security Treaty, went mad and committed suicide in a grotesque fashion. The author once again resorts to the elder-and-younger brother pattern: while Mitsusaburō is a brooding, impractical intellectual, his younger brother Takashi is an active man. Ōe also places the setting of the novel in the familiar countryside of Shikoku. That these characters are in search of their identity is evident from the visit they pay to their native village, as well as their family name Nedokoro, which means 'where the root is'. Ōe's description of the village where the protagonists' ancestors used to be the local headmen is as masterly as in *The Catch*. In addition to his superb sense of place the author employs his historical imagination: the political situation in which Takashi becomes involved is overlapped with that of the first year of the Man'en era or 1860. In that year a revolt by the peasants against the great grandfather of the Nedokoro family was led by his younger brother. The revolt was a failure and the younger brother is said to have escaped to Edo and later made his career under the

Meiji government. It is with the younger brother of the great grandfather that Takashi identifies himself. In 1960 the Nedokoros are no longer powerful in the province. The village economy is under the control of an upstart Korean who owns a large supermarket. Conflict arises between him and the native villagers whose lives he makes unbearable. As might be expected, Takashi becomes the leader of the villagers' strife with the upstart millionaire or 'the emperor of the supermarket' as he is called. But Takashi becomes isolated and deserted by the villagers as a result of his raping a girl. He commits suicide and the villagers' battle fails. Takashi's death is preceded by his confession that he had incestuous relations with his idiot sister many years ago. It is followed by a further recognition that the younger brother of the great grandfather actually did not escape from the village but was kept imprisoned till his death in a dungeon on the Nedokoro estate.

What emerges from this gloomy family chronicle in which the past and present are overlapped? Are Ōe's characters able to re-discover their lost identity in it? The answer is no. As shown in 1860 the family of Nedokoro contained within itself two anti-thetical elements: the great grandfather, as the retainer of the family tradition and the patriarchal authority; and his younger brother, who rebelled against him in collaboration with the peasants and was eventually defeated. In 1960 the relationship between Mitsusaburō and Takashi corresponds to that of the great grandfather and his younger brother. Mitsusaburō as an urban intellectual, however, has already lost identity with his ancestors, while the object of Takashi's rebellion is the commercialism that destroys the village community. But Takashi himself cannot embody an absolutely positive value, for he is responsible for the death of a village girl and his own idiot sister. He functions only as a mediator for discovering the identity which is universal and unchanging throughout history. It seems that Ōe wants to say that such an identity is embodied in the nature of the countryside, belief in the spirit of the forest, and rituals such as the *nenbutsu* (invocation) dance, all shared by the people of the village community. Such is the identity that Mitsusaburō and Takashi should be searching for. It could have existed in an ideal community where there was harmony between man and man and between man and Nature. Unfortunately, however, for neither Mitsusaburō nor Takashi, living in the industrial society of 1960, is it possible to attain this state without some sacrifice: in Takashi's case, his own death; and in Mitsusaburō's case, patience to come to terms with reality, reconciling himself with his adulterous wife and bringing up Takashi's body. It is far from heroic, but that is the only alternative for Mitsusaburō.[16]

While producing a number of novels year after year, Ōe has also for some time been actively engaged in voicing his political opinions in public. In 1960 Ōe, Ishihara Shintarō and Etō Jun (1933–) all collaborated to organise the Wakai Nihon no Kai (the Young Japan Group), which criticised the way in which the government handled the revision of the Security Treaty and expressed deep concern over the subsequent political chaos.[17] In the same year Ōe visited the Chinese mainland and vigorously praised the communist regime until the first Chinese nuclear tests, which he criticised. In 1963 he paid a visit to Hiroshima, the record of which was published as *Hiroshima Notebook* (*Hiroshima nōto*, 1965). His concern for Hiroshima is not based on any specific ideological standpoint but derives from his genuinely humane sympathy with the survivors who have suffered from the same kind of humiliation and existential anxiety as represented in his novels. For these people neither the government's aid nor the ideologically biased anti-nuclear campaign would do. The *Hiroshima Notebook*, however, does not end with entire pessimism about the situation but with admiration and hope for the attempt on the part of the survivors to recover from the persistent after-effects of radiation and the effort of half a dozen conscientious local intellectuals to help them.

The *Hiroshima Notebook* was followed by *Okinawa Notebook* (*Okinawa nōto*), which was in a way a logical development of the previous book. Here again the author looks at the situation from his unique position. At that time, while the Japanese government was doing its best to get Okinawa back from America, the opposition parties and various left-wing groups were protesting against the presence of the American bases. But they all overlooked the fact that whoever governed Okinawa, whether the Japanese government (1868–1945) or the post-war American administration, there always existed the indigenous populace who were sacrificed for some external aim. It was with these people that Ōe sympathised. His sympathy is at one with his aspiration to the communal identity shared by the local people in *The Football in the First Year of the Man'en Era*.

We are entering the sphere where literature and politics meet. Ōe's aspiration to the communal identity shared by the indigenous people involves a difficult question: how could it transcend its own specificity and attain universality? A tentative answer to this question may be found in Ōe's account of his trip to South-East Asia in the autumn of 1970:

'After staying a few weeks in India, I became aware that I was beginning to take my Japanese identity as something of only relative importance. This awareness of mine appeared in the forefront of my consciousness in the holy land of Benares in the valley of the Ganges when I heard on the B.B.C. radio news about how a Japanese writer committed *seppuku* after crying "Long Live the Emperor". For the last few years I have been preoccupied with Okinawa and obsessed with an overwhelming and shameful question: "what is it to be a Japanese? how can I transform myself into a Japanese different from what he is now?" . . .

'When from India I look back upon Japan, it becomes crystal clear that the view of the Emperor given by that writer who committed suicide was nothing but a fiction, a personal mysticism.

'Also I cannot but realise how we are bound by a false Japanese identity. Yes! it is not so much that we are dissatisfied with our false identity as that we are proud of it. Are we ever ashamed of ourselves as "economic animals"? Have we sufficiently disapproved of having ourselves defined as "an economic power"?'[18]

In India Ōe came across a gregarious, poverty-stricken people. Instead of recognising them as Indians, he sees in them humanity at large driven to extreme deprivation. He goes on to say:

'In the climate of India and surrounded by the people there I became more and more aware of the falsity of the assumption that Japan is an economic power and will predominate in the twenty-first century.

'. . . Japan is wrapped in "ethnocentrism", which, however, looks so illusory as to fade away in the eyes of the "human beings" in the streets of Calcutta.'[19]

According to Ōe, the Emperor System, Japan as an economic giant, and Mishima's suicide are all based on a false standard of values. Perhaps he is over-simplifying the matter. That Mishima's idealism was not compatible with the recent material prosperity of Japan is well known. But Ōe's sin of over-simplification is venial. It is more important to note the different ways in which Mishima and Ōe seek Japan's identity. Mishima's search moves upward towards the idealised concept of the Emperor, while Ōe's moves downward towards the populace; Mishima's imagination binds itself within the framework of the national polity, while Ōe's releases itself beyond and transcends the boundary of the state. The indigenous populace embodies a medium through which Ōe can search for his identity, yet he is capable of transcending geographical particularities and attaining identity in a universal perspective:

'Through my Indian experience the voice of "humanity" free from the illusion of "ethnocentrism" indicates where a new hope exists, yet curiously intermingled with deeper despair. I find myself on the threshold of a new vista at the end of my trip to India, Asia and Okinawa.'[20]

In this chapter I have tried to show how Abe Kōbō and Ōe Kenzaburō are both concerned with the search for identity, each in his own way. Abe's unique position may become clear by comparison with his predecessors. The Japanese I-novelists, for instance, believed or at least tried to believe that there was the ego or the core of individual personality to be searched for through their attempts to write novels, although their purpose was never really fulfilled. Even Mishima, who was an opponent of the tradition of the I-novels, treated the growth of his own ego under the guise of a mask. Abe, on the contrary, seems to suggest that, whether disguised under a mask or not, there is no personal identity other than that which is inevitably bound to the material world. In this Abe represents the truly existentialist standpoint that existence precedes essence.

The search for identity presupposes a community in which the ego is to be realised as a social self. For Abe, however, a community is an illusory idea which he rejects outright. His works provide a picture of life in which man is utterly lonely, deprived of communication with his fellow men and determined by physical reality. And yet what Abe intends to prescribe in his works is not despair but tough reasonableness with which to accept the inescapable reality of life; only by doing so can man justify his own existence. In contrast to Abe, Ōe seems to aspire to a community in which the personal identity is to be realised. The difference between the two in this respect is probably due to the fact that as a child one spent the life of an expatriate while the other was deeply rooted in his native rural community. However, it is extremely difficult for Ōe, now living in the midst of industrial society, to celebrate the pastoral. As a result he portrays characters overwhelmed by the strain of urban society, or else he is 'of the Devil's party': in depicting a tension between the social restraint and spontaneous impulse, he represents the latter by anti-social characters, such as juvenile delinquents, sexual perverts and criminals, who are apparently intended to be fallen angels. Unfortunately, Ōe's aspiration to a community is thus expressed by showing the difficulty of its realisation.

The history of modern Japanese literature, as in other aspects of culture, has been streaked with the cross-currents of the native tradition and Western influence. There were writers, such as Tanizaki and Kawabata, who embodied the traditional sensibility almost spontaneously. Mishima's artificially acquired Western taste, on the other hand, was deliberately counterbalanced by his fortified Japanese consciousness. Abe differs from any of these predecessors. He was brought up as an expatriate in a place somewhat like a barren wilderness, where neither the culture of his homeland nor that of the West was available in tangible form. In such a circumstance there was nothing for him but to conceive of culture, of whichever hemisphere, in the abstract. This could have been a disadvantage, but, in Abe's case, it enabled him to create a literary universe which transcends the author's nationality. He is probably the first Japanese writer whose works, having no distinctly Japanese qualities, matter to the Western audience because of their universal relevance.

With Ōe it is a different matter. On the one hand he looks Westernised in his attempts to assimilate various features of contemporary European and American authors. On the other, however, he presents his themes in a specifically Japanese context. I have tried in this chapter to underline his concern with the communal identity to be sought in indigenous culture. This is likely to derive from his anxiety about his own and his countrymen's precarious footing in contemporary Japanese society, where the native tradition is jeopardised by the ever-accelerating modernisation which was started under Western influence in Meiji and has perhaps got out of hand. A description of the situation in these terms might sound fictitious to Abe for whom there exists no distinction between the native and foreign cultures, while it is an overwhelming reality to Ōe. From this difference in their attitudes to the cultural *milieu* of present-day Japan emerge the two types of literature: one has so nearly effaced Japanese elements as to attain universality in both its themes and its techniques; the other, despite its Westernised façade, houses sentiments that epitomise the dilemma of the nation at the present time. In this sense, Ōe's is a search for the identity of the race as well as an individual.

PART III

SOCIETY

10

NEW RELIGIONS IN JAPAN:
AN APPRAISAL OF TWO THEORIES

EIMI WATANABE RAJANA

In this paper, two frequently expressed theories of the development of Japan's New Religions will be discussed. The two theories, designated respectively the 'Emperor-Substitute Theory' and the 'Urban Anomie Theory', have this in common; they both hold that the New Religions function as substitutes or alternatives for traditional institutions or norms that have ceased to function or are malfunctioning in one way or another. This seems to be the most widespread view of the New Religions. When they are criticised as being 'magical, superstitious, feudalistic', and so forth, the implication is that they possess these 'pre-modern' characteristics, appealing to certain segments of the population who for one reason or another have been unable to make the transition into the 'modern scientific age'. Yet it must be said that such a view of the New Religions cannot account for the fact that they continue to exist, and to attract (though decreasingly so), a substantial number of new converts amongst the younger and more educated groups. It is the purpose of this chapter to examine the two current theories to see whether there is an alternative viewpoint that might overcome this difficulty.

EMPEROR-SUBSTITUTE THEORY

There is a group of theorists who connect the enormous upsurge of New Religions in the immediate post-war period to the loss of divinity by the Emperor. McFarland, in his *Rush Hour of the Gods*, sets forth the Emperor-Substitute Theory, in which the leaders of the New Religions are regarded as substitutes for the Emperor who had been deprived of his divine status:

'After World War II, when the Emperor renounced all claim to divinity and his constitutional status was altered and when freedom of religion was guaranteed, the heads of the New Religions had an opportunity to become Emperor substitutes among a people from whose lives the lodestone had been removed. In many instances, consciously or unconsciously, they had essayed that role, with the result ... that the image of the divine Emperor seems to be projected in the "living *kami*" of the New Religions.'[1]

The post-war constitution designated the Emperor as 'the symbol of the state and of the unity of the people, deriving his position from the will of the people with whom reside sovereign power'. This effectively abrogated the sanctity and the inviolability of the Emperor. This, McFarland and others maintain, caused a spiritual vacuum which was to be filled by the leaders of the New Religions.

When one examines the case of such religions as the Dancing Religion, led by Kitamura Sayo, this thesis appears plausible. Sayo is unequivocal about her own divinity, preaching to others in the following way:

'Be grateful that you were born in this century. Three thousand years ago it was Buddha who preached this Gospel, two thousand years ago it was Christ, today I am the Christ ... my body is His temple and descended from Heaven. He dwells in Me and chooses pious people. God convokes them with His holy power. He purifies their spirits so that they may become His innumerable angels and may guide and reform, one by one, all the other spirits, astray. This is God's way. Since I serve as God's mediator, no fear have I. Because God has rested His authority in Me I shall redeem the sincere and pious.'[2]

Sayo's forceful declaration of her divinity and the success of her religion after five years of proselytising in gaining over a hundred thousand converts, suggests that the idea of an alternative divinity was a cogent attraction in that period.

This 'Emperor-Substitute Theory' assumes that the heads of the New Religions were similar to the Emperor in some way. Yet Sayo, for example, apart from her claim to divinity, had little in common with the Emperor. The Emperor had been a remote divinity, a being on whom a commoner was not allowed to set eyes (quite literally). Sayo, in contrast, was a familiar divinity; she travelled throughout the country to spread her ideas, phrasing her sermons in coarse language and illustrating them with events from the daily life of a farmer. Whereas the Emperor's charisma had rested on his office, Sayo derived hers from the force of her own personality (to the extent that the continued existence of the religion was doubtful upon her death). The Emperor needed a mythology extending over two millenia and the entire organisation of the state to sustain his authority (which was not really his own), but Sayo relied upon her own personality, that of 'an ordinary farmer's wife'.

If Sayo is to be compared to the Emperor then it might be said that she is much more than the Emperor, for she alone achieved that which the Emperor could not have managed to attain by himself.

Underlying this Emperor-Substitute Theory is the basic premise that the Emperor, or what he personified, had been the loadstone in the lives of the people. The propagation of the Emperor ideology had been systematic and thorough, so that at least on the surface the majority of the populace participated in the cult of the Emperor. Citizens paid regular and frequent visits to shrines, children sang patriotic songs, and tales of loyalty and obedience to the Emperor and to the country filled their textbooks. No doubt many internalised this ideology and transposed it into a form of personal belief. But the large number of those who rejected and resisted it openly (and were consequently penalised for it) leads one to conjecture that a considerable part of the population had their doubts about the ideology, although they had not expressed themselves truthfully in public. A survey conduced by Jiji Press in 1946 revealed that the percentage of Japanese who believed in religion, including Shintoisim, was 56 per cent. It is unlikely that the remaining 44 per cent had discarded their belief in the short period of one year since the end of the war. Is it not more logical to hypothesise that for a larger proportion of the population the shintoistic beliefs, including the Emperor ideology, had not been internalised into a personal belief?

Ronald Dore, surveying Tokyo citizens in 1951, commented that:

'As far as shrine-visitors are concerned, fifty-five people out of a hundred said that they went less frequently now than during the war. Of these fifty-five, thirty-two said that the greater frequency of their war-time visits was due to compulsion—for to refuse to partake in an organised visit was to lay oneself open to being branded a *hikokumin*.'[3]

The visits of the remaining twenty-three out of the fifty-five (the majority of whom were women) had been spontaneous. In the same survey, of the 53 per cent who possessed a *kamidana* (Shinto alcove) in their homes, the largest proportion stated that they worshipped at the *kamidana* out of habit, followed by those who worshipped to show respect (to their ancestors), then those worshipping for personal productive or protective prayer, and lastly those worshipping for '*kami* [Shinto deities] and nation'. Dore interprets this appearance of a small minority who mentioned worshipping for '*kami* and nation' as 'some small evidence of the success of the policy of the political and military leaders since the Meiji period deliberately to cultivate the Shinto religion as a means of fostering national unity'.[4]

If however, the political and military leaders had been as successful as Dore maintains, one would expect more people to have gone to shrines spontaneously to pray for the '*kami* and nation' (and not, as many women did, for the safety of their menfolk), and more people to worship at their *kamidana* for the '*kami* and nation', instead of out of habit. The results of Dore's survey shows, rather, that state Shinto had not been internalised to the extent frequently supposed, but remained a system of behaviour which had been forced upon the Japanese people to a large extent.

If this be the case, and I suspect it to be so (though it cannot be confirmed due to lack of concrete evidence), for many the Emperor had not been the loadstone of their lives, and therefore there was no need to substitute what had never been there. In other words, the Emperor-substitute thesis is applicable only if the Emperor had been internalised as part of the personal belief system.

To conclude this section, I would argue that the Emperor-substitute thesis has limited applicability; it is relevant for explaining the success of such religions as the Dancing Religion (which, in the main, spread among the rural population), but is insufficient as an explanation for the rise and development of multitudes of other religions. It will be suggested that the sufferings due to extreme living conditions, to broken families, and to loss of loved ones had led people to grope for anything which promised a better future; thus the search was *not only* for an Emperor-substitute.

URBAN ANOMIE THEORY

The second part of this paper examines another type of explanation of the New Religions, in terms of their being substitutes for social institutions. This is connected with the process of urbanisation, as suggested in the following quotations from Ikado Fujio:

'It seems natural that religions with powerful organizations such as *Sōka Gakkai*, *Risshō Kōseikai*, the P.L. Association, *Seichō-no-Ie* (House of Growth) etc. have made a great advance in the socially unstable sectors of the urban population. . . . The socially unstable groups in urban society are composed of psychologically insecure persons who are for the first time cut off from any substantial contact with their home village, who are without connection with any big company or patronage of any powerful person and who are shut off from opportunity to climb up the social ladder. They are the ones who, feeling tied down to the mediocre middle all their lives, seek an authority that may be able to soothe their feelings of discontent.[5]

'People who came from the rural areas and therefore were formerly in one way or another part of the traditional system of established religions, are more or less cut off from such an institution when they are in cities. The postwar development of mass communication media has prompted the expression of individual interests, and in the course of time, the so-called "non-religious people" appeared openly in cities, having been released from the control of the established religion of the *ie* (house) which forced belief and membership on them.[6]

The growth of the New Religions, especially those with an extensive organisational structure, is in this argument attributed largely to the process of urbanisation and the resultant anomie. The underlying premise is that before the process of urbanisation, the migrants lived in well-integrated *Gemeinschaften* in security. One should be wary when making such a basic assumption; one needs to keep in mind that over the past half century or so the majority of migrants had been second and other junior sons of rural families who had no prospect of succeeding to and inheriting the *honke* (main house) name, status, and property. There were push factors, for example, economic necessity and non-inheriting status, as well as the pull factor of the growth of industries, which induced the movement of the population to urban and industrial centres. Thus, it is not totally accurate to suppose that by migrating, such persons are forsaking institutional security; rather, they might be leaving affective relationships based on personalities or kinship.

There are many concrete examples in the New Religions of migrants who do feel isolated and insecure in the city, and seek companionship and security in the religious organisation. Such is the case of a 31-year-old male member of Rissho Kosei Kai, a tailor's apprentice from Fukushima living in at his workshop; for him, the primary significance of the *hoza* (group counselling session) was 'to talk with companions'. But no concrete evidence has been provided to prove that the majority of the members of the New Religions, or that a disproportionate number, are migrants. James Allen Dator, in his Soka Gakkai survey of 1965, asked his sample of 980 adult citizens in Tokyo (Soka Gakkai and non-Gakkai) how long they had lived at their present address. The answers (in percentages) were as follows:[7]

	TOTAL	SOKA GAKKAI	CHRISTIANS	SHINTO BUDDHIST	NEW OTHER RELIGIONS
Half or more of their lives	37%	—	19	60	40
Five to ten years	30%	55	41	22	42
Less than five years	33%	45	40	18	18

From this data it appears that Soka Gakkai members, together with Christians, are the most recent arrivals in their present address. Dator delves deeper by asking those who had moved where they lived previously:

'Between 73 and 79 per cent of all religious groups including Soka Gakkai, had lived near Tokyo, . . . 4 per cent said they had moved to Tokyo from some other urban area, and only 12 per cent said they had lived in a rural area. The Soka Gakkai respondents did not differ significantly from these overall totals.'[8]

This result, and the evidence that Christians are nearly as mobile as Soka Gakkai members, suggest that the geographical mobility may be due to social mobility rather than to rural-urban migration. Soka Gakkai members might be moving because of changing social circumstances; but the type of mobility portrayed here does not support the thesis that Gakkai expansion is due to anomie caused by urban migration.

Ikado, in the passage previously quoted, mentions another group, apart from the migrants, whom he considers as being 'socially unstable' and thus susceptible to the message of the New Religions. These are the 'psychologically insecure persons . . . who are without connection with any big company or patronage of any powerful person and who are shut off from the opportunity to climb up the social ladder.'[9]

A number of surveys have shown that, occupationally, Soka Gakkai members are disproportionately in the 'labourer' category.

'Nine national surveys indicate that housewives and laborers of all types are extraordinarily numerous in the Gakkai, while official, managerial, professional and technical personnel, white-collar workers, students, and persons engaged in agriculture, forestry, and fishing are by contrast rare.'[10]

A study made by the Prime Minister's Office revealed that Komeito supporters (more or less the same as Soka Gakkai members) are '50 per cent more likely to be employed in non union enterprises than other employed respondents'.[11] Self-employed persons, if theirs is a small-scale enterprise, are as economically insecure as non-unionised workers. Most small factories tend to do subcontracting work for larger enterprises, and in periods of economic decline large enterprises will ruthlessly terminate their relationship with subcontractors before dismissing their own employees.

It is not economic insecurity as such, however, that members hope to have appeased by joining the New Religions. Rather, it is despair about future advancement, the lack of gratification which work might offer, that members seek solace for. In a questionnaire survey of one hundred new members of the Men's Division of Soka Gakkai, respondents were asked what problems they had before joining.[12]

Anxiety about the future	46%
Lack of friends	32%
Financial difficulties	20%
Ill health	15%
Disharmony with rest of family	15%
Others	14%

Comparison of the members who joined Rissho Kosei Kai between 1945 and 1952 and those who joined between 1961 and 1968, as to their motives for joining, show the following results:[13]

THOSE WHO JOINED 1945–52

(1) *I was persuaded into it*
(2) *Because of illness*
(3) *Because of economic difficulties*

THOSE WHO JOINED 1961–8

(1) *I was persuaded into it*
(2) *I was impressed by the doctrine*
(3) *Because of illness*

Though the sample is small, it is significant that none of the recent entrants mention 'economic difficulties', whereas those in the earlier group do not mention 'I was impressed by the doctrine'. The economically insecure group do not appear to seek solutions for their economic problems to the extent that it occurred in previous years.

Probably because of the close-knit hierarchical nature of the organisation of the New Religions, they, especially Soka Gakkai, have often been described as being 'fascist' and 'authoritarian' (the orderliness and homogeneity of behaviour has also contributed to this reputation). This has prompted Dator and White to concern themselves with examining authoritarianism, 'mass man', alienation and so forth, amongst Soka Gakkai members. Both Dator and White adapted tests devised by American psychologists[14] to measure the degrees of alienation, anomie and authoritarianism among Gakkai members. Both conclude, approximately, that their Gakkai samples do not differ significantly from the general Japanese population and that they cannot deduce from their survey that Gakkai members are particularly alienated, anomic, or authoritarian:

'We conclude, then, that on most social and personal matters, Sokka Gakkai members are seldom "better" and usually are somewhat "worse" than the general population, though often they are no worse, and occasionally they are somewhat better, than are members of either the traditional or the new religions.'[15]

'Thus one surmises that the Gakkai member is closer to the average Japanese than to the average Japanese Communist or to the mass man model.'[16]

As seen from these quotations, both Dator and White are most cautious about drawing any definitive conclusions from their studies. Even so, I venture to maintain that these test results are almost totally unreliable as indicators of what they claim to measure, for the following reasons:

(a) There is immense difficulty in operationalising such concepts as anomie, alienation, or authoritarianism, whether it should be a subjective or an objective measurement.

(b) The tests were designed for American samples, which makes some of the questions inappropriate. For instance, 'There's little use writing to public officials because often they aren't really interested in the problems of the average man' is used by Dator as a measure of anomie. Since Japanese people in general are not so much in the habit of writing to officials, data derived from such a question is of little value. Similarly, Dator's usage of voting in elections as an indicator of 'citizenship duty' fails to bring out the point. As one well knows, Gakkai members are strongly urged to vote for Komeito. High rates of voting among Gakkai members indicate their faith or obedience to the religious organisation, and not so much their sense of 'citizenship duty'; this is further supported by the fact that one-third of Gakkai members had been non-voters before the formation of Komeito.

(c) In both tests, Gakkai members cluster around the mode more than the non-Gakkai population. This suggests that members have been socialised to some degree by joining the Gakkai, and are thus 'contaminated'. By testing individuals who are already Gakkai members, they cannot measure whether the organisation attracts authoritarian, anomic or mass man; the socialisation process of Gakkai itself might have 'cured' such characteristics, or it might have made them conscious of such anomic tendencies that were insignificant previously.

For these reasons then, data based on such personality tests are unreliable as indicators of whether anomic individuals are attracted to Soka Gakkai or not. One has to rely on such objective criteria as occupational background, and conclude from that that they are likely to constitute such individuals who do not have other organisational attachments, whose futures are relatively insecure, and whose prospects for social advancement are faint.

What mechanism do the New Religions contain that attracts such people? In most of the New Religions there are personalised, problem-solving mechanisms which cater for individual needs: for example, the *hoza* (group counselling session) in Reiyukai and Rissho Kosei Kai, the *zadankai* (discussion meeting) in Soka Gakkai. This is possible, in spite of the large numbers of their membership, because human relations are firmly rooted in the line of the converter-converted. Ikado calls this the 'direct sales method',[17] in contrast to the sale through the 'wholesale method' of the missionary work of established religions. Each member has his own *michibiki-no-oya*, the parent-who-converted, who is personally responsible for his welfare.

Robert Nisbet has emphasised that large organisations 'will become as centralised and as remote as the national state itself unless these great organisations are rooted in the smaller relationships which give meaning to the ends of the large associations'; without these smaller relationships, the large association can only 'intensify the process of atomization which such association can and should counteract':

'No large association will remain an object of personal allegiance, no matter how crucial its goals may be, unless it is constantly sensitive to the existence of the informal but potent relationships of which it is really composed.'[18]

The smaller relationships of 'parent-child' (vertical relationships), the geographically based neighbourhood groups and the age groups (horizontal relationships) in the New Religions combine to provide this 'informal but potent relationship' which Nisbet regards as essential for maintaining the personal allegiance of members to the large organisation.

However, a closely knit organisation is only one-half of the means of integrating individuals to larger society. Even if he is well integrated to the organisation, if the organisation itself is estranged from the larger society, the individual will not be approaching his integration into society itself. William Kornhauser has emphasised this point;[19] for him, a 'mass society' is characterised by a lack of operative intermediate relations which should provide an effective link between the individual and primary groups and the nation state; in such a society, atomised individuals who have no intermediate or proximate relations are accessible to mass movements (Kornhauser's Mass Man).

Some of the elaborately organised and multi-faceted New Religions, particularly Soka Gakkai, I believe, are among the most effective 'intermediate organisations' today. Through their pursuits in the spheres of politics, arts, publishing, business, education, welfare services, etc., they remain in close contact with other organisations, religious and secular, which operate in the same spheres. Through connections with political parties or individual politicians at the national or local level (I need not stress the importance of the religious organisations for the politicians), New Religions can be effective pressure groups, or a medium through which members voice their opinions. White investigates the 'secondary ties' (associational connections) which Gakkai members maintain, following Kornhauser's formula that the mass man lacks secondary ties (that is, connections with intermediate organisations). White concludes that 'Gakkai members have secondary ties and that these ties are not restricted to Gakkai-related associations.'[20] Although White admits that 'membership in the Gakkai constitutes one such relationship for each Society member', he does not emphasise that the Gakkai at present is perhaps more effective as an intermediate organisation than local neighbourhood groups or the P.T.A., which constitute most of the remaining secondary ties. Thus membership in Gakkai itself by definition excludes the Gakkai members from being 'mass men'; by the fact of membership in the Soka Gakkai, adherents are no longer unattached, isolated or marginal. New Religions, by appealing to the strata that are generally unattached to other effective inter-mediate organisations, such as trade unions, business or professional groups, are far from being mass movements; they are viable inter-mediate organisations which enable these individuals to participate in the life of the nation.

CONCLUSION

To conclude, my main contention concerning the two theories examined here is that both view the New Religions in a negative light, that is, as compensation for some kind of deficiency (this is perhaps a typical way of looking at sectarian behaviour). These theories are not incorrect, but they are insufficient; one ought to seek alternative—and more positive—explanations of the New Religions, of their origins, development and their existence today. The New Religions, as has been shown, are not primarily the closely knit, closed organisations which terms such as 'pressure chambers', '*takotsubo*', or 'antidotes to anomie' imply, but organisations which relate atomised individuals to larger society. They are not little pockets of traditionalism which provide momentary repose for those who cannot keep up with the changing times. Rather, they help to integrate individuals who have few alternative means of participating in the larger society.

11

THE USE AND MEANING OF
LEISURE IN PRESENT-DAY JAPAN

SEPP LINHART

In the Western world the impression of the Japanese as very diligent, hard workers is possibly the strongest stereotype about them. This stereotype seems to have been created sometime after the First World War, when thanks to a labour force which was being recruited rather slowly Japan was able to impress the world for the first time with her economic successes, having overcome the hurdles of incipient industrialisation. Usually accompanied by a negative statement ('the Japanese are very diligent, but . . .'), this stereotype is still very much in use. Unlike some other foreign views of the Japanese, this opinion has also been taken up enthusiastically by the Japanese themselves. The Japanese National Character Survey every five years asks for the strong points of the Japanese, and always *kinben* (diligent, hard-working) is chosen by a majority as the most popular characteristic.[1] Every Japanese, reporting in a newspaper his experiences in a foreign country, tells his fellow countrymen how little Europeans and Americans work, and nowadays—after the advance of Japanese enterprises into South-East Asia—Japanese managers are complaining constantly about the low working ethos of the South-East Asians.

The working spirit of the Japanese is not always appreciated abroad. For instance, South-East Asians often call it inhuman, or some such expression, and Americans speak of unfair competition. In Japan herself the first doubts about the values of diligence and hard work have now begun to arise. Those values have hitherto been accepted unrestrictedly by a great majority of the people. Today, though, paralleling the questioning of them, there is even a growing dissatisfaction with an economic policy that is still primarily concerned with higher growth rates, while constantly neglecting to improve the infrastructure and to accumulate social stocks.[2] Inflation and pollution have brought about calls in favour of changing from the current policy that openly favours enterprises and industry to a policy aimed directly at the improvement of the life of all citizens of the nation. Instead of a quantitative widening of the country's economy, a qualitative widening of the economy is demanded. As a consequence of such a policy, new markets for the industry of environmental protection and for the leisure industry could be created. Yet the growing domestic criticism of the above-cited values ('we are working too much') cannot be comprehended as questioning the meaning of one's work. Rather, it seems as if it was at least partly produced by Japan's growing leisure industry, for whose development the attitudes of Japanese employees—work hard and enjoy your leisure only when it cannot be helped—constitute obstacles which are difficult to overcome. The Ministry for Trade and Industry, too, has recognised the importance the leisure industry will have in the near future and established in 1972 a Centre for the Development of Leisure (*yoka kaihatsu sentā*), the most important function of which is to create the prerequisite need for leisure among the people.

Such efforts for the development of a leisure industry might surprise the Japan expert, who knows that for more than ten years Japan has been enjoying a 'leisure boom'. On the other hand, it must not be overlooked that even today only two strata of Japanese society have, in the popular view, the full right to enjoy their leisure: youth, especially students, who are not yet members of the production process; and the elderly, who already have retired from active work. Ten years ago it was the students who during their summer vacations poured into Hokkaido to discover Japan's northernmost island. Nowadays it is again the students who, during their spring and summer vacations, travel to America, Europe and South-East Asia. Advertising for travelling abroad is also aimed at elderly couples who, because they do not have to care for their children financially any longer and because they are no longer needed as members of the labour force, are rather responsive to such temptations. But the majority of the population takes part in the leisure boom only to a very small extent. Therefore, I would like to describe in the following sections the restrictions to the development of leisure, and the use of leisure in today's Japan, as well as attitudes towards work and leisure as they are indicated in the results of several national opinion polls.

DAILY, WEEKLY AND YEARLY RHYTHM OF WORK AND LEISURE

In industrial societies, there exists a dominant rhythm of work and leisure in the life of the individual, which has its origin in the fact that the employee has to be on his job at specified times. The daily rhythm is a result of most people working by day and sleeping at night; the weekly rhythm is determined by the weekend intervals; and the yearly rhythm is set through national holidays and seasonal vacations. This rhythm constitutes the conditional frame for the use of leisure, and in order to understand Japanese leisure behaviour we first have to take a look at it.

The most thorough investigation on how much time people spend for various activities per average week-day, Saturday and Sunday, is carried out every five years by the Japanese television and broadcasting company N.H.K. on a national sample.[3] In 1970, men aged 20 years and over spent per average week-day about ten hours and thirty minutes for sleeping, eating and personal hygiene; they worked for nine hours, including domestic work and commuting to work; and for five hours and a quarter they performed some leisure activity.[4] On Saturdays, work-related time was half an hour shorter and free time a quarter of an hour longer. On Sundays, Japanese men worked three hours and forty minutes less while enjoying two more hours of leisure. Work-related time of women is longer than that of men, on Sundays as much as two hours and fifteen minutes; therefore their free time on Sundays decreases by one hour.

Of course, such averages do not tell us much about individual cases. For our purpose, it is more informative to differentiate according to occupations, excluding the persons in each occupation who were not working on the day of the investigation, be it for illness, vacation or some other reason. This gives the following results. On week-days as well as on Saturdays, more than 90 per cent of the individuals of each occupation were working. On week-days, the average working hours ranged from seven hours and forty-eight minutes to nine hours and eleven minutes. The order according to length of working hours was: independent operators (artisans, small shop-owners), professionals (and managerial occupations), blue collar workers, commercial workers, white collar workers, peasants. The average working hours on Saturday are considerably shorter only for white collar and professional workers, while peasants and commercial workers work even longer. On Sundays, the order from longest to shortest working hours is quite different: commercial workers, peasants, independent operators, blue collar workers, white collar workers, professionals. Only for two out of five Japanese is Sunday a day on which no work has to be done. About 25 per cent of all employed Japanese work more than eight hours on Sunday and 40 per cent work more than six hours. With the exception of blue and white collar workers, more than 50 per cent of all the Japanese in other occupations are working on Sunday too.

These data show us that in Japan the individual's free time on weekends is very limited when compared to the European and American state of affairs. By the end of the 1960s, the five-day-week had been introduced all over Western Europe and North America, whereas in Japan the movement for the introduction of the two-day weekend was just beginning at that time. In 1971, a genuine five-day-week had been introduced by only 0·4 per cent of all Japanese companies, while in 89·1 per cent of all firms a full six-day-week is still in existence.[5] The materialising of the five-day-week gives clear evidence of the dual structure of the Japanese economy. In 1971, in only 55 per cent of all firms with more than a thousand employees had people to go to work for six days a week, as compared with 93 per cent for enterprises employing between thirty and ninety-nine workers. Returning to our problem, we can state that Saturday for the majority of the Japanese is still an ordinary working day and that for the weekly rhythm of leisure the interval given by Sunday is of primary importance.

The amount of free time is about five hours on week-days including Saturday, and seven hours on Sunday. But on Sunday there is a three hours' range of variation as to the amount of available leisure-time between individuals in possession of maximum free time (professionals) and those with a minimum of free time (peasants). In this investigation the following activities were listed under the heading of leisure-related time: private socialising, relaxing, enjoying a hobby or some other form of entertainment, reading, listening to the radio, or watching television. Because the last two activities often occur simultaneously with others, we get the somewhat unrealistic impression of rather long daily leisure hours. Extra-professional time not spent at home increases on Sunday, but except for the independent operators fewer people from all occupations leave their home on Sunday.

In examining the annual rhythm of leisure, national holidays and vacations have to be considered. At present, Japan celebrates twelve national holidays. Of special importance is the so-called 'Golden Week', when there are three such holidays (in the period from 29 April to 5 May), as well as the New Year, when usually all firms close their doors for at least three days. During these periods, the Japanese employee can stay away from work for some days in succession and take a rest. Paid holidays are another opportunity not to attend work for some days. The attitude of the Japanese employee towards the use of his holidays is quite different from that of his Western colleague. In 1969, one out of five employees had not made any use at all of his right to holidays, and 40 per cent used less than half of their holidays due.[6] Cross tabulations show differences according to sex, age and occupation. More women than men, more younger individuals than older ones, and more blue collar than white collar workers make use of their holidays. The custom to take longer holidays is virtually unknown. When in another investigation by the N.H.K. it was asked how much summer vacation people took during the summer of 1967, two-thirds said they had taken less than three days off, and only 15 per cent went for holidays as long as one week or more.[7] As for the reasons why they did not make more use of their holidays, 61 per cent said that it was not necessary to take more days off, 29 per cent reported that they had been too busy, while 8 per cent said that they did not go on holiday as in their opinion it would have been unfair to their working colleagues. As much as 54 per cent of all interviewed male employees made use of their holidays only if they were ill or if some urgent family affair made it absolutely necessary, and not more than one out of four men used his holidays for such leisure activities as travel, sport and entertainment. Again there exist differences: the younger generation and women are more inclined to make use of their holidays for their own leisure.[8]

Japanese employees usually do not use up all of their holidays but keep some days in case they get ill. If they have no holidays left and fall ill on a working day they will not get the attendance allowance (*shukkin teate*) and their half-yearly bonus will be much smaller. That means that full use of one's holidays at an early time of the year carries with it a certain financial risk. On the other hand, not to make use of one's holidays seems to be advantageous for advancement in the firm. Therefore, female employees, who usually in big organisations cannot do much more than serve tea and run errands, as well as blue collar workers, whose chances for advancement are very limited because so many university graduates are available, can make a fuller use of their vacations (and do so with far fewer worries) than white collar workers. This is especially true for a system in which advancement is linked to the number of years spent with the firm. For a white collar employee hoping for a career it is very important not to make a bad impression on the management, but that could not be avoided if one took leave for a fortnight. Most employees are convinced that if they stay away from the firm for too long it would burden their fellow workers far too much. So they prefer to take longer weekends if they feel a need for a rest. Of course, the Japanese leisure industry has adapted itself to that form of holiday-making and Japanese travel bureaux offer many one-to-three-day group journeys across the country. Holidays with the whole family for one or more weeks either at the seaside or in the mountains are virtually unknown. Hence the annual rhythm of leisure is still very similar to the one in traditional society with its emphasis on *o-bon* (Festival of the Dead) and the New Year's festival.

There exist not only the N.H.K. time budget studies but also a number of other empirical studies on the different ways of using leisure in Japan. Needless to say, the use of leisure varies according to sex, age, social stratum and type of work, but we shall first try to characterise Japanese leisure compared with leisure in Europe or the United States.

In a recent publication by the Leisure Development Centre it was pointed out that the typical pattern of Japanese leisure is passive leisure. In the Soviet Union, West Germany, the United States and France, men as well as women show a much more active behaviour pattern during their leisure than the Japanese,[9] whose typical leisure activities are watching the television, listening to the radio, reading newspapers, journals and books, as well as relaxing and sleeping. Akuto Hiroshi, after analysing the use of leisure of men and women by age-group, says: '. . . those who enjoy a great amount of leisure are among the men in their high teens and twenties, among woman individuals up to their high teens, that is only the very young generation. Leisure-time of people in their forties and especially of women is spent very badly. Most of them have not yet gone further than thinking that leisure means watching television. That means that we have to state, when thinking about the Japanese people as a whole, that their leisure has not yet developed either quantitatively or qualitatively.'[10] In a somewhat different form, Akuto's statement written in 1972 reminds us of the view of Ikeuchi, which dates from 1960. The latter correctly stated that the leisure boom was not by any means as substantial as generally believed, basing this conclusion on the first empirical study of leisure in post-war Japan undertaken by the University of Tokyo in 1959 as a response to the leisure boom of the late 1950s.[11]

According to an opinion poll taken from a national sample in November 1971, the most frequent Japanese leisure activities, in decreasing order, are: watching television (82 per cent of all interviewed), reading the newspapers (50 per cent), enjoying the company of one's family (34 per cent), lounging about at home (29 per cent), speaking with friends, neighbours or one's lover (24 per cent), shopping in shopping streets or department stores (24 per cent), reading journals (24 per cent), travelling, hiking, angling and diving (21 per cent). On the other hand, such leisure activities as sports, *pachinko* (pinball games), mahjong, *go* and the movies range far down in the same list. Typical leisure activities of the young generation up to 29 years include playing a musical instrument, going to the movies, engaging in sports, attending concerts or shows, playing mahjong, painting, listening to records, visiting a sporting event, an exhibition or a museum, and writing poems. Young people do such things much more frequently than older people. On the other hand, the list of characteristic leisure activities of individuals of 30 years and over is rather limited. It consists of enjoying the company of one's family, religious activities, writing a diary, home craftsmanship, and needlework.[12]

Leisure activities of women are much more limited than those of men. They do not do much sport, and usually are not allowed to take part in gambling, be it *pachinko*, mahjong or horse races. Almost their only compensation apart from shopping in the big attractive department stores is *keikogoto*, which includes flower arrangement (*ikebana*), calligraphy, tea ceremony and playing the *koto*. These are all activities that are usually done not for their own sake but as a part of the traditional bride school or *hanayome shūgyō*, a *sine qua non* for getting a distinguished husband. Differences between blue collar and white collar workers consist in the latter reading more newspapers and books, devoting more time to their hobbies, and going more frequently on a trip at weekends, while more of the former watch television. Of some interest is the fact that the inhabitants of Tokyo show a much more active leisure pattern than the inhabitants of any other region, on week-days as well as on Sundays.[13] This makes it clear that the location of one's home or office is of considerable importance for behaviour during one's non-professional time. The employee of a firm located somewhere at Marunouchi in Tokyo, only five minutes walk from the Ginza, has much more opportunity to stop over on his way home than his colleague in the countryside. Tokyo's surroundings offer far more opportunities than any other region for gambling, which is so popular among the younger generation that one-third of the 20 to 24 years' age-group is indulging in it on Sundays.

THE MEANING OF WORK AND LEISURE

As has been pointed out frequently, leisure is something which cannot be enjoyed unless a certain stage of affluence has been reached. In today's Japan a rather high stage of affluence has been reached, but as we have seen above, Japanese society still has a very long way to go before it can be called a leisure society in terms of international comparison. Considering that money as well as time are basic conditions for a fuller leisure life and that often more money can only be obtained at the expense of time—by working overtime or doing a second job—many opinion surveys have asked whether people would prefer to get more money or more free time instead. To quote a recent example from a national poll taken during July 1972 by the Prime Minister's Office, 49 per cent made a decision in favour of more money as compared to only 18 per cent who voted for more free time.[14] As can be expected, these answers correlate highly with an individual's economic standing. People with a high income are very eager for more free time, and those with a low income want more money as they cannot make use of their free time without money to spend. But when in the same poll a similar question was asked on the relation of working hours and income, 34 per cent said they would rather have shorter working hours than an increase in their income, while only 31 per cent said they would prefer a higher income even at the expense of more working hours.[15] The answers to the latter question show a certain satisfaction with present income—compare for example the results of a 1963 survey in one of Japan's largest steel firms, where 73 per cent said higher wages ought to be given before working hours should be decreased and only 18 per cent voted for fewer working hours in first place[16]— and it can be expected that pressures to reduce working time will be of increasing importance in future trade-union bargaining with management.

In order to judge whether this is a sign that the Japanese are no longer the working bees that they still are assumed to be in the West, we have to analyse some questions put by opinion surveys concerning the meaning of work and leisure. It is a frequently heard opinion in Japan that the Japanese use their free time for recreation for the sake of their work (*hataraku tame ni asobu*), while Europeans and Americans work in order to enjoy their leisure (*asobu tame ni hataraku*). Are those generalisations true? As early as 1959 a group of scholars of the University of Tokyo, investigating leisure in Tokyo, asked which preferences would be given in relation to six statements about work. One was 'Work is work and play is play. Work diligently during set working hours, and when released from work, forget it and play.' This was chosen by 39 per cent. Twenty-nine per cent said: 'I like to work, but I need to have enough time for the rest and relaxation essential to build up my energy for working.' Nineteen per cent agreed that: 'Since working is a human duty, I must work to the limit of time.' And 12 per cent chose: 'Work is a form of enjoyment; I haven't especially thought about it.' The two other alternatives were: 'Work is a means of subsistence. I try to do a suitable amount of it, then as much as possible enjoy myself playing'; and 'There is no point in making drudgery of human life. I think it is good to do what you yourself want to do.'

These, together with the 'Don't know' category, made up only 9 per cent.[17] The *Kokumin seikatsu kenkyūsho* used the same questions later on. In 1970 the positive 'Protestant Ethic' responses, as Dator calls them ('Work is duty' and 'Work is enjoyment'), were only favoured by 19 per cent; the mixed 'Protestant Ethic' responses ('Work is work, play is play' and 'Rest in order to work') got 68 per cent; while negative 'Protestant Ethic' responses even at this date amounted to only 9 per cent.[18] So altogether we have to say that in more than ten years the basic values towards work had not undergone much change.

Blue collar workers, too, who for example in Great Britain are said to have an instrumental orientation towards work, in Japan often have a work-centred orientation. This can be shown by the results of a survey by Rikkyō University in August 1967. Here 1,181 workers of big firms were asked a simple dichotomous question in relation to their attitudes towards leisure. Fifty-five per cent of them said they thought it was also necessary to enjoy human life and therefore leisure should be pursued with all one's might, while 45 per cent agreed to: 'Work is forever the central point of human life and therefore leisure has to be governed by work.' As usual, younger workers were more strongly in favour of the first opinion and older workers favoured the second.[19]

In a survey by the N.H.K. in 1967 which gave three alternatives as to the meaning of work, 29 per cent agreed with 'Work is the greatest joy in life'; 48 per cent said 'Born a human being it is your duty to work', while 22 per cent responded 'Working is necessary for making a living', showing thus a strict instrumental attitude towards work. The first answer was more frequent among white collar workers than among blue collar workers.[20]

Asked in August 1971 whether they rested for work or whether they worked to be able to enjoy their leisure, one-third of 1,673 respondents chose the first and one-quarter the second alternative. Another 35 per cent said work and leisure were of equal importance to them.[21] When the same question was used in 1972 in a much bigger national sample of 15,000 people, only men over 30 agreed with 'leisure for work', while male teenagers and those in their twenties, as well as all age-groups of women, preferred working as a means for enjoying leisure.[22]

The results cited above give us a picture of a society where the attitudes towards work and leisure are slowly changing from a very one-sided over-emphasis on work to a more balanced outlook on work and leisure, seeing both as necessary. Whereas in the former puritan ethic, leisure was seen as a kind of evil, nowadays it is thought of as something necessary for recreation and personal development.

LEISURE AGE OR LEISURE SOCIETY?

We have so far discussed the restrictions put on leisure by the time available to the individual, the use of leisure by the average Japanese, and the meaning of work and leisure for modern man in Japan. The results have not given convincing proof that the present age is a 'leisure age' for Japan, nor that Japanese society is a 'leisure society', though both terms are often used to describe the present scene. But it is evident that the Western observer who compares Japanese conditions with those of his own country has an outlook different from that of a Japanese cultural critic, who usually will make a comparison with pre-war times, when Confucian values still had a firm hold on Japanese society.

Another point has to be stressed which makes us doubt the overall importance of leisure in contemporary Japan, a point related to the characteristics of Japanese social structure. It is the intermingling of work and leisure, the extension of working life into private life. Dumazedier defines leisure in the following way:

'Leisure represents a liberation from other forms of time utilisation. It is an end in itself, characterised by the fact that the individual needs take precedence over those of the collectivity. It is a time for relaxation, entertainment and for fuller development of the individual and his personality. Determined in relation to work, extra-professional time and free-time, leisure is a sort of quarternary product of industrial civilisation.'[23]

If we accept this definition, we have to admit that until now we have been speaking about extra-professional time or free time rather than leisure. Dumazedier takes as a starting-point for his definition of leisure the individual's needs, but we have to ask here whether such individual needs are of equal value and importance in a collectivity-oriented society like the Japanese. The individual in Japan is not what he is in the West, and *kojinshugi* (individualism) is even today often mistaken for *rikoshugi* (egoism).

The two groups of overwhelming importance in the social life of the individual are the family and the firm. Traditionally the latter has precedence over the family if a conflict situation arises. Many leisure activities of the Japanese employee are performed either under an official programme of his company—be it the *undō-kai* (sports field-day), autumn's *ian-ryokō* (firm's excursion trip), or membership in a sports or cultural circle of the firm—or unofficially as a member of the work-group. This includes socialising after work, as well as standing in as fourth man, if required, in a mahjong party on Saturday afternoon. I was very impressed when two members of the lower-middle management of a big company discussed with me the steps they should undertake to liberate their firm's workers from the grip of the left-wing trade union by means of developing adequate leisure programmes in the company. They themselves, though, did not give a single thought to their own free time, which would decrease considerably if such programmes could be realised, because, of course, they themselves would have to function as leaders.

Sunday is usually the only day the *sarariiman* (salaried worker), be it blue or white collar, spends in the company of his family; and the activities of men on Sunday are commonly called *katei sābisu* (family service). Although free-time activities together with one's wife are somewhat uncommon, spending the Sunday with one's children (naturally including the company of the wife) has become almost a norm for many Japanese men. This children-centred leisure on Sunday might consist of a visit to a department store, where lunch is taken and the children are allowed to play in the toy department, or an excursion to a children's playland, or simply playing catch-ball on nearby open ground. Such activities, which represent the typical leisure activities of Japanese employees, clearly do not fit the leisure definition given by Dumazedier. They have a strong obligational character, especially as they are spent together with the members of the two groups—firm and family—to which the married Japanese employee is linked with life-time commitment.

Matsumoto has presented the hypothesis that the shelter of the personal in-group community, as a member of which the average Japanese spends not only the working hours but also a major portion of his free time, provides institutional means for dissipating tensions and stresses for the Japanese individual in the form of seasonal recreation and after-work socialising.[24] If this hypothetical assumption is true, we have to ask in further investigations whether there is much need for individual-centred leisure in Japan at all.

12

UNION-MANAGEMENT CONFLICT
IN A JAPANESE COMPANY

R. C. CLARK

I am going to describe how a conflict between the union and the management of a medium-sized Japanese company was resolved. The company in question, of which I made a study in 1970–1,[1] was a corrugated board company with eight factories in various parts of Japan, employing about a thousand people. It had certain distinctive features: a rather young president, and an unusual relationship with its parent company; but there was no reason to suppose that it was wholly unrepresentative of Japanese companies of its size. I hope to show, by describing a dispute that took place within it, how a union which was unable to employ any of the tactics such as striking or going slow, which one would normally associate with strong unions, and which in the opinion of its own members was a weak and ineffectual union, was nevertheless able to gain advantage of an undoubtedly strong and resolute management.

I shall have to begin by enumerating certain peculiarities of Japanese industrial society, the most notable of which is 'life employment'. It is perhaps most convenient to think of 'life employment' in Japanese companies in the same way that one would think of 'equal pay for equal work' in Britain: a principle sufficiently honoured in practice to be considered a major characteristic of the employment system, but with too many qualifications and exceptions to be taken as a complete description of that system. Ideally, Japanese companies take on employees straight from school and universities and retain them until they have reached the age of 55. To encourage their employees to stay, they pay them more with every succeeding year and also offer them semi-automatic promotion according to age and length of service up a series of ranks. A good comparison here would be with the British police force, where a man would start as a constable, become a sergeant, then a deputy inspector, and so on. In the ideal case, then, the older an employee is the more money he gets, the higher his position is, and the greater his incentive to be a loyal company servant.

The life employment ideal was always, perhaps, impracticable in the smaller Japanese companies in which a large proportion of the working population is employed, because these smaller companies are unable to compete with the larger ones in recruiting direct from schools, and because, lacking financial reserves, they have little alternative to dismissing staff during business recessions. Recently, however, even large companies have found it increasingly hard to maintain life employment practices because of changes in the labour market.

In Japan today so many companies are competing for the young school-leavers who are coming on to the labour market, while these young school-leavers are becoming relatively fewer, not least because so many of them are now going on to universities, that there is an acute shortage of young labour. Young workers are therefore in a position to change jobs, and many of them do. The probability that a young worker who has newly joined the labour market can get a better job outside the firm he is working in diminishes as he grows older. At the beginning of his career the probability is great. By the time he is 25 or so, however, he is less interesting to employers other than his own, while at the same time he has accumulated considerable credit with his own employer, credit which is not easily transferable. At this age, also, he is likely to marry and so increase his responsibilities and decrease his chances of moving. The difference in probability is so great that it is permissible to speak of mobile and immobile workers. In the company I studied there was a very considerable difference in the behaviour of these mobile and immobile workers.

Nevertheless, in spite of increasing difficulties, Japanese companies go to considerable lengths to try and maintain 'life employment' and the related practice of pay by age and length of service; and the fact that they do so has important consequences for social relations among their employees. The distinction between worker and manager, for example, is made very arbitrary if everyone who is taken in from school or university passes semi-automatically up the promotion ladder. In the company I studied everyone began on the shop floor or in menial office work. By the age of 30 a man would probably be promoted to the first of several standard ranks, and thereafter promotion would take place every four years or so until he was in his mid-forties. It happened that the line between managers and workers was drawn between team heads and sub-section heads (Figure 1), but it could equally well have been drawn between sub-section heads and section heads, or section heads and deputy managers.

NON-UNION MEMBERS	President (*Shachō*) Vice-President (*Senmu*) Managing Director (*Jōmu*) Director (*Torishimari-yaku*)	UPPER MANAGEMENT
	Department Head (*Buchō*) Deputy Department Head (*Jichō*) Section Head (*Kachō*) Sub-Section Head (*Kakarichō*)	MIDDLE MANAGEMENT
UNION MEMBERS	Team Head (*Hanchō*) Ordinary Company Member (*Hirashain*)	

Figure 1. The Composition of the Company

A team leader knew that within a fairly short time he was likely to join the official management ranks as a sub-section head; while his immediate superiors in the sub-section rank, who were officially managers, were equally well aware that they had only recently been workers. Today's team leaders and sub-section heads had spent, say, ten years together as workers, and would hereafter spend at least the same length of time together as managers, assuming that life employment was the rule. The distinction between a manager and a worker was only a temporary and technical one, neither the employees nor the company itself placing any great emphasis upon it.

A second peculiarity of Japanese industrial society is the way in which Japanese unions are organised. Typically they are enterprise unions rather than trade unions. They are associations not of people of similar skills and functions in different companies but of all the workers of one company, regardless of their differences of function and training. The enterprise unions are therefore to some extent comparable with the joint shop stewards committees that have appeared in Britain in recent years.

Enterprise unions, though they certainly have many advantages over trade unions, reinforce a tendency towards isolation in Japanese firms which is primarily a result of 'life employment' practices. The majority of people in a Japanese company may have been in it since school or university, surrounded by the same faces, and fixed between the same sets of subordinates and superiors. Relations between employees develop an intensity rare in Western firms, and this intensity is not lessened, as in the West, by a trade-union organisation which encourages the individual worker to participate in activities beyond his firm. On the contrary, enterprise unions are inherently exclusive.

211

The union at the company studied here, which I shall call Marumaru, was a typical enterprise union. In 1969 it had succeeded in persuading the company to establish a closed shop, so that every non-manager, that is every employee beneath the rank of sub-section head, was a union member. Since most of those below this rank were also below the age of 35, and most of those above the rank were older, the union membership comprised most of the young people of Marumaru.

As I said earlier, one could perceive a distinction at Marumaru between mobile young employees who could afford to think of leaving the company and so behaved rather casually towards it, and the immobile employees, those over the age of 25, for whom the best future lay with the company, and who therefore gave every appearance of having adapted themselves to its demands. Marumaru was a very young company, the average age of the employees being about 30, so that the proportion of mobile young employees in the company membership was quite large; and since older company employees were usually not union members the proportion of mobile employees in the union membership was even higher and may well have constituted a majority. If these young workers, with little to lose by overt opposition to the company, had been able to gain control of the union organisation, then the union might well have been a militant one, and its militancy might have imposed a considerable strain on social relations in the company.

In fact, however, the union was firmly in the control of its older members, men of the team-leader rank who could shortly expect to move up into management. The supreme body of the union was the annual general meeting, which was attended by one delegate for every twenty union members in each factory branch, and also by the outgoing executive committee. The delegates to the general meeting were elected in some branches and appointed as a result of 'discussions' in others. The main purposes of the general meeting were to establish the objectives of union policy and to elect the Three Officers of the union, the chairman, vice-chairman and secretary of the executive committee. This election took place in an interesting manner. The outgoing Three Officers had been sounding out volunteers to succeed them for two or three months before the general meeting, and there had even been discussions with the directors of the company over who might be suitable. By the time of the general meeting, therefore, everyone knew who the Three Officers would be, and they were elected unanimously without ever having stood as candidates. The outgoing chairman merely asked the delegates to write on pieces of paper whom they thought the Three Officers should be. He then collected the names and announced that there had been an overwhelming vote for the three people whose election rumour had long predicted. This method of choosing the Three Officers guaranteed that they would be staid and sensible people of ten years' service in the company who would certainly keep the company's interests in mind quite as much as the union's.

In theory, the Three Officers were no more than the three senior members of the central executive committee which met once a month to handle the union's affairs. The other members of the central executive committee were elected or chosen in some other manner by the factory branches, each factory having one Representative on the committee. In fact, however, the Three Officers were very much more influential than the factory Representatives, because they controlled the amount of information available to other union leaders, because they undertook most of the all-important informal negotiations with the company's labour department, and because, having no constituency, they were able to be very flexible in their dealings both with management and with their union colleagues.

The union was, then, an oligarchy presided over by the Three Officers, but many of the other union leaders were, like the Three Officers, older men of the team-leader rank and so fundamentally sympathetic to the very moderate policies which the Three Officers invariably pursued. On the other hand, the great number of union members who were mobile clearly had little concern for the company —they were leaving it in large numbers—and they would undoubtedly have been happy to support a more militant policy. Most of them, aware of the union's oligarchic tendencies and its subservience towards the company, were indifferent to it and showed little interest in union activities, except, perhaps, when the bonus negotiations were on. This indifference naturally helped to perpetuate the union's oligarchy.

The people on the management side who actually dealt with the union were all in the middle standard ranks. Every month there would be a meeting between union leaders and management in each factory. The factory manager, his deputies and the section and sub-section heads would represent the management side, while the union was represented by its branch officials, most of whom were team leaders. Every two months 'central friendly talks'—*chūō (rōshi) kondankai*—would take place between the union central executive committee, the Three Officers and the factory Representatives, and a deputation of head office managers headed by the director in charge of the labour department. The upper managers and those with real authority, the president, the vice-presidents, and the senior managing directors, rarely met the union leaders at all. The president had only had one interview with the union leadership in three years.

If the leaders of the Marumaru union were all halfway to management, it was equally true that the representatives of management had all relatively recently been union men themselves. Some of them were ready to express overt sympathy with union objectives. Many of them had known their opposite numbers for many years from a time when they had all been in the union together. It was not uncommon, for example, for a manager to come into the union office, a little hut in the grounds of the Yokohama factory, and give the union secretary a few words of advice, based on his own union experience, on what union policy should be; the following day might find manager and unionist arguing against each other at a 'friendly talk'. This understanding between the union leaders and the middle and lower management was, as I hope to show, the most important asset the union possessed in its dealings with management.

The case study I am going to describe involved events which took place not at the factory where I myself was working but in another factory near the town of N-, where the management was trying to introduce a new system of shift working. I did not myself attend any of the discussions over the shift-work problem, though I was given the minutes of all the central and factory meetings which took place, so that I was able to infer from them what had taken place between each meeting. More important, I was able to interview most of the people involved in the problem, from the president to shop-floor workers.

Work in the factories at Marumaru went on day and night each working day of a six-day week. Workers were divided into three sections, each section taking one of three shifts for a week and then moving to another shift in the following week. Sundays and national holidays were days of rest. Within each section there were two subsections, one to run the corrugator, the huge machine that made paper board into corrugated sheet, and one for the printing and processing machines, which made packing-cases from the sheets coming off the corrugator.

At some time before May 1970, the factory management at the N-factory told the local union branch that it wished to install a second corrugator. It had long been considered that a second corrugator would eventually be needed at N- to meet the increasing demand, but it had earlier been assumed that the factory would be able to manage with one corrugator until 1971. The company had a standing agreement with the union which permitted the management to organise continuous work shifts, with work going on even on Sundays and holidays, while a second corrugator was being put into any factory. The extra production gained from working on Sundays would make up for any loss incurred during the installation of the second corrugator, and at the same time allow for a smooth increase in production until the new machine began working. The N- union branch therefore automatically agreed to the company's request for continuous work shifts. The work force was reorganised into four sections instead of the normal three, so that in any one day three sections would take one shift each while the fourth rested. By the terms of an agreement announced in early May, the management received permission to operate this '4-group 3-shift' system from May until the end of August, by which time the second corrugator was expected to be running.

Now a corrugator is a very large machine with a variety of components and auxiliary machines which have to be specially ordered to fit the needs of a particular factory. Ordering a corrugator, building it, transporting it to the factory, and assembling it there, having rearranged the other machines to make room for it, would all take a long time, perhaps between five and eight months. If, therefore, the company had only decided to order the corrugator in May, there would have been little chance of its being in service in August. This the union, or at least the Three Officers of the executive committee, knew very well. In making the agreement with the company they were, for Marumaru's sake, misleading their own members as to the length of time they would have to do continuous shift work.

But the union leaders had themselves been misled in turn, for no corrugator had been ordered or was to be ordered that year. The N- factory differed from the other large Marumaru plants in that the board and boxes it produced were used to pack not manufactured goods but fish and vegetables. Demand therefore varied greatly with the time of year (Figure 2). The demand in December and January was well within the capacity of a single corrugator working a six-day week; it was only in the summer months that demand was beginning to exceed that capacity. The problem of meeting demand at N- was not necessarily to be solved simply by putting in a new corrugator. Even if a new machine made it possible to produce enough board in summer, the factory would find itself with two large and expensive machines doing the work of one in the winter months. Until the demand in summer outgrew the capacity even of a machine working continuously it would be more economical to use one machine only and work it full time in the summer and less intensively in the winter. The main disadvantages of this solution would be the discomfiture of the work force and the considerable difficulties over the upkeep and repair of machinery.

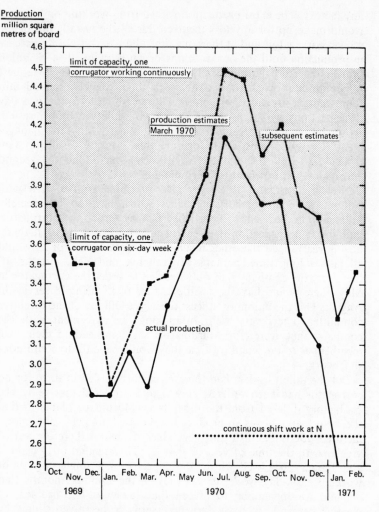

Figure 2. Production and Estimates at N-factory

As Figure 2 shows, there were good reasons for not putting in a corrugator at any time in 1970, but there was an especially strong argument against putting one in in the late August or September, when it would be too late to be of help in the summer peak period and would probably lie idle until the late spring of 1971.

Even if the upper management had, as it was later to claim, thought of putting in a corrugator and then changed its mind, it should have informed the union of its decision and returned the factory to normal working. In fact no announcement was made, and the work force went on to continuous shifts without either the union or even the middle and lower factory management realising that no corrugator was coming. It was only after about a month, in early June, when still no building or redisposition of machinery was taking place, that rumours began to be heard that there would be no corrugator. At this point the N- factory manager was transferred and a new man came in from another plant. The new manager told me that he himself knew, on his appointment, that no new corrugator was to be put in in 1970 but that he had not realised that his subordinates and the union leadership had not been told. It was only on 29 June, when the factory had been on two months of continuous work, that an official announcement was made at the factory 'friendly talks'. I quote from the company's minutes:

Company   Originally we were thinking of putting in a corrugator, but we looked into it, and because the factory was not ready for it and we had not reached a level of production at which a new corrugator would be needed, it was decided to try and get production up to the point where we could put one in. It is not that we are not going to put one in, simply that we have postponed it.

The union branch leaders, their fears confirmed, took what appeared to be an attitude of pained displeasure:

Union   Don't you think we should have heard this explanation a little earlier? We had an agreement that the 4-group 3-shift system should go on until the end of August. Even now your explanation does not explain anything and we feel we have been tricked.

Company   It is a matter of business. We have to change to fit the conditions. There may have been a problem in letting you know sooner rather than later. But not only did the company announce the plan; it also gave it careful consideration. There is absolutely no question of trickery. It is a matter of having production match sales, and it is all we people in the factory who have to decide when to put the corrugator in.

Union   If we continue there will be resentment at not being able to rest on Sundays and at having to do overtime to help out on the processing side [where far more corrugated sheet than usual had to be made up into boxes]. It is not desirable from the point of view of safety; and there

217

are also complaints from the corrugator teams. We
would like the system ended by December.

Despite the alleged trickery, then, the union was prepared to allow
the company to go on with continuous work five more months than
had originally been agreed on the assumption that a corrugator
would be installed. I say 'the union', but according to the local
branch leaders at N-, with whom I subsequently had long talks,
the branch would have wanted the continuous shifts stopped
immediately, but its views were overridden by the Three Officers
of the central executive committee. The division between branch
and centre became more marked as summer progressed, putting the
chairman of the executive committee, who happened to be an
employee at the N- factory, in an unpleasant position.

I should like at this point to discuss how the shift-work problem
appeared to each of the four main parties to management-union
relations: the upper management, the middle managers, the union
leaders, and the mass of the union membership.

The original decision to initiate continuous shift work at N-
had come from the upper management, probably from the president
himself, though it was characteristic of decisions at Marumaru that
no one knew who had taken them until after they had been successfully effected. The president and the other members of the upper
management were all in the Tokyo head office, very far from N-,
and they only heard of the contention caused by the new shift
system through their middle managers. These middle managers,
who constituted the second party to the debate, had actually to
execute the decision to introduce the new shift system and to
represent it to the union and its membership. They themselves were,
however, far from anxious to identify themselves with the decision.
Both at the time and after the problem had been settled they frankly
admitted that the upper management had made a mistake in introducing the new shift system in such a roundabout way. And while
these managers were having to bear the ill-will aroused by the move
to continuous shifts they were themselves quite as inconvenienced
as any unionist by the introduction of the new schedules, which
meant Sunday working for them as well as the union members.
The middle management, then, was certainly quite as anxious
as the union leadership to have the problem brought to an
end.

Among the union leaders there was, as I have indicated, a division
between the branch leadership and the Three Officers, but this
division was caused less by a fundamental difference of opinion than
by the differing circumstances of the two sets of leaders. The branch

218

leaders were of the same age and position in the company as the Three Officers, and they were just as unwilling as the Three Officers to call a strike or initiate some other action which might jeopardise their own careers and, indeed, harm the company they had served so long. But the branch leaders were more exposed to the opinions of the ordinary union members and less closely in touch with the management than the Three Officers, so that they could afford to appear to be more militant.

As for the ordinary union members, though it was common for the union leaders to assert that there was great discontent in the ranks, in fact the union membership was surprisingly little aroused. Workers complained that the continuous work shifts deprived them of opportunities to be with their children on Sundays. They also considered that the number of days assigned them in the shift cycle was insufficient compensation for having to work on Sundays. Finally, they were annoyed at what they considered the duplicity of management. But it could not have been said that there was serious unrest on the shop floor. The leaving rate of young people, which was usually a good indication of whether a factory was a happy one, was only fractionally higher than in the previous year. And if it was merely tolerable at this stage, the 4-group 3-shift system actually become popular with shop-floor workers later on, when the company increased the number of rest days in the shift cycle. Then the branch leaders, far from receiving even lukewarm support from their constituents, found themselves campaigning on a point of principle for the withdrawal of a scheme which the union membership had come to like.

The active parties, then, were the managers of middle rank and the union leaders, the managers regretfully pressing the new shift system on the factory, the union leaders protesting against the change, while at the same time bearing the company's interests in mind. Though these two groups were set in overt opposition to each other, the opposition was muted; and for reasons I have already discussed there was in fact a strong sense of understanding and sympathy between them.

No important developments took place between the June factory 'friendly meeting' at N-, from the minutes of which I have just quoted, and the July meeting. At the July meeting the discussion continued where it had ended in June, with the branch leaders accusing the management of breaking faith, while the managers defended what they claimed to be their prerogatives and called for the union's co-operation in everyone's best interests. At the end of the meeting the union branch announced its intention of referring the matter to the central committee.

Union We have fully explained all this to our members. We have exactly the same views as you when it comes to expanding production. Only we don't see the point of the system. It is exhausting physically and it is becoming a prime reason for the loss of labour. We are going to refer this to the central committee. We do not think we will get anything done at this level no matter how much we talk.

In point of fact, the Three Officers had been involved in the continuous shift-work problem from the very start, but far from wanting to bend the whole effort of the union to try and force a solution, they had been anxious to keep any public contention to as small a group of people as possible. They had therefore left the branch leaders to deal with the problem locally as long as they could, and they had meanwhile neglected to keep the union member-ship in the other factories informed. The first public announcement about the shift-work problem at N-, this after three months of shift working, was now made by the union secretary in the following union bulletin:

To protect the workers' fundamental rights!

For us a place where it is pleasant to work, a happy workplace, an attractive workplace are, from the point of view of the balance between labour and management, fundamental rights of the worker which we must protect. They are things which have been absolutely established by law and contract and moreover con-firmed in customary dealings between labour and management. But we are more than wage labourers. We live by offering our labour as cogs in an enterprise, and in accordance with the labour we offer we should receive a fair deal in the form of working conditions of equivalent value. According to the Labour Standards Law certain items are clearly stated as working conditions in a broad sense: a factory's operational equipment, which influences working efficiency and the maintenance of working capacity; factory discipline, which is closely associated with the treatment of the workers, and so on. But are these things being clearly carried out in all the factories? And if they are, are they not being done bureaucratically? Isn't it an administration that alienates workers? Is the will to work encouraged by warm leadership? We feel doubts on these and other matters. We continue to have the same feelings as when we entered the company, because people do not enter the company with the intention of leaving, so those who do leave are driven out. And what are the complicated reasons that cause them to leave? How did the phenomenon come about?

They have to be thought out carefully. But to take as an example, the 4-group 3-shift system at N- factory, are not the directors making the workers work simply as a means to make a profit? How did they deal with things apart from profit, the dissatisfactions of the workers with the workplace and their superiors resulting from the agreement to go on 4–3 shifts until the installation of a corrugator in August, and the imbalance in the corrugating division resulting from the irregular 4–3 system, and the carry over to the processing division [working on Sundays]? They only make their business plans on the spur of the moment, and there is considerable distrust of their not keeping their promises. From now on, as a union, we shall have to think of when it will be introduced in all the factories, and we will have to think deeply, from the foundations, of the nature of the relationship between management and labour, together with emphasising respect for the workers.

The ordinary worker in any of the factories except N- who read this notice through, even if he knew what a 4-group 3-shift system was (which was unlikely), would have been left with a confused and false impression of what was happening at N-. The essential fact that the company had entered into an agreement on a certain condition and then failed to fulfil that condition was only obliquely referred to and not clearly expressed. The muddled account that was given of the problem appeared to suggest that the matter was already in the past, that there was no more to be done for N-, and that all the union could do was to try and prevent the 4-group 3-shift system from being adopted elsewhere. But if the bulletin failed to inform the ordinary union members it had the effect of a strong emotional signal to those in Marumaru who knew the facts already: the people at the N- factory, and the union leaders and middle managers in other factories as well.

While the bulletin was being distributed, talks were going on between the Three Officers and the labour department at the head office to try and solve the problem, and a compromise solution was reached. The company agreed to improve the continuous work cycles by adding another day's rest, so that workers now received an extra three weeks holiday a year in return for having to work on Sundays and national holidays. In return the union agreed to run the 4-group 3-shift system ostensibly 'on a temporary basis' after the end of August, but in reality until a new corrugator was put in in 1971—that is at the time originally planned. Before the agreement could be announced there had to be at least a pretence of a public discussion of the issue at the August 'central friendly talks' between the central executive committee of the union and the usual deputation of head office managers. These talks took place not in the head office, as was customary, but at the N-factory, and the N- branch leaders were allowed to be present as observers.

The head of the labour department began, according to the company's minutes, by recounting how the company had gradually introduced first a 2- and then a 3-shift system. Continuous shift work with a logical development, and its introduction at N- was of significance for the company as a whole.

Company   We have heard your demand that the system be ended. We started it as a precondition to the installation of a corrugator at N- and we have to go on and solve the problem. From now on we would like to start running the 4-3 system at other factories, too, and we should like your co-operation in this.

This remark, made four months after the new shift system had first been put into operation—and of course after its withdrawal had been informally agreed—was the first indication that N- was indeed a test case. The debate then continued with apparent furiousness, the Three Officers demanding a return to normal shift work, and the management arguing the necessity of going on with continuous working. Finally, a member of the local branch leadership who did not know about the informal agreement between the Three Officers and the management made an impassioned plea for the abolition of continuous shifts. After his outburst the meeting was brought to a hasty end when the company decided to curtail its recapitulatory arguments and instead to produce a corrugator.

N-Factory   We have been listening to what union members have
Manager   to say about this problem. I came in June to take up a position in which I had to carry out a new policy. We have made a start and we cannot go back, I would like to go on with 4–3 shift work and put in a new machine. I discussed things with the directors in July; if a date for the installation is announced we will think again. . . . If the union has a plan, please discuss it with the director in charge of labour relations.

Labour   We heard in July what the factory manager had to
Director   say. We have considered the estimates for the forth-coming year, and the point at which we shall reach the 5 million square metres a month mark will be

222

	August 1971. Since we have to have two corrugators by then we have ordered one. But it is not a machine you can get hold of right away. We are ordering it so that it will be ready by June and running in July [i.e. the installation would take nine or ten months]. The production department is at present negotiating to get it earlier.
Union	We understand. We should like to think about it and then talk to the labour department about it tomorrow.
Labour Department Head	We have made a start, and to keep up production we have to go on with the 4–3 system. We should like you to recognise that the system is a means of shortening working hours and that it will allow us to progress to a forty-hour week, and so let us continue working it.

With these remarks the 4-group 3-shift problem officially came to an end. The secretary issued a bulletin which explained the workings of the system. The workers (and managers) at N- gladly received their extra day's holiday; and the subject did not come up again at the central friendly talks. Only the N- branch leadership remained dissatisfied, though, as I remarked earlier, the branch leaders were as far from being dissidents without a permanent place in Marumaru as the Three Officers, while their constituents were very content with the new shift cycle.

As a result of the problems that had arisen at N-, the president decided to drop all plans to work other factories continuously. Later that year another factory reached a position where 4-group 3-shift working, this time on the processing side, would have been economically desirable, but the factory continued or normal shifts nevertheless. Ironically, the president was not aware, when he came to the decision, that 4-group 3-shift working had been happily accepted by ordinary union members at N-. It therefore seemed as though the union, despite having lost the battle at N-, had prevented the company from adopting the 4-group 3-shift system elsewhere, and so could have been said to have won the war—though whether the victory was to the advantage of the rank and file union members was another question.

The significance of the story of the 4-group 3-shift system is that it shows not only the strength but also the source—or at least the immediate source—of the union's influence. Evidently the union did not derive its power from the will to action of its ordinary members. Its weapon was the moral sympathy it leaders could enlist among their friends and working colleagues in the junior management. These junior managers had little authority, so that they were unable to translate their sympathy directly into action on the union's behalf. There were, however, in a position to communicate the dissatisfactions of the union leadership to upper management, sometimes, as in the shift-work case, in amplified form. The upper management, however determined it might be to execute a project, had to consider the dangerous extent to which discontents and reputed discontents could resonate inside a company made a particularly close community by the life-employment system. A large number of the people in Marumaru had, after all, worked together for many years; and because of the prevailing tradition that common social life should extend outside working hours, everyone knew everyone else's backgrounds, personalities, aspirations and faults. Moreover, everyone could expect to continue to be in the company with the same set of co-workers for many years to come. Under these circumstances a controversy like that engendered by the 4-group 3-shift system could give rise to great bitterness and transform a happy workplace into a very unpleasant one. It is not hard to imagine, for example, how the quarrel between the chairman of the union executive committee and the N- branch, or the forthright criticism of upper management by union and lower management affected social relations at the N- factory, and impelled the upper management to bring the dispute to an end, even if it meant conceding to the union.

A second but less immediate and therefore less obtrusive reason why management had to pay attention to union demands was that it was conceivable that if the union were continually thwarted new and more militant union leaders would come to be elected. These leaders would come not from the team leaders and senior workers but from the young mobile employees with little loyalty to the company. On occasion the union leaders would refer to this possibility in bargaining with the management, remarking that they, the present union leaders, fully understood the company's point of view, but the younger union members were far more unsympathetic to the company; only if the management went far towards conceding to the union would it be possible for the leadership to calm and appease their constituents.

It is worth emphasising once more how much this passive power of the union depended on the system of pay by age and seniority, the life-employment system, and the fact that the union was an enterprise union. The close association between the union leaders and the middle management, the need to avoid contention in a closed society, and the potential rivalry, based on a difference of interests, between the union leaders and the rank and file—all these aspects of the 4-group 3-shift problem and its solution were related to the characteristic features of Japanese industrial society which I noted at the beginning of this paper.

It is only reasonable to think that the political mechanism by which union-management relations worked at Marumaru, since it depended on these common features of Japanese companies, should be reproduced in other companies as well; and that cases like the one I have described should be fairly typical in Japanese industry. There have been very few case studies of Japanese unions, but two I am familiar with do indeed have something in common with the Marumaru case. In the 1950s Nakano,[2] describing a union election, revealed an alliance between middle management and union leadership and an antagonism between union leaders and ordinary members. More recently Cole[3] has written of an oligarchic pro-company union whose leaders used a transparent device to induce the membership to approve a low wage offer from the management.

One might add, parenthetically, that similar union-management relations could be expected to be found in the West in those institutions, not necessarily companies, where 'life employment', a continuous promotion system, and a comparative lack of contact with outside bodies are seen. I have already mentioned the police force as an organisation roughly similar to a Japanese company; but industries like banking and insurance also furnish examples of Japanese-type organisations.

The weakness of this kind of labour-management relations is that the union is unable to represent interests very far removed from those of management. Fujita and his co-workers[4] have commented on the long-term instability of Japanese enterprise unions. They have put forward a theory that unions change according to a cycle. First there are young unions, like that at Marumaru, led by older workers sympathetic to management. The older workers lose the confidence of their members and a new leadership arises from among the young workers, some of whom are disposed to militancy. The militant leadership of the union eventually ends in a crisis when a new docile union is formed by the secession of a majority of the workers from the now intolerably militant original union.

It was possible to see how such a series of events could take place at Marumaru. It was certain, for example, that in the future the proportion of older workers who had come from other companies rather than from school and college would be much greater. These workers would be senior in terms of age but not of length of service, and they might well present considerable problems both for union

leaders and for the management. Yet management did have considerable scope for adjusting for this and other changes. It could redefine
union membership so as to include a solid contingent of sub-section
heads—such an idea was indeed under discussion when I left
Marumaru. Or again, management could seek to persuade individual
dissidents to leave the company, or at least moderate their activities.
Whatever might happen over the years, in the meantime industrial
relations appeared impressively stable, so stable that they allowed
a very serious problem like that of the continuous work shifts
to be solved relatively smoothly and in such a way as to leave no
lasting effect on the parties involved.

13

REGIONAL DEVELOPMENT POLICY IN JAPAN: SOME ASPECTS OF THE PLAN FOR REMODELLING THE JAPANESE ARCHIPELAGO

JOHN SARGENT

Tanaka Kakuei's *Plan for Remodelling the Japanese Archipelago*[1] was published as a paperback book in the summer of 1972, at a time of mounting concern within Japan over the social and economic costs of ultra-rapid industrial development. Indeed, the previous five years had witnessed a striking change in Japanese attitudes towards economic growth. Whereas well-nigh universal pride in the achievements of Japanese industry had characterised the late 1950s and the early years of the Income Doubling Plan, a growing sense of disillusionment became apparent towards the end of the 1960s. By the end of the decade, manufacturing industry was increasingly seen as a major source of pollution, and as a prime cause of the deterioration of the urban living environment. Through extreme examples such as Yokkaichi, where the growth of a giant petro-chemical complex had given rise to a disease known as *Yokkaichi zensoku* (Yokkaichi asthma), and Minamata Bay, where the discharge of effluent from a local factory had caused widespread mercury poisoning, industrial pollution was bringing Japan some degree of international notoriety. Meanwhile in the great conurbations, the contrast between industrial development and the backward state of essential services such as sewerage facilities and water mains saw becoming increasingly apparent, both to the Japanese and to foreign observers. Nowhere amongst the industrial countries of the world was the contradiction summarised by Galbraith as 'private opulence and public squalor' more conspicuous than in Japan.

In the midst of growing obsession within Japan over the negative aspects of industrial growth, the Tanaka plan, written in a popular style and clearly aimed at a wide audience, appeared to offer a solution to Japan's environmental problems through a dramatic and ambitious scheme involving the dispersal of industry from the overcrowded conurbations and the establishment of growth points in the peripheral regions.

There can be no doubt that the publication of Tanaka's book was to some extent motivated by political considerations, for its appearance coincided almost exactly with the announcement that Prime Minister Sato was about to retire from public office, and it was already obvious that Tanaka was a leading contender for the premiership. It is difficult to estimate the extent to which *Remodelling the Japanese Archipelago* contributed to the success of Tanaka's campaign, but within a few weeks following its publication the book had become a best-seller, and by the end of 1972 it had sold over 800,000 copies.[3]

Before proceeding to outline the main proposals of the Tanaka plan, it is first necessary to provide a brief summary of recent regional development policy in Japan, for many of the projects put forward by Tanaka are related to previous planning experience.

Within most of the world's industrial regions, the negative aspects of industrial development are conspicuously apparent in the form of congestion, urban sprawl and pollution. Meanwhile districts remote from industrial centres almost invariably suffer from the effects of rural depopulation and of relative economic stagnation. In these respects, the experience of Japan has been far from unique. However, what clearly sets Japan apart from her industrial competitors is acute shortage of usable land, and hence an unusually high degree of industrial concentration within a narrow and restricted axial zone. Thus only 16 per cent of the surface area of Japan is cultivable, and industry and population are overwhelmingly concentrated in a narrow belt running from the eastern edge of the Kanto Plain to northern Kyushu. The latest National Development Plan, published by the Economic Planning Agency in 1969, indicates that although this belt accounts for only 31 per cent of the total area of Japan, it nevertheless contains $63 \cdot 4$ per cent of the Japanese population and $83 \cdot 6$ per cent of the total value of factory shipments.[4] However, the geographical concentration of industry and population is even greater than these figures suggest, for within this so-called Pacific Belt the bulk of industrial production is located in the three conspicuous bay-head conurbations of Keihin, Hanshin and Chukyo, centring on Tokyo-Yokohama, Osaka-Kobe and Nagoya respectively. In 1970, these three conurbations taken together contained 63 per cent of the value of factory shipments[5] and 45 per cent of the population of Japan.[6] It is within these major industrial regions that problems of congestion and pollution are most acute, and where the poor quality of the urban living environment is most pronounced.

Regional development planning in Japan has attempted not only to restrict the concentration of industry in the conurbations but also to encourage economic development in the mainly agricultural outer regions, which, since 1955, have suffered the effects of a sustained exodus of population to the cities of the Pacific Belt. As early as 1956, the first serious attempt was made to restrict the growth of the Keihin conurbation. Thus the Capital Region Development Plan, which took as its model the 1944 plan for controlling the development of the Greater London region, aimed to limit the growth of the built-up area of Tokyo by the establishment of a green belt, beyond which several new towns were intended to provide foci for industrial growth independent of the metropolis. Unfortunately this approach, which has proved to be not entirely successful even in its application to the London region, was doomed to failure in the radically different conditions of Greater Tokyo. During the mid-1950s, the speed and scale of population growth in the Tokyo region was such that by the time the plan was published the proposed green belt area had almost disappeared beneath a swiftly advancing wave of factories and housing, while the much vaunted new towns have become little more than vast dormitory settlements housing Tokyo commuters. The equivalent plan for the Hanshin region took a similar approach, and was no more successful.

The inauguration of Prime Minister Ikeda's Income Doubling Plan in 1960 heralded the next stage in Japanese regional planning policy. Although Ikeda's original intention was to encourage further industrial growth in the Pacific Belt, pressure from within the Liberal Democratic party brought about official acknowledgement that regional disparities in economic growth should be rectified.[7] Accordingly, the Overall Development Plan of 1962 proposed a three-fold division of Japan into overcongested areas (Tokyo, Osaka, Nagoya, Kitakyushu, and other industrial districts within the Pacific Belt), adjustment areas (mainly the whole of central Honshu outside the Pacific Belt), and development areas (the remaining outer regions). The main purpose of the plan was to restrict any further increase in population and industry in the conurbations while at the same time encouraging the establishment of factories in the development areas, by means of local investment in social overhead capital, and by the provision of other incentives such as exemption from municipal property tax for a specified period. The function of the intermediate adjustment areas was never clearly defined, but they were essentially viewed as hinterlands within which future industrial growth should be carefully monitored in order to prevent the development of congestion.

One of the main results of the 1962 plan was the establishment in the outer regions of fifteen New Industrial Cities, which were intended to be major foci for industrial expansion. The announcement of this programme immediately initiated vigorous competition among local authorities for designation of their areas as New Industrial Cities. When the final allotment was made, it was clear that the location of the cities often owed more to the degree of local support for the Liberal Democratic party than to economic rationality. Furthermore, in each New Industrial City area, local authorities were expected to provide most of the expenditure needed for the provision of factory sites and the laying out of the infrastructure. In rural districts which had received designation, local revenues were usually too low to provide adequate funds, and in the outermost regions, New Industrial Cities were generally unsuccessful. In some cases, such as Hyūga-Nobeoka in Kyūshū and Jōban-Kōriyama in Tōhoku, the creation of New Industrial Cities has had little effect upon the rate of emigration, and population has continued to decline.[8] The most successful New Industrial Cities were those established in districts such as south Okayama, where industry was expanding well before 1962. On the whole, the 1962 plan did little to rectify regional imbalances in industrial growth.

In 1969, regional development policy was taken a stage further by the introduction of the New National Overall Development Plan.[9] Although its publication attracted little attention outside academic circles, this plan in fact contained many of the ideas subsequently elaborated by Tanaka in *Remodelling the Japanese Archipelago*. Rather than concerning itself with detailed proposals, the 1969 plan instead offered a number of basic guidelines for regional development within Japan up to the target year of 1985. Aimed at the encouragement of economic development throughout the entire Japanese archipelago and not only in the Pacific Belt, the plan also stressed the need to conserve the natural environment, and embodied the view that those responsible for causing industrial pollution and congestion should bear the costs needed to eradicate these problems. This latter concept was to be given great prominence in the introductory chapter of *Remodelling the Japanese Archipelago*. The 1969 plan proposed a division of Japan into seven major planning regions centred respectively upon Sapporo, Sendai, Tokyo, Nagoya, Osaka, Hiroshima and Fukuoka, and strongly emphasised the need to improve the national communications network through the construction of motorways and railways of the *shinkansen* (bullet train) type. Moreover, the plan advocated the construction of a small number of large-scale industrial development projects in the peripheral regions of the country. The concept of combining an extention of the communications network with the development of large-scale industrial complexes was to become a central feature of the Tanaka plan, and it is to an examination of the main proposals of the Tanaka plan that this paper now turns.

Tanaka's book begins by acknowledging the costs of post-war industrial growth. Thus Tanaka asserts that it was in 1968, the year of the hundredth anniversary of the Meiji Restoration, that the advantages of concentrating industry and population in the large conurbations began to be outweighed by the disadvantages. It is then argued that should past trends be allowed to continue unchecked, problems of population growth, pollution, power supply and traffic congestion will inevitably intensify. Each of these problems is then examined in detail.

Tanaka first indicates the unusual concentration of population in the three major urban and industrial regions, and points to the extreme difficulties of commuting which this concentration has caused. He suggests that in the Tokyo region, a continued growth of population stimulated by the natural reproduction of the existing population rather than by migration, will bring about an increase in numbers to 40 million by 1985.

As regards the likely intensification of pollution, Tanaka's vision of the future is equally pessimistic. The results of a Ministry of International Trade and Industry survey are quoted to show that in 1968 the amount of sulphur dioxide released into the atmosphere above Tokyo was equivalent to slightly more than half a million tons of sulphur. On the basis of current trends, the ministry estimates that by 1975 this rate of emission will have risen to 1·4 million tons. Tanaka argues that the maximum application of devices to cut down the discharge of sulphur dioxide will reduce this total by only 20 per cent, leaving one million tons of sulphur equivalent to be released into the atmosphere.

The problem of power shortage is then briefly outlined. Within the industrial regions, Tanaka argues, the continuation of present trends will inevitably lead to a severe crisis in electricity supply by 1985. These trends include not only the growing geographical concentration of industry but also a significant switch in the pattern of electricity consumption, due to the increasingly widespread use of certain electrical appliances. Thus the use of room coolers, which have now become indispensable items in many city offices and households, has contributed towards a shift in the annual peak demand for electricity from December to August, when output from hydro-electric power stations is usually low. Moreover, Tanaka identifies the construction of office blocks as a further prime cause of increased demand for electricity within the conurbations. He quotes as an example the 36-storey Kasumigaseki Building, the electricity consumption of which is alleged to be equivalent to that of 16,000 ordinary houses. In theory, the answer to the growing problem of electricity shortage would be investment in more thermal electric power stations, but Tanaka admits that such a solution has become almost impossible, due to the intense opposition of local authorities, many of which now identify oil-burning power stations as major producers of atmospheric pollution.

A further source of crisis in the conurbations is worsening traffic congestion. Tanaka points out that as regards the total number of insured motor vehicles, Japan in 1972 ranked second in the world, with a total of 21 million vehicles. The Japanese government estimates that given the continuation of present trends, this already large number will almost double to a total of 40 million vehicles by 1985. This dramatic increase is contrasted with the provision of good roads, in which respect Japan still lags far behind the other industrial nations. Thus Tanaka indicates that in 1972 the length of motorway in use in Japan amounted to 709 km., in contrast with 4,453 km. in West Germany, 3,907 km. in Italy, and 1,938 km. in France.

Other problems considered by Tanaka include the ever-present vulnerability of the congested metropolitan region to a major earthquake. Recent disastrous fires in large buildings, notably in crowded department stores, have cast doubts on the assertion that tall buildings in Tokyo are invulnerable to earthquake damage, and in the event of a major earthquake the many underground shopping centres which have been built in recent years in response to land shortage would be put at grave risk.

Taking into account these and other factors such as soaring land prices, inadequate housing and labour shortage, Tanaka concludes that the major conurbations of Japan have reached crisis point. The solution, he argues, is the employment of radical measures to achieve the dispersal of industry to the peripheral regions of the country, and this decentralisation constitutes the main theme of the Tanaka plan.

As in the 1969 plan, the Tanaka programme takes 1985 as its target year. The Tanaka plan, however, is based on a far more optimistic forecast of future economic expansion, for it assumes a growth in gross national product of 10 per cent per annum, from 73 billion yen in 1970 to 304 billion yen in 1985.

The plan aims to reduce industrial concentration in the Pacific Belt coastlands to the levels indicated in Table 1. These changes in industrial concentration will be achieved through two main approaches. Firstly, and in accord with the aims of the 1969 plan, large-scale complexes of heavy industry will be established in the extremities of the country, at locations far removed from the conur-

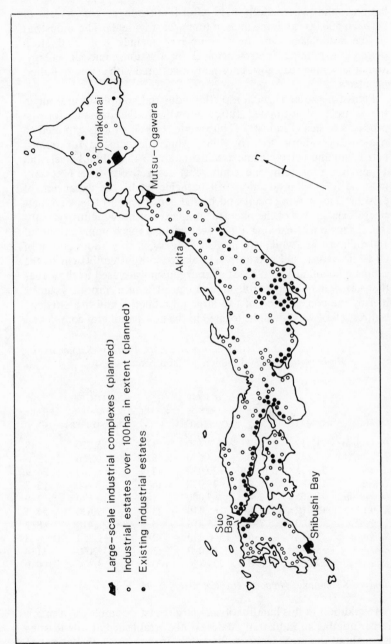

Figure 1. *Location of Planned Large-Scale Industrial Complexes and Estates*

bations, and where deep bays afford anchorages for vessels of between 500,000 and one million tons (see Figure 1). The industries to be established in these complexes include iron and steel, petroleum refining, petro-chemical production, nuclear energy, and other similar categories normally associated with severe pollution problems.

Plans for the construction of the industrial complexes are put in the context of estimated future growth in the demand for the products of heavy industry. Thus crude steel demand is expected to rise to 200 million tons by 1985, while the demand for refined petroleum and petro-chemicals will amount to 15 million barrels and 17 million tons (ethylene equivalent) respectively, The necessary increase in steel production will be achieved by the expansion of existing steel-making plant and by the construction of massive new steel works in two of the planned complexes of heavy industry. Thus the expansion of existing plant will yield a maximum output of 160 million tons, while two new steel works, each with an output of 20 million tons, will make up a total steel output equivalent to the estimated demand for 1985. Similar arguments are used to show that the 1985 demand for petroleum and petro-chemical products can be met by the construction of five large oil refineries and five ethylene centres, all of which will be located in the new peripheral complexes.

Table 1: Estimated Future Growth in Value of Factory Shipments by Regions (in thousand million yen and percentages)

| | 1970 | | 1985 | | | |
AREA	ESTIMATE	SHARE %	IF PAST TRENDS CONTINUE	SHARE %	WITH RE-DISTRIBUTION OF INDUSTRY	SHARE %
Hokkaido	1,512	2·2	3,450	1·3	15,850	5·8
Tōhoku	3,174	4·6	8,670	3·2	36,350	13·3
Kantō	25,155	36·4	120,030	43·9	68,060	24·9
Tōkai	11,488	16·6	38,370	14·0	37,440	13·7
Hokuriku	1,665	2·4	5,000	1·8	10,670	3·9
Kinki	15,719	22·8	65,410	23·9	39,630	14·5
Chūgoku	5,100	7·4	15,850	5·8	22,410	8·2
Shikoku	1,772	2·6	6,450	2·4	11,750	4·3
Kyūshū	3,475	5·0	10,090	3·7	31,160	11·4
Japan	69,060	100·0	273,320	100·0	273,320	100·0

Source: K. Tanaka, *Nippon Rettō Kaizō-ron*, p. 94.

In addition to this handful of very large coastal complexes, a much larger number of industrial estates will be established at inland sites throughout the provinces (see Figure 1). These estates, the layout of

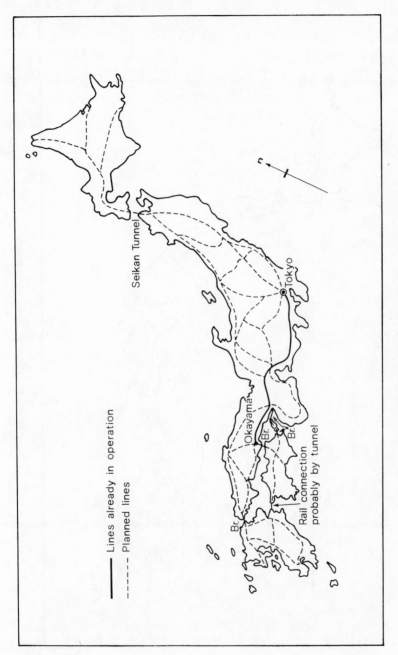

Figure 2. Planned Network of Shinkansen Railway Lines

Motorways in use
Planned motorways

Sapporo

Tokyo

Nagoya

Osaka

Kitakyūshū

Figure 3. Planned Motorway Network

which will be carefully planned so as to preserve green spaces and to avoid overcrowding, will accommodate labour-intensive and non-polluting industries such as electrical machinery and light engineering. Many of the industrial estates will be located with respect to the accessibility of motorway interchanges and freight loading points on the railway network.

Indeed, the success of these schemes for a new pattern of industrial location depends very heavily on a complete modernisation and extension of the existing communications system, and the second part of the Tanaka plan describes the layout of motorways, *shinkansen* (express railways of the New Tokaido Line type), and oil pipelines which must be established by 1985.

According to Tanaka, the *shinkansen* network will be extended to a total length of 9,000 km. (see Figure 2), while motorways (Figure 3) and pipelines will amount to 10,000 km. and 7,500 km. respectively. The growth of the *shinkansen* network will be accompanied by a massive modernisation of the ordinary J.N.R. (national railways) lines involving electrification and, where necessary, the doubling and quadrupling of existing track. Meanwhile, *shinkansen* trains will be speeded up by the use of linear motors capable of hauling rolling stock at speeds of up to 500 km. per hour. Tanaka also emphasises that in rural areas, rail services on unprofitable branch lines will be maintained by the state as part of the overall programme for the dispersal of industries to the countryside.

The extension of the motorway network is also seen as a major means of achieving a more balanced distribution of industry. In this connection, Tanaka quotes as an example the experience of Rittō-machi, a town in Shiga prefecture, which is situated close to the Meishin motorway linking Kobe and Nagoya. Although formerly devoid of industrial development, Rittō-machi now contains over 200 factories, all of which have appeared since the completion of the motorway in 1964.

Thus, developments in communications are meant to open up hitherto neglected regions of the country. In many respects, for example, the island of Shikoku will be transformed, should the aims of the Tanaka plan be realised. By 1985, according to Tanaka, three island-hopping bridges will span the Inland Sea between Honshu and Shikoku. These bridges will carry roads, railways and pipelines for oil and water. The Yoshino river, Shikoku's only source of abundant fresh water, will be tapped by aqueducts which will carry water over the mountains to the dry Sanuki plain in the north of the island. Meanwhile, two deep water bays (Tachibana Bay and Sukumo Bay) will be developed as anchorages for giant oil tankers. At sites on the shores of these bays, oil storage depots will supply local refineries and will also feed pipelines which will carry oil to industrial centres in northern Shikoku and in western Honshu. Thus, argues Tanaka, giant tankers will no longer need to enter the congested navigation lanes of the Inland Sea.

Much mention is made of oil pipelines, in the provision of which Japan lags far behind the United States and Western Europe. In 1969, for instance, Japan possessed less than 100 km. of pipeline, in contrast with 228,000 km. in the u.s.a. and 15,000 km. in Europe. The Tanaka plan estimates that by 1985, pipelines will carry 40 per cent of Japan's freight in oil and oil products.

Another striking feature of the Tanaka plan is the intention to create an unspecified number of new cities in the provinces. These cities, which will contain populations of about 250,000, will differ from the existing Japanese new towns (described by Tanaka as 'human deserts') in that they will function as industrial, cultural and administrative centres. In many cases, the industrial estates mentioned earlier will be associated with the foundation of these new cities. In fact, the cities will not be built on entirely new foundations, for according to Tanaka, they are to be created either by the expansion of existing small cities, or by the merging of contiguous rural local authorities to form large administrative districts which will then be provided with the necessary urban and industrial nuclei for new town development.

As regards the main conurbations of central Honshu, the Tanaka plan envisages ambitious programmes of urban renewal. Although the precise details of these schemes are not revealed, the principle of building high-rise blocks to make maximum use of land and, indeed, to free land for amenity use, is given particular emphasis. Tanaka even suggests the drafting of legislation to impose a *minimum* height on new building, a notion which contrasts oddly with his earlier condemnation of high buildings as major users of electricity. Thus if the Tanaka plan is realised, the construction of buildings below seven storeys will be prohibited within the major conurbations. The state, argues Tanaka, should play an important role in the provision of new housing, but will act in co-operation with large corporations, which will function as private developers.

Clearly, the aims of the plan for remodelling the Japanese archipelago are extraordinarily ambitious, and their realisation calls for an enormous amount of capital expenditure. In this connection, taxation is stressed as a means of raising the necessary funds, and also as a device for encouraging companies to locate their factories in the outer regions. Already, a 1·5 per cent surcharge on corporation tax has been imposed on companies located in the conurbations. For companies willing to migrate to the provinces, long-term exemption from municipal property tax, together with depreciation allowances and investment grants, will be offered by way of inducement. Tanaka stresses that wherever necessary the state should supply grants to local authorities to reimburse them for the cost of inducements. In this respect, the Tanaka plan seeks to avoid the overburdening of local authority finances which was a major weakness of the 1962 plan for creating New Industrial Cities.

As regards the provision of funds for the entire plan, particular emphasis is given to the introduction of a vehicle weight tax, the main purpose of which will be to finance road and railway construction. Such a tax, it is claimed, would have the additional advantage of keeping a large number of heavy commercial vehicles off the roads.

When published in the summer of 1972, the Tanaka plan undoubtedly attracted widespread interest throughout Japan. Tanaka's promise, made shortly after his election to the premiership, that the realisation of the plan would be the major objective of his domestic policy, suggested to many Japanese that for the first time the Liberal Democratic party was prepared to take a serious approach towards solving the manifold problems of the overcrowded cities. Moreover, the grandiose and imaginative schemes proposed by the Tanaka plan seemed fully in accord with Japan's world-wide reputation for devising dramatic measures to solve her post-war problems. At the same time, it was thought that the enactment of the plan might put an end to frequent criticisms from abroad to the effect that the Japanese 'economic miracle' had been achieved at the expense of the creation of a satisfactory living environment. Here was a chance for Japan to show the world that she was quite capable of coping with the negative aspects of industrial growth. In all, the Tanaka plan seemed to offer an approach towards domestic problems which was in every way as revolutionary as the new foreign policy aimed at a *rapprochement* with China. For all these reasons, the Tanaka plan helped to boost the initial popularity of the Tanaka administration.

Meanwhile, from the viewpoint of the Liberal Democratic party, the plan offered a means of retrieving the support of the urban electorate, whose increasing allegiance to opposition parties was in some measure due to the seemingly indifferent attitude of previous governments towards the steady deterioration of living conditions within the major conurbations. Also, the plan, with its promises of rapid economic development in the outlying rural districts, was perhaps seen as a device for retaining the support of the farming population, whose traditional attachment to the Liberal Democratic party had begun to waver, mainly due to the reluctance of the government to continue with its policy of generous subsidisation of rice production. In this connection, it is perhaps significant that Tōhoku, the primary rice-producing region of Japan, stood to benefit more than any other peripheral region from the planned dispersal of industry embodied in the Tanaka proposals (see Table 1). Furthermore, despite its strictures upon the location of factories in overcrowded districts, the plan appealed strongly to that other pillar of the Liberal Democratic party, namely the business world, for it offered a wide range of profitable opportunities for investment in the infrastructure, at a time when foreign markets in both America and Europe seemed to be increasingly sensitive to the inroads made by Japanese exports. Thus from the standpoint of the Liberal Democratic party, the plan had much to commend it.

The reaction of the opposition parties to the plan was, however, predictably hostile. Thus during the election campaign of December 1972, the Japan Socialist party identified the Tanaka plan as a major cause of the rapid escalation of land prices which had occurred during the previous six months, while the Kōmeitō claimed that the plan for remodelling the Japanese archipelago was really nothing more than a scheme for ensuring the purchase of the archipelago by big business interests. The Democratic Socialist party contended that the only beneficiaries of the plan would be the real estate companies and civil engineering firms. In August 1972, the Japan Communist party published a tract entitled 'The New Policy of the Tanaka Cabinet and Its Reality', which alleged that the Tanaka plan had not only encouraged wholesale land speculation by large corporations, but was also attempting to destroy Japanese agriculture from the roots upwards. The opposition parties also shared the belief that the Tanaka plan would spread pollution throughout the country, and claimed that the plan completely ignored the growing desire of local governments for greater autonomy.[10]

It can be demonstrated that, although exaggerated for electioneering purposes, many of these accusations were to some extent substantiated by the course of events during the last six months of 1972. Nevertheless, it would be unfair to dismiss the Tanaka plan merely as a scheme for serving the interests of the Liberal Democratic party and the Japanese business world. After all, an essentially similar approach towards regional development planning has been followed in the United Kingdom since the early 1930s.[11] In recent years, for example, successive British governments have aimed to encourage industrial growth in regions suffering either from high unemployment or from excessive rural depopulation, by the application of fiscal incentives, while at the same time attempts have been made to restrict the growth of large cities by the imposition of controls on office building. Thus after 1966, British government cash grants for new plant and machinery were provided at double the national rate in the case of companies wishing to locate their factories in the Development Areas, while in 1967 regional differentials in selective employment tax were introduced in order to give the Development Areas a cost advantage over other regions.

Meanwhile, many European countries have attempted to create foci for industrial growth in peripheral regions suffering from the combined effects of rural depopulation and economic underdevelopment. In Italy, for example, the *Cassa per il Mezzogiorno* has attempted for more than a decade to encourage the growth of manufacturing industry in the impoverished regions of the south, not only through investment in the infrastructure but also by the establishment of new industrial complexes. A prime example of this latter policy was the construction of an integrated iron and steel works at Taranto in the early 1960s.[12]

Such developments both in Italy and elsewhere in Europe have not always fully succeeded in slowing down the rate of emigration, and their shortcomings may, perhaps, serve to indicate some weaknesses in the concept underlying the Tanaka plan. In the *Mezzogiorno*, for instance, the growth of large-scale capital-intensive industries such as steel and chemicals has brought about a sharp rise in productivity per worker but has not led to a dramatic expansion in the number of local job opportunities. Furthermore, it can be argued that the creation of a single large-scale industrial complex at the centre of an extensive region of economic underdevelopment does little to halt the rate of emigration from villages at the peripheries of that region. Meanwhile, it is not always certain that the improvement of communications leads to growth within backward areas. Indeed, without careful ancilliary planning measures, the opposite effect may well result, and the new highways and railways may only serve to accelerate the movement of population to the more advanced regions of the country. In general, however, regional development plans roughly similar to that proposed by Tanaka have long been accepted as necessary by several of the industrial countries of Western Europe.

Within Japan, however, early interest in the Tanaka plan was rapidly replaced by growing scepticism and disillusionment. Firstly, initial attempts to implement the plan coincided with an extremely rapid rise in land prices. In January 1972, a government survey revealed that the average price of urban land in forty-six selected cities had risen by 24 per cent during the previous twelve months.[13] A subsequent survey carried out by *Nippon Fudōsan Kenkyū-jo* showed that urban land prices for Japan as a whole had risen by 31 per cent during the year ending in October 1973.[14] In some areas, this rise can certainly be attributed to the Tanaka plan. In Niigata prefecture, for instance, land prices have soared since the middle of

1972 owing to the purchase of large tracts of land by corporations and real estate companies. In many cases, these transactions have involved the purchase of land close to the planned route of the *Jōetsu shinkansen* as indicated in the Tanaka plan.[15] On the national scale, however, land prices were already rising steeply before the publication of the Tanaka plan. Thus a recent report of the Economic Planning Agency suggests that the acquisition of land by corporations has been a conspicuous feature of the last six or seven years, and has not been confined to the period since mid-1972. Between 1967 and 1971, the report points out, the area of land owned by individuals increased by 2 per cent, in contrast with a 16 per cent increase in the area of land owned by corporations.[16] Although the Tanaka plan undoubtedly stimulated land speculation by corporations, it was probably the unusually large accumulation of foreign exchange reserves, and the consequent availability of funds for investment within Japan, which was the underlying cause of the increase in the purchase of land by large corporations between 1967 and 1973. Whatever the real cause, however, the Tanaka plan has been widely criticised for encouraging land speculation, and for causing a rapid rise in the price of land.

Secondly, in the drafting of the Tanaka proposals, government planners appear to have greatly underestimated the strength of local opposition to industrial development. Thus attempts to establish the large-scale complexes at Mutsu-Ogawara and around the shores of Shibushi Bay have met with unexpectedly fierce opposition from local communities.[17] Similarly, the proposed construction of an oil unloading terminal and associated oil storage facilities at Sukumo Bay in western Shikoku has aroused the antagonism of the local fishing industry.[18] In each of these three areas, local opposition has been strong enough to hamper seriously progress with the respective development plans.

Indeed, the publication of the Tanaka plan coincided with a dramatic growth in the number of organisations formed at local levels to combat industrial pollution and the alleged diversion of local government expenditure away from housing and welfare and into public works schemes devised for the benefit of industry. In recent years, the term *taishū undō* (mass movements) has been used to describe these organisations, which include *jūmin undō* (residents' movements) and *shimin undō* (citizens' movements). Perhaps the most conspicuous of these movements are those formed to claim compensation for the victims of mercury poisoning, which has been caused by industrial pollution in the vicinity of Minamata Bay, and to protest against the effects of sulphur dioxide pollution from the refineries and petro-chemical plants at Yokkaichi, but similar organisations are active in many localities within the industrial regions of the Pacific Belt. The Environment White Paper of 1972 identified 673 organised groups which may be classified as *taishū undō*.[19] Most of these groups share the belief that the government has neglected the rights of local communities to have their proper say in the formulation of regional development policy and many of them, with considerable justification, view the Tanaka plan as a prime example of planning carried out entirely by Tokyo politicians and bureaucrats, without reference to local needs.

Meanwhile, any appeal the Tanaka plan may have initially held for the Japanese electorate has been considerably diminished by the swift decline in the popularity of the Tanaka cabinet. This disillusionment may, perhaps, be partly attributed to the cabinet's inability to achieve any dramatic results from the much-acclaimed improvement of relations with Peking, but it is more probable that the main source of discontent has been the apparent failure of the Tanaka administration to control the rate of domestic inflation. Mainly owing to the recent world-wide rise in prices of food and industrial raw materials, upon the import of which Japan is unusually dependent, the rate of inflation within Japan is currently one of the highest among the industrial countries of the world. In this context, the Japanese electorate is likely to demand that priority be given to the introduction of an effective policy for price control rather than to an expensive and inflationary plan for remodelling the archipelago.

Whatever the views of the electorate, the proposals contained in the Tanaka plan call for massive capital investment in the infrastructure, and any deterioration of the Japanese balance of payments brought about by the rising cost of imports will inevitably limit the availability of investment funds. Ultimately, the success of the Tanaka plan depends on the continuing prosperity of the Japanese economy.

14

JAPAN'S POLICY TOWARDS
FOREIGN TRADE:
THE STRATEGIC OPTIONS

CHRISTOPHER HOWE

Japan's policy towards foreign trade in the post-war period has reconciled the necessities of diplomacy with the pursuit of economic self-interest in a highly effective manner. Thus while Japan's diplomatic position has required close economic relations with the United States, limited official trade contacts with China and formal adherence to the principles of multilateralism and liberalism in world trade, in practice, while benefiting from liberal trade policies in Europe and America (particularly in the 1960s) Japan's own liberalisation of trade was very slow prior to the 1970s, and the foreign exchange market still remains subject to numerous restrictions. A gap between formal policy and behaviour is also evident in Japan's relations with China. This is illustrated in the 1960s and early 1970s by the rapid growth of mutual trade in spite of the absence of either diplomatic relations or formal inter-governmental arrangements for controlling the size and nature of trading relations.

THE PERFORMANCE OF TRADE AND THE BALANCE OF PAYMENTS

Japan's trade under this post-war policy has established a fairly consistent pattern in respect of its rate of growth and of its commodity and regional structures. The rate of growth of exports between 1950 and 1970 was a steady 16 per cent per annum in real terms. This rate was approximately half as high again as the rate of growth of real output and double the rate of growth of world trade.[1] Rapid as this export growth has been, it has not raised Japan's share of world trade to any remarkable level, nor has the trade sector as a whole become noticeably large in relation to total national income. In 1972, for example, Japan's share of total world exports was 7·7 per cent. This was only slightly higher than the U.K. share at 6·6 per cent, and markedly smaller than West Germany's share of 12·6 per cent.[2] Thus Japan's share of world exports is, for example, less than half of Japan's share of world steel output.

The relative weight of trade in the Japanese economy is indicated by the value of exports and imports relative to National Income. For the 1960s, the ratio of trade to National Income has been in the region of 25 per cent. In comparative perspective, this figure is lower than that of most members of the European Economic Community, and in historical perspective, it is far below the peak value of 47·6 per cent achieved by Japan in 1937.[3]

The structure of Japan's post-war trade has shown regular patterns. In commodity terms, imports have remained predominantly of food and raw materials throughout the whole post-war period, while exports have mainly consisted of manufactured goods. Within the latter category, however, the relative importance of the light and heavy industry sectors has been reversed. The data in Table 1 illustrate the way in which the changing nature of Japan's comparative advantage has been reflected in the relative decline of labour-intensive industrial exports.

Table 1: The Structure of Japanese Exports 1950–1972

	1950	1960	1965	1972
Total	100	100	100	100
Food	6·26	6·31	4·07	2·27
Crude raw materials	2·77	2·24	1·49	0·92
Industrial products	90·83	91·06	93·87	96·70
of which light industry		(46·68)	(31·86)	(18·70)
heavy industry		(44·38)	(62·01)	(77·20)
Other	0·14	0·39	0·57	0·11

Sources: *Tōkei nenkan*, various years; *White Paper on International Trade, 1973*, summary in Ministry of International Trade and Industry (M.I.T.I.) Background No. 73–27 (M.I.T.I. Information Office, July 1973).

Turning to the regional structure of trade, Table 2 shows the share of North America and Asia in Japan's exports and imports. The table shows the way in which North America has continued to grow in importance as an export market throughout the whole twenty-two-year period, while as a source of imports it has been declining. The data for Asia indicate that the importance of Asian imports has been maintained throughout the whole period of rapid Japanese growth, and although exports to the region have declined, the area still accounts for a sizeable share. Moreover, in considering the Asian data, we must remember that Japan's absolute size is such that seen from the Asian perspective, these proportions represen very substantial trade penetration. Indeed, in the case of South-Eas' Asia, one authoritative estimate has suggested that if present trends continue, Japanese goods will account for more than half of total imports by 1985.[4]

Table 2: The Share of North America and Asia in Japan's Imports and Exports, 1950–1972 (percentage shares)

Destination of exports

	NORTH AMERICA	ASIA
1950	21·65	46·28
1960	27·17	36·11
1965	29·33	32·63
1972	35·10	25·30
of which		(21·60 South-East Asia)

Sources of imports

	NORTH AMERICA	ASIA
1950	43·26	32·62
1960	34·59	30·50
1965	28·96	33·48
1972	29·95	32·14

Sources: As for Table 1.

The effect of these trade developments on the balance of payments is shown in Table 3.

Table 3: Japan's Balance of Payments, 1960–1973/4 (million U.S. dollars)

	TRADE BALANCE	CURRENT BALANCE	BASIC BALANCE
1960	268	143	88
1964	377	—480	—373
1965	1,901	932	517
1966	2,275	1,254	446
1967	1,160	—190	—1,002
1968	2,529	1,048	809
1969	3,699	2,119	1,964
1970	3,963	1,970	379
1971	3,976	—	—
1972	5,024	—	—
1973/4 (fiscal)	5,600 (est.)		—2,000/—3,000

Sources: Tōkei nenkan, 1971; White Paper on International Trade, 1973; Financial Times (24 August 1973).

Note: The trade balance is defined as exports minus imports. The current balance is the trade balance plus net payments for services and transfers. The basic balance is the current balance adjusted for long term capital movements.

From this, one can see that in spite of the positive trade balance throughout, it is only in the late 1960s that the overall current account shows real strength. As recently as 1967, Japan actually had a current account deficit and in 1970, when the current balance was nearly two billion U.S. dollars, long-term capital movements reduced the basic balance to 379 million U.S. dollars. According to forecasts made in mid-1973, the prospect for the fiscal year 1973/4 was that although the trade balance would continue to grow, the basic balance would show a deficit of two to three billion U.S. dollars.

This brief factual account of the past suggests three important analytical questions: (1) How dependent on trade has the past rate of growth of the economy been? (2) How do we explain the dramatic strengthening of the trade account in recent years? (3) How useful is the pattern of the past as a guide to Japan's trade policy and performance in the future? Of these three questions, it is the last two with which we are mainly concerned. With regard to the first question, the evidence suggests that until the mid-1960s at least, trade was not an important exogenous force in the economy. For while it is true that Japan's dependence on raw-material supplies from abroad has made export growth a necessary condition for domestic growth, the primary stimulus has come from high domestic rates of investment and other internal characteristics of the economy. The link between domestic growth and foreign trade (as Mr Kanamori has pointed out) is that domestic demand and investment were concentrated in sectors that were rapidly growing in world trade. This made the task of marketing an adequate share of exportables that much easier,[5] although until the mid-1960s, the trade balance appears more as a constraint than an engine of growth.

The transformation of the balance of payments in recent years can be mainly explained by two factors. The first of these is that by a combination of domestic management of the economy and a continued growth of labour productivity, prior to the exchange rate upheavals of 1971, Japan was able to maintain a lower rate of increase of export prices than any major competititor.[6] Thus although the nature of Japan's comparative advantage was changing in a way that made the export of relatively labour-intensive products progressively more difficult, overall, Japan's trade competitiveness was improved. The second factor was that in a period when the United States in particular was experiencing excess demand, Japan's high rates of investment ensured that there was adequate capacity for export growth. This capacity factor was compounded by a sharp deceleration in the growth of domestic demand between 1970 and 1972 which led to an accumulation of inventories and provided financial incentives to increase exports.[7]

Finally, we come to the question of the durability of post-war patterns of growth and trade, and while there is no simple answer to this, it is the thesis of this chapter that there are three new factors emerging which will have inescapable repercussions for Japan's future growth and which will create new sets of choices for Japan's foreign trade policy-makers. The three factors are: (1) the crisis in Japan's relationship with America; (2) political and economic developments in Russia and China that are altering the attitudes of both countries towards their trade relations with Japan; and (3) political, demographic and economic developments in Japan itself which are changing the criteria for economic policy-making and which are bound to have repercussions in the foreign trade sector.

THE STRATEGY OF LIBERALISATION

The crisis in Japan's relationship with America is not confined to economic and trade issues. It involves a whole range of diplomatic, political and strategic matters. Within the sphere of economics and trade, the crisis reflects the fact that, in its latter stages, the recent growth of the Japanese trade surplus has been largely at the expense of the United States. Thus by 1972, nearly two-thirds of the American deficit was accounted for by the deficit with Japan. This situation has been regarded by the Americans as intolerable and their response has resulted not only in a state of confrontation with Japan, but in American contributions to the disintegration of the international monetary system and to the state of general ferment in trade relations throughout the world. In one sense, Japanese responsibility for American balance of payments problems is quite limited; since although the American and Japanese payments' turning-points occurred during the mid-1960s, it is only comparatively recently that a real symmetry between the two accounts began to develop (see Table 4).

The origins of the American deficit have little to do with Japan and if the beneficiary of the American deficit had not been Japan it would have been someone else. Nonetheless, it is a necessary characteristic of Japan's trading relations that they tend to produce a series of bilateral surpluses and deficits. This is because the commodity structure of Japan's trade reflects the basic determinant of Japan's raw-material scarcity, and unless countries and regions that supply these resources can absorb adequate Japanese imports to enable a bilateral balance to be achieved, then Japan must earn surpluses elsewhere to pay for them. At present, Japan runs surpluses in North America, Europe, South-East Asia and Africa to pay for

248

*Table 4: The Trade Balances of Japan and the United States, 1967–
1971 (million U.S. dollars)*

	U.S. CURRENT BALANCE	U.S. TRADE BALANCE WITH JAPAN	JAPAN'S CURRENT BALANCE
1967	3,435	200	513
1968	129	−559	1,934
1969	52	−868	3,191
1970	1,692	−16	3,463
1971	−3,391	−2,390	7,782

Sources: U.S. and Japanese balances from *United Nations Statistical
Yearbook, 1972* (New York, United Nations, 1973); U.S.
balance with Japan from *Tōkei nenkan, 1971* and *White Paper
on International Trade, 1972.*

Note: The U.S. and Japanese current balances are calculated according
to I.M.F. conventions which differ somewhat from those used
to calculate the balance in Table 3. The trade balance data are
based on customs returns.

deficits in Finland, South Africa, Australasia, the Middle East and
Canada. The history of international trade is full of examples of
complicated patterns of trade and settlement of this kind. The
problem in the Japanese case is that the scale of the operation has
now become very large indeed and that for a variety of reasons, the
United States' share of Japan's total surplus requirements reached a
level that was unsustainable within a liberal framework of trading
relations. Thus the current American-Japanese problem is neither
accidental nor inevitable but should be seen as a momentarily acute
aspect of a general problem.

The Japanese response to the situation has taken place at two
levels. First, there is what might be termed the higher level of
international trade and financial diplomacy. At this level, Japanese
policy has been aimed at preserving as much of the liberalism of the
G.A.T.T. philosophy of international trading relations as possible and
as much of the stability and predictability of the old fixed exchange
rate, I.M.F.-dominated world as is realistic in a period when more than
half of the world's currencies are floating and the future of the I.M.F.
is in considerable doubt. For a country with Japan's record of
domestic protection and currency inconvertibility, this is all rather
ironic, but none the less rational for that. At the lower level of
policy and action, Japan has taken a number of steps in an effort to
reduce her trade and basic surpluses overall, and her surplus with
America in particular. These measures include a series of revalua-
tions of the yen, an acceleration of trade and capital liberalisation,
specific efforts to improve the bilateral imbalance with America by

planned import agreements, and a new policy towards foreign aid and Japanese investment abroad. Most of these measures have been conceived and implemented on a very substantial scale. The yen revaluation against the dollar is now of the order of 35 per cent and is the most substantial re-adjustment of its kind since the war. The liberalisation of trade is necessarily a slower process, but the fact that the process is definitely extending to the dismantling of non-tariff and quota barriers suggests that in the long run its effects may be large.

The liberalisation of capital flows into Japan on the other hand is not relevant to short-term problems except in the sense that the new measures (which allow 100 per cent foreign control in a very wide range of sectors) will reduce American dissatisfaction with Japan's commercial policies in general. Japan is now also committed to a marked improvement with regard to aid quality. In the past, a high proportion of Japan's 'aid' was in fact granted on commercial or near commercial terms, so that although gross aid amounted to a respectable proportion of gross national product (G.N.P.), net aid in 1972 was only 0·23 per cent of G.N.P. Official policy now envisages that this figure be raised to 0·70 per cent in conformity with O.E.C.D.– D.A.C. policy decisions.[8] In the case of Japanese foreign investment, the size of future outflows is likely to be very substantial, since in addition to continuing investment in raw-material extraction, Japan is now increasingly investing in manufacturing and other sectors in both advanced and underdeveloped economies. The Minister of Finance, Mr Aichi, has predicted that by 1983, the outstanding value of Japanese investment will be 23 billion U.S. dollars, compared with a 1973 value of 6 billion U.S. dollars.[9]

The effectiveness of this bundle of high level policy activities and lower level practical measures cannot yet be measured precisely. At the high level, the G.A.T.T. negotiations that began in Tokyo in autumn 1973 will be an important determinant of the framework for international trade for the rest of the decade. At present, the outcome of these talks is not predictable since although it is clear that President Nixon is anxious to make the talks successful on the lines of the Kennedy Round, his domestic political problems may constrain him from being as effective as he could wish. In the monetary field, the outlook is even less obvious. It seems safe to predict that a return to fixed parities is improbable, but it may prove possible to make real progress towards the establishment of new mechanisms to create liquidity and to provide automatic incentives for nations with balance of payments imbalance to adopt appropriate internal policies for their correction.

At the level of practical measures to reduce Japan's trade surplus, success seems more probable. One reason for this is the sensitivity of Japan's trade performance to relative price factors. The appearance of the trade surplus was largely due to price advantage, and its decline is likely to be brought about by a combination of the effects of the revaluation and of domestic inflationary forces. The power of domestic inflationary forces was probably underestimated in 1972. In particular, the short-term effects of the dollar devaluation on Japan's terms of trade were absorbed without adequate realisation that the inevitable revision of contracts for raw materials would impart a sharp upward movement to import prices in 1973. The fact that contract revision took place at a time when commodity prices were rising has made the effect on costs even more serious. The other cost factor behind the recent domestic price rise is that long-term demographic and attitudinal changes are now combining to create a new situation in the labour market. The labour supply and the age structure of the population are now reflecting the effects of declining fertility in the 1950s and transfer of labour from the rural sector and low productivity urban sectors is progressively more difficult.[10] These quantitative forces seem to have been reinforced by a new degree of militancy among organised labour. This has been visible in the spring offensives of 1972 and 1973, both of which produced generalised wage settlements that exceeded the rate of growth of aggregate productivity. The net effect of these domestic forces is reflected in the 15 per cent rise in the wholesale price index between July 1972 and July 1973.[11] If Japan continues to maintain a rate of price increase higher than that of major trading competition, then this must ultimately have an effect on the trade balance.

The other component of the basic balance—long-term capital flows—is more immediately responsive to policy decisions and is already showing signs of contributing to a solution of the payments problem. And the level of outflows in the first five months of 1973 has been sufficiently large to bring the basic balance of payments into deficit in every month.

Whether the changes in Japan's trade and payments that have been initiated in 1973 will satisfy her trading partners remains to be seen. At best, the net effect of the recent upheavals will be: (1) continuance of a stable, multilateral trading framework; (2) Japan's basic balance of payments (that is, trade and long-term capital accounts) will be brought into balance, probably in the first instance as a result of change on capital account. In addition, one distinctive new trend will be (3) the achievement by Japan of more satisfactory bilateral balances with surplus areas such as North America and with deficit areas, especially Iran, South-East Asia and Australia. This will be the result not only of pressure from surplus areas who will not tolerate large unmanageable deficits in their trade with Japan, but from deficit areas, who are actively demanding trade outlets for the products of their industrial sectors. This pressure will be particularly strong from countries such as Iran, who anticipate a period when natural resources will have been depleted and who are therefore anxious to bring about rapid transformations in their economic structure, if possible through trade.

THE STRATEGY OF REGIONALISATION

If events do not mature smoothly and the readjustment of Japan's economic relationships within a liberal, multilateral framework proves very difficult, then Japan might seriously consider the development of some different trade strategies. A theoretical possibility is a definite switch away from a policy of growth through specialisation and use of the international trade sector. This policy had its advocates in the immediate post-war period among scholars who argued, with some reason, that pre-war dependence on trade had been a factor in the development of militarist expansionism and who felt that trade links with the United States would have too powerful an effect on the future institutional characteristics of the Japanese economy.[12] At the present, while domestic policy towards the future economic structure will be more influenced by external factors than in the past, the prospect of a systematic withdrawal from the international economic community is inconceivable, since it would involve a decline in real income that would be political suicide for any government that attempted to implement such a policy.

A more realistic possibility is that if the liberal economic order falls short of Japanese needs and aspirations, then there could be a renewal of Japanese interest in the development of a trade policy that was regionally oriented. Several straws have been blowing in this wind for a long time. One of these is the proposal for an Asian-Pacific Free Trade Area.[13] In part this is a proposal for a formalisation of existing trends in the region in a way that would increase the size and predictability of intra-regional trade and at the same time, through planned specialisation agreements, reassure Japan's regional trading partners that the growth of trade will be compatible with their domestic industrialisation ambitions. However, the prospects for a Free Trade Area on the lines advocated by Kojima and others seem bad. Japan's preponderance in the *existing* pattern of trade in the region is at present already too great for many countries in the region, and even without a Free Trade Area, the forecasts for the future suggest that Australian and South-East

252

Asian dependence on Japan will grow to a point where Japan will account for 40 per cent to 50 per cent of total exports and much higher percentages of exports of specific raw materials.[14] In addition, realisation of large export increases from the Australian-Pacific region to Japan would have implications for investment as well as trade, since Japanese investment would be required to produce the levels of output necessary to satisfy Japanese demand. In view of the doubts already being expressed by countries in this region concerning economic dependence of this order, inter-governmental agreement to accelerate such dependence seems unlikely.

For the Japanese too, the acceleration of specialisation within the Asian-Pacific region would create problems, since further specialisation would be bound to create pressures to reduce the protection of Japanese agriculture. Economically this would be good, but the process of reallocating resources from the agricultural sector would be a difficult one with political repercussions that would be most unwelcome to the Liberal-Democrats, whose rural political base has already been subject to erosion.

Another substantial and more flexible way in which Japan's trade policy might take on a regional colouring is through the establishment of a Yen Currency Area. The dollar devaluation and the general currency uncertainties have created genuine problems for trading nations in the region and the establishment of some form of yen bloc is arguably a solution to some of these problems. Initially such a bloc would involve the wider use of the yen for contract purposes. Ultimately, it would lead to a dismantling of exchange controls to give foreign holders of yen a greater degree of freedom than they have now. One attraction of this sort of development is that the range of options is wide. The development of the bloc might, for example, be confined to a small group of technical changes, or it might be expanded to create a fully fledged yen area, similar in principle and in effect to the plans for European monetary harmonisation. Such an area, together with a dollar and Euro area, would form part of a monetary analogue of tripolar systems of political and strategic alliance.

RELATIONS WITH CHINA AND THE SOVIET UNION

A third, and most concrete way in which Japan's trade could be more regionalised would be through the development of closer economic ties with China and the Soviet Union.

In recent years, the Chinese have emphasised the policy of 'self-reliance'. We may define this type of policy as one aimed at eliminating the crucial role of external resources in the economic system and such a policy has consequences for both the internal allocation of resources and foreign trade policy. Internally, the consequences of self-reliance in China have been a new emphasis on agriculture and the oil industry, as well as new policies towards the development of indigenous technology. In trade terms, the policy led to a new flexibility in the choice of trading partners—although as long as food imports were important the choice was constrained to countries that could supply it.

Chinese policies of self-reliance reflected the collapse of the Sino-Soviet political relationship and the problems posed for the continued growth of foreign trade by China's agricultural difficulties in the late 1950s. Given these circumstances, the new trade strategy was a rational one. For while the trade sector did remain crucial (for food imports) the flexibility of the new approach and the reallocation of resources to agriculture both produced tangible benefits. However, as a long-term strategy, a policy that aimed at minimising the role of trade in the Chinese economy was deficient. One reason for this is that although it is true that China's endowment of natural resources, her enormous internal market and wide-ranging technical capability all appear to make the country an ideal candidate for a policy of economic autarchy, there is one commodity in which China is not only deficient, but in danger of becoming increasingly relatively deficient *vis-à-vis* the rest of the world. This is the commodity of knowledge. China's systems of education and research may well have features that make them appeal to those concerned with the inadequacies of Western oriented educational and scientific research systems in underdeveloped countries, but it remains true that China cannot afford to remain isolated from the mainstreams of invention and technical development that flow around the rest of the world, to a considerable extent along the channels of trade and investment. This is partly because China's political aspirations must ultimately be reflected in certain levels of economic and technical capability and partly because the Chinese themselves insist that they will not accept a pattern of trade in which they export raw materials in exchange for manufactures. The reason for this is that they feel that trade relations of this kind are essentially those of the metropolitan state and its colonial dependency. However, in order to develop the export of manufactures, the Chinese are bound to remain in contact with non-Chinese technology and taste, and this cannot be done simply by importing foreign technical and fashion literature.

The other aspect of the trade-growth strategy of the 1960s that is unsatisfactory is that however much the Chinese may wish to avoid dependence on credit, it is arguable that use of medium-term credits would enable the Chinese to enter a phase of very rapid industrialisation, unconstrained either by the short-term growth or fluctuations in the output of exportable goods. This would be a genuine Great Leap Forward of the kind that was achieved with Russian assistance in the 1950s. The benefits of such a development might be very substantial—particularly if China is caught in a more serious type of population trap than is generally appreciated. Evidence on this subject is scarce, but what we have suggests that although planned fertility decline may be feasible, economic improvement may have important repercussions on the still high level of mortality. If this is so, the problem of reducing the net growth rate of population may be very hard and the case for accelerating economic growth by expansion of the modern sector very strong.

The effect of these developments in China could be that the Chinese will wish to expand trade very rapidly in the next few years and that they may well cast Japan in an important role in this expansion. In many ways, Japan has the capacity to do for the Chinese in the 1970s and 1980s what the Russians did in the early 1950s, and although past patterns could not repeat themselves mechanically, a close economic relationship with Japan would enable the Chinese to get access to almost the whole range of modern industrial technology, to large quantities of technical assistance, and also to credit. One confirmation of the correctness of this analysis of the Chinese approach is the fact that Chou En-lai's initiative towards Japan with regard to trade matters came in 1960, at a time when the implications of the break with the Soviet Union were becoming apparent. In addition to these economic considerations, economic links that improved Sino-Japanese political relations would also fit well into Chinese attempts to create a worldwide anti-Soviet diplomatic alliance.

From the discussions in the earlier part of this chapter one can perceive motives which might prompt the Japanese to respond to Chinese pressures for trade expansion. Such an expansion would clearly represent a movement towards diversification of trade. It could also be part of a strategy to expand trade in the Asian-Pacific region which, in so far as it was done through planned, bilateral agreement, would enable Japan to become slightly less dependent on the vagaries of multilateral interdependence.

These considerations are of a rather general character. More concrete are Japanese aspirations to secure supplies of raw materials of which China already had considerable quantities and which optimists anticipate may be discovered in increasing quantities in the future. These materials include agricultural products, minerals and oil.[15]

255

A third, more intangible but still important force pushing the Japanese towards China, is the backwash of political reconciliation. Now that the long period of mutual isolation is over, the Japanese seem anxious to improve relations with China at every point. Enthusiasm is high. In outlining plans for a China Fair, the president of the Osaka Chamber of Commerce described China as: 'A large, dynamic, reborn nation' to which 'until the late eighteenth century, Japan had continued to owe almost its entire cultural development.'[16] This enthusiasm is, of course, shot through not only with hopes of economic gain but also with a sense of guilt for past Japanese actions in China. China's refusal to accept reparations has made a favourable trade policy the only way of assuaging this by economic means.

The power of the forces pulling China towards the Japanese economy is revealed by the rapidity with which trade has already grown in recent years. Table 5 illustrates the growth of trade from the low point of 1960.

Table 5: The Relative Importance of Sino-Japanese Trade to Each Partner, 1960–1985

	1960	1966	1971	1985 (est.)
Trade with Japan as percentage of total Chinese trade	0·6	15·5	19·6	40·0
Trade with China as percentage of total Japanese trade	0·2	3·2	2·1	4·0

Sources: As Table 3; F. H. Mah, *The Foreign Trade of Mainland China* (Edinburgh, University Press, 1972), p. 14; Hisao Kanamori, *Nihon keizai no shōrai*, pp. 232–3.

For much of the period 1960–71, the institutional and political conditions for trade were unpropitious. During the 1960s, trade was allowed by the Chinese to flow through two main channels. These were the *Liao-Takasaki* or Memorandum Trade, and the Friendly Firm Trade. Memorandum Trade was a device proposed by the Chinese to give a quasi-official status and stability to trade with Japan. It allowed each party to set up an official apparatus in the other's country, the first Memorandum agreement being for five years, starting in 1962. Thereafter agreements were annual and business negotiation was preceded by lengthy political argument. Although Memorandum Trade arrangements had great significance in terms of providing contact at a time when diplomatic relations did not exist, 90 per cent of trade was carried through the channel of Friendly Firm Trade. Under this arrangement, Chinese authorities dealt directly with firms, who were designated as being 'friendly' towards China and who had to subscribe to several sets of principles enunciated by the Chinese. This whole apparatus provided the Chinese with a valuable instrument for manipulating Japanese businessmen and conducting propaganda activities against the Sato government.[17] It is remarkable that trade continued to grow through these channels (with only a slight hesitation) in spite of intense political frictions arising from the Cultural Revolution and from Prime Minister Sato's visits to Taiwan and the United States in 1966 and 1967. The future level of trade is difficult to predict, but Japanese Ministry of Trade and Industry estimates have suggested that trade will grow for the rest of the 1970s at almost 20 per cent per annum. This is approximately twice the rate of growth projected for Chinese trade as a whole.[18]

The developments described above and the possibilities for Sino-Japanese trade in the future constitute an important departure from the recent past. It would however be a mistake to overestimate what it all means from the Japanese perspective. To begin with, there is a marked asymmetry in the significance of Sino-Japanese trade to the two partners. For while Japan is China's most important trading partner and will continue to be so, China accounts for only 2 per cent of current Japanese trade and even an expansion at the highest end of present predictions would only raise the share to about 4 per cent by the 1980s (see Table 5). In addition, both sides have significant policy constraints on the growth of mutual trade. On the Chinese side it is probable that even if significant credit is accepted—and current indications are that it will be—there will be a limit to how far the Chinese will wish to go. Given the large present Chinese deficit with Japan (see Table 6), it is possible that this limit will operate at a level that constrains trade to a rate of growth below that currently being forecast.[19]

Another policy constraint imposed by the Chinese is that of refusing to accept a 'colonial' structure of trade, that is, a structure which involves exporting raw materials in exchange for manufactured goods. In conjunction with the previous problems, this could be very important, because the obvious way to achieve a rapid expansion of trade would be for China to import, on credit, capital goods related to the mineral and agricultural sectors, and then to repay the loans with exports produced in these sectors. But this possibility will be restricted if China insists on too rapid a transformation in the structure of exports.

Japan too has several potential constraints on trade with China. One of the most sensitive of these is that future growth of trade with China would necessarily involve increases in agricultural imports. China already accounts for two-thirds of Japan's imports of farm

Table 6: Japan's Trade with China, 1960–1972 (millions U.S. dollars)

	EXPORTS TO CHINA	IMPORTS FROM CHINA	TOTAL	BALANCE OF TRADE
1960	2·7	20·7	23·4	− 18
1961	16·6	30·9	47·5	− 14·3
1962	38·5	46·0	84·5	− 7·4
1963	62·4	74·6	137·0	− 12·2
1964	152·7	157·9	310·5	− 5·1
1965	245·0	224·7	469·7	+ 20·3
1966	315·2	306·2	621·4	+ 9·0
1967	288·3	269·4	557·7	+ 18·9
1968	325·4	224·2	549·6	+101·2
1969	390·8	234·5	625·3	+156·3
1970	568·9	253·8	822·7	+315·1
1971	578·5	323·3	901·8	+255·2
1972	606·3	490·9	1,097·2	+115·4
1973				

Sources: *Nihon tōkei nenkan, 1971,* 'Japan-China Trade Eyes Large Expansion; Inter-Governmental Pact seen by Year end', *The Japan Economic Review* (15 March 1973); 'China's Foreign Trade in 1971', *Current Scene,* Vol. 10 (October 1972).

products and any future growth would not only add to the domestic political problems referred to earlier, but would also make the promised expansion of farm imports from the United States much more difficult.[20] Dramatic changes in imports from China would also accelerate the re-adjustment problems of the many small-scale firms in both the trading and manufacturing sectors.

The other factor which is going to affect Japan's attitude to trade with China is fear of antagonising trading partners of much greater economic and political significance. Even Taiwan is important here. Taiwan's total foreign trade is (incredibly enough) larger than that of the Chinese People's Republic and is growing much more rapidly. Japan's exports to Taiwan have increased from about parity with the People's Republic in the mid-1960s, to nearly double its level in 1972. Trade and investment naturally felt a certain impact from the diplomatic consequences of Japan's reconciliation with the People's Republic, but the legal and institutional obstacles to trade with Taiwan have been overcome by a sleight of hand comparable to that exercised on Sino-Japanese trade prior to 1972. Apart from Taiwan, the Japan-China trade will be subject to pressure from other important partners in the region, particularly South Korea and Indonesia.

The most serious threat of all to Japanese expansion of trade with China is that posed by the problems surrounding Japan's relations with the Soviet Union. At the political level, the Soviet Union is bound to oppose the Chinese diplomatic offensive to isolate the Soviet Union and has considerable capability for doing this. The military capacity of the Soviet Union is now superior in many respects to that of the United States and Western Europe. To Japan, with binding international commitments and strong domestic opposition to rearmament, the persuasive power of this capacity must be even more overwhelming. There is also the question of the return to Japan of the northern islands, on which at present the Soviet Union has made no significant concessions. On both these counts, the Soviet Union has considerable capacity to influence Japanese policy towards China.

The economic dimension to this triangular relationship arises from the fact that the Soviet Union and Japan have a strong mutual interest in economic co-operation. On the Soviet side, domestic economic problems are leading to a new approach to non-communist trading partners who, it is hoped, will be persuaded to enter large, long-term trade agreements involving the extension of credit.[21] Japan is one of the most promising partners in this respect, since she is well placed to provide the capital necessary to develop oil and other natural resources in Asiatic Russia which would, in the long run, be paid for by exports of these materials to Japan. As argued earlier, long-term, bilateral contracts of this kind for raw-material exploitation are most attractive to Japan. Thus in a sense, the Chinese and Russians are competing with each other for a new role in Japan's regionally oriented trade policy; and the Japanese will find that they cannot afford to go too far in foregoing substantive political and economic gains from closer relations with the Soviet Union, in exchange for the relatively small economic gains likely to arise from an improvement in relations with China.

THE IMPLICATIONS OF DOMESTIC ECONOMIC POLICY FOR FOREIGN TRADE

The relationship of domestic to foreign trade policy is far too large a topic to be dealt with in any detail here. But because there are a number of trends in domestic policy-thinking of immediate relevance to the issues discussed in earlier parts of this chapter, it is essential at least to mention briefly what these are.

In late 1973, the most urgent dilemma facing the policy-makers was the possible incompatibility between measures necessary to control inflation and the objective of reducing the current account strength of the balance of payments. We have already pointed out that, through its effect on price competitiveness, domestic inflation is likely to help *reduce* the trade surplus. If, however, measures to control inflation ultimately involve a sharp reduction in the rate of growth of the economy, we may expect a sharp *improvement* in the trade surplus due both to a reduction in demand for imported raw materials and to the stimulus to exporting that would be provided by the appearance of excess capacity and an increase in inventories. This relationship between internal and external equilibrium is an established feature of the post-war Japanese business cycle. But whereas in the past the favourable effects on the trade balance have occurred at a point fairly close to external balance, in 1973 or 1974 a sharp improvement might occur while the balance was still too favourable to Japan to be internationally acceptable.

If we move now from the short-term to the long-term problem, we have to ask the question: what are the implications of the idea— widely discussed in Japan—that the rate of growth of the economy should be reduced permanently, for example, by reducing the length and intensity of the working day. There is some evidence that such a measure might produce an enormous balance of payments surplus. One such piece of evidence is an important article by Houthaker and Magee in which they estimate income elasticities of demand for world exports. Briefly, this shows that in the Japanese case, the effect of a unit of growth in the world economy on the demand for Japanese exports is nearly three times as great as the effect on Japan's demand for imports resulting from a unit of Japanese growth. The implication of this is, that consideration of demand factors alone would lead one to the conclusion that equilibrium growth (in the sense of growth accompanied by trade balance) requires that Japan grows nearly three times as fast as the rest of the world![22] And it may indeed be the case that the balance achieved up to 1969 was the result of such a differential in growth performances. The conclusion that this suggests is that a slowing of Japan's growth, unless accompanied by a slowing of world growth, is likely to produce large trade surpluses. However, the incompatibility of trade and internal policy objectives may not be as stark as these data suggest. One reason for this is that the Houthaker, Magee study was based on data for the late 1960s and there are reasons for thinking that in the new climate of liberalisation and external contact of the 1970s, the income elasticity of demand for foreign goods may have altered. And it is certainly the case that imports as a share of total domestic consumption of manufactured goods are unexpectedly low in Japan—even by comparison with such a naturally self-sufficient economy as the United States.[23]

Supply considerations also suggest that the future relationship between growth and trade may be different from that of the past, and these considerations are closely linked to current policy proposals to alter the structure of the economy. One proposal is that the share of industry in future growth should be reduced in favour of an expansion of urban infrastructure and of social and welfare expenditures. Such a policy could be expected to reduce the growth of the supply of goods that are potentially exportable (or are substitutes for imports); and it would do this *without* reducing the growth in demand for imports that may be expected to follow future expansion of national product.[24]

The second policy proposal is, more precisely, a group of ideas concerning the actual composition of the industrial sector itself. These proposals are even more directly relevant to trade prospects than those mentioned above. One idea in this group is that the government should encourage a shift of exports from light industry to 'high value added' and 'knowledge intensive' industries. Since the types of industry referred to here are in fact relatively capital-intensive industries, this policy may be considered as one of encouraging changes that liberalisation and growth could be expected to bring about in any case. Rising relative labour costs and growing investment in human capital have already (as noted earlier) changed the nature of Japan's comparative advantage as an exporter; and the liberalisation of the home market will mean that the old export industries will no longer be able to survive even within the protected home market. A policy that accepts these trends and tries also to encourage a shift into those parts of the capital-intensive sector that do not have unwelcome environmental effects, is therefore a reasonable one. What is less reasonable and less realistic are related proposals to reduce *absolutely* the level of output of nine heavy industries thought to be major contributors to pollution. These industries include steel, oil refining, automobiles and chemicals.[25] It is difficult to see how these proposals could have much operational significance at the present time, since the nine industries include industries that are large and rapidly growing exporters. It seems unlikely that any government could pay the costs (in terms of real income foregone) that would result from a run-down of industries in which Japan has a real and increasing comparative advantage. Even a small beginning in this policy could have large effects on Japan's future in international trade.

CONCLUSION

This chapter has shown that the framework—both internal and external—within which Japan's foreign trade decisions have been made, is changing fundamentally. This framework has economic and political dimensions. Economically, the conflicts between a liberal, multilateral world and a more regionally polarised one are still being played out, and we cannot yet see how Japan will emerge in this process. On the domestic front it is economic development that is changing the premises on which policy decisions are to be made and which will lead ultimately to departure from past patterns of trade. If trade strategy were to be formulated on economic criteria alone, the choices of the policy-makers would be difficult enough. Japan's contemporary problem, however, is that basic changes in the economic and international relations spheres have coincided. Thus economically, the Chinese and the Russians are competing as rival, underdeveloped countries for Japan's credit and imports; America and China are competing as exporters of agricultural goods to Japan; and Japan and America are competing in East Asia for access to oil supplies. And all these economic rivalries and complementarities are interwoven with the readjustment of political relations that is following from the withdrawal of America from South-East Asia, from the emergence of Japan from American tutelage, and from the Chinese diplomatic offensive against the Soviet Union. What Japan must do in the 1970s is devise a trade strategy that satisfies the demands of her new political position without sacrificing indispensable supports of future economic growth.

POSTSCRIPT

This chapter was prepared before the autumn of 1973 and does not therefore take account of the worldwide economic and financial consequences of the rise in the price of crude oil. It appears, however, that in almost every important respect, the oil crisis will strengthen the significant currents in Japan's economic and foreign trade strategy, discerned and partly explained in the body of this chapter.

With regard to the question of the balance of trade, the oil price rise has accelerated the Japanese move into a deficit position. This has occurred partly as a direct consequence of the increased foreign exchange cost of oil and partly as a result of a further loss of competitiveness due to the general rise in Japanese prices. Indeed the net effect of the oil problem on the yen-dollar exchange rate has been a yen devaluation that has almost eliminated the losses suffered by the dollar from mid-1972 to mid-1973.

The influence of these developments on Japan's long-term strategy is less easily demonstrated, but the general effect seems bound to be to undermine the case for full multi-lateralism. In this chapter, I forecasted that bilateral trading arrangements with surplus countries such as Iran would probably grow in scale. The current trend towards bilateralism between Europe and the oil producers is bound to be reflected in similar Japanese ventures. Quite what the impact of the oil problem will be on the Asian pattern of trade is less clear. Indonesia will obviously remain an attractive trading partner, but the problems of the Chinese-Japanese-Soviet trade triangle may intensify. Both China and the Soviet Union are potential exporters of oil to Japan but in each case, there are serious technical obstacles to be overcome before either could account for a significant share of Japan's oil imports. Thus the Japanese will have to adopt strategy that allows them time to perceive which partner is likely to prove most rewarding in terms of this product.

The future of Japanese domestic economic policy will also reflect the oil problem. The impact of oil deflation has reduced the rate of growth for the fiscal year 1974–5 to $-1\cdot6\%$ and only moderate growth can now be in prospect for the latter half of the 1970s. One result of this will be to make even more costly and improbable, major changes in domestic policy that will have a high cost in terms of growth and international competitiveness. However, the full economic and political implications of this deceleration, if it materialises, may well prove more subtle and complex than anything we can envisage at the present time.

NOTES

Introduction

1 These questions (as well as others concerning economic development in the twentieth century) were discussed at the conference in a paper by Professor G. C. Allen, entitled 'Japan's Economic Development: Commercial, Financial and Technical Factors'. This paper has been published elsewhere.

2 The conference also discussed a paper entitled 'Japan and World Politics', in which Professor Johan Galtung considered the international implications of Japan's newfound strength. This paper has been published elsewhere.

Chapter 1

1 *Gunken seido*, a system of sub-prefectures and prefectures. See Inoue Kiyoshi, *Meiji ishinshi kenkyū kōza*, Vol. 4 (Tokyo, 1958), volume title *Nihon no gun-kokushugi*; Ishii Takashi, *Meiji ishin no kokusaiteki kankyō* (Tokyo, 1966). In English, Honjo Eijiro, *The Social and Economic History of Japan* (Kyoto, 1935), chapter on Léon Roches and Bakufu reforms (in which dates have not been converted to the Western calendar).

2 Lord Redesdale, *Memories* (London, 1915), Vol. 1, p. 395.

3 *The Modern History of Japan* (London, 1963), p. 97. See also, by the same author, *The Meiji Restoration* (Stanford, 1972).

4 Redesdale, op. cit., Vol. 2, p. 418.

5 Haraguchi Kiyoshi, *Boshin sensō* (Tokyo, 1963), p. 67. I do not always agree with Haraguchi, a former student of Tōyama Shigeki, but a veneer of Marxism has not prevented him from writing a carefully researched, accurate and useful study, with well-chosen excerpts from primary sources. Many hundreds of pages have been devoted to the civil war in a host of large-scale historical and biographical works in Japanese on this period, but this book is, as Haraguchi points out, the first study of the subject *per se*. Likewise, so far as I have been able to discover, this present paper (a by-product of a larger work on the last Shogun which this writer is beginning to work on) is the first historical analysis of the civil war in a Western language.

6 Ibid. Japanese dates have been changed to their equivalents in the Western calendar.

7 Ibid., pp. 67–8.

8 Ibid., p. 68. Haraguchi suggests that Iwakura's shift was affected by Yoshinobu's quick response on 11 January to a request for funds. From Osaka, Yoshinobu ordered Bakufu officials in Kyoto to deliver 1,000 *ryō* immediately, from Tokugawa domain revenues.

9 *Dai Nihon gaikō monjo* (Tokyo, 1936–49), Vol. 1, Pt. 1, pp. 169–73.

10 Haraguchi, op. cit., p. 68.

11 *Ōkubo Toshimichi monjo* (Tokyo, 1927–9), Vol. 2, p. 108. According to Satow, who reports a meeting which he and Mitford had with Terajima, all three agreed that the proposed notification to the effect that the Emperor had taken over the government, including the administration of foreign affairs, 'in the present undecided state of affairs would be premature'. Sir Ernest Satow, *A Diplomat in Japan* (London, 1921), p. 306. The reference to foreign laughter in Terajima's letter to Ōkubo may have been added by Terajima to give point to this by invoking the emotional force of shame, especially potent for the Japanese, particularly at that time.

12 *Nihon gendaishi I: Meiji ishin* (Tokyo, 1951), pp. 291–4.

13 Beasley, op. cit. (1972), p. 296.

14 Haraguchi, op. cit., p. 72; Hirao Michio, *Boshin sensōshi* (Tokyo, 1971), pp. 8–9. Haraguchi says about 10,000 pro-Tokugawa troops moved on Kyoto; Hirao says about 15,000.

15 One result was that for the first time it was possible for the new government not only to levy, but also to collect exactions from the important merchant houses of Osaka.

16 This account of the Toba-Fushimi hostilities is based on Hirao Michio, *Boshin sensōshi*, pp. 11–22. After the battle, Satow spoke to some Aizu participants who were wounded, and reports: 'They asserted that they would have beaten the enemy if they had been properly supported, but Tōdō had turned traitor at Yamazaki (on the right bank of the river, nearly opposite Yodo), which was the most important point of the defence, and Keiki's general Takenaga had gone over to the enemy at Yodo itself. Moreover, the drilled infantry were useless; if one man ran the rest followed like a flock of sheep (as we should say). They estimated the Satsuma force at the low figure of 1,000, but said the skirmishing of the enemy was very good, and they were armed with breech-loaders' (Satow, op. cit., pp. 314–15). As can be seen, this Aizu account is, understandably, somewhat biased, overstressing the importance of the turn-coating of Tōdō and Yodo, and scoffing overmuch at the Western-trained Bakufu units.

17 *Boshin nikki*, pp. 14, 42, cited in Haraguchi, op. cit., pp. 80, 86.

18 *Fukkoki* (Tokyo, 1929–31), Vol. 4, p. 609.

19 Haraguchi, op. cit., pp. 160–3.

20 Ibid., p. 87.

21 Ibid., p. 165.

22 Examples can be found in *Fukkoki*, Vol. 9, p. 660, and Vol. 11, p. 457.

23 The battle of Hakone is described in Hirao, op.cit., pp. 70–6.

24 Haraguchi, op. cit., p. 84. This is a good example of Japanese pragmatism of the type of the 'situational ethic', reminiscent of the division of military clans in the civil wars of the South-North Court Period (1336–92) to assure that they would be on the winning side, while making certain their nominally opposing members did not actually meet in combat.

25 *Boshin nikki*, p. 89.

26 Haraguchi, op. cit., pp. 99–100, note 13.

27 *Fukkoki*, Vol. 2 (2 March).

28 Haraguchi, op. cit., p. 95.

29 See Beasley, op. cit. (1972), pp. 297–8, and Gordon Daniels, 'The Japanese Civil War (1868)—a British View', *Modern Asian Studies*, Vol. 1 (July 1967), p. 263. This is an interesting presentation of observations of a British medical doctor on the northern campaign where he had been sent to care for the wounded. Gordon Daniels has also contributed a valuable article, 'The British Role in the Meiji Restoration: A Re-interpretive Note', *Modern Asian Studies*, Vol. 2 (October 1968), pp. 291–313, which refutes the usual oversimplification that while France supported the Bakufu, the British shifted their support to Chōshū and Satsuma. There are many Japanese eye-witness accounts, of which a recent ten-volume compilation is of particular interest and usefulness: *Bakumatsu ishin shiryō sōsho* (Tokyo, Jimbutsu Ōraisha, 1968–9). For the negotiations for the surrender of Edo, see Hirao, op. cit., pp. 46–52.

30 Haraguchi, op. cit., pp. 105–6.

31 Ibid., pp. 108–11; Hirao, op. cit., pp. 95 ff.

32 Ibid., pp. 112–13.

33 Ibid., p. 118.

34 Ibid., pp. 116–23, 127.

35 Ibid., pp. 206–9. The Ueno battle is described in Hirao, op. cit., pp. 53–62.

36 Ibid., pp. 210–11.
37 Ibid., p. 214.
38 Hirao, op. cit., p. 137; Haraguchi, op. cit., p. 230.
39 Haraguchi, op. cit., pp. 215, 234–5.
40 *Sendai hanki*, in *Fukkoki*, Vol. 12, pp. 386–7. Various parts of the country experienced depredations by bands falsely claiming to be Imperial troops, but it is not quite clear whether this refers to them or simply to properly Imperial but similarly 'unjust' soldiers.
41 Haraguchi, op. cit., pp. 233–5. Hirao lists 31 *han* as members of the 'Shiraishi alliance', an addition of six *han* who associated themselves with the alliance after 23 June. The total assessed yields of these 31 *han* equalled 1,886,000 *koku* (pp. 139–40). Adding Aizu (230,000) and Shōnai (140,000), the total becomes 2,256,000.
42 Ibid., pp. 191–7.
43 Ibid., pp. 236–9; *Sendai hanki*, in *Fukkoki*, Vol. 12, pp. 99–106, and *Fukkoki*, Vol. 7, p. 297. A letter from the government's chief of staff to the Kanagawa procurator accuses several named Japanese merchants from Yokohama of sailing with Snell to Niigata to trade in weapons (ibid., p. 297).
44 Haraguchi, op. cit., p. 239. The activities of the naval vessels under Enomoto in supporting the Shiraishi alliance are described in Hirao, op. cit., pp. 185 ff.
45 Ibid., pp. 240–2. Dr William Willis, from his observations in Aizu, describes it as very badly governed, and found much resentment against the *han* government among the heavily taxed peasantry. He succeeded in influencing the Imperial command in the northern campaign to stop the killing by Imperial troops of prisoners of war, and considered the Imperial army much more efficient and humane than their enemies. Daniels, 'The Japanese Civil War (1868)—a British View', op. cit. Comparing the behaviour of Imperial and enemy troops, my interpretation of the evidence differs from that of Haraguchi, who is much harder on the government troops than on the anti-government soldiers.
46 Ibid., pp. 245–6.
47 A term used by Inoue Kiyoshi, in *Nihon no gunkokushugi*.
48 Hirao, op. cit., pp. 10, 16.
49 Of a total number of government troops given in official records, 114,739, plus 400 non-combatants, 3,331 died in battle, plus 219 others dead (total: 3,550); seriously wounded, 3,845. Of these numbers, Satsuma troops totalled 7,306, of whom 514 died and 713 were wounded; Chōshū (total unknown): 427 died, 517 wounded; Tosa troops totalled 2,717, of whom 106 died and 168 were wounded. The far northern domain of Akita (*daimyo* Satake) which, after having refused aid to the government troops in mid-June, later went over to the government side, fielded more men even than Satsuma, a recorded 8,698, of whom 351 died, with an unknown number wounded.

Accurate figures for the pro-Tokugawa forces do not exist. Based on incomplete records, an estimate of 4,690 deaths makes a minimum total of 8,240 dead in the civil war. If unrecorded deaths and deaths of civilians are included, it is very possible that 10,000 would actually be nearer the mark. For the wounded, statistics for the pro-Tokugawa forces are too incomplete to permit an estimate which can claim any accuracy. But if the government totals for dead and wounded are taken as typical, roughly 20 per cent more wounded than dead, the total wounded in the civil war would come to perhaps about 12,000. Hirao, op. cit., p. 217. (Projection of conjectural totals author's own.)
50 *Nihonjin no hyakunen*, Vol. I, *Kindai Nihon no yoake* (Tokyo: Sekai Bunkasha, 1969), p. 132. Internal military struggles were not, of course, at an end in 1869. It may be of interest to compare these casualty statistics with those

of the most important of the samurai rebellions which followed: 'More than 60,000 imperial troops fought against the rebels and they suffered 16,000 casualties, 7,000 of these being combat deaths. Only a few hundred of the 30,000 Satsuma troops survived the conflict.' James H. Buck, 'The Satsuma Rebellion of 1877', *Monumenta Nipponica* XXVII, 4 (Winter 1973), p. 427.

51 Haraguchi, op. cit., pp. 255–60, citing the *Kōgisho nikki, Kenseihen shoshū*, in *Meiji bunka zenshū*, page numbers not cited. For details about the careful steps taken to abolish the domains, see Beasley, op. cit. (1972), pp. 326–49.

52 On Yamagata, and the importance of the civil war in furthering his career, see Roger F. Hackett, *Yamagata Aritomo in the Rise of Modern Japan, 1838–1922* (Harvard, 1971). There are several references in Hirao to the important role played by Itagaki Taisuke, first in deciding Tosa to join battle on the side of Satsuma at Toba-Fushimi, and then as a staff officer in the northern campaign.

Chapter 2

1 The *Kaigai shinbun* was being published in the foreign settlement by Joseph Heco, a castaway who had reached the United States where he had been educated, converted to Christianity and given American citizenship. As the name suggests, the *Kaigai shinbun* offered foreign news, which was translated from English newspapers. It was Heco's intention, at least, to publish his newspaper about twice a month. Heco did not indicate the publication date on any of his issues. At the head of each issue, he informed his readers of the arrival date of the ship that brought the newspapers serving as his source. The earliest issue was translated from newspapers that reached Yokohama in an English vessel in Genji 2–3–13, which corresponds to 8 April 1865. In the modern printed edition of the *Kaigai shinbun* (in the *Bakumatsu Meiji shinbun zenshū* (hereafter cited as *BMSZ*), Vol. 2), the last issue, the twenty-fourth, is based upon newspapers brought by an English ship that reached Yokohama in Keio 2–8–25 (3 October 1866). The 1865 date of the initial issue differs from the one reported in Heco's *Narrative of a Japanese* (Vol. 2, p. 53), namely 28 June 1864. A number of hypotheses have been suggested to cope with the problem thereby created. Those interested in pursuing the points under dispute might start with the bibliographical note by Ishii Kendō in *BMSZ*, Vol. 2, pp. 5–12; Ono Hideo, 'Heco no "Kaigai shinbun" ni tsuite', *Shinkyū jidai*, Vol. 1, No. 1 (February 1925), pp. 29–35; and Chikamori Haruyoshi, *Joseph Heco* (Tokyo, 1963).

2 The first issue of the paper is a rarity and I have never seen it. I depend for my dating on a letter sent from Nagasaki on 28 June 1861 by Guido Verbeck who told his correspondent: '. . . Last week the first number of the *Nagasaki Shipping List and Advertiser* was published.' (The letter is in the Verbeck Papers kept in the Gardner A. Sage Library, New Brunswick Theological Seminary, New Brunswick, New Jersey, U.S.A.) Ebihara Hachirō, whose book, *Nihon ōji shinbun zasshishi*, is a study of the early foreign language press in Japan, gives the date as Bunkyū 1–6–22 which corresponds to 27 July 1861 (see p. 15). Since there is no reason to doubt Verbeck's reliability on this point, it appears that Ebihara has given the 22 June date, which confirms Verbeck, in the Japanese calendar rather than in the Western Gregorian calendar.

3 Ebihara, op. cit., and Robert M. Spaulding, Jr, *Bibliography of Western-Language Dailies and Weeklies in Japan, 1861–1961* (mimeographed, n.d., n.p.).

4 From mid-1863, Bakufu translators had been scanning the Yokohama foreign press for the information of senior officials. The Yokohama papers, besides being written in the language of the country that loomed largest diplomatically on Japan's horizon, had the advantage of being obtainable close at hand. The practice of translating from them began at this time because a

military-diplomatic crisis had enveloped Tokugawa relations with England after Satsuma samurai had cut down Charles Richardson, a British visitor from Shanghai, in September 1862. By the end of March 1863, a force of British warships was assembled at Yokohama and in the late spring, it was widely anticipated that hostilities would soon break out. The translations have been reprinted in *BMZS*, Vol. 1.

5   Press reports of the Hibiya park riot and events leading up to it are reproduced in Nakayama Yasumasa (ed.), *Shinbun shūsei Meiji hennenshi*, Vol. 12, pp. 477 ff. A full treatment of the anti-peace treaty movement can be found in Chapter 7 of Okamoto Shumpei, *The Japanese Oligarchy and the Russo-Japanese War* (New York and London, 1970).

6   Eric W. Allen, 'International Origins of the Newspapers: The Establishment of Periodicity in Print', *Journalism Quarterly*, Vol. 7 (1930), p. 310.

7   The civil war *shinbunshi* are reprinted in *BMSZ*, Vols 3–5, and *Meiji bunka zenshū* (Tokyo, 1928; hereafter cited as *MBZ*), Vol. 17. On the word *shinbunshi*, Ono Hideo, 'Waga kuni shoki no shinbun to sono bunken ni tsuite', *MBZ*, Vol. 17, kaidai, p. 3; Suzuki Hidesaburō, *Honpō shinbun no kigen* (Kyoto, 1959), Chap. 1; and Roswell S. Britton, *The Chinese Periodical Press, 1800–1912* (Shanghai, 1933), pp. 5–6.

8   Ono Hideo, *Kawaraban monogatari* (Tokyo, 1960).

9   Britton, op. cit., Chap. 1.

10   Allen, op. cit., p. 318.

11   Marius B. Jansen (ed.), *Changing Japanese Attitudes towards Modernization* (Princeton, 1965), p. 24.

12   The reports of the Ikeda mission are reprinted in *Bakumatsu ishin gaikō shiryō shūsei* (Tokyo, 1942–4), Vol. 6, pp. 141–50. The other reports recommended that the Bakufu enter into treaty relations with European and Asian countries, that students be sent abroad and that Japanese be permitted to trade with and travel to foreign countries.

13   *BMSZ*, Vol. 3, p. 211.

14   Ibid., p. 236.

15   Ibid., p. 132.

16   Ibid., p. 188.

17   The *Shinbunshi inkō jōrei* are reprinted in the *Chūgai shinbun*, No. 1 (18 April 1869), *MBZ*, Vol. 17, p. 369.

18   Takayanagi Shinzō, Ishii Ryōsuke (eds), *Ofuregaki Kanpō shūsei* (Tokyo, 1958), Item 2,020.

19   Mori Wataru, 'Meiji gannen Fukuchi Ōchi gokuchu benmeisho', *Bungaku* (1968), Vol. 36, No. 11, pp. 1,340–5. Fukuchi's memoirs of his career as a journalist, *Shinbunshi jitsureki*, published in 1894, are reprinted in *MBZ*, Vol. 17.

20   Ōtsuki Fumihiko, *Mitsukuri Rinshō kun den* (Tokyo, 1907), p. 69.

21   For example, in June 1872, Tokyo journalists were for the first time permitted to attend court hearings and report them in the press: *Gendai nihon bungaku dainenpyō* (Tokyo, 1931), p. 11. Three years later, on 22 February 1875, Dajōkan decree No. 30 permitted the public to attend hearings of civil suits. On 9 June 1873, the government's revenue and expenditure were made public for the first time: Hioki Shōichi, *Bunka dainenpyō* (Tokyo, 1955), Vol. 5, p. 260.

22   *Hōki bunrui taizen*, Dai ippen, monjo mon, shuppan, pp. 405–6. Nishida Taketoshi expresses the opinion that although the instructions were issued to the Kyoto authorities, they very likely had a general application throughout Japan: Nishida, *Meiji jidai no shinbun to zasshi* (Tokyo, 1961), p. 38.

23   Kido's letter to Shinagawa Yajirō, 28 January 1871, *Kido Kōin monjo*, Vol. 4, pp. 161–3. Part of this letter is quoted in Tsumagi Chūta, *Shōgiku Kido*

kō den (Tokyo, 1927), Vol. 2, pp. 1,395–7. It is translated into English in Tsunoda Ryusaku *et al.* (eds), *Sources of Japanese Tradition* (New York, 1958), p. 652. A part of the letter is also reprinted in Nishida Taketoshi's bibliographical notes in *BMSZ*, Vol. 6 (Part 1). Kido himself wrote very little about the *Shinbun zasshi* and what there is, is quoted in Tsumagi and in Nishida. The first 60 issues of the *Shinbun zasshi* (of a total of 357) are reprinted in *BMSZ*, Vol. 6 (Part 1) and Vol. 6 (Part 2).

24 Diary entry for 5 April 1871, quoted in Tsumagi, op. cit., p. 1,397.

25 Ōtsu Junichirō, *Dai nihon kenseishi*, Vol. 2, p. 284.

26 The scanty information about Kido's assistants can be found in Nishida's bibliographical notes in *BMSZ*, Vol. 6 (Parts 1 and 2) and in Nishida, op. cit., p. 26.

27 Nishida, *Meiji jidai no shinbun to zasshi*, op. cit., p. 25.

28 'Yamanashi ken shinbunshi', in Nihon shinbun kyōkai, *Chihō betsu Nihon shinbunshi*, p. 213. The first issue of the *Kyōchū shinbun* is reproduced in Miyatake Gaikotsu, *Bunmei kaika: shinbun hen* (Tokyo, 1925), pp. 81 ff. (Unless otherwise noted, references in the text to prefectural *shinbunshi* can be found in *Chihō betsu Nihon shinbunshi*.)

29 The text of the decree is reprinted in Nakayama Yasumasa (ed.), *Shinbun shūsei Meiji hennenshi* (Tokyo, 1936), Vol. 1, pp. 496–7. The *Kyōchū shinbun* report of the riot is on pp. 517–21.

30 Tokutomi Sohō, 'Shinbun oyobi shinbun kisha no hensen', which is Vol. 10 of the *Sohō sōsho* (Tokyo, 1929), pp. 80–5.

Chapter 3

1 Itō Takashi, *Shōwa shoki seijishi kenkyū* (Tokyo, Tōdai shuppankai, 1969), pp. 127–33.

2 A good official account of naval expansion plans is given in *Yamamoto Gombei to kaigun* (Tokyo, Hara Shobō, 1966), pp. 405–30.

3 *The Times* (9 December 1920).

4 Oka Yoshitake, *Tenkanki no Taishō* (Tokyo, Tōdai shuppankai, 1969), pp. 168 ff.

5 Public Record Office, Foreign Office 371/6701 [F 2333], Eliot to Curzon (25 May 1921).

6 Library of Congress microfilm. Japanese War Ministry archives, R 101 F 07122 (T534), 'Beikoku gumbi no waga kokubō ni oyobosu eikyō', memo by Major General Sugano Naoichi (December 1918).

7 Cf. W. R. Braisted, *The United States Navy in the Pacific, 1909–22* (Austin, Texas, 1971), pp. 537–9.

8 *The Times* (9 December 1920).

9 *Kokumin shinbun* (9 April 1921); Public Record Office, Foreign Office 371/6678 [F 1872], Eliot to Curzon (16 April 1921).

10 *Japan Advertiser* (23 January 1921).

11 *Taiheiyō sensō e no michi* (Tokyo, Asahi, 1963), Vol. viii, pp. 3–7, memo by Katō Tomosaburō (27 December 1921) (work hereafter cited as *TSM*).

12 Public Record Office, Foreign Office 371/6701 [F 2333], Eliot to Curzon (25 May 1921).

13 *Gaimushō no 100-nen* (Tokyo, Hara Shobō, 1969), Vol. 1, p. 816. For advance discussions, see ibid., pp. 810–17. It should be remembered that it looked beforehand as though army reduction would also be at issue.

14 *Gaimushō no 100-nen*, Vol. 1, pp. 820–1; *Shidehara Kijurō* (Tokyo, Shidehara Heiwa Zaidan, 1955), pp. 208–15.

15 *Katō Kanji Taishō den* (Tokyo, Katō Kanji Denki Hensankai, 1941), pp. 709–27. I shall generally refer to Katō Tomosaburō hereafter as 'Baron Katō'. This usage has been adopted not out of lowly deference to his aristocratic title, but in order to distinguish him from Katō Kanji, who had not been similarly ennobled.

16 Cf. Fukai Eigo, *Kaiko 70-nen* (Tokyo, Iwanami, 1941), pp. 163–4.

17 *Shidehara Kijurō*, p. 207.

18 Ibid., pp. 207–8.

19 (Sir) Arthur Willert, *Washington and Other Memories* (London, 1972), p. 153, reflects a common attitude by describing the Washington Conference as 'a showpiece of Anglo-American co-operation'.

20 Ibid., p. 154.

21 Arthur, Lord Lee of Fareham, *A Good Innings*, 3 vols (privately printed, 1939), Vol. 2, Chap. 30.

22 Willert, op. cit., p. 156.

23 Braisted, op. cit., pp. 598–9.

24 Ichihashi Yamato, *The Washington Conference and After* (Palo Alto, 1928), p. 40.

25 *Settsu* was one of two Dreadnought battleships of 21,000 tons laid down in 1909.

26 *TSM*, Vol. 8, pp. 3–4, memorandum of 27 December 1921.

27 Arai Tatsuo, *Katō Tomosaburō* (Tokyo, Jiji tsushinsha, 1958), pp. 66–7; *Gaimushō no 100-nen*, Vol. 1, pp. 833–4.

28 *Katō Kanji den*, pp. 761 ff.

29 Ichihashi, op. cit., p. 83.

30 See *TSM*, Vol. 8, pp. 3–7.

31 'Probability' is used in English in the Japanese text. But is it 'possibility' that is intended?

32 Arai, op. cit., pp. 79–80.

33 Cf. the opinion of Ichihashi, op. cit., pp. 85–6: 'Kato was made a "victim" of domestic politics. He must have felt keenly the loss of the late Premier Hara, who would undoubtedly have saved him from such an embarrassment. Premier Takahashi was not the statesman to win over the members of the Privy Council or those of the Foreign Affairs Advisory Council, the real authors of the instructions. Baron Katō intimated to the writer even the names of the men who were working against him.'

34 *Katō Kanji den*, pp. 745–60, especially pp. 758–9.

Chapter 4

1 See for instance, Inoue Kiyoshi, *Nihon no rekishi* (Tokyo, Iwanami Shinsho, 1966); Robert A. Scalapino, *Democracy and the Party Movement in Pre-war Japan* (Berkeley, University of California Press, 1962); James W. Morley, *Dilemmas of Growth in Pre-War Japan* (Princeton, Princeton University Press, 1971).

2 For instance, Takeyama Michio, *Shōwa seishin-shi* (Tokyo, Shinchōsha, 1956); Hayashi Fusao, *Daitōa sensō kōteiron* (Tokyo, 1964).

3 For instance, James B. Crowley, *Japan's Quest for Autonomy* (Princeton, Princeton University Press, 1966); Richard H. Minear, *Victors' Justice* (Princeton, Princeton University Press, 1971).

4 Hugh Byas, *The Japanese Enemy, His Power and His Vulnerability* (New York, Knopf, 1942), pp. vii–viii.

5 Hugh Byas, *Government by Assassination* (New York, Knopf, 1942), pp. 13, 226.

6 John K. Fairbank, Edwin O. Reischauer and Albert M. Craig, *East Asia. The Modern Transformation* (Boston, Houghton Mifflin, 1965), p. 588.

7   Edwin O. Reischauer, 'What Went Wrong?', in Morley, op. cit., pp. 507–8. Italics are mine (B.S.).
8   As related by an eye-witness. For instance, Sir Vere Redman, 'Rebellion on a Snowy Morning', *The Japan Times* (25 February 1966).
9   William Henry Chamberlin, *Japan Over Asia* (Garden City, Blue Ribbon Books, 1942), p. 258.
10   Joseph C. Grew, *Ten Years in Japan* (New York, Simon and Schuster, 1944), p. 177.
11   Suzuki Hajime, *Tennō sama no sain* (Tokyo, Mainichi Shinbunsha, 1962), p. 197. The victim was Suzuki Kantarō, who later recovered from his wounds and was prime minister of Japan at the end of the Second World War. See also Ben-Ami Shillony, *Revolt in Japan* (Princeton, Princeton University Press, 1973), p. 138.
12   Crowley, op. cit., p. 384. Italics are mine (B.S.).
13   Especially by Paul W. Schroeder, *The Axis Alliance and Japanese-American Relations, 1941* (Ithaca and London, Cornell University Press, 1958); and recently, in even stronger terms, by Richard H. Minear, op. cit.
14   Byas, *Government by Assassination*, pp. 41–4.
15   Imamura Hitoshi, *Daigeki-sen* (Tokyo, Jiyū Ajia-sha, 1960), pp. 40–1.
16   *The Osaka Mainichi and the Tokyo Nichi Nichi* (3 March 1936), p. 4.
17   For instance, 'Ni ni roku jiken no nazo o toku', *Kaizō* (February 1951), p. 157; Kōno Tsukasa, *Yugawara shugeki* (Tokyo, Nihon Shūhōsha, 1965), p. 186. Konoe later claimed that the Kōdōha might have saved Japan from the Pacific War. As quoted in Crowley, op. cit., p. 323.
18   John Toland, *The Rising Sun* (New York, Random House, 1970), p. 36; David Bergamini, *Japan's Imperial Conspiracy* (New York, William Morrow, 1971), p. 621.
19   Mishima Yukio, *Eirei no koe* (Tokyo, Kawade Shobō, 1970), pp. 223–4, 229.
20   Mishima Yukio, 'Nihon-shugi chimidoro no saigo', *Shūkan Yomiuri* (23 February 1968), p. 12.
21   An English translation of the story is found in Yukio Mishima, *Death in Midsummer and Other Stories*, translated by Geoffrey W. Sargent (New York, New Directions, 1966), pp. 93–118.
22   Kōno Tsukasa, *Ni ni roku jiken to Mishima Yukio-shi*, published by the author (Tokyo, 15 February 1971), p. 7.
23   For the controversy surrounding Nonaka's death, see: Saitō Ryū, *Ni ni roku* (Tokyo, Kaizōsha, 1951), p. 203; Isobe Asaichi, 'Kōdōki', in Kōno Tsukasa, *Ni ni roku jiken* (Tokyo, Nihon Shūhōsha, 1957), p. 90; 'Ni ni roku jiken no nazo o toku', *Kaizō* (February 1951), p. 162. See also, Shillony, op. cit., p. 196.
24   Criticism of the rebels for having failed to live up to Bushidō was voiced after the rebellion by the chief of staff of the First Division: Kōno, op. cit., p. 448.

Chapter 5

1   A useful guide to the work of Japanese local historians is the three volumes by Furushima Toshio (ed.), *Chihō Shi Kenkyū no Genjo* (*The Present State of Local History Studies*) (Tokyo, 1968). In Akita the Akita Kindai Shi Kenkyūkai publishes the *Akita Kindai Shi Kenyū* (*Akita Modern History Studies*) annually, and in 1968 produced *Kindai Akita no Rekishi to Minshū* (*Modern Akita: History and People*), a valuable introduction which focuses on social change and the growth of class consciousness. A more detailed study is planned. More official in character are the sixteen-volume prefectural history, the *Akita Ken Shi*,

NOTES

issued by Akita Ken (Akita 1960–6), and the two-volume *Akita Ken Seishi* (*Political History of Akita Prefecture*), compiled by the Akita Ken Gikai Akita Ken Seishi Hensan Iinkai (Akita, 1955); but, as is often the case, these works are less comprehensive for the last half-century than for preceding periods.

2 *Kindai Akita no Rekishi to Minshū*, Appendix, Chart 6.

3 Ibid., p. 161. The figure for the former category was still 61·49 per cent in 1933, when it exceeded that of any other Tōhoku prefecture: *1936 Kahoku Nenkan* (*Yearbook of the Kahoku Shimpō of Sendai*), p. 160. In 1931, 57,458 taxpayers were unable to pay on time, and by the following year the amount of debt owed by Akita farmers was 177,000,000 yen, the highest per household in Tōhoku and four times the value of all agricultural production in Akita in 1932: *Kindai Akita no Rekishi to Minshū*, p. 161.

4 *Akita Sakigake Shimpō* (25 March 1930). Hereafter cited as *Sakigake*.

5 *Kindai Akita no Rekishi to Minshū*, Appendix, Chart 12.

6 Ibid., p. 158.

7 *1936 Kahoku Nenkan*, p. 135.

8 Ibid., p. 132.

9 *Kindai Akita no Rekishi to Minshu*, Appendix, Chart 5. 1 *chō* = approximately 1 hectare or 2·45 acres.

10 See especially the *Sakigake* editorial of 10 January 1936, in which this famous phrase is invoked as a conclusive argument against bureaucratic domination. The attachment of the editor, Andō Wafū, to representative government stretched back more than half a century.

11 The number of election offences was easily the highest in the Tōhoku region in 1930, i.e. 778. The national total was 14,242. Over 90 per cent involved vote-buying. *Sakigake* (22 April 1930).

12 *Sakigake* (23 February 1932). The other three were Inukai, Adachi and Ozaki.

13 He happened to be partly incapacitated from an accident, as well as under criminal investigation, but these were probably not the real reasons for his non-selection.

14 *Sakigake* (4 and 6 February 1932). Tsuchida Mansuke, Akita's elected member of the House of Peers, had apparently pledged his support to Soeda, an old friend and sometime business associate.

15 On 18 February 1932 the *Sakigake* described Inomata's problem on the occasion of the latter's visit of respect to his ex-patron's grave three days before the election. Between 1930 and 1932 a split had developed between him and Sakakida's son and ex-supporters, but no explanation was offered by the paper. Details of voting figures for Akita elections 1928–42 are given in the Appendix to this article, pp. 110–12.

16 See, for example, the report in the *Sakigake* of 25 January 1936 headed 'Strong Opposition of New Men to Precedence of Previous Representatives'.

17 In 1930 the size of the electorate in each *gun* was as follows: 1st electoral district—Minami Akita 27,895, Kita Akita 25,219, Yamamoto 20,923, Katsuno 11,115, Kawabe, 8,097, Akita city 8,319. 2nd electoral district—Semboku 30,561, Yuri 23,020, Hiraka 21,954, Ogachi 19,352.

18 *Sakigake* (24 January 1932).

19 He became Minister of Justice after the election anyway.

20 *Sakigake* (24 January 1932). Though apparently ambitious, Akashi was not a party member.

21 Ibid. (26, 28 and 29 January 1932).

22 *Sakigake* (28 January and 6 February 1932). On Ikeda, see the short biography in Akita Ken Sōmubu Hisho Kohōka, *Akita no Senkaku* (Akita, 1969), Vol. 2, pp. 335–51; also *Akita Ken Shi*, Vol. 6, p. 31.

23 *Sakigake* (29 January 1932). Ikeda attended this meeting, but previously it had been suggested that he was fed up with politics and lacked campaign funds. Ibid. (28 January 1932).

24 Ibid. (3 February 1932). It was reported in the same issue that in an attempt to overcome the difficulties of distance and communication, the branch office of the party was moved to Kawamura's residence in Tokyo, but, as will be seen, this did not solve the problem. For so much of the selection process to take place outside Akita was untypical, and is probably to be explained by the need to gain the full approval of central headquarters if the benefits of belonging to the party in power were to be fully enjoyed. See also ibid. (31 January 1932). The account given here of the events of the next two weeks is also based on *Sakigake*, especially the issues of 5, 6, 8, 9, 10, 12 and 13 February.

25 However, Sugimoto again had serious doubts about standing on 11 February because of campaign expense difficulties, and the question was only finally settled after the pro-Seiyūkai prefectural governor, Uchida Takashi, paid a surreptitious visit to Tokyo. Ibid. (14 February 1932).

26 The exact methods by which *yūryokusha* delivered votes was never entered into by the *Sakigake*, although it did on one occasion comment that: 'Instead of individual house-visiting, it would be more rational for *yūryokusha* to make public speeches of policy agreement' (11 February 1930). One must assume that as landlords *yūryokusha* were in a position to exert irresistible pressure on their tenants, though in an uncertain number of cases the promise of a vote may have been regarded as the repayment of a favour. Whatever the means, it is clear that many *yūryokusha* could guarantee a block of votes. For example, in Tateai, the home village of the Tsuchida family, Tsuchida Sōsuke secured 346 out of 425 votes in 1937 (the remainder going almost entirely to the proletarian candidate). *Sakigake* (6 May 1937). The fact that election returns were recorded not just for the whole electoral district but for each town and village made it possible for an approximate check to be made by *yūryokusha* despite the secrecy of the ballot.

27 *Sakigake* (15 February 1930; 13 February 1932).

28 *Sakigake* (2 February 1932). The official limits were based on the number of electors per member. They were reduced in 1936.

29 *Akita Ken Seishi*, Vol. 1, p. 672. Record of interview with Arthur Tiedemann in 1951.

30 In a contribution entitled 'Senkyo Shukusei to Chihō Jichi', in *Shimin* (August 1935). Mizuno added that probably not more than ten candidates in either of the major parties could afford the cost of election from their own pockets.

31 *Akita Jānaru* (1 October 1968).

32 *Sakigake* (14 April 1937).

33 Ibid. (21 February 1930).

34 Ibid. (4 May 1937).

35 Ibid. (10 February 1936). The struggle between Kawamata, who was based on Yokote in Hiraka *gun* and was the leader of the peasant movement in Akita, and Tsuchida Sōsuke, the heir to the 'Tsuchida kingdom' in southern Akita, was considered the most interesting aspect of the election in the second district.

36 Ibid. (8 February 1930). In 1930 the movement for women's electoral rights was strong, and there were forty women's societies in Akita. Shida's wife was a leader in the movement. On the Seiyūkai side, Suzuki, a lawyer by profession, was known to have cultivated bureaucrats, teachers and railway staff, and had 'recorded in the recesses of his brain the electors in every household' in Akita city. Ibid. (13 February 1932).

37 Examples of these, and an array of other military terms, are too numerous to

cite. On one occasion, however, the metaphor was changed and an unusual note of humour introduced, when a national list of candidates was drawn up, divided as in *Sumō*, into East and West, with Ozaki Yukio and Inukai Ki given the distinction of *yokozuna*, and the rest ranked below in accordance with the number of successful campaigns fought. Ibid. (14 February 1932).

38 Some illustrations of this practice are given in the prefectural police history, *Akita Ken Keisatsu Shi*, Vol. 2, pp. 56–7. The extent of official partiality should not be exaggerated, however. Although, according to one account, in 1930, when there was a Minseitō government, Seiyūkai election offences outnumbered Minseitō by 7,905 to 3,647, the ratio was not so high as in 1928, when the Seiyūkai was in power and was responsible for 4,596 offences against the Minseitō's 1,920: Koyama Matsukichi, 'Senkyo burōkā no kenkyo to keisatsukan', *Shimin* (August 1935), p. 17. The figures given here for 1930 differ from those in the *Akita Sakigake Shimpō* (22 April 1930), where the Seiyūkai is credited with 8,543 and the Minseitō with 3,470.

39 In 1930 only 538 Minseitō supporters were actually prosecuted, compared with 2,825 Seiyūkai offenders: Koyama, loc. cit.

40 Interview (25 April 1972).

41 *Akita Jānaru* (1 October 1968).

42 See *Sakigake* issues of 2, 5, 7, 13, 14, 18 and 20 February 1932.

43 On 20 February 1932, the *Sakigake* also commented that he had paid no attention to his public duties for a fortnight.

44 Lists of taxpayers eligible to vote in elections to the House of Peers were published every seven years for each prefecture. Since taxes were divided into three categories—land, business and income—and since the land tax was broken down into the various villages in which land was owned, these lists represent a valuable source for tracing changes in fortune and patterns of land-ownership in Japan after 1890. The value of such *jinushi meibō* is discussed in an article by Taguchi Katsuichirō, 'Shōwa Jūyonen Rokugatsu Tsuitachi Chō, Kizokuin Tagaku Nozeisha Giin Gosenjin Meibō ni Tsuite', *Akita Kindai Shi Kenkyū*, Vol. 13 (1967). From the examples given by Taguchi, it transpires that Oyamada's fears were not realised. By 1938 he had risen to tenth place. In addition to these official registers there exist also commercially published lists of taxpayers—a sort of prefectural *Who's Who*—including even those paying as little as five yen. One such list is among the papers of the Tsuchida family microfilmed by the *Kindai Rippō Katei Kenkyūkai*, which has in recent years been engaged in the collection of private materials relating to modern Japanese constitutional history under the auspices of the Law Faculty of Tokyo University.

45 According to the *Sakigake* (15 February 1932), Sugimoto had 'made big' in the lumber industry, which was important in Akita.

46 *Akita Ken Seishi*, Vol. 1, p. 672.

47 According to *Sakigake* (18 January 1936), 495 *buraku* (hamlets) had established *bōhan kumiai* (organised groups for the prevention of offences). On 6 February 1936, it reported that the government had spent three million yen distributing posters attacking election corruption.

48 *Akita Ken Keisatsu Shi*, Vol. 2, p. 60. 202 persons were involved. In 1937 the figures were twenty-two offences and sixty-seven offenders. The Tsuchida family documents contain a detailed breakdown of expenditures of Tsuchida Sōsuke in the 1936 election, but unfortunately this list is only a copy of the one which he, like all candidates, had to furnish to the governor. It is difficult to credit the amount of 6,152 yen, which was all Tsuchida admitted to, the more so because members of his family were suspected, though not charged, by the police of buying a village representative for 200 yen. Tsuchida's residence was searched during the investigation. See *Sakigake* (18, 21 and 23 February 1936).

49   There was some sign of this in the prefectural assembly election of September 1935, when an unusually large number of unendorsed candidates stood, several with success. *Akita Ken Seishi*, Vol. 1, p. 760. In the 1939 prefectural election candidates are reported to have campaigned as individuals without putting forward a party programme. Ibid., p. 778.

50   It is impossible to assess the relative importance in local politicians' motivation of personal rivalry and concern with prestige on the one hand and a desire to promote the economic development of the prefecture on the other. It is clear from newspaper reports, the five-volume work on the shapers of modern Akita, *Akita no Senkaku*, and the *Akita Ken Seishi* that local politicians of both parties shared the view, regardless of whether official party policy proclaimed the need for retrenchment, that it was vital for the government to spend more money on Tōhoku in general and Akita in particular. It may well have been this common sense of priorities which reduced the significance of policy differences during elections and allowed greater emphasis on personal and *gun* rivalries. I have, however, come across no suggestion in newspaper coverage of elections that voting preferences were influenced in favour of the party in power by the expectation that it would maintain control of the cabinet and favour its areas of support with government funds.

51   Of the candidates put forward by the Taisei Yokusankai 213 were new, compared with 253 previous members. *Kahoku Shimpō* (4 May 1942). This proportion of fresh blood was much the same as in Akita, where in addition to Machida, Shida, Nakada and Oyamada, the official list included three newcomers to national elections—Futada Zeigi, Fujihi Ryōji and Saitō Kenzō. Only the last-named, however, had not been a prefectural assembly member.

52   In addition there were three other candidates—the perennial Kon Sakunosuke, the ex-proletarian lawyer, Furusawa Ayaru, by this time a member of the *Tōhōkai*, and Hatakeyama Jūyū, a company employee who had not been prominent in prefectural politics, but was to be a Minshūtō member of the Diet from 1949 to 1952.

53   This information comes from a pamphlet in the collection of documents belonging to Shioda Dampei, now in the *Kindai Rippō Katei Kenkyūkai* collection in the Meiji Shimbun Zasshi Bunko at Tokyo University.

54   *Akita Jānaru* (1 October 1968).

55   In February 1936, for instance, the Akita branch is recorded as having received from headquarters 2,500 posters proclaiming 'Make manifest the military spirit in the election!'. *Sakigake* (5 February 1936). The nearest thing to a voting recommendation was a reader's letter from a member advocating the selection by the local reservists of a candidate from their own number. Ibid., (16 January 1936). It seems significant that the writer should need to use a liberal newspaper for his purpose. There are some indications that the local leadership of the Zaigō Gunjinkai was dominated by landlord families.

56   In 1932, apart from Akashi Tokuichiro, three bureaucrats were considered. All had left the prefecture to follow careers elsewhere. In 1936 one was mentioned again, together with another Akita native, a Professor Tani of Nihon University. In 1937 only a single name cropped up.

57   According to Katano, there was no formal party organisation in the *gun*, only clubs or similar associations. *Akita Ken Seishi*, Vol. 1, p. 668.

58   Katano mentions 300 Seiyūkai members (paying dues of 200–300 yen a year). Ibid., pp. 668, 672. The Tsuchida documents contain a detailed list of Minseitō members in Hiraka amounting to 366 names.

59   The Tsuchida's correspondence includes letters from Katō Kōmei, Wakatsuki Reijirō, Nagai Ryūtarō, etc., and they were interested in agriculture, especially horse-breeding, on a national level. Shida was related to Wakatsuki by

marriage, and was interested in relations with Russia, national parks, and the political rights of women, Koreans and Taiwanese. Such examples were probably not untypical.

60 *Sakigake* (17 April 1937).

61 See for example, the letter from 'A new elector' (10 September 1931), and the leader entitled 'Politics and Youth' (18 February 1936).

62 Ibid. (14 January 1936); *Akita Ken Seishi*, Vol. 1, pp. 754–5. In 1936 Suzuki Ankō left the Seiyūkai, but his action was clearly influenced by failure to secure the party endorsement he sought. He certainly did not turn his back on politics completely, for in 1937 he surprisingly campaigned on Tsuchida's behalf, stating that the premature dissolution of the Diet was wrong and that existing members should be returned. The statement loses some of its force, unfortunately, in the light of reports earlier in April of Suzuki's manoeuvres to secure endorsement again. See *Sakigake* (11, 13, 14 and 22 April 1937).

63 The awakening of a new consciousness during the 1930 election, which took place at a time when there were great hopes that a solution could be found to Japan's economic difficulties in a change of government policy, was emphasised by Andō Wafū in his interpretation of the election results. See, in particular, the editorial entitled 'Political Awareness of the Young Men of the Farming Villages' (1 March 1930). Part of the explanation for the later drop in interest was given by Seiyūkai secretary, Iizuka, in an interview in 1936, when he commented that real decisions were taken *achira*, that is in Tokyo. It should, however, be noted that in 1937 the *Sakigake* was still hopeful that the parties would regain power. See, especially, the editorial entitled 'Absolutely Favourable Opportunity for Party Revival' (3 April 1937). The 1932 election was something of a special case, in that for much of the campaign public attention was focused on the Shanghai Incident.

64 See, for example, the editorials of 5 and 6 February 1936.

65 *Nihon Seitō Shi Ron* (*An Examination of Japanese Political Party History*) (Tokyo, 1968), Vol. 4, pp. 1–3.

66 It is worth noting in this connection that in 1932 neither Ishikawa Teishin, who was a protégé of Inukai, nor Nakada Gichoku, who was backed by the Odate Bokudōkai, a club the name of which reveals its connections with the Seiyūkai leader, succeeded in securing party endorsement, even though Inukai was prime minister.

67 *Sakigake* (3 and 8 April 1937). In four electoral districts in other prefectures candidates were returned without a contest as a result of party co-operation. *1937 Asahi Nenkan*, pp. 120–2.

68 Undoubtedly the frequent splinterings of parties and the consequent regrouping of factions in different coalitions with different names in previous decades also made it difficult for a sense of attachment to parties to develop.

69 Such a conclusion ought not to be regarded as definitive, not only because Akita was only one among more than forty prefectures, but also because it may have preserved an unusually strong sense of local identity, based on its distance from the centre, its history, and possibly even a certain consciousness of and pride in, its own intellectual tradition. Hirata Atsutane, Satō Nobuhiro and Andō Shōeki were occasionally invoked as the Tokugawa ancestors of Akita citizens, being regarded as men who had condemned the social evils of their time, and a more recent local figure, Ishikawa Rikinosuke, was revered as an exponent and practitioner of agricultural self-help through co-operation and planning—the most important strand of *Nōhonshugi* in Akita in the 1920s and 1930s. See 'Nōhon Ideorogii Oboegaki' by Makino Hisanobu, *Akita Kindai Shi Kenkyū*, No. 18 (1972).

70 Unless Akita was very untypical, the 81 per cent of candidates elected under

nominal Taisei Yokusankai endorsement must have been a fairly inflated figure in terms of real success.

Chapter 6

1   The amplest account appears in J. K. Fairbank, E. O. Reischauer, A. M. Craig, *East Asia. The Modern Transformation* (Tokyo, 1965), p. 108; and G. R. Storry, *A History of Modern Japan* (London, 1960), p. 227. Hugh Borton, *Japan's Modern Century* (New York, 1955), p. 384 gives a briefer mention. J. W. Hall, *Japan, from Prehistory to Modern Times* (Tokyo, 1971), p. 347, E. O. Reischauer, *Japan the Story of a Nation* (previously entitled *Japan, Past and Present*) (Tokyo, 1971), p. 214, and W. G. Beasley, *The Modern History of Japan* (London, 1963), provide the briefest versions of all. Hall provides the estimate of '100,000 deaths'; Fairbank, Reischauer and Craig state that 'over 100,000' were killed. Reischauer mentions that two great raids on Tokyo together took 'well over 100,000 lives'. The second raid referred to here is probably that of 25 May 1945 which is estimated to have destroyed 16·8 square miles of the city.

2   Ishida Takeshi, *Hakyoku to Heiwa (1941–52)* (*Catastrophe and Peace*), *Nihon Kindaishi Taikei* (Tokyo, 1968), Vol. 8; Tōyama Shigeki, Imai Seiichi, Fujiwara Akira, *Shōwa shi* (*Shōwa History*) (Tokyo, 1959); Inoue Kiyoshi, *Nihon no Rekishi* (*History of Japan*) (Tokyo, 1966), Vol. 3, p. 205.

3   Katō Hidetoshi, Imai Seiichi, Shiota Shōbei, Usui Katsumi, Itō Mitsuharu, *Shōwa shi no Shunkan* (*Moments of Shōwa History*) (Tokyo, 1966), Vol. 2, p. 104.

4   Hayashi Shigeru, *Taiheiyō Sensō* (*The Pacific War*), *Nihon no Rekishi* (Tokyo, 1967), Vol. 25, pp. 403–8.

5   Tsurumi Shunsuke, Hashikawa Bunsō, Imai Seiichi, Matsumoto Sannosuke, Kamishima Jirō, Katō Hidetoshi, *Hateshinaki Sensen* (*The Endless Front*), *Nihon no Hyakunen* (Tokyo, 1967), Vol. 3, pp. 307–13.

6   W. F. Craven and J. L. Cate (eds), *The Army Air Forces in World War II*, Vol. 5: *The Pacific-Matterhorn to Nagasaki June 1944–August 1945* (Chicago, 1953) (hereafter referred to as Craven and Cate), p. 639. Referring to the raid of 25 May 1945: 'The attack was, however, highly successful. Photos showed that the fires kindled by 3,262 tons of incendiaries had destroyed 16·8 square miles, the greatest area wiped out in any single Tokyo raid, though the attack of 9 March had accomplished almost as much with about half the bomb weight.'

7   For example, the United States Strategic Bombing Survey (Pacific War), *The Effects of Strategic Bombing on Japanese Morale* (Washington, 1947), p. 3. 'The mass movement from the cities began after the great fire raids on Tokyo in March 1945.'

8   Although Tokyo's Metropolitan government produced a detailed account of the city's war damage over twenty years ago, that is, *Tōkyō-to Sensai shi* (*A Record of War Damage in Tokyo Metropolis*) (1953), organised attempts to collect and correlate material relating to Tokyo's air raids only gained momentum during the past four years. These activities have been centred on the Tōkyō Kūshū o Kiroku Suru Kai (The Society for Recording Tokyo's Air Raids), one of whose members, Saotome Katsumoto, has written the only book devoted to the raid of 10 March 1945: *Tōkyō Daikūshū* (*The Great Tokyo Air Raid*) (Tokyo, 1971).

9   As yet there is no comprehensive social history of Japan during the Pacific War and no integrated study of government social policy in the period.

10   'The East China airfields, constructed with so much back-breaking labour, and at considerable American expense, were overrun by the enemy. As the

Americans abandoned them one by one, they blew up the expensive equipment and valuable stores brought in ton by ton, by American planes over "The Hump" of the eastern spur of the Himalayas. By mid-September 1944, Operation Icho-Go had achieved its objectives.' O. Edmund Clubb, *Twentieth Century China* (New York, 1964).

11　Craven and Cate, op. cit., p. 609.

12　General Curtis E. LeMay and MacKinlay Kantor, *Mission with LeMay* (Garden City, New York, 1965) (hereafter referred to as LeMay), p. 329; Craven and Cate, op. cit., p. 101.

13　LeMay, op. cit., p. 345; Craven and Cate, op. cit., p. 576.

14　Craven and Cate, op. cit., p. 101.

15　Ibid., p. 573.

16　Ibid., p. 571; LeMay, op. cit., pp. 347–8.

17　Craven and Cate, op. cit., p. 608.

18　Ibid., p. 573; Tōkyō Kūshū O Kiroku Suru Kai (The Society for Recording the Tokyo Air Raids), *Tōkyō Daikūshūten* (*The Great Tokyo Air Raid Exhibition*), Booklet (Tokyo, 1972), p. 4.

19　Craven and Cate, op. cit., p. 611.

20　Ibid., p. 608.

21　Saotome, op. cit., p. 202.

22　For example Hayashi, op. cit., p. 404.

23　Craven and Cate, op. cit., p. 614; *New York Herald Tribune* (11 March 1945); *New York Times* (10 March 1945).

24　Craven and Cate, op. cit., pp. 613–14; LeMay, op. cit., p. 349.

25　Tōyama, Imai, Fujiwara, op. cit., p. 188.

26　For the limitations of Japanese defences see: Craven and Cate, op. cit., p. 613; LeMay, op. cit., pp. 346–7; United States Strategic Bombing Survey (Pacific War), *The Strategic Air Operations of Very Heavy Bombardment in the War Against Japan* (*Twentieth Air Force*) (Washington, 1946), pp. 19–21.

27　*Kindai Nihon Sōgō Nempyō* (*A Comprehensive Chronology of Modern Japan*) (Tokyo, 1968), p. 274.

28　United States Strategic Bombing Survey (Pacific War), *Field Report Covering Air-Raid Protection and Allied Subjects, Tokyo, Japan* (Washington, 1947), pp. 5–8.

29　Ibid., pp. 14–18.

30　Ibid., p. 92.

31　Saotome, op. cit., p. 19.

32　*Field Report Covering Air-Raid Protection and Allied Subjects, Tokyo,* p. 78.

33　Ibid., p. 6.

34　*Kindai Nihon Sōgō Nempyō,* p. 336.

35　Accounts of evacuation can be found in Tōkyō-to, *Tōkyō-to Sensai shi,* pp. 177–251; *Field Report Covering Air-Raid Protection and Allied Subjects, Tokyo,* pp. 151–9.

36　*Field Report Covering Air-Raid Protection and Allied Subjects, Tokyo,* pp. 137–45.

37　Hayashi, op. cit., p. 403.

38　Fire prevention is described in: *Field Report Covering Air-Raid Protection and Allied Subjects, Tokyo,* pp. 71–4.

39　M. Amrine, *The Great Decision, the Secret History of the Atomic Bomb* (London, 1960), pp. 77–8.

40　Saotome Katsumoto, 'Sangatsu Tōka Shitamachi Daikūshū' (10th March, the Great Shitamachi Air Raid'), in *Asahi Shinbun* (Tokyo edition) (18 July 1970).

41 *Asahi Shinbun* (11 March 1945); Craven and Cate, op. cit., pp. 615–16.
42 *Field Report Covering Air-Raid Protection and Allied Subjects, Tokyo*, p. 183.
43 Craven and Cate, op. cit., p. 617.
44 Saotome Katsumoto, op. cit., in *Asahi Shinbun* (18 July 1970).
45 *Field Report Covering Air-Raid Protection and Allied Subjects, Tokyo*, p. 58.
46 Ibid., p. 77.
47 *New York Times* (11 March 1945).
48 *New York Times* (10 March 1945).
49 *New York Times* (11 March 1945).
50 *Field Report Covering Air-Raid Protection and Allied Subjects, Tokyo*, p. 183.
51 Ibid., p. 160.
52 Ibid., loc. cit.
53 Ibid., pp. 90–1.
54 Ibid., p. 169.
55 Ibid., p. 161.
56 Ibid., p. 156.
57 Ibid., p. 155.
58 Saotome, op. cit., p. 202.
59 *Field Report Covering Air-Raid Protection and Allied Subjects, Tokyo*, p. 3.
60 Casualty statistics are very difficult to evaluate. The problem is briefly discussed in Hayashi, op. cit., p. 416, and Saotome, op. cit., p. 190.
61 Hayashi, op. cit., p. 404; Tōkō Kūshū O Kiroku Suru Kai, op. cit. (Foreword); Saotome, op. cit., p. 178.
62 Saotome, op. cit., p. 62.
63 Ibid., p. 68.

Chapter 7

1 Basic biographical information concerning Matsui Sumako is taken from Toita Kōji, *Joyū no Ai to Shi* (Kawade Shobō, 1963).
2 Toita, op. cit., pp. 28–30. On the fighting in 1868, see the chapter by C. D. Sheldon, pp. 27–51.
3 Ozaki Hirotsugu, *Joyū no Keizu* (Asahi Shinbun-sha, 1964), p. 99.
4 Matsui Sumako, *Botanbake* (Shinchō-sha, 1919), pp. 6–7. She later claims that she did make an effort to improve (pp. 12–13). This autobiography was originally published in 1913. The edition used here was a reprint issued at the time of Matsui Sumako's suicide.
5 Ibid., pp. 48–50.
6 Matsumoto Kappei, *Nihon Shingeki-shi* (Chikuma Shobō, 1967), p. 227.
7 Contraction of venereal disease from the husband was a common problem for wives in Meiji and Taishō Japan. See Fukuchi Shigetaka, *Kindai Nihon Josei-shi* (Sekka-sha, 1963), pp. 75, 97–8.
8 Quoted in Toita, op. cit., p. 41.
9 Nangō Terumi, *Matsui Sumako* (Bun'ei-sha, 1968), p. 55.
10 By Toita, op. cit., p. 43.
11 Matsui, op. cit., pp. 36–44.
12 A small ceremony took place, but the 'marriage' was not registered. See Ozaki, op. cit., p. 102.
13 Toita, op. cit., p. 43.
14 Ibid., p. 44.
15 Shingeki history of this period has been admirably documented by Akiba Tarō, *Nihon Shingeki-shi*, 2 vols (Risō-sha, 1955). It is also discussed in this volume in the contribution by A. Horie-Webber, pp. 147–65.

16　An earlier experiment—a medical school called Saiseigakusha—had in 1884 encountered problems similar to those of Bungei Kyōkai. Fukuchi, op. cit., p. 75.
17　Toita Kōji, *Shingeki no Hitobito* (Kadokawa Shinsho, 1954), p. 53.
18　Yamada Ryūya and Yoshida Kōsaburō in Toita Kōji, *Taidan Nihon Shingeki-shi* (Seia-bō, 1961), pp. 55–6.
19　Quoted in Ozaki, op. cit., p. 118.
20　Quoted in Toita, op. cit. (1963), pp. 81–96.
21　Fukuchi, op. cit., pp. 81–3.
22　Information on the *Seitō* movement is mainly taken from Ide Fumiko, *Seitō* (Kōbun-dō, 1961).
23　Ibid., pp. 57–9.
24　Ibid., pp. 60–1.
25　Matsui, op. cit., pp. 181–2.
26　Imai Seiichi (ed.), 'Taishō Demokurashī', *Nihon no Rekishi*, Vol. 23 (Chūō Kōron-sha, 1966), pp. 110–11. The extra scene is quoted in full in Toita, op. cit. (1963), pp. 96–7.
27　Kawatake Shigetoshi, *Shingeki Undō no Reimeiki* (Yūsankaku, 1946), p. 276.
28　Ibid., p. 278.
29　Matsui, op. cit., p. 183.
30　Ibid., p. 184.
31　Ide, op. cit., p. 32.
32　Matsui, op. cit., pp. 158–64.
33　*Tōkyō Asahi Shinbun* (6 January 1919).

Chapter 8

1　*Tokyo Shinbun* (16 April 1950) (*Shingeki Nendaiki*, Vol. 3, p. 192).
2　'Gekidan Tampō', *Higeki Kigeki* (November 1971), p. 69.
3　Tsuda, 'Shingeki no Daidokoro', *Higeki Kigeki* (April 1971), p. 14.
4　Ibid., pp. 13–16. (See also *Asahi Shinbun, Yūkan* (1 September 1971), p. 7.)
5　Ibid., pp. 14–15.
6　Ibid., p. 16.
7　Ibid., p. 15. (See also *Asahi Shinbun, Yūkan* (31 August 1971), p. 7.)
8　*Asahi Shinbun, Yūkan* (20 August 1971), p. 6. The categories in the questionnaire were as follows: (1) I intend to participate positively in the activities and management of the *gekidan;* (2) I have the intention, but I may not be able to do so fully because of my present personal circumstances; (3) As for the activities of the *gekidan*, it will suffice for them to be reported to me at the general meetings; (4) I have lost my grip on the meaning of belonging to Mingei; and (5) I want to resign from the *gekidan*.
9　*Asahi Shinbun, Yūkan* (25, 30 August 1971, 7 October 1971), resp. p. 7; *Asahi Shinbun* (25 December 1971), p. 3.
10　*Asahi Shinbun* (28 October 1971), p. 3.
11　Ibid., *Yūkan* (7 April 1971), p. 9.
12　Ibid. (28 September 1971), p. 9; see also 'Haiyū Shōgekijō no Kaisan', *Higeki Kigeki* (December 1971), p. 54.
13　*Asahi Shinbun, Yūkan* (22, 24 December 1971), resp. p. 9.
14　Kawamoto, 'Gekidan Tanpō-Mingei', *Higeki Kigeki* (November 1971), pp. 72–3; Kōchi, 'Gekidan Tanpō-Haiyu-za', *Higeki Kigeki* (November 1972), pp. 65–6; see also *Asahi Shinbun, Yūkan* (7 October 1971), p. 7.
15　See the references given in notes 9, 10, 11, 13 and 14 above; 'The Tottering Ideals of Shingeki', *Asahi Shinbun, Yūkan* (17 December 1971).

16 'Gekidan-sei', *Asahi Shinbun, Yūkan* (31 August, 1, 2 September 1971), resp. p. 7; see also 'Gekidan Tanpō' ser., *Higeki Kigeki* (December 1971–December 1972).

17 'Gendai Engeki no Teimei o Tsuku', *Higeki Kigeki* (November 1972), pp. 23–35.

18 Y. Katō, 'Bunmei Kaika', *Meiji Bunka Zenshū* (Nihon Hyōronsha, 1928), Vol. 20, p. 5. *Chonmage* was the male hair-style of the late Tokugawa period, that is, long hair tied at the top of the head. *Zangiri* was hair cut short in the Western fashion, as adopted in the Meiji period.

19 'Shinbun Zasshi', Meiji 5, Mar. ed. (S. Kawatake, *Nihon Engeki Zenshi*, Iwanami, 1959, pp. 756–7).

20 M. Kawatake *Mokuami Zenshū* (Shunyōdō, 1923), Vol. 16, pp. 407–627.

21 For background information on the Kabuki drama, and explanations of the technical terms used here, see E. Ernest, *The Kabuki Theatre* (London, Secker & Warburg, 1956) and A. C. Scott, *The Kabuki Theatre of Japan* (London, Allen & Unwin, 1955).

22 T. Ihara, *Kabuki Nendai-ki* (Iwanami, 1962), Vol. 7, p. 181.

23 Ibid., pp. 233–6.

24 N. Tamura, *Zokuzoku Kabuki Nendai-ki* (Ichimura-za, 1922), pp. 243–4.

25 'Kabuki Shinbun' (August 1886) (S. Tsubouchi, 'Meiji Gekikai Shōshi', *Shōyō Zenshū* (Shunyōdō, 1924), Vol. 10, pp. 25–7).

26 Ibid., p. 25.

27 Suematsu, 'Engeki Kairyō Iken', 1887, *Meiji Bunka Zenshū*, Vol. 12, pp. 222–9.

28 Ibid., p. 230.

29 Ibid., p. 231.

30 Ibid., p. 233.

31 Ibid., p. 229.

32 Ibid., pp. 229, 234, 235.

33 Sotoyama, 'Engeki Kairyō-ron Shikō', *Meiji Bunka Zenshū*, Vol. 12, pp. 203–19.

34 'Gekijō no Setsu', *Meiji Bunka Zenshū*, Vol. 12, p. 261.

35 Tsubouchi, 'Engeki Kairyō-kai no Sōritsu o Kiite Hiken o Nobu', *Meiji Bunka Zenshū*, Vol. 12, pp. 251–6.

36 Mori, 'Engeki Kairyō Ronsha no Henken ni Odoroku', Meiji 22 (*Ōgai Zenshū*, Ōgai Zenshū Kankō-kai, 1924, Vol. 3, pp. 20–4).

37 Tamura, *Zokuzoku Kabuki Nendai-ki* (1921), pp. 464–8.

38 Ibid., p. 466. Suematsu himself is said to have undertaken the task of revising these texts, but the extent of his textual reform is not known.

39 Kawatake, *Nihon Engeki Zenshi*, p. 811.

40 Ibid., p. 812.

41 Apart from these Kabuki reform movements, there was a movement characterised as Sōshi Shibai or Shosei Shibai during the later part of the Meiji period. This group of amateur performers started by dramatising the current social and political events of the period, and later established itself as Shin-pa, the new sect, opposed to the old sect of Kabuki. The Shin-pa performances received popular support during the Meiji 30s. It produced plays by contemporary writers, using for the first time actresses to play female roles; at the height of its activities, a Shin-pa group led by Kawakami Onjirō even toured Europe and, on its return, produced adaptations of Shakespeare's *Othello, The Merchant of Venice* and *Hamlet*. However, the novelty of Shin-pa was to be overshadowed by the rise of the Shingeki movement, and its artistic integrity came to be questioned by the Shingeki advocates as a mere imitation of Kabuki. Thus, in effect, Shin-pa made little contribution in determining the course of the modern Japanese

theatre; nevertheless the transitional role it played during the Meiji 30s should not go without notice. See Kawatake, *Nihon Engeki Zenshi*, pp. 985–1,017.

42 On Tsubouchi, see also the chapter by Brian Powell, pp. 139–40.

43 Tsubouchi, 'Kabuki no Tetteiteki Kenkyū, *Shōyō Zenshū*, Vol. 10, pp. 63–4.

44 'Bungei Kyōkai Kaisoku', Meiji 42, *Shōyō Zenshū*, Vol. 12, p. 612.

45 'Bungei Kyōkai Isshin no Shui', Meiji 42, *Shōyō Zenshu*, Vol. 12, p. 587.

46 Tsubouchi, 'Yochōchō no Engeki Kenkyūsho', Meiji 42, *Shōyō Zenshū*, Vol. 12, p. 628.

47 Kawatake, *Nihon Engeki Zenshi*, p. 1,043.

48 Tsubouchi, 'Yochōchō no Engeki Kenkyūsho', op. cit., pp. 627–33.

49 The plays produced by Bungei Kyōkai were the following: *Hamlet*, *The Merchant of Venice* and *Julius Caesar* (Shakespeare), *Magda* (Harman Sudermann), *A Doll's House* (Henrik Ibsen), *The Man of Destiny* and *You Never Can Tell* (G. B. Shaw), *Alt Heidelberg* (Meyer-Förster), and Tsubouchi's *Kanzan Shutoku*, *Ohichi Kichizo*, *Hachikazuki Hime*, *Kotto-netsu* and *Kitahara to Utamaro*. Kawatake, 'Koki Bungei Kyōkai', *Shōyō Zenshū*, Vol. 12, Appendix, pp. 31–44.

50 The Bungei Kyōkai movement was dissolved in 1913 by Tsubouchi himself. The dissolution is generally attributed to a scandal, namely the love affair between a junior leader of the Kyōkai, Shimamura Hōgetsu, and a student actress, Matsui Sumako (see Brian Powell's chapter, pp. 143–5). But it is also said that Tsubouchi's moderate policies were increasingly becoming a target for criticism by the young members of the Kyōkai and that this division within the Bungei Kyōkai was also a factor that led Tsubouchi finally to dissolve the movement. See note 52, below.

51 K. Matsumoto, *Nihon Shingekishi* (Tsukuma-shobō, 1966), p. 46.

52 While acknowledging the merits of the Ibsenian modern theatre of Realism, Tsubouchi believed that the greatest model for a new Japanese theatre was the Shakespearian theatre of Romanticism (see 'Chikamatsu, Shakespeare and Ibsen', Meiji 42, *Shōyō Zenshū*, Vol. 10, pp. 769–813). Thus, he chose three of Shakespeare's plays for the Bungei Kyōkai repertoire, and himself wrote several epic plays (notably *En no Gyōsha*), modelled upon Shakespearian drama. However, the tide of the day was against him. The young Shingeki advocates of the time, who were obsessed with the latest trend of literature, Naturalism, preferred Ibsen, and criticised Tsubouchi's views as mediocre and his attitude as old-fashioned and moderate.

53 Tsubouchi, 'Hamlet Kōengo no Shokan', Meiji 44, *Shōyō Zenshū*, Vol. 12, pp. 667.

54 Tsubouchi, 'Bungei Kyōkai Isshin no Shui', Meiji 42, ibid., pp. 587–8.

55 See note 43.

56 J. Tanizaki, 'Seishun Monogatari', *Tanizaki Junichirō Zenshū* (Chūo-kōronsha, 1968), Vol. 13, p. 311.

57 H. Masamune, 'Hōmei o Tsuioku suru', *Masamune Hakuchō Zenshū* (Shinchō-sha, 1968), Vol. 12, p. 252.

58 Takeda Shōken, 'Shokoku Onna Banashi', in Matsumoto, op. cit., p. 48.

59 S. Kubo, 'Osanai Kaoru', *Gendai Nihon Kiroku Zenshū* (Tsukuma-shobō, 1971), Vol. 18, p. 193.

60 Osanai's letter to a Kabuki actor, Danko, written on 8 December 1908 (I. Ōyama, *Kindai Nihon Gikyoku-shi* (Ōhū-sha, 1969), p. 308).

61 M. Shimomura, *Shingeki* (Iwanami, 1956), p. 11.

62 The other European plays produced were: *To the Stars* (L. Andreyev), *The Miracle of St Anthony* and *Death of Tintagiles* (M. Maeterlinck), and one by E. Brieux translated into Japanese as *Shinkō*.

63 Kubo, op. cit., pp. 191–4; Matsumoto, op. cit., pp. 14–21.

64 Shimomura, op. cit., p. 11. Upon producing the first production, *Borkman*, Osanai is said to have tried to get an Austrian actor to teach him directing. But having failed in this attempt, he based his direction on the information gathered from the cuttings of newspaper reviews of the German production and a description of it, which his friend sent him from Munich. Thus his goal for the first trial was a modest one: he stated that 'our attempt will have been worthwhile if we can capture even a little of the rhythm of everyday speech in this modern Western play . . . and master suitable gestures to accompany it' (Matsumoto, op. cit., p. 15). The result is indicated in the following review of the production by Masamune, then a theatre critic: 'Although it made a great impression on the young belletrists . . . the production was not a success by any means, the obvious reason being that Japanese Kabuki and Western drama have nothing in common. Sadanji [in playing the lead] could not grasp the essence of the character however hard he tried, nor could Osanai be said to have had a particularly deep knowledge. Sadanji simply shouted his lines loudly and failed to express Ibsen's solemn depth' (Masamune, 'Ibsen ni Tsuite', *Zenshū*, Vol. 13, p. 76). Compare note 66 below.

65 Kawatake, op. cit., p. 1,057. The Japanese plays produced were: *Umesuke to Sō* and *Kōchiya Yohei* (Yoshii Isamu), *Kanraku no Oni* (Nagata Hideo), *Daiichi no Akatsuki* (Akita Ujaku), and *Ikutagawa* by Mori Ōgai.

66 From the various accounts given by the Jiyū Gekijō audience, we may judge that the enthusiastic support aroused by its productions was mainly due to the novelty and exoticism of modern ideas and Western fashions of life provided by these European plays, rather than to the legitimate appeal of a successful theatre. This is illustrated in Kawatake's recollection of the opening night of *Borkman*: 'We were enthralled simply by the fact that Ibsen was for the first time being transplanted into a Japanese theatre, and felt fanatical about seeing it three-dimensionally on stage' (Kawatake, op. cit., p. 1,051). For similar accounts see: Tanizaki, op. cit., pp. 386–7; Shimazaki, 'Jiyū-gekijō no Atarashiki Kokoromi', *Zenshū*, Vol. 8, pp. 463–8; Masamune, 'Osanai Kaoru no Nokoshita mono', *Zenshū*, Vol. 12, pp. 460–3.

67 See *Kanraku no Oni* (H. Nagata), *Daiichininsha* (S. Mayama), *Hideko Kaburagi* (S. Doi), *Shakai no Teki* (T. Iniwa). In fact, some of these plays show a curious poetic conflict: while they adopt the Japanese dramatic ideas of their original models, the actions of the Japanese heroes seem to be frustrated. Their natural impulses as characters and the thematic ideals seem to be in conflict. Consequently, the plays leave us with an ambivalent impression.

68 Masamune, 'Ibsen ni Tsuite', op. cit., pp. 75–7.

69 Jiyū Gekijō was dissolved in 1919 because of financial difficulties and the fact that its Kabuki actors were becoming increasingly busy with their traditional roles.

70 The Tsukiji Shōgekijō movement was founded in 1924, with its own theatre, the first for Shingeki alone, by Osanai and Hijikata Yoshi, who had just returned from a stay in Europe and the U.S.S.R., where he studied the latest trends of the theatre. At the start of the movement, Osanai declared that since he could not find sufficiently stimulating native plays, he would not produce them at Tsukiji. This remark was met by loud protests from some Japanese writers, and created a controversy between them and Osanai. (For example, see Yamamoto, 'Tsukiji Shōgekijō no Hansei o Unagasu', *Zenshū*, Vol. 9, pp. 368–76, 387–96.) Thus during the first two years of its activities, Tsukiji Shōgekijō did not produce a single Japanese play, while introducing a new foreign play every ten days. Finally, succumbing to pressure, it produced Tsubouchi's *En no Gyōsha* as its fiftieth production, and from then on chose some native plays for the repertoire. However, the statistics show the character of the movement: during its five-

year span, it presented 107 plays, of which only 22 were by Japanese authors (*Tsukiji Shōgekijō*, Mar. edn, 1928). The Tsukiji Shōgekijō movement was dissolved in 1928 on the death of Osanai. By this time, the latest ideology abroad, socialism, had begun to invade the minds of the Shingeki advocates. In the 1930s and into the period of the Second World War, the Shingeki movement took on socialist slogans and fought with the government censor. An order for its suppression came in 1940, leaving only one, nonideological group, Bungaku-za, to continue its activities during the war.

71 Osanai himself finally admitted this in a speech delivered just before his death in 1928. See Osanai, 'Nihon Engeki no Shōrai', *Nihon Gendai Bungaku Zenshū*, Vol. 17, pp. 124–38.

Chapter 9

1 Postscript to the revised version of *The Road Sign at the End of the Road* (Tōjusha, 1965).

2 *Abe Kōbō Zen-sakuhin* (*Complete works of Abe Kōbō*), 15 vols (Shinchō-sha, 1972–3), Vol. 3, pp. 297–8.

3 *The Face of Another*, translated by E. Dale Saunders (New York, Knopf, 1966), pp. 109–10.

4 Ōe is also aware of the racial problem in Japanese society and deals with it in terms of lost identity. See the discussion of Ōe's *Outcries*, p. 178, below.

5 It is interesting to note that Ōe treats the psychology of the perverted characters who perform erotic acts in a train in *The Sexual Man*. See p. 178 below.

6 *The Face of Another*, op. cit., pp. 146–7.

7 Ibid., p. 162.

8 Ibid., pp. 163–4.

9 Introduction to the selected works of Abe Kōbō in the *Warera no bungaku* series, No. 7 (Kōdansha, 1966), p. 480.

10 The vision of this state includes the celebration of sexual power, with which Ōe becomes more and more preoccupied in his later works. It is noteworthy, however, that in his later works the sexual urge becomes more and more perverted under the social strain and cannot be celebrated as in the present work.

11 Ōe's preoccupation with sexual perversion in his works may be compared with Mishima Yukio's treatment of the subject. But the resemblance between the two in this and other matters is superficial. There are real differences between them, some of which will be mentioned later in this chapter.

12 One of the recurrent patterns in Ōe's fictional structure is the use of elder and younger brothers as in *The Catch*, *Plucking Buds and Shooting Lambs*, *Today the Struggle*, *The Football in the First Year of the Man'en Era*, etc. Ōe's use of this pattern is clearly intentional. In *Plucking Buds and Shooting Lambs* the young brother functions in a significant way. Unlike other boys, he does not originally come from a reformatory but, given up by his father, voluntarily participates in the experience of the juvenile delinquents. Neither purely a member of the delinquents nor belonging to the hypocritical society of the adults, he is in a sense the representative of genuine innocence. He is therefore a mirror for his brother and his companions and functions in structure as a point of view.

13 Each decade in the post-war history of Japan seems to have a marked character. For instance, in 1960 there was a vain and abortive attempt by the leftists to overthrow the direction of politics operated under the Japanese–American Security Treaty. The failure of their attempt made them realise that the re-orientation of Japanese politics by means of abolishing the Treaty and the reformation of society at large along socialist lines was an illusion. In the

meantime, the Japanese economy was achieving a spectacular growth which entailed a conflict in economic interest between the United States and Japan, and the re-shaping of American policy towards the Far East. This new situation was typically symbolised by President Nixon's announcement of a new economic policy in the summer of 1971 and the accelerated Sino-American *rapprochement*. In the circumstances, the Japanese–American Security Treaty has automatically lost much of its meaning. The irony of the situation is that it has proved the illusoriness of not only the post-war American policy towards the Far East but also the grounds on which the left-wing criticism of the American policy was founded.

14 Outcries are uttered twice in the novel: once near the beginning by a youth who dies of a car accident; later, by the girl whom one of the central characters strangles to death.

15 The first year of the Man'en era corresponds to 1860 in the Christian era. In fact football, which is played in the novel in 1960, did not exist in Japan in 1860. The author's intention is to overlap 1860 with 1960, thus paralleling past and present and implying continuity in history.

16 A similar kind of readiness to accept the reality is discernible in the hero of *A Personal Matter* (*Kojinteki na taiken*, 1964), which the present chapter has no space to discuss.

17 Soon afterwards they parted company. Etō harshly criticised Ōe's growing inclination to radicalism as well as his literary works. Ishihara became in 1968 a L.D.P. member of the House of Councillors, winning the largest number of votes throughout the country; in December 1972 he became a member of the House of Representatives, again winning the largest number of votes in his Tokyo constituency.

18 *Asahi Shinbun* (11 January 1971), evening edn.

19 Ibid. (12 January 1971).

20 Ibid. (13 January 1971).

Chapter 10

1 H. Neill McFarland, *The Rush Hour of the Gods* (New York, Macmillan Co., 1968), pp. 75–6.

2 Harry Thomsen, *New Religions of Japan* (Tokyo, Charles E. Tuttle, 1963), p. 205.

3 Ronald Dore, *City Life in Japan* (London, Routledge, 1958), pp. 309–10. *Hikokumin*: 'traitor'.

4 Ibid., p. 308.

5 Ikado Fujio, 'Trend and Problems of New Religions: Religion in Urban Society', in K. Morioka and W. H. Newell (eds), *The Sociology of Japanese Religion* (Leiden, Brill, 1968), p. 106.

6 Ibid., p. 104.

7 James Allen Dator, *Soka Gakkai, Builders of the Third Civilization* (Seattle, University of Washington Press, 1969), p. 93 (data incomplete in text).

8 Ibid., p. 93.

9 Ikado, op. cit., p. 106.

10 Jàmes W. White, *The Soka Gakkai and Mass Society* (California, Stanford University Press, 1970), pp. 69–70.

11 Quoted in White, op. cit., p. 71.

12 Murata Kiyoaki, *Japan's New Buddhism* (New York and Tokyo, John Weatherhill, 1969), p. 159.

13 Watanabe Eimi, 'Rissho Kosei Kai', in *Contemporary Religions in Japan*, Vol. 9 (1–2) (1968), p. 96.

14   Dator uses tests devised by (1) Alan Roberts and Milton Rokeach, 'Anomie, Authoritarianism and Prejudice', *American Journal of Sociology*, Vol. 61 (January 1956), p. 357; (2) Wayne Thompson and John Horton, 'Political Alienation as a Force in Political Action', *Social Forces*, Vol. 38 (March 1960), p. 195; (3) Horton and Thompson, 'Powerlessness and Political Negativism', *American Journal of Sociology*, Vol. 67 (1962), p. 486; (4) Angus Campbell *et al.*, *The Voter Decides* (Peterson, Evanston Row, 1954), p. 104. White uses T. W. Adorno *et al.*, *The Authoritarian Personality* (New York, 1950).

15   Dator, op. cit., p. 105.

16   White, op. cit., p. 214.

17   Ikado, op. cit., p. 111.

18   Robert A. Nisbet, *The Quest for Community* (New York, Oxford University Press, 1953), p. 277.

19   William Kornhauser, *The Politics of Mass Society* (London, Routledge).

20   White, op. cit., p. 183.

Chapter 11

1   See Tōkei sūri kenkyūsho, *Nihonjin no kokuminsei* and *Dai-ni Nihonjin no kokuminsei* (Tokyo, 1961 and 1970).

2   One example of such criticism is: Shigeki Koyama, 'Nihon shakai no kindai-sei to hoshusei', *Shūkan Ekonomisuto* (6 February, 1973), pp. 62–6, and 13 February, 1973, pp. 84–9.

3   N.H.K. hōsō yoron chōsasho, *Shōwa 45-nendo kokumin seikatsu jikan chōsa* (Tokyo, 1971). All the data on the time budgets are taken from this investigation unless otherwise indicated.

4   The total sum of time spent on the various activities is 24 hours 45 minutes, because some activities are done simultaneously with others. This is especially true for watching television, which has become a secondary activity for many Japanese. Therefore, when we consider as pure leisure-time the time which is spent only for leisure activities the amount of leisure-time on weekdays is only 3 hours 36 minutes.

5   Investigation of the Ministry of Labour, quoted in: Keizei kikaku-chō, *Shōwa 47-nen-han kokumin seikatsu hakusho. Nihonjin to sono shakai* (Tokyo, 1972), p. 398.

6   Ibid., p. 173.

7   N.H.K. hōsō yoron chōsasho kokumin yoron han, 'Nihonjin no shokugyō-kan (sono 1)—kokumin yoron chōsa no bunseki o chūshin to shite', *Bunken geppō*, Vol. 18, No. 1 (January 1968), p. 38.

8   Keizai kikaku-chō, op. cit., pp. 173–4.

9   Tsūshō Sangyōshō yoka kaihatsu sangyō-shitsu, *Waga kuni yoka no genjō to yokajidai e no tenbō* (Tokyo, 1973), p. 37. It contains the following table (in per cent):

		JAPAN		U.S.A.	FRANCE	GERMANY	U.S.S.R.
		1965	1970	1965/6	1965	1966	1966
	passive leisure	65·2	63·5	48·8	52·4	42·0	36·6
Men	*active leisure*	34·8	36·7	51·3	47·7	58·0	63·5
	passive leisure	73·1	73·8	44·2	52·8	46·6	39·8
Women	*active leisure*	26·8	26·2	55·6	47·3	53·3	60·2

Japan: over 20 years of age   Other countries: 18 to 65 years

10   Akuto Hiroshi, 'Kachi ishiki no henkō', in Akuto Hiroshi, Tominaga Kenichi and Sofue Takao, *Hendō-ki no Nihon shakai. Sono kōzō to ishiki no bunseki* (Tokyo, 1972), p. 42.

11 Ikeuchi Hajime, 'Sangyōjin no yoka-riyō no jittai', *Rōmu kenkyū*, Vol. 13, No. 9 (1960), p. 34.
12 Makita Michio, 'Yoka kōdō no bunrui o megutte', *Bunken geppō*, Vol. 22, No. 7 (July 1972), pp. 17–18.
13 Sōrifu kōhōshitsu, 'Shūkyū futsuka-sei. Yoka', *Yoron chōsa*, Vol. 5, No. 1 (January 1973), Tables pp. 70–3.
14 Ibid., p. 63.
15 Ibid., p. 98.
16 Tōkyō daigaku bungakubu shakaigaku kenkyūshitsu, *N-sha jūgyōin no yoron chōsa. Zensha kurosu shūkeihyō* (Tokyo, 1964) (mimeographed).
17 Okabe Keizō, 'Goraku shikō to seikatsu yōshiki no henka', *Shisō*, No. 431 (May 1960), p. 598.
18 Quoted in Fukutake Tadashi, *Gendai Nihon shakairon* (Tokyo, 1972), p. 126.
19 Rikkyō daigaku sangyō kankei kenkyūsho, *Zoku daikigyō burū karā wākā no seikatsu to iken* (Tokyo, 1969) (mimeographed), p. 124.
20 N.H.K. hōsō yoron chōsasho kokumin yoron han, op. cit., p. 35.
21 Kokumin senkōdo chōsa iinkai, *Nihonjin no manzokudo. Kokumin senkōdō yobi chōsa* (Tokyo, 1972), p. 167.
22 Quoted by Akuto, op. cit., p. 35.
23 Joffré Dumazedier, 'Development of the Sociology of Leisure', *Current Sociology*, Vol. 16, No. 1 (1968), pp. 35–6.
24 Y. Scott Matsumoto, 'Social Stress and Coronary Heart Disease in Japan: A Hypothesis', *The Milbank Memorial Fund Quarterly*, Vol. 43, No. 1 (January 1970). Reprinted in *Selected Readings on Modern Japanese Society*, compiled and edited by George K. Yamamoto and Tsuyoshi Ishida (Berkeley, 1971).

Chapter 12

1 The study was part of the research undertaken for my Ph.D., presented in a thesis entitled 'Social Relations in a Japanese Company' in 1971. It was sponsored by the London Cornell Fund and London University.
2 T. Nakano, 'Rōdō kumiai ni okeru ningen kankei' ('Human Relations in a Labour Union'), *Shakaigaku Hyōron*, Vol. 7 (1952), pp. 57–69.
3 Robert E. Cole, *Japanese Blue Collar: The Changing Tradition* (Berkeley, University of California Press, 1971).
4 W. Fujita, S. Ujihara and N. Funahashi, *Nihongata Rōdō Kumiai to Nenkō Seido (Japanese-Type Labour Unions and the Age-Seniority System)* (Shimbunsha, 1963).

Chapter 13

1 K. Tanaka, *Nippon Rettō Kaizō-ron* (Nikkan Kōgyō Shimbun-sha, 1972). Now available in English translation as *Building a New Japan: A Plan for Remodelling the Japanese Archipelago* (Tokyo, Simul Press).
2. J. K. Galbraith, *The Affluent Society* (London, Hamish Hamilton, 1958), p. 200.
3 *Asahi Nenkan* (1973), p. 315.
4 Keizai Kikaku Chō, *Shin Zenkoku Sōgō Kaihatsu Keikaku* (Ōkura-shō Insatsu-kyoku, 1969), p. 12.
5 Keizai Kikaku Chō Chōsa-kyoku, *Chi-iki Keizai Yōran* (Keizai Kikaku Kyōkai, 1972), p. 125.
6 Shōwa Yonjūgonen Kokusei Chōsa, *Zenkoku Todōfuken Shi-ku-chō-son betsu Jinkō* (Sōrifu Tōkeikyoku, 1971).

7 S. Ōkita, *Regional Planning in Japan Today*, in W. W. Lockwood (ed.), *The State and Economic Enterprise in Japan* (Princeton University Press, 1965), p. 622.

8 Keizai Kikaku Chō Sōgō Kaihatsu-kyoku, *Shin Sangyō Toshi nado no Genjō* (Ōkura-shō Insatsu-kyoku, 1969), pp. 32-3.

9 Keizai Kikaku Chō, op. cit.

10 *Asahi Nenkan* (1973), p. 315.

11 G. McCrone, *Regional Policy in Britain* (London, Allen & Unwin, 1969), pp. 91-105.

12 J. P. Cole, *Italy* (London, Chatto & Windus, 1968), pp. 248-9.

13 *Nihon Keizai Shinbun* (8 January 1972).

14 *Nihon Keizai Shinbun* (2 October 1972).

15 M. Satō, 'Jōetsu Shinkansen no Tochi Kassen', *Chuō Kōron*, Vol. 88, No. 2, pp. 72-86.

16 *Nihon Keizai Shinbun* (2 October 1972).

17 *Asahi Nenkan* (1973), pp. 555-6.

18 G. Murase, Kōchi-ken Sukumo Wan Genyu Kichi Kōsō, *Keizai Hyōron*, Vol. 20, No. 10; '*Rinji Zōkan Tokushu Keiei-Kaikeigaku*' pp. 154-63.

19 *Asahi Nenkan* (1973), p. 554.

Chapter 14

1 Japanese data from *Tōkei nenkan* (*Japan Statistical Yearbook*), various years from 1952 (Tokyo, Bureau of Statistics, Office of the Prime Minister).

2 Data from *International Financial Statistics*, Vol. 26, No. 8 (Washington, International Monetary Fund, 1973).

3 *Nihon keizai tōkei* (*Historical Statistics of the Japanese Economy*) (Tokyo, Statistics Department, Bank of Japan, 1962). Further revisions of the National Income data used to calculate nominal trade ratios in Table 39 of this volume are unlikely to alter the picture significantly.

4 Hisao Kanamori, *Nihon keizai no shōrai* (*The Future of the Japanese Economy*) (Tokyo, Nihon keizai shinbunsha, 1971), p. 221.

5 Hisao Kanamori, 'Economic Growth and Exports', in Lawrence Klein and Kazushi Ohkawa, *Economic Growth: The Japanese Experience since the Meiji Era* (Homewood, Illinois, Richard D. Irwin Inc., 1968).

6 Comparative data on prices of exports of manufactures are in *Keizai yōran, 1972* (*Handbook of Economic Statistics, 1972*) (Tokyo, Keizai Kikakuchō Chōsakyoku, 1972). The role of prices in explaining Japan's recent export performance is confirmed by the analysis in *White Paper on International Trade, 1972* (Tokyo, Japan External Trade Organisation, 1972), Chapter 1.

7 *Keizai hakusho, 1971* (*Economic White Paper, 1971*) (Tokyo, Keizai Kika-kuchō, 1971), Part 1, Chaps 2 and 4; and Part 2, Chap. 2.

8 'Japan's New Principles of Foreign Aid Clarified', *The Japan Economic Review* (15 February 1973).

9 'Tokyo's Tight Money Policy may Reverse U.S. Trade Imbalance', *The Times* (12 May 1973). Estimates and a good discussion of future capital flows are in Hisao Kanamori and Sueo Sekiguchi, *Sekai o ugokasu Nihon keizai* (*The Japanese Economy Propels the World*) (Tokyo, Nihon Keizai Shinbunsha, 1972), Chap. 6.

10 Detailed analyses of these problems are in *Rōdō Hakusho, 1971* (*Labour White Paper, 1971*) (Tokyo, Ministry of Labour, 1971), pp. 47-110; and Funahashi Naomichi, *Tenkanki no chingin mondai* (*Wage Problems in the Transition Period*) (Tokyo, Nihon Hyōronsha, 1971).

11 'Japan Raises Official Discount Rate to 7 per cent', *Financial Times*

(29 August 1973). Between 1963 and 1970, the average annual rate of increase of retail prices was approximately 4 per cent (*Keizai hakusho, 1971*, p. 307).

12   For example, Matsui Kiyoshi, *Nihon no bōeki* (*Japan's Foreign Trade*) (Tokyo, Iwanami Shoten, 1954).

13   Kiyoshi Kojima, *Japan and a Pacific Free Trade Area* (Berkeley and Los Angeles, University of California Press, 1971).

14   An Australian view of these problems is H. W. Arndt, *Australia and Asia: Economic Essays* (Canberra, Australian National University Press, 1972). Arndt suggests that by 1980, Japan will be taking 38–42 per cent of Australia's exports.

15   'Interest Grows in China's Oil Wealth', *The Japan Economic Review* (15 November 1972). This article reported that members of the China Committee for Promotion of International Trade told a private delegation of Japanese businessmen that exports of crude oil to Japan were definitely envisaged for the future. On present information, the scope for these in the next few years would be microscopic in relation to Japan's total oil imports. However, even notional imports would be psychologically welcome to Japan and the possibility of extensive off shore and other developments could change the supply prospects radically during the next decade.

16   'China Fair and Japan's Hopes on It', *The Japan Economic Review* (15 May 1973).

17   The best account in English of the development of the framework of Sino-Japanese trade is a forthcoming article by Dan F. Henderson and Tasuku Matsuo, 'Japan's Trade Experience with the People's Republic of China'. An important Japanese source is Japan External Trade Organisation, *Nitchū bōeki shusatsu—Chūgoku ichiba e no approach* (*Handbook on Sino-Japanese Trade— An Approach to the Chinese Market*) (Tokyo, Nihon Bōeki Shinkokai, 1971).

18   'Japan–China Trade Eyes Large Expansion; Inter-Governmental Pact seen by Year-End', *The Japan Economic Review* (15 March 1973). Some detailed estimates of China's future foreign trade are: Robert F. Dernberger, 'Prospects for Trade Between China and the United States', in Alexander Eckstein (ed.), *China Trade Prospects and U.S. Policy* (New York, Praeger, 1971); and Ishikawa Shigeru (ed.), *Chūgoku keizai no chōki tenbō IV* (*The Long-Term Prospect for the Chinese Economy*), (Tokyo, Ajia Keizai Kenkyūsho, 1971), Vol. 2.

19   The Chinese justify departure from the principle of balanced trade by speaking of the necessity for achieving balance over a longer period, rather than holding to a strict annual balance. The first article cited in note 18 above quotes the Chinese as saying : 'we are desirous of a better balance of trade only on a long range without being too mindful of a short-run imbalance such as seen of late'.

20   Competition between China and the United States is particularly acute in the cases of soy beans and livestock.

21   The Soviet need for trade and assistance is partly due to the effect of large defence expenditures on investment, but even more important is the failure of the civilian economy to maintain satisfactory rates of technical progress. This problem has been exhaustively analysed by Michael Boretsky, 'Comparative Progress in Technology, Productivity and Economic Efficiency: U.S.S.R. *v* U.S.A.', in Joint Economic Committee, Congress of the United States, *New Directions in the Soviet Economy* (Washington, U.S. Government Printing Office, 1966).

22   H. S. Houthaker and Stephen P. Magee, 'Income and Price Elasticities in World Trade', *Review of Economics and Statistics* (May 1969), Vol. 51.

23   United Nations, *Handbook of International Trade and Development Statistics* (New York, 1971). This study shows that in 1969–70, 5·89 per cent of manu-

factures consumed in Japan were imported, compared with 18·86 per cent in the U.K. and 5·35 per cent in the United States.

24 The economic implications of improvement in the quality of urban living are discussed in *Keizai hakusho, 1971*, pp. 186–217. A valuable survey relevant to this problem is Kagaku Gijutsu-chō Shigen Chōsakai, *Kore kara no toshi seikatsu kankyō* (*The Future Urban Living Environment*) (Tokyo, Treasury Printing Office, 1972).

25 Ministry of International Trade and Industry, *Envisioning the Future Industrial Structure*, Background information 73–31 (24 July 1973); 'Priority Switched from Exports to Promotion of Public Welfare', *The Japan Economic Review* (15 April 1973); Kiichiro Satoh, 'Reform of Japan's Industrial Structure', *Keidanren Review* (Spring 1973), No. 26.

INDEX